The Art Business: Art World, Art Market

This book provides a comprehensive overview of the professional activities of the art business. Addressing this fast-moving industry, *The Art Business: Art World, Art Market* analyses the sector's institutions and structures, including galleries, auction houses and art fairs. The rapid development of art finance and its deployment of art as an asset class are covered, and up to moment observations are delivered on the quickly evolving auction system that includes dramatic changes at the major auction houses, Sotheby's and Christie's. This edition highlights growing crises in the market including the ever more unbearable costs of art fair attendance and the lack of a reliable system for establishing ownership and title of artworks. Ever more pressing ethical issues such as toxic museum donors, cultural heritage compliance, and problems of corrupt provenances are explored in detail. Enhanced by new data analytics on the US art market, the author also distils advice and guidance for working art professionals hoping to build their careers.

The result is an up-to-date picture of an art business suitable for students and practitioners across the creative sector.

Jeffrey Taylor is US Fulbright Scholar at the European Humanities University (EHU) in Vilnius, Lithuania.

Discovering the Creative Industries

Series Editor: Ruth Rentschler

The creative and cultural industries account for a significant share of the global economy. Gaining and maintaining employment and work in this sector is a challenge and chances of success are enhanced by ongoing professional development.

This series provides a range of relatively short, student-centred books which blend industry and educational expertise with cultural sector practice. Books in the series provide applied introductions to the core elements of the creative industries. In sum, the series provides essential reading for those studying to enter the creative industries as well as those seeking to enhance their career via executive education.

Fundraising for the Creative and Cultural Industries

Leading Effective Fundraising Strategies

Michelle Wright, Ben Walmsley and Emilee Simmons

Managing the Arts and Culture

Cultivating a Practice

Edited by Constance DeVereaux

Managing Organizations in the Creative Economy

Organizational Behaviour for the Cultural Sector

Paul Saintilan and David Schreiber

Transformational Innovation in the Creative and Cultural Industries

Alison Rieple, Robert DeFillippi and David Schreiber

The Art Business

Art World, Art Market

Jeffrey Taylor

For more information about this series, please visit: www.routledge.com/Discovering-the-Creative-Industries/book-series/DCI

The Art Business

Art World, Art Market

Jeffrey Taylor

Second Edition

LONDON AND NEW YORK

Designed cover image: © Yingshan Zhang / Getty Images

Second edition published 2024
by Routledge
4 Park Square, Milton Park, Abingdon, Oxon, OX14 4RN

and by Routledge
605 Third Avenue, New York, NY 10158

Routledge is an imprint of the Taylor & Francis Group, an informa business

© 2024 Jeffrey Taylor

First edition published by Routledge 2018

British Library Cataloguing-in-Publication Data
A catalogue record for this book is available from the British Library

ISBN: 978-0-367-53451-6 (hbk)
ISBN: 978-0-367-51323-8 (pbk)
ISBN: 978-1-003-43175-6 (ebk)

DOI: 10.4324/9781003431756

Typeset in Calvert
by codeMantra

Contents

Contents

Preface to the Second Edition

The second edition of this book provides important updates to all the chapters with numerous recent events from the quickly evolving art business. In addition to updating all of the original chapters, a new Chapter 20 has been provided on Art Advisors, Art Finance, and Non-Fungible Tokens. The need for such a chapter came about because these rapidly emerging sectors all necessitated discussion especially on the perils present.

In the Introduction, I explain the concentric circle model of Art World, Art Business, Art Market. This book concerns itself with the two inner circles of that model, and particularly all the professional activities associated with art. It can be employed as a textbook for higher education courses in topics such as Gallery Management, Visual Arts Management, Arts Administration, as well as Curatorial Practice, and Museum Studies. The chapters progress from very general topics in which any student who aspires to a career in the art business should expect to be relatively competent towards chapters that become increasingly specific in their focus by the book's end. These early chapters lay out the essential sectors of the art business: the primary art market, the secondary art market, auction houses, art fairs, antiques, and museums. Potential graduates of professional programs in visual arts management might conceivably end up in any of these sectors, and so all of them should be covered.

The latter chapters of the book could be more described as a handbook, with more technical discussions of highly professional activities that may only become relevant to someone once they have graduated and are facing these sorts of tasks. These chapter topics include transportation, customs, cultural heritage compliance, and taxation. Some chapters also explore specialized areas of activity such as curatorship, appraising, and connoisseurship. The book endeavors to balance a need to describe general structures and practices in a theoretical discourse, while also providing narrative examples to help illustrate these points. Furthermore, each chapter concludes with a case study that should re-emphasize some of the chapter's most important ideas. Often these case studies can be cautionary tales of things that have been known to go wrong in the art business, and hopefully students will be fore-warned. For the new Chapter 20, for example, the case study examines the fraudulent schemes of Inigo Philbrick. Each chapter also provides ten terms relevant to that sector or activity, which are frequently employed by professionals, but students would be unlikely to know its precise meaning in an art context.

The art business is global, and therefore, I attempt to present it in a global perspective and not give overemphasis to simply one location. That said, New York will, of course, figure more prominently than any other city as it remains the undisputed capital of the art business. One common configuration is that art worlds tend to evolve into centers and peripheries, and this book aims to address the concerns of art professionals working in either centers or peripheries, large cities or small towns. In some chapters, there may be a great many different local and national variants in sectors such as: taxation, cultural heritage compliance, or customs, and for these topics I attempted to provide as diverse a set of examples, as possible. This book should, therefore, be relevant to students and practitioners in any location within the global art business.

Acknowledgments

Upon the publication of this second edition, I would need to gratefully thank Fulbright for my current position as a US Fulbright Scholar at the European Humanities University (EHU) in Vilnius, Lithuania. The research provision of this fellowship has allowed time and access to the research facilities of EHU and city of Vilnius that were essential to a careful revision and expansion of this book. I must also acknowledge the National Endowment for their Arts (NEA) for their Research: Art Works grant that allowed me and my team to produce our *Report on the US Art & Design Market* that provides much of the underlying research incorporated into this second edition.

This original writing of the book was made possible through an opportunity provided by the Frick Collection and the Frick Art Reference Library, and specifically their Center for the History of Collecting, which allowed me to serve as 2016 Leon Levy Fellow, and to conduct an extensive study in the historical art market's disruptions and problems. In addition, I must thank the Eugene and Emily Grant Family Foundation award I received in 2013 for allowing for an in-depth consideration of the crisis of forgery. In past years, I have also been the beneficiary of the Kress Foundation's program on technical art history at Yale University. Furthermore, many ideas for this book emerged from advanced study events provided by the National Endowment for the Humanities and the Harriman Institute at Columbia University.

From an educational perspective, I must first acknowledge the role of my PhD dissertation advisor Ilona Sármány-Parsons at the Central European University (CEU), who encouraged me towards a study of the art market as an academic topic. In general, the milieu of CEU formed so many of the intellectual foundations necessary for this critical undertaking, and I must especially single out Istvan Rév, who taught me to think in a way capable of comprehending the art world in its totality. I would never have been able to complete my dissertation and subsequent first book (which allowed me to develop a conceptual approach to the art market) if not for the very professional staff at the Budapest Museum of Fine Arts Library and the Archives of the Hungarian Academy of Science Art History Institute. Director of the Institute József Sisa has consistently been a role model of the cooperatively minded cross-disciplinary art historian. My colleagues at the Frick Art Reference Library (especially Christina Peter) and their Center for the History of Collecting (Inge Reist, Esmée Quodbach, and Samantha Deutch) provided excellent support and guidance to their world-class resources which so-much informed the writing of this book. Many of my university colleagues have frequently assisted with anecdotes and research opportunities, and I must particularly single out my colleague Bernadette Salem, who continually urged me on towards the completion of this second edition. I have consistently benefited from the trainings and conferences provided by the Appraisers Association of America, who continue to be a leading repository of knowledge on the vast and disparate corners of the art, antiques, and collectibles markets. The team of researchers who joined our NEA project to measure the US Art & Design Market also significantly assisted with the research inherent in this second edition. I must particularly acknowledge: Gayla Ruckhaus for her sampling of the US gallery landscape, Paulina Szarleja for her surveying and preparing the data for publication, James Grau for his study of related art market research projects, and Steven Graning, for work on the sources for this edition.

On a professional level, at the forefront of those to be mentioned are the many unforgettable characters who make up the Central European art market and who populated my apprenticeship in the trade. Many of them forming negative examples, but a few being true role models of what it meant to be a scrupulous connoisseur and also a good actor: Judit Virág in auctions, Zelko Kvarda in antiques, and Gergely Barki as a museum curator. Many of the top professionals in New York's art services industries would contribute their insights and anecdotes which have been consolidated into this book's chapters. Especially, I must acknowledge Andrea Megyes and the team at Dietl International for their descriptions of how transport, customs, and cultural heritage compliance happen at its highest level of professionalism. Above all, I must acknowledge my business partner Thiago Piwowarczyk at New York Art Forensics for the constant advice and support, as well as sharing many of the experiences that serve as the foundation to this book's knowledge.

I am extremely grateful to the universities who have given me the chance to pursue this subject on an academic level: The International Business School of Budapest, the *Institut d'Études Supérieures des Arts* (IESA) in Paris, SUNY Purchase, Western Colorado University, and especially my current home at the EHU. The EHU's mission to provide a liberal arts and design-focused education for students from Belarus, Russia, and Ukraine in the safe, cultural vibrant, and free environment of Vilnius, Lithuania remains an inspiring example to the enduring soft power inherent in art.

Introduction

The Art Business, Art World, Art Market

The public space occupied by art has become so massive and ubiquitous that we have coined a term to articulate its vast reach: the art world. The term includes every activity and venue where art is present: museums, art galleries (both commercial and noncommercial), schools where art and art history are taught, and all the publications (books and journals) devoted to art would form just a short list of the full expansiveness of the term. It encompasses the activity of both professionals and amateurs, and it is often given to geographic or chronological designations to describe these categories in a more contained understanding: for example, the New York art world, or the nineteenth-century Paris art world.

A more discrete term would be the art business, which refers to all the activities surrounding the production, commerce, and exhibition of art. Furthermore, the term encompasses all the activity of people professionally engaged with art. This art business includes both commercial for profit enterprises and also nonprofit entities that employ people and earn income through art. If money changes hands, whether to purchase objects or to purchase an entry ticket or an art publication, then it would be considered an activity within the art business. This book concerns itself with art professionals and their institutions that make up the art business.

We can imagine the art world as a concentric circle that surrounds the art business. That circle would then contain

DOI: 10.4324/9781003431756-1

two very distinct inner circles, divided into their distinct forms of consumption. One offering experiential consumption of art and the other offering ownership consumption of artworks. In addition, there would be some professional activities that would serve both circles and not be subsumed in either, for example, transportation, customs, and conservation.

The experiential consumers largely patronize nonprofit and state-owned museums and public art collections. Therefore, this sector can be more simply understood to reference the museum sector, where the business model is to offer an experience with artworks, but not ownership of them. In recent years, this sector that had been almost exclusively nonprofit and state-owned has now also witnessed the appearance of for-profit entities, such as Meow Wolf, that are also selling forms of experiential consumption.

The other distinct inner circle is the one that sells ownership of artworks, or ownership consumption. It can more precisely be called the art market, which is the commerce in art where transfers of ownership occur. The entities of this sector include auction houses, commercial galleries, art fairs, and related supporting professions, such as art advisors and appraisers. The term art market may also be divided into two distinctly different markets: the primary art market and the secondary art market. The primary art market refers to artworks being sold for the first time and essentially functions as a synonym for the contemporary art market. The secondary art market refers to artworks sold for the second (or third or fourth) time and is often understood to mean the trade in older artworks.

This book can be read as a handbook to those professional activities of the art business, and each chapter is intended to be self-contained so that it can be read on its own. The chapters proceed systematically through first the areas of the ownership consumption, especially its types of commercial entities. Then experiential ownership and museums are considered especially with their focus on curatorship. Finally, the book concludes with a series of chapters relevant to practitioners in either sector, including transportation, customs, cultural heritage compliance, marketing, conservation, and connoisseurship.

Introduction

ART AS A CONCEPT

Art as a concept is relatively new. All cultures have had a concept of treasure—essentially materials that are highly prized and have exchange value. Treasure, although it may have been constructed with great care and craftsmanship, still draws its value primarily from its input materials. Art, however, draws its value primarily from a knowledge of who made it, and, as a concept, has existed rarely in history. If we consider the Metropolitan Museum of Art in New York, the museum's entire first floor containing its massive Egyptian, Greek, Roman, African, Pre-Columbian Americas, and Oceanic collections might be colloquially referred to as "art" (because of the building in which they are located), but virtually none of it was produced according to our modern notion of art. Most of it was produced to serve a religious function, and if not that, then as a form of state propaganda to glorify the ruling power. The makers of those objects were not artists in the way we conceive of the profession now. They were not expected to express their own creative impulses, nor were they expected to innovate new methods of representation, and their names are largely not recorded.[1] They were crafting objects that would serve as repositories of divine power and lavished attention to detail in order that it should be worthy of that role.

The long transition from art's religious purpose to one that is purely secular and unencumbered with any other assigned purpose other than to be art, took centuries to occur and only became widely accepted in the nineteenth century. Even today, art continues to borrow from the terminology of religion to express its value and describe the act of creation. In fact, the cult of art is now frequently referred to as a sort of secular pseudo-religion that embodies all that is good and valuable in civilization, and which gives meaning and purpose to people.

THE PHENOMENON OF COLLECTING

Other species have been known to hoard,[2] but *Homo sapiens* are the only species known to collect. Various attempts have been made to explain this peculiar phenomenon. Objects might be collected because they have acquired symbolic meaning that differentiates them from other, more mundane objects.[3] This prioritization of the objects that collectors' prize evolved into a sophisticated system of symbolic goods that acquire cultural capital and can be converted into numeric denominations of financial capital.[4] By the nineteenth century, class distinctions brought on by industrialization further emphasized the need for prestige goods and their conspicuous consumption.[5] Despite advancing innovations in printing and photography allowing for a wider, more egalitarian dissemination of artistic images, the art world continued to fetishize the one-of-a-kind object as holding some very specific "aura."[6] Furthermore, the prices achieved by these unique objects express not just their position within social networks, but also webs of meaning that are understood by those networks.[7]

Something that might be identified as an aesthetic impulse can already be recognized among our ancestors in the Acheulean hand-axes that began to appear as early 150,000 BCE,[8] which lavished excessive care on the appearance of the tool beyond what would have been necessary to achieve its function and would indicate their forms to be a product of "cultural concepts."[9] As an almost universal phenomenon, cultures have created objects, particularly those imbued with sacred and political significance, that are finely crafted and composed of valuable input materials. We can term these objects as treasure, and if other cultures come into possession of these objects, they too can also value them based on a common appreciation for the input materials, even if the context of the objects has been lost. An important paradigm shift, however, began to occur as a result of the Axial Age (900–300 BCE)[10] when philosophical and religious systems began to emerge that gave new importance to the individual. The names of sought-after craftspeople became known and began to be recorded in proto-art histories.[11] Art then emerges as a new system of valuation for objects, one not based on input materials, but rather on a knowledge of who made them.

The earliest records of the appearance of art collecting, that is, collecting objects based on a prioritization of their makers, can first be identified in the Hellenistic period (323–31 BCE) in the Eastern Mediterranean.[12] Subsequently, a similar phenomenon can be observed in the Later Eastern Han Dynasty in China

Introduction

(25–220 CE).[13] The common characteristic that both societies had developed was a historical perspective that allowed them to look upon past eras as a sort of lost golden age. In Greece, the high Hellenic period of the construction of the Parthenon in Athens had given way to a disastrous Peloponnesian War[14] and subsequent invasion by the Gauls (279 BCE).[15] The restoration of the Eastern Han Dynasty (25–220 CE) was characterized by strong nostalgia for the earlier Western Han (202 BCE–9 CE) and all that had been destroyed during the turbulent period of interregnum and the short-lived Xin Dynasty (9–23 CE).[16] The loss of much of the cultural material from these earlier times was further emphasized by a literary historical tradition that celebrated these prior eras and identified their cultural producers by name. At this time, we can observe the peculiar human habit of collecting,[17] and particularly the targeted collection of objects made by those named in these texts.

The earliest recorded example of targeted collecting of named masters can be identified at the Sack of Corinth in 146 BCE, when the Roman general Lucius Mummius held an auction of the loot. Pliny the Elder places the event as the moment when Romans developed a taste for Greek art:

> For upon the sale of the spoil on that occasion, King Attalus having purchased, at the price of six thousand denarii, a painting of Father Liber by Aristides, Mummius, feeling surprised at the price, and suspecting that there might be some merit in it of which he himself was unaware, in spite of the complaints of Attalus, broke off the bargain, and had the picture placed in the Temple of Ceres; the first instance, I conceive, of a foreign painting being publicly exhibited at Rome.[18]

In this scene, we observe forces of a nascent art market at work, the dynamics of which were familiar to King Attalus II of Pergamon[19] but surprised the Roman Mummius. Attalus, however, had been educated in the gymnasia of Athens,[20] where he had been inculcated with a knowledge of an art history that was already many centuries in development, and therefore, would have known of the esteemed position held by

Aristides within its hierarchy.[21] The period of the later Roman Republic and Empire would witness the emergence of a fully formed art world or what Joseph Alsop would term the Eight By-products of Art.[22] Once a society has embraced the concept of art, which, distinct from treasure, values the object primarily based on a knowledge of who made it, then eight by-products can subsequently be observed. One, art collecting occurs when wealthy individuals begin to prioritize the acquisition of objects made by certain artists. Their collecting is informed by, two, art history, which sets up a hierarchy of past masters. The art market, three, then prices artworks according to their standing within the hierarchy established by art history. Once these three basic elements are in place, then five more phenomena quickly appear. At this time in the Mediterranean world of antiquity, forms of public collections began to emerge, either in the holdings of sacred institutions,[23] libraries,[24] or public spaces.[25] These collections, which increasingly venerated the makers of their objects, can be considered early forms of what is the fourth of these by-products, art museums. Number five, art faking, appears as a result of the dramatically higher prices commanded by works by canonical artists and therefore incentivizes attempts to fraudulently attribute similar pieces.[26] With so much value riding on a knowledge of attribution, then any change in that knowledge can produce, six, the process of revaluation. Interest in the artworks of earlier eras spurs a wider interest in collecting the material culture of those eras, a trade we call antiques, which is seven. The eighth by-product, super-prices, produces much of the dynamism on the art market because like material objects can command dramatically higher prices based on an attribution.[27] All of these linked phenomena would exist until the fall of the Roman Empire in the West. It would be replaced by a commerce that would operate on much of these same principles, the trade in sacred relics.[28]

The fair as a model of conducting commerce, in any commodity, remains one of the oldest formats of trade. In fact, it nearly always predates the models of fixed retail commerce such as shops. This was the case in ancient times, and with the collapse of much of civilization in the Dark Ages in Europe, commerce emerged slowly in medieval times first in the form of fairs and markets, and only later into fixed commercial venues.[29] The merchants coming to the fairs were bringing in goods that were otherwise scarce in that area and earning a profit from being able to sell these goods where they were otherwise unavailable. Their overhead costs came in the form of transportation and security, but they saved money by being able to do business with only a temporary facility and be present only when consumer demand had been consolidated. The earliest art fairs began along that model. The first one we know of, the Pand market, was located in the courtyard of the Church of Our Lady in Antwerp in Flanders (today's Belgium).[30] This fair featured primarily printed works, especially woodcuts, often of devotional topics popular with the private piety movement of the fifteenth century, which sought an alternative to a corrupt institutional church. As the markets expanded across Northern Europe, printers began speculating in popular motifs and sending examples to many locations.[31] The commerce in oil paintings, however, was more controlled by the local Guilds of St. Luke, which would not allow outside works to be sold within a city's domain.[32]

The creation of the French *Académie royale de peinture et de sculpture* was, in many ways, an attempt to circumvent the power of the guilds through the protection of the king.[33] When the Academy began holding shows in the seventeenth century of the latest works by the teachers and their students, it would form the basis for the dominant model of art commerce up through to the beginning of the twentieth century. The Paris Salon, named for the *Salon Carré* where the early exhibitions of the *Académie des Beaux-Arts* were held, became, by the eighteenth century, the once-a-year exhibition of contemporary art.[34] Following the French Revolution exhibitions were opened to all artists. By the later eighteenth century, other art centers would also imitate the model: The Royal Academy began holding exhibitions in London in 1768.[35] Civic-minded patrons would found art unions [*kunstverein*] across the emerging cities of Central Europe, which resembled small municipally organized versions of the Salon system.[36] By the later nineteenth century, those art unions would be superseded by organizations that aspired toward national representation, with the organization often identified with its purpose-built facility, a *kunsthalle*, such as the Vienna *Künstlerhaus*[37] or the *Műcsarnok* in Budapest.[38]

These salons would face a phenomenon of secessions, or alternative exhibition societies, as these salons were overwhelmed by waves of artist proletariat in the late nineteenth century. These massive market-monopolizing institutions would begin to fracture toward the end of the century and would increasingly be replaced by entrepreneurial dealers[39] who more successfully solved the overarching, never-ending crisis of the art market: who would allocate the market's most precious asset, its wall space. The ultimate dialectic triumph of the dealer, of which the 1913 Armory Show will be a crucial event, must first pass through a process of market pluralization, often associated with break-away salons, known as secessions. The unrelenting force causing the perpetual crisis in the Salon system was the expanding stream of young people throwing themselves into the profession of artist. The market would shatter into many facets—official salon, alternative salon, self-staging movements, and new commercial galleries—all driven by a mad scramble for new business models in the face of this massive glut of supply.

CENTERS OF THE ART WORLD

From the Renaissance period to the present, the art world has always had a center. The fifteenth century saw Florence emerge as a center of humanism and artistic innovation but would cede primacy to Rome in the sixteenth century. Rome would remain the undisputed art center until the middle of the nineteenth century.[40] During the 1850s, the reorganization of Paris along Baron Haussmann's principles also saw it become the world center for the leisure economy. During these same years, the secondary market (the market for older art works) and the antique market also began to migrate from Holland to Paris and particularly to its primary auction house, Drouot.[41] As a result of the French Revolution, however, much of the prime secondary market material began to be sold in London. During this period, the two leading auction houses, Christie's and Sotheby's, came of age. It is also in London that the House of Duveen was founded as an antique purveyor to the Royal Family.[42]

Like other art centers on the European periphery, New York witnessed its own secession, when a number of artists decided to compete with the dominant National Academy of Design (essentially the New York equivalent of the Salon) and hold an extraordinary exhibition involving vast amounts of European modernist art.[43] Unlike other secessions, New York's 1913 Armory Show happened only once, but it spawned a series of new artist organizations and, more importantly, served as a symbolic moment when the gravity of the art world began to shift across the Atlantic. European dealers had been colonizing New York for many decades already, with Michael Knoedler taking control of a gallery established in 1846 to be a representative of the French lithographer, Goupil & Cie.[44] In the 1880s, the dealer of the Impressionists, Paul Durand-Ruel, established a presence in New York, where his faltering business was rescued by American interest in the movement, which had been largely scorned in Europe.[45] In the 1890s, the Duveen firm opened its New York branch, and it was there that young Joseph Duveen cultivated the taste for old master paintings among the new millionaire class.[46] During the period between the two World Wars, the migration intensified among dealers, artists, and collectors. Many leading figures of the European avant-garde—Marcel Duchamp, Max Ernst, Piet Mondrian, and Andre Breton—would make New York their home.

New cultural institutions also began to proclaim an emboldened self-confidence. The Whitney Museum was founded to expressly promote American art. The Museum of Modern Art quickly became one of the dominant international tastemakers in determining the trajectory of canonical modern art. Both Solomon and Peggy Guggenheim (related—uncle and niece—but two very distinctly different people) played essential roles in the promotion of abstract art as New York's signature style. Solomon Guggenheim, under the influence of Hilla Rebay, founded the Museum of Non-Objective Art in 1939, which would ultimately become today's Guggenheim Museum.[47] Peggy Guggenheim founded a short-lived institution called Art of This Century, which both served as a museum for European Abstract and Surrealist art, and also as a commercial gallery where it helped launch the careers of Jackson Pollock and Mark Rothko.[48] New dealers with strong commitments to the New York school, now called abstract expressionism, such as Betty Parsons and Sidney Janis, began to fundamentally alter the way art was sold.

Parsons introduced unframed canvases in a white, unadorned room. Janis relentlessly pushed up the prices of his leading artists, especially, as with Pollock, after they were dead.[49]

From the late 1940s on, New York became the undisputed center of the art world. It had already been the center of high-end secondary market dealing since the early twentieth century, but by the mid-century, the primary market too had moved to New York. While the secondary market has remained fixed on the Upper East Side of Manhattan on Madison Avenue, the primary market made three major moves in the later twentieth century, migrating from 57th Street to Soho in the 1980s, and to Chelsea starting in the late 1990s.[50] Now the Chelsea contemporary art district is reputed to contain at least 300 galleries.

In the 1980s, the big auction houses, Christie's and Sotheby's, entered the U.S. market and increasingly began to shift the gravity of their most important sales from London to New York. Paris still plays a primary role in the antique trade with the agglomeration of flea markets known as *Marché aux Puces de Saint-Ouen* continuing to serve as a leading wholesale center (especially for U.S. antique dealers) for furniture and a vast array of applied arts. London's role in secondary and antique markets declined precipitously in recent years as the city's ever rising real estate costs vastly exceed what can be earned in re-sale trades. Nonetheless, London had found a new role for itself as a rival to New York in the area of contemporary art and presented the first serious competitor to New York's pre-eminence in almost half a century. That ascendancy, however, came to an abrupt halt with the 2016 Brexit referendum, and the UK's subsequent departure from the European Union.[51] Nonetheless, no other city has emerged to steal the title of the world's second art center, though many are making claims to it. Paris recently added the Paris+ art fair, part of the Art Basel chain, in an attempt to reassert its historical stature.[52] Berlin was, for a long time, expected to assume a more significant stature, but failed to generate a significant home market.[53] In Asia, just as Hong Kong appeared to have won the battle for art center of Asia, it just as quickly lost that title. Among the other aspirants: Seoul, Beijing, Shanghai, Taipei, Singapore, Mumbai, or Tokyo, none have been able to assert anything more than local and national dominance. That lack of a dominant Asian art center may more reflect that their markets remain based in their own national school. In the United States, the leading rival to New York, Los Angeles can boast enormous buying power and a plethora of working artists but lacks other significant component parts of global art center. For the moment, New York remains the only city to possesses the commensurate concentration of all sectors: primary market, secondary market, auction houses, museums, working artists in all media, and associated professions such as conservators of all media, publishing, academics, art handlers, and appraisers. Nowhere else do we such see a constant flow of artworks from all over the globe as that into and out of New York.

Even though New York's primacy remains unchallenged, new centers of gravity have begun to emerge at a surprising pace across the United States and globally. All the major American metropolises (Boston, Washington, D.C., Chicago, Los Angeles, San Francisco, and Miami) boast significant self-confident art scenes. Historical towns with strong tourism industries based around their coastal waters or their skiing and outdoor recreation, such as Provincetown, Jackson, Santa Fe, and Aspen, develop as art centers because of the concentration of both artists and collectors. One of the leading global trends is the practice of repurposing industrial structures for reuse as artists' studios, galleries, or exhibition spaces. This phenomenon is occurring all across the industrialized world, from the 798 Art District in Beijing to the Box Factory of this author's hometown of St. Joseph, Michigan.

Despite the seeming existential threat posed by Covid-19, the art world has bounced back to be bigger than ever. The does not mean, however, that it is not also riven with near constant crisis. The infrastructure and support for contemporary art across the globe continues to grow, but other sectors, especially antiques, remain in a prolonged depression.[54] The secondary market galleries complain that much of its business is being cannibalized by the auction houses.[55] Furthermore, the art fair phenomenon, which has become a parallel retailing platform to the ones based around permanent venues, may have finally reached its peak saturation, and Covid-19 certainly accelerated the shake-out of less-resilient fairs. If one tendency is sure, it is that next year tens of thousands of new BFA and MFA graduates will throw themselves onto the market in the hope of having a career as a working artist. As these artists struggle to be shown and sold, innovative conceptions will emerge out of that struggle, and the art world will continue to evolve.

CASE STUDY: THE SALON DES REFUSÉS

No single event did more to set in place the modernist art market than an event in Paris in 1863 called the *Salon des Refusés*.[56] In the nineteenth century, Paris had grown into the leading center of an increasingly global art world. Although primary market dealers did exist at this time, the dominant platform for the sale of contemporary art works remained the yearly Paris Salon. By 1863, the event was held annually in the massive Grand Palais, an exhibition hall capable of routinely showing up to 4,000 artworks.[57] Nonetheless, by 1863, Paris had already attracted so many aspiring artists that the Salon for 1863 received over 7,000 submissions.[58] The Salon's jury was composed of mostly elderly members of the Academy and other decorated artists, who accepted less than half of the entrants that year. Outrage among the rejected artists, the *Refusés*, led the emperor Louis-Napoléon Bonaparte to offer them to show their works, and let the public decide.[59]

Only a small number of those who were refused actually elected to take part in the show.[60] The two most memorable entrants, though, would leave a lasting impression upon the development of modern art. Édouard Manet had submitted his *Le Déjeuner sur l'herbe* [Luncheon on the Grass],[61] which horrified viewers with an obvious reference to a well-known piece in the collection of the Louvre, *Le Concert champêtre* [Pastoral Concert] by Titian/Giorgione. The other notable entrant was James McNeill Whistler's *Symphony in White, No. 1: The White Girl*,[62] which appeared absurd in its flattened exercise in variants of white pigment. Both would become giants in the history of art. Manet is widely regarded as the founder of the mega-movement called Modernism. Whistler stands as one of the most esteemed American painters, and his solo exhibitions in London in the 1870 and 1880s would serve as landmarks in the evolution of curating.[63] The most important achievement of the *Salon des Refusés* would be the construction of a key component of the modernist paradigm: the maverick.[64] Until this time, an ideal artist's career was understood to be one of straight upward trajectory. With the emergence of modernist heroes such as Manet, Whistler, and subsequent trailblazers Paul Cezanne, Georges Seurat, and Vincent van Gogh, however, the narrative arc became more complex. An artist must first pass through a period of being misunderstood and denigrated. The modernist maverick should only achieve widespread admiration at the end of their life or posthumously. The art market then prizes these bold and unappreciated early works above all else, and any collector prescient enough to purchase them can subsequently reap enormous rewards when the artist reaches canonical status.

INTRODUCTION—TERMS

Treasure—valuable materials which may also carry value similar to or be easily convertible into currency. Treasure may be objects fashioned with excellent craftsmanship, but value is still primarily derived from the input material.

Primary Art Market—the market in artworks being sold for the first time. It is frequently referred to as the contemporary art market.

Secondary Art Market—the market in artworks being sold for a second (or third, fourth, etc.) time. Usually implies the sale of older works, often where the artist is dead.

Antiques—a phenomenon which occurs in all mature art markets, which is the capacity of applied arts, and ultimately any object of human creation, to acquire value as a result of age and subsequently follow the commercial hierarchies of the art market.

Art history—a crucial prerequisite for the existence of a secondary art market. A historical perspective and the selective elevation of certain past practitioners creates the hierarchy with which the market determines valuation.

Super-Prices—a phenomenon which occurs only in the art market where materially identical works can hold vastly different values (even in ratios of 10,000 to 1 or more) based strictly on the work's authorship.

Revaluation—the capacity of artworks to rise or fall dramatically in value, usually related to new information about the work's authorship.

Applied Art—objects created by a formula of use-plus-beauty, that is, artworks that are produced to be both beautiful but also functional.

Fine Art—objects created by a formula of art-as-end-in-itself. In the nineteenth century, this concept became associated with the *l'art pour l'art* [art for art's sake] movement.

Collector—the prime mover of the art market. The desire of collectors to own certain artworks, and their willingness to outbid all other collectors for those artworks, provides the core dynamic that drives the market.

Notes

1   The *Euphronios Krater*, signed by Euphronios, the Athenian vase painter, when it was in the collection (1972–2008), would have been a notable exception. See: Povoledo, E. "Ancient Vase Comes Home to a Hero's Welcome." *The New York Times*, Jan. 19, 2008.

2   For discussion of magpies, for example, see: Shephard, T., Lea, S. and Hempel de Ibarra, N. "The Thieving Magpie'? No Evidence for Attraction to Shiny Objects." *Animal Cognition*, vol. 18, no. 1, Aug. 2014.

3   Schultheis, F. "The Art, the Market, and Sociology: Concluding Remarks." In Glauser, A., Holder, P., Mazzurana, T., Moeschler, O., Rolle, V., and Schultheis, F., eds., *The Sociology of Arts and Markets: New Developments and Persistent Patterns*. Palgrave Macmillan, 2020, pp. 411–419.

4   Bourdieu, P. *Distinction: A Social Critique of the Judgment of Taste*. Trans. R. Nice. Harvard University Press, 1984.

5   Veblen, T. *The Theory of the Leisure Class: An Economic Study of Institutions*. MacMillan, 1899. p. 59.

6   Benjamin, W. "The Work of Art in the Age of Mechanical Reproduction." In Arendt, H., ed., Zohn, H. trans., *Illuminations: Essays and Reflections*. Schocken, 1969, pp. 218–242.

7   Schultheis, F. *Talking Prices: Symbolic Meanings of Prices on the Market for Contemporary Art*. Princeton University Press, 2005.

8   Lycett, S. J. "Acheulean Variation and Selection: Does Handaxe Symmetry Fit Neutral Expectations?" *Journal of Archaeological Science*, vol. 35 2008, pp. 2640–2648.

9   Bar-Yosef, O. "The Known and the Unknown about the Acheulean." In Goren-bar, N. and Sharon, G., eds., *Axe Age: Acheulian Tool-Making from Quarry to Discard*. Equinox, pp. 479–494.

10 Jaspers, Karl, *Vom Ursprung und Ziel der Geschichte*, München: Piper, 1949, p. 2.

11 An example of these proto-art histories would be the discussion of the painter Parrhasius contained in: Xenophon, *Memorabilia*. Ithaca, NY: Cornell University Press, 2001, Book 3, Chapter 10.

12 Alsop, J. *The Rare Art Traditions: The History of Art Collecting and Its Linked Phenomena Wherever These Have Appeared*. New York: Harper & Row 1987, pp. 28–29.

13 Ibid., pp. 29–31.

14 Thucydides. *History of the Peloponnesian War*. Ed. M. I. Finley, trans. R. Warner. New York: Penguin, 1972.

15 Pausanias. Trans. W. H. S. Jones, *Description of Greece*. Harvard University Press, 1918. 10.19.5–23.8.

16 Twitchett, D. and Loewe, M. (eds.), *The Cambridge History of China: Volume I: the Ch'in and Han Empires, 221 B.C. – A.D. 220*, Cambridge: Cambridge University Press, pp. 223–290.

17 Dillon, A. "Collecting as Routine Human Behavior: Motivations for Identity and Control in the Material and Digital World." *Information & Culture*, vol. 54, pp. 255–280.

18 Pliny the Elder. Ed. John Bostock, M.D., F.R.S. H.T. Riley, Esq., B.A. Book XXXV: An Account of Paintings and Colours, Chapter 8 — "At What Period Foreign Paintings Were First Introduced at Rome." *The Natural History*. Taylor and Francis, 1855.

19 Kaye, N. "The Dedicatory Inscription of the Stoa of Attalos in the Athenian Agora: Public Property, Commercial Space, and Hellenistic Kings." *The Journal of the American School of Classical Studies at Athens*, vol. 85, no. 3, July September 2016, pp. 537–558.

20 Troncoso, V. A. "The Hellenistic Gymnasium and the Pleasures of Paideia." *Symbolae Hilologorum Posnaniensium Graecae et Latinae*. Adam Mickiewicz University Press, Poznan, XIX, 2009, pp. 71–84.

21 Most of these proto-art histories are lost, but they are the source from which Pliny the Elder drew from for his chapters on art in *The Natural History*. For more discussion of these sources, see: Coulson, William D. E. "The Reliability of Pliny's Chapters on Greek and Roman Sculpture." *The Classical World*, vol. 69, no. 6, 1976, pp. 361–372.

22 Alsop, *The Rare Art Traditions*, pp. 16–17.

23 Pausanias, in *Description of Greece,* enumerates the holdings of many of the most important temples and holy places, for example in Thespiae, 9.27.1–4.

24 The competition between the libraries of Alexandria and Pergamon was particularly fierce for collecting the rarest and oldest extant manuscripts. See: Coqueugniot, Gaëlle. "Where was the Royal Library of Pergamum?: An Institution Found and Lost Again." In König, J. et al. eds., *Ancient Libraries*. Cambridge: Cambridge University Press, 2013, pp. 109–123. Also, the library at Pergamon was known to contain a copy of Phidias' sculpture of *Athena Parthenos*, See: Hill, D. K. "A Copy of the Athena Parthenos." *The Art Bulletin*, vol. 18, no. 2 June, 1936, pp. 150–167. The *Mouseion* of Alexandria, although the origin of the modern word museum, however, would better be understood at the time, as a gathering of scholars under the protection of the muses.

25 The Portico of Philippus serves as an example of this sort of public space. See: Heslin, P. *The Museum of Augustus: The Temple of Apollo in Pompeii, the Portico of Philippus in Rome, and Latin Poetry*. J. Paul Getty Museum, 2015.

26 Taylor, J. "Art Forgers and the Deconstruction of Genius." *Journal for Art Market Studies*, vol. 1 2021, pp. 2–3.

27 See: Pliny the Elder, *The Natural History*, Book XXXV, for many of the important masters known and prized by the classical art world.

28 Geary, P. J. "10. Sacred Commodities: The Circulation of Medieval Relics." In *Sacred Commodities: The Circulation of Medieval Relics.* Cornell University Press, 2018, pp. 194–218.

29 Casson, M. and Lee, J., "The Origin and Development of Markets: A Business History Perspective." *Business History Review*, vol. 85, no. 1 2011, pp. 9–37.

30 Ewing, D. "Marketing Art in Antwerp, 1460–1560: Our Lady's Pand." *Art Bulletin*, vol. 72, no. 4 1990, pp. 558–584.

31 Campbell, L. "The Art Market in the Southern Netherlands in the Fifteenth Century." *The Burlington Magazine*, vol. 118, no. 877, 1976, pp. 1s88–198.

32 Montias, J. "The Guild of St. Luke in 17th-Century Delft and the Economic Status of Artists and Artisans." *Simiolus: Netherlands Quarterly for the History of Art*, vol. 9, no. 2, 1977, pp. 93–105.

33 Landois, P. "Academy of Painting." In *The Encyclopedia of Diderot & d'Alembert* (1751, 2003). Collaborative Translation Project. Trans. R. Benhamou (2003). Ann Arbor: Michigan Publishing.

34 Crow, T. *Painters and Public Life in 18th Century Paris.* New Haven, CT: Yale University Press, 1987.

35 Sawbridge, P. *A Little History of the Royal Academy.* London: Royal Academy of Arts, 2019 (2022).

36 Romain, L. (1984) "Zur Geschichte des deutschen Kunstvereins. In: Arbeitsgemeinschaft deutscher Kunstvereine." In *Kunstlandschaft Bundesrepublik.* Stuttgart: Klett-Cotta, pp. 11–37.

37 Officially the "Gesellschaft bildender Künstler Österreichs" and later known as "Genossenschaft der bildenden Künstler Wiens." See: Neuwirth, W. M. (11961) *Das Wiener Künstlerhaus: Die Geschichte des Wiener Künstlerhauses Das geistige Antlitz - 100 Jahre Künstlerhaus 1861–1961.* Auszug eines Aufsatzes in der Festschrift anlässlich des hundertjährigen Bestehens des Wiener Künstlerhauses.

38 The organization was the *Országos Magyar Képzőművészeti Társulat* [National Hungarian Artist Society]. See: Taylor, J. *In Search of the Budapest Secession: The Artist Proletariat and the Modernism's rise in the Hungarian Art Market, 1800–1914.* Budapest: Central European University Press (Helena History Press), 2014, pp. 26–41.

39 Jensen, R. *Marketing Modernism in Fin-de-Siècle Europe.* Princeton, NJ: Princeton University Press, 1996, pp. 22–46.

40 Bowron, E. P. and Rishel, J. J. *Art in Rome in the Eighteenth Century* [Exhibition Catalogue]. Philadelphia Museum of Art (Rizzoli), 2000.

41 McClellan, A. "Edme Gersaint and the Marketing of Art in Eighteenth-Century Paris." *Eighteenth-Century Studies*, vol. 29, no. 2, Winter, 1995/1996, pp. 218–222.

42 Secrest, M. *Duveen: A Life in Art.* Alfred A. Knopf, 2004, pp. 19–40.

43 Brown, M. W. *The Story of the Armory Show.* Abbeville Press, 1988, pp. 45–62.

44 Goldstein, M. *Landscape with Figures: A History of Art Dealing in the United States.* Oxford University Press, 2003, p. 26.

45 Thompson, J. A. "Durand-Ruel and America." In Patry, S. ed., *Inventing Impressionism: Paul Durand-Ruel and the Modern Art Market.* London National Gallery, 2015, pp. 136–151.

46 Secrest, pp. 41–57.

47 Birnie Danzker, J.-A., Salmen, B., and Vail, K., *Art of Tomorrow: Hilla Rebay and Solomon R. Guggenheim.* Guggenheim Museum, 2005.

48 Davidson, S. and Rylands, P., eds. *Peggy Guggenheim & Fredrick Kiesler: The Story of Art of This Century.* Peggy Guggenheim Collection, 2005.

49 Goldstein, M. *Landscape with Figures: A History of Art Dealing in the United States.* Oxford: Oxford University Press, 2000, pp. 215–300.

50 Fensterstock, A. *Art on the Block: Tracking the New York Art World from SoHo to the Bowery, Bushwick and Beyond.* St. Martins Press, 2013.

51 Middleton, W. "Is Brexit Going to Cause a Crisis in the London Art Scene?" *Town and Country*, Nov. 5, 2019.

52 Greenberger, A. "Paris+, Explained: Why Art Basel Arrived in Paris, and What's Happening to FIAC." *ARTnews*, Oct. 16, 2022.

53 Brown, K. "The Organizers of Berlin's Most Important Art Fair Have Canceled All Future Editions Due to Financial Shortfall." *Artnet*, Dec. 11, 2019.

54 Tarmy, J. "Your Unloved Heirlooms Might Mean Serious Money." *Bloomberg*, July 1, 2021.

55 Ahlstrom Christy, C. "Art Market Transformed by Shifting Boundaries." *Property Journal*, July 15, 2022.

56 Boime, A. "The Salon des Refusés and the Evolution of Modern Art." *Art Quarterly*, vol. 32, Winter, 1969, pp. 411–426.

57 For example, the Salon of 1861 had 4,097 artworks. See: *Explication des Ouvrages de Peintre, Sculpture, Gravure, Lithographie, et Architecture des Artistes Vivants Exposés au Palais des Champs-Élysées - 1861.* Charles de Mourges Freres, 1861.

58 The *livret* for 1863 lists 2,923 works, and Boime cites 4,000 rejected works.

59 "Voulant laisser le public juge de la légitimité de ces reclamations," according to *Le Moniteur Universal*, Apr. 24, 1863.

60 The *livret* for the Salon des Refusés lists 687 works. *Catalouge des Ouvrages Refusés par le Jury de 1863.*

61 Lot 363 in the *livret*, titled *Le Bain* [The Bath].

62 Lot 596 in the *livret*, titled *Dame blanche* [White Woman].

63 Jensen, R. *Marketing Modernism in Fin-de-Siècle Europe.* Princeton University Press, 2022, pp. 42–48.

64 Robertson, I. "The International Art Market." In Robertson, I., ed., *Understanding International Art Markets and Management.* Routledge, pp. 13–60.

Primary Market Galleries

Chapter 1

TWO-AGENT MODEL

A large part of the commerce in newly made artworks goes on unnoticed, and essentially outside of the activity of primary market galleries. It happens through simple commissions between collectors and artists. In such cases, it would be difficult to speak of the existence of a market because neither seller nor buyer is a full-time professional merchant, and artworks do not enter a marketplace with dynamics of supply and demand. This model only involves two agents and almost invariably involves producing artworks with contracted features, and a pre-agreed price to be paid. For nearly the entire history of art, only this business model existed. It was how altarpieces and statues of monarchs were produced, and still exist widely, especially in the genres of painted portraits and large-scale public sculptures. This model of creating artworks derives from the ancient system of guild production when the costs of materials and production might easily exceed 50 percent of the object's final cost. Artists were treated as craftspeople and not expected to excessively concern themselves with expressing an aesthetic vision. Their concerns were more about quality, refinement, and attention to detail. Newer business models, such as open studio events, have helped revive this business model, allowing artists to deal directly with collectors and circumvent galleries entirely.

DOI: 10.4324/9781003431756-2

THREE-AGENT MODEL: PRODUCTION ON
SPECULATION AND THE ROLE OF THE DEALER

The creation of a primary art market based on the three-agent model is closely linked to the wider development of early capitalism and proto-industrialization in the sixteenth and seventeenth centuries. The declining costs of production, such as the introduction of linen canvases, and the wider availability of certain pigments such as cochineal acquired through European imperialism,[1] began to allow artists to make speculative ventures of painting pictures before any collector had ordered, or even expressed interest in such a work. A defining feature of early capitalism entails the specialization of the means of production, especially in breaking down what were formerly holistic tasks.[2] The guild method of making a painting would have involved all of the tasks being done all under one master's roof: preparation of a wooden support, grinding pigments, mixing pigments with binders, preparing brushes, painting the work, and finally framing the work.[3] By the early modern period (1500–1789), we can observe specialization in all these separate tasks, all essential to the making of a painting: canvas and brush suppliers, paint manufacturers, and framers, all of whom act as suppliers to the painters. As painters end up owing money to these suppliers, their creditors accept artworks in barter arrangements.[4] In order to redeem the artwork for cash, these supplier began to use the walls of their business as an improvised gallery of paintings for sale.

By the early nineteenth century, a new breed of dealer emerged from the book and print trade. These businesses sold books (used and new) as well as a vast collection of printed lithographs and engravings. They formed an international network of dealers in prints, some of which they printed themselves and others received on consignment from other firms.[5] They usually carried a variety of printed materials such as maps and sheet music.[6] Original artworks, such as an oil on canvas painting, were more important as the source for serially produced lithographs, and if the lithographs sold well enough, then the painting might ultimately be sold for a good price as well.[7] What was lacking in these early dealers was a concerted long-term interest in the careers of their artists.[8] They saw themselves as merchants of pictures, not of artists.

SALON VERSUS GALLERY

For good reason, dealers did not see themselves as concerned with the careers of artists: in the nineteenth century, careers were not made in galleries, they were made in the Salon.[9] Painters did not aspire to sell their paintings through a dealer, they hoped to sell them at the Salon. By the middle of the century, nearly all Western capitals and major cities had a local version of the Salon, and these yearly events galvanized emerging art centers across the globe. Artists preferred the Salon system because there was a public triumph: medals and scholarships could be won, a painting could be selected for reproduction as a lithograph, and the sale of an artwork would be publicly announced.[10] Furthermore, the organizers usually only took a 10–20 percent cut on the sale and paid promptly. The problem with the Salon system lay in its success: it attracted far too many artists by the end of the century, and increasingly up to half of all submissions could be rejected. Many disputes that arose at that time had to do with how Salon juries needed to be re-organized, with the electorate of such juries made more democratic. Nonetheless, no re-organization ever satisfied everyone, and as the Salons became more lenient, the viewing public simply found an ever-greater morass of tightly packed clashing styles, techniques, and themes.[11]

The Salon system began to be supplanted by a new generation of dealers who took an entrepreneurial approach to building the careers of their artists.[12] Paul Durand-Ruel pioneered this approach by supporting and promoting the artists of the Impressionist movement. The venture nearly led him to bankruptcy, but ultimately began to pay off in the 1890s when American and Russian collectors began to take an interest in the new movement.[13] This entrepreneurial dealer method would become the dominant business model of the twentieth century. This new type of dealer supported their artists financially, even when faced with a lack of sales to collectors. They would increasingly use their gallery primarily for solo exhibitions where artists experimenting with a new technique could show their vision in an adequate critical mass of works for the audience to appreciate their intentions.[14]

By the middle of the twentieth century, the Salon system had largely been vanquished. To our modern mind, the idea that the market's most precious asset, its wall space, could be divided up by committee (the jury was essentially a committee), strikes us as quaint and also a recipe for mediocrity, as well as never-ending disagreement. Modern art requires bold, uncompromising vision, and the petty despotism of the sole-proprietor gallery offers a far more consolidated decision-making structure. Nonetheless, Salons provided an undeniably valuable public, large-scale art experience, which galleries do not offer. Therefore, the Salon system was revived in the 1970s in the form of Art Basel and the contemporary art fair, the key difference being that the nineteenth-century Salon had a jury of artists who juried other artists. The twenty-first century art fair also has a jury, but it is a jury of dealers jurying other dealers.

ALPHA GALLERIES

At the pinnacle of the primary art market sit a handful of elite galleries, which can be referred to as alpha galleries. These galleries occupy multiple locations: Gagosian has 22 venues worldwide, and David Zwirner has seven. They have gallery locations that specialize in contemporary sales, and others that deal in secondary sales. Other galleries that are often referred to as alpha would be White Cube, Thaddeus Ropac, Pace, and Hauser & Wirth. These galleries act almost as tastemakers in and of themselves, in that when they bring a new artist into their stable, it is a sign of that artist having "made it." The galleries work along many platforms simultaneously. They stage mega-installations (e.g., Richard Serra, *Junction*, 2011 at Gagosian and Doug Wheeler, *SA MI 75 DZ NY 12*, 2012, and Yoyo Kusama, "*Who Have Arrived In Heaven*," 2013) that act as essentially free, museum-type art experiences. These kinds of exhibitions may not produce any readily salable objects but act as a statement of awesomeness by the gallery, and in fact museums often purchase the entire installation. These galleries also stage major retrospectives on canonical artists (Warhol, Giacometti) that also function as free museum shows, but where works can be discreetly purchased if a significant enough offer is made.

These galleries maintain a stable of approximately 30–50 artists who are on exclusive contract with a stipend. Therefore, the gallery essentially pays the artist a regular salary (against sales), which is paid regardless of actual sales. Each artist usually gets a solo exhibition once every two years. Furthermore, for many of their artists, the alpha galleries maintain a print division that sells lower cost, numbered lithographs and silkscreens. These galleries may have over 100 employees, including many specialists normally only found in museums, such as registrars. They occupy the most prominent and expensive locations at major art fairs and if they fail to attend, as Gagosian did not participate in the 2016 Armory Show, their absence is noted.[15] Their business models are complex and reliant on many different sources of revenue: prints can provide steady modest income and investments in new artists can be subsidized by discreet high-profit private sales of secondary market masterpieces.[16] The gallery frequently maintains a hierarchy of which collectors, depending on the status of their existing collection, receive primary access for purchasing new works from their in-demand artists.[17]

CHELSEA-TYPE GALLERIES

In the 1990s, the center migrated to Chelsea, an area in Manhattan's Lower West side between 10th and 11th Avenues, and it continues to reign as New York's dominant contemporary gallery district. Originally, it was its low costs and highly functional warehouse architecture (complete with freight lifts and easy truck accessibility) that attracted dealers over from Soho. Now, rents easily approach $20,000 per month for a modest-sized, non-street-level gallery space.[18] Many tenants have left or threatened to leave for lower cost locations in Brooklyn's Bushwick or Queen's Long Island City, or even across the Hudson to Jersey City. Nonetheless,for much of the last decade, no clear Next Chelsea made itself apparent in the critical agglomeration of galleries necessary to contest Chelsea's supremacy. Recently, however, the Lower East Side neighborhood of TriBeCa has been gathering momentum and attention.[19] Chelsea's current dominance is also buoyed by inherent strengths that only seem to be growing stronger. The area's gentrification and West Side building boom only bring in more well-heeled clientele, while the expanding High-Line and new Whitney Museum, and now the completion of The Shed[20] along the Hudson have truly turned the neighborhood into a contemporary art amusement park, especially on Thursday evenings, when at least 30 galleries hold openings with free wine.

A typical Chelsea gallery occupies one of the upper floors of the industrial warehouses and office buildings that used to service the piers that stretched out into the Hudson River. The prime street-front retail tends to be dominated by the Alpha caliber galleries. Most Chelsea galleries make use of the synergy of so many galleries all existing in a single building, and this pulls collectors and the general art audience up the stairs to the upper floors. With often three to five galleries per floor, visitors are drawn along in a sort of covered bazaar of contemporary art. Galleries in the same building also tend to coordinate their openings so that at least three to four are happening every Thursday evening.

The interior layout of these galleries tends to involve a high desk/counter toward the entrance where an intern can sit and monitor who comes in, though not necessarily greet anyone. The counter contains a guestbook, where visitors write comments and leave email addresses if they want to be on the gallery mailing list. Somewhere, in this area, will be a price sheet for the works on display. Prices are not normally posted on labels next to artworks. The gallery will have one main exhibition area which will generally be used for solo exhibitions. If the exhibition space can be divided in to two distinct units, then the gallery might have multiple simultaneous solo exhibitions. In addition to the exhibition areas, galleries will usually have a cramped storage area and an office. Ideally, the office will be large enough for staging private viewings of artworks with important collectors. Sometimes, galleries will hold a smaller, less desirable space in the same building and call it a "project" space. Such a space can actually be rented out to third-party exhibitors, either artists or curators, while giving the appearance of the exhibition having occurred at a gallery in Chelsea. In the trade, though, they tend to be known as "vanity galleries" and can even be regarded as something of scam preying upon artists desperate enough to pay to have a show.

Similar to the Alpha galleries, a Chelsea-type gallery might keep a stable of 18–24 artists who are represented by the gallery.

In many cases, these contracts might be exclusive, but perhaps not with a worldwide exclusivity, but rather only for the New York or US market. More cash-rich galleries may be able to pay stipends, but most have straightforward consignment arrangements, keeping anywhere from 40 to 60 percent of the sale price. The difference in percentages retained by the gallery usually reflects power relations indicative of how much the dealer and artists believe they need each other. Other costs which could either be met by the artist or absorbed by the gallery include the cost of framing and the transportation of the artworks to the gallery. At any given time, the gallery may be holding one or two solo shows in their exhibition space but will be working constantly to promote and sell all their represented artists through the back office, through showing collectors the examples they keep in the storage area. Furthermore, most of these galleries will participate in two to four art fairs a year, with the more established ones attending main fairs such as Art Basel Miami Beach, and the less established ones attending satellite fairs.[21]

The Chelsea-type galleries exist in all major art markets and as opposed to those in New York, those in other cities are more likely to be fortunate enough to occupy prime street-front retail locations in their leading gallery district, such as London's Mayfair or the Marais in Paris. What all these galleries have in common is a principal reliance on the sale of contemporary art as their primary source of revenue, and their business model emphasizes the building of artists' careers through a series of solo exhibitions and art fair exposure. Although they may not have as much leverage as an alpha gallery, a Chelsea-type gallery will also be greatly concerned over who is collecting their artists' work. The stature of a private collection, and ideally public collection, that is, a museum which buys an artists' work, goes a long way toward establishing canonical status and the super-values that go with such status. It is this long-term focus on the trajectory of their artists' careers that defines the operation of these galleries.

REGIONAL GALLERIES

The alternative to running a Chelsea-type gallery for the sale of contemporary art would be the regional gallery model. This model is far more numerous and widespread than the Chelsea model, and it is also generally much less expensive to operate. Regional galleries are frequently owned and operated by an artist who opened the business in order to give themselves a place to exhibit and sell. They usually invite five to ten other artists from the area to also exhibit there. Each exhibitor is given a designated location and they fill it with as much inventory as possible. The entire gallery uses a salon-style hanging approach, and no space goes unused. The gallery may also carry 3D pieces and sculpture on pedestals in the middle of the room and sell hand-made jewelry at the gallery's reception desk.

The gallery is called regional because it draws its artists from its region and also sells art that usually represents the region: its landscapes and familiar motifs. The difference between the regional model and the Chelsea model has everything to do with the difference in the collector base. Chelsea-style galleries exist in very large art centers with a wealthy local collector base. Their exhibitions rotate because their collectors come back month after month and expect to see something different each time. A regional gallery's collector base is transient. Most regional galleries exist in towns heavily dependent on the tourism economy, and tourists then make up a large part of the regional gallery's clientele. These collectors may only visit the gallery once, and so all the inventory must be available immediately, which is why it is hung salon style. Pieces on the wall largely do not move unless they are sold. Artists frequently become frustrated with the regional model because they believe it does not give them enough focus to catapult them into the upper levels of the art world, and the venue can feel more like a shop than a gallery. Nonetheless, in many markets the regional model is the only one that can work because Chelsea-type galleries require far-higher price-points in order to sustain that higher-cost model.

ARTIST-LED GALLERY MODELS

Similar to the way in which a frustrated artist might start a regional gallery to represent themselves and some of their colleagues, an artist may also opt to simply form a gallery which strictly sells their own work. This model, in fact, can be frequently found in gallery districts, especially those with distinct regional motifs. The artist may often serve as their own gallerist while also using the gallery as their studio, and in that way more resembles an open studio arrangement. Some of these self-representing artists can become quite successful and create a brand with chains of galleries selling the artist's work. Thomas Kinkade would be the best-known example of such an artist, but many others can be found among the galleries located in resort towns.

A different form of artist-maintained model would be the co-op gallery, which has member artists who all share duties of sitting in the gallery and acting as salesperson. They also then share opportunities for solo exhibitions and are allowed to keep a certain amount of their own material always in stock for sale.

OTHER MODELS FOR EXHIBITING AND SELLING CONTEMPORARY ART

In addition to the Chelsea-type and regional gallery models, a large variety of other business types also manage to sell contemporary art to collectors. Many of these types are essentially two-agent models, with the artist dealing more or less directly with the client, with the exhibiting entity being more of a passive platform than an active participant in the sale. Examples of these kinds of venues are public libraries, restaurants and cafes, open studio events, and local art fairs where artists can rent a stand. Small-scale salons are still often organized on many different organizing principles (region, medium) with juries and large collective exhibitions of many artists' work. In many cities, nonprofit art centers function in similar ways to that of Chelsea-type galleries in that they stage solo exhibitions, and the artworks are very much for sale, with the venue keeping a percentage of the sale (usually around 20–40 percent). Furthermore, the largest network of nonprofit exhibitions spaces exists on university campuses. Although these galleries and museums generally have a non-commercial profile, exhibitions serve to build careers and collectors can always make inquiries about works on display.

Other methods by which new artworks enter the hands of collectors can come through a raffle or charity auction process. These methods often occur with smaller value works and graphics, which are used as fundraisers for nonprofit galleries, art centers, and small museums. Other artists might choose to be represented by an art agent who does not keep a physical venue other than a small office, and some artists will simply sell their work directly on the internet through their own website, or any of the expanding platforms for selling art.

At the higher end, both Sotheby's and Christie's hold auctions devoted to primary market material, that is, new artworks that have not yet ever been sold and are coming straight from the studio.[22] Larger scale, public artworks such as murals and sculpture continue to be commissioned by governmental entities, architects, developers, and public art funds. At the lower end, print galleries and auction houses located in shopping malls, casinos, resorts, vacation towns, and cruise ships sell prints and new artworks (often referred to as "hotel art") of uncertain value.

SERIAL ART WORKS

The primary art market is frequently perceived to be mostly about paintings, that is, one-of-kind original artworks. In fact, a very large sector of it, and this has always been the case, occurs in the sale of serial artworks, that is, artworks that are produced in a series, and so are not original. This is the case with the enormous photography business. Furthermore, printing (woodcuts, lithographs, engravings, and later, photo-transfer) remains the most entrepreneurial and speculative area of the market because of the large investments in production and inventory. Prints also pose additional problematics for verifying their authenticity and for maintaining the "aura" of rarity, which still remains the driving force of the market.[23] Serial artworks usually sell for significanlty lower prices than original ones and offer an option for newer, less-wealthy collectors. Nonetheless, for them to have much value at all, they must possess a guaranteed rarity that comes with the print being part of a limited edition; for example, 100 prints, each one numbered with its own number out the total of 100 (with an additional 10–20 as artist's proofs). A photographer may print very few prints, or even just one. A scrupulous gallery keeps tight administration on the process and ensures that the printing plate/screen/negative is destroyed after the series is produced. This close control of both the production and sales process allows the gallery to verify the actual rarity of their product. The biggest threat to the serial art world is unauthorized reproduction.

This problem can occur where the printing process is not properly monitored and (materially identical except for perhaps a fake signature and numbering) unauthorized material gets sold into the market. This situation afflicts many of the twentieth century's biggest names: for example, Dali[24] and Warhol.[25]

In order to add a layer of authority to serial artworks, many galleries offer certificates of authenticity to verify that this is their print and in the numbering that is reported. However, buyers should beware, because these certificates are just as likely to be forged as the artworks themselves. Validating the authenticity and rarity of a serial artwork will always remain one of the central challenges of this sector of the primary market. The administration and stewardship essential to the print business has been adapted to other problematic sectors such as video art, digital art, conceptual art, and land art. All of these media face challenges on the marketplace because of the ease of their reproducibility or the fact that the artwork is not an easily commercially exchangeable object. Therefore, dealers in these media also use a combination of certificates of authenticity that verify the limitedness of the edition and then maintain good administration of which collectors own which pieces (which can be necessary if a piece needs to be digitally "replaced"). The phenomenon of Non-Fungible Tokens represents a technological solution through blockchain to similarly guarantee the rarity of what are otherwise infinitely reproducible artworks.[26]

IMPORTANCE OF MULTIPLE REVENUE STREAMS

It should again be stressed that the alpha galleries of the primary market often sustain themselves and earn a large proportion of their profits from either serial artworks or secondary market sales. In general, this lesson can be applied to the rest of the primary market. Most successful long-lasting galleries survive on a mixture of revenue streams. Many Chelsea-type galleries may in theory earn most of their income from contemporary art sales of works from the stable of artists they represent, but increasingly these galleries will also represent a deceased artist's estate and sell off works that remained in the artist's studio, and this kind of work more often resembles the secondary market.[27] Many galleries sell both original artworks such as paintings and also serial artworks such as prints, photographs, and bronze sculpture. Galleries and their dealers may often maintain multiple business profiles in related professions, such as being an art advisor, interior designer, framer, conservator, or appraiser. Given the fickleness of the contemporary art market, multiple revenue streams remain a vital part of any successful business strategy.

CASE STUDY: AMBROISE VOLLARD

Some dealers have exerted enormous influence over the composition of canonical membership in art movements. Paul Durand-Ruel largely determined who became the widely known figures among the Impressionists.[28] Betty Parsons and Sidney Janis did much to shape Abstract Expressionism.[29] Ambroise Vollard, however, more than anyone, created the canon for the mega-movement known as modernism. Students of art history will be familiar with an expression "the Four Horsemen of Post-Impressionism," referring to Paul Cezanne, Vincent van Gogh, Paul Gauguin, and Georges Seurat. These artists are understood to have led art from Impressionism into full-fledged, avant-garde modernism. The first director of the Museum of Modern Art (MoMA), Alfred Barr, drew what has now become a widely disseminated diagram that served as the dust jacket for the catalog of the museum's 1936 exhibition of Cubism and Abstract Art.[30] It shows how these four painters had been the source for all subsequent movements: Fauves, Cubism, Futurism, and early forms of abstract art. That hierarchy has been further re-referenced to generations of museum-goers because the first room of the MoMA's permanent collection that presents a history of modernism usually always contains works by Cezanne, van Gogh, Gauguin, and Seurat.[31] Ambroise Vollard dealt in the works of all four of them, and for two of them, Cezanne and Gauguin, Vollard is largely the only reason any of us have ever heard of them.

His rise in the Paris art market would appear an unlikely one. He did not come from a dynasty of dealers like

---

Durand-Ruel or Georges Petit. He began by staging small exhibitions in an apartment of works by Manet that were still in the possession of his widow. He then resurrected the career of Cezanne, who had retired back to his home in Provence,[32] Among the many other major names in art for which Vollard had served as dealer are: Matisse, Degas, Renoir, Bonnard, Vuillard, Denis, Derain, Redon, Henri Rousseau, and Rouault. Vollard gave Pablo Picasso his first show in Paris in 1901 but failed to ever offer the artist a permanent contract. Vollard did not necessarily comprehend the importance of Cubism, despite the fact that Picasso painted a Cubist portrait of the dealer that still stands as one of the definitive works of the early period. Picasso would move on to other dealers. Vollard also failed to appreciate Pointillism and did not continue to pursue the works of Seurat. Nonetheless, most dealers would consider their career a success if they had managed to discover one or two canonical masters. Vollard's long list of successes reads as a "who's-who" of Parisian modernism, and he achieved this with a sales strategy that often stood in marked contrast to his competitors. He kept a disorderly shop, where he sometimes slept in his chair, and generally did little to help his clients find the painting they were looking for.[33] Rather than represent artists he preferred to buy works outright, sometimes whole studios, and then hold the pieces for years while an artist's reputation and the prices went up.

PRIMARY ART MARKET—TERMS

Emerging artist—the preferred term for an artist who is at the beginning of their career, having had only a few gallery exhibitions. Savvy collectors aim to purchase works from an artist at this stage in their career.

Mid-career artist—the term for an artist who has had numerous gallery exhibitions, has a cadre of collectors, and has probably been working professionally for at least ten years. These artists are hoping to make the next step up into future canonical status.

Alpha gallery—one of a handful of top galleries who maintain venues in major art centers across the globe. They will be present at every major international art fair.

Studio show—a method of circumventing the gallery system where artists have exhibitions of their work inside their own studio. These shows often occur in coordination with other artists who have studios in the same building.

Pop-up gallery—a gallery which occupies an improvised space which has been acquired for a short-term lease at little or no rent.

Opening—the event that marks the beginning of a temporary exhibition. These may include both VIP and public events, usually in the evening with the artist present.

Solo show—exhibition where the work of only one artist is shown. It offers an opportunity for an artist to fully present their work with proper contextualization and adequate numbers of pieces to really express an aesthetic direction.

Group show—exhibition involving works by multiple artists. Group shows may be showing the works of an artists' collective or movement, or they might have a unifying theme which should be apparent from the exhibition's title.

Consignment—the payment model used by most galleries: an artist consigns their artwork to the gallery. If the artwork is sold, then the gallery pays the artist their share (typically between 40 and 60 percent of the sale price).

Stable of artists—most Chelsea-type galleries maintain contractual relations with a limited number of artists they represent, often referred to as a stable. These artists are supposed to sell their works only through the representing gallery, and in exchange are promised a solo exhibition, usually every two years. Therefore, a stable tends to be no bigger than 18–24 artists.

Notes

1 Lee, R. L. "Cochineal Production and Trade in New Spain to 1600." *The Americas*, vol. 4, no. 4, Apr. 1948, pp. 449–473.

2 Smith, A. *An Enquiry into the Nature and Causes of the Wealth of Nations*. Random House, 1947, pp. 3–5.

3 Prak, M. "Guilds and the Development of the Art Market during the Dutch Golden Age." *Simiolus: Netherlands Quarterly for the History of Art*, vol. 30, no. ¾, 2003, pp. 236–251.

4 Montais, J. M. (1988) "Art Dealers in the Seventeenth-Century Netherlands." *Simiolus: Netherlands Quarterly for the History of Art*, vol. 18, no. 4.

5 Szabolcsi, H. "A Bécsi Artaria Magyar Kapcsolatairól." In András, E., ed., *Angyalokra Szükség Van. Tanulmányok Bernáth Mária Tiszteletére*. Budapest: MTA Műv. Tört. Kutatóintézet, 2005, pp. 15–19.

6 Ridgewell, R. "Music Printing in Mozart's Vienna: The Artaria Press." *Fontes Artis Musicae*, vol. 48, no. 3, 2001, pp. 217–236.

7 Geraldine, D., Huemer, C., and Oosterlinck, K. "Art Dealers' Inventory Strategy: The Case of Goupil, Boussod & Valadon from 1860 to 1914." *Business History*, Nov. 2020, pp. 1–32.

8 Galenson, D. and Jensen, R. "Careers and Canvases: The Rise of the Market for Modern Art in the Nineteenth Century." *Van Gogh Studies: Current Issues in 19th-Century Art*. Van Gogh Museum, Waanders Publishers, 2007, pp. 146–147.

9 White, H. C. and White, C. A. *Canvases and Careers: Institutional Change in the French Painting World*, rev. ed. University of Chicago Press, (1965) 1993.

10 Galenson, pp. 146–148.

11 Brauer, F. *Rivals and Conspirators: The Paris Salons and the Modern Art Centre*. Newcastle upon Tyne: Cambridge Scholars Publishing, 2013, pp. 138–157, 347–348.

12 Boime, A. "Entrepreneurial Patronage in Nineteenth-Century France." In Carter II, E. C., Forster, R. and Moody, J. N., eds., *Enterprise and Entrepreneurs in Nineteenth- and Twentieth-Century France*. Johns Hopkins University Press, 1976, pp. 137–207.

13 Thompson, J. A. "Durand-Ruel and America." In Patry, S. ed., *Inventing Impressionism: Paul Durand-Ruel and the Modern Art Market*. London: National Gallery Company, 2015, pp. 136–151.

14 Monet's Haystack exhibition would lead Bertha Honoré Palmer to collect the artist's works and eventually own three of the paintings from the series. See: Brettell, R. R. "Monet's Haystacks Reconsidered." *Art Institute of Chicago Museum Studies*, vol. 11, no. 1, Autumn, 1984, pp. 4–21.

15 Neuendorf, H. (2017) "The Armory Show Lures Gagosian Back to the Piers for a Slimmed-down 2018 Edition." *artnet news*, Nov. 6.

16 Segal, D. "Pulling Art Sales out of Thinning Air." *The New York Times*, Mar. 7, 2009.

17 Eckardt, S. "Hilde Lynn Helphenstein Wants to Be the Art World's Anthony Bourdain: The Brains Behind @jerrygogosian is Building a New Kind of Creative Career." *W Magazine*, Sep. 20, 2022.

18 Kinsella, E. "It's a 'Leaser's Market' With 'Unheard-Of' Rents: Why Blue-Chip Galleries Are Doubling Down in New York's Chelsea." *Artnet*, Sep. 6, 2018.

19 Larkin, M. "New York's Hottest New Gallery District Looks Familiar." *New York Times*, Nov. 10, 2021.

20 Wainwright, O. "The $500m Shed: Inside New York's Quilted Handbag on Wheels." *The Guardian*, Apr. 5, 2019.

21 Kinsella, E. "Are Art Fairs Good for Galleries—Or Killing Them? The Short-Term Costs, the Long-Term Costs." *Artnet*, May 31, 2014.

22 "From the Studio to the Auction Block: How the Path Between These Two Poles Shrank in the 21st Century—and What It Means for the Art Market." *Artnet News and Morgan Stanley*, Nov. 3, 2022.

23 Benjamin, W. "The Work of Art in the Age of Mechanical Reproduction." In Arendt, H., ed., Zohn, H., trans., *Illuminations: Essays and Reflections*. Schocken, 1969, pp. 218–242.

24 Levin, H. "Confessions of Art Fraud King Michael Zabrin." *Chicago Magazine*, Oct. 25, 2011.

25 Dorment, R. "What Is a Warhol? The Buried Evidence." *The New York Review of Books*, June 20, 2013.

26 Sloane, K. and Taylor, J. "Art Markets without Art, Art without Objects." *The Garage Journal: Studies in Art, Museums & Culture*, vol. 2, 2021, pp. 159–161.

27 Hanson, S. "The Great Artists' Estates Race." *The Art Newspaper*, May 17, 2017.

28 Patry, S., ed., *Inventing Impressionism: Paul Durand-Ruel and the Modern Art Market*. London: National Gallery Company, 2015.

29 Goldstein, M. *Landscape with Figures: A History of Art Dealing in the United States*. Oxford University Press, 2000, pp. 247–267.

30 Barr, A. *Cubism and Abstract Art*. Modern Museum of Art, 1936, back cover.

31 After the MoMA's 2019 renovation, a room devoted to modernity now precedes the first room of the permanent collection.

32 Jenson, R. "Vollard and Cezanne: Anatomy of a Relationship." In Rabinow, R., ed., *Cézanne to Picasso: Ambroise Vollard, Patron of the Avant-Garde*. New York: Metropolitan Museum of Art, 2006, pp. 29–47.

33 Dumas, A. "Ambroise Vollard Patron of the Avant-Garde." In Rabinow, R., ed., *Cézanne to Picasso: Ambroise Vollard, Patron of the Avant-Garde*. New York: Metropolitan Museum of Art, 2006, pp. 3–27.

Secondary Market Galleries

Chapter 2

THE INTERSECTION OF ART HISTORY AND THE MARKET

Emergence of secondary markets precedes primary markets because an art history that establishes a canon arrives as the first ingredient in cultivating the phenomenon of collecting. Classical historians such as Xenocrates of Sicyon and Pliny the Elder established a hierarchy of masters for the ancient art market.[1] Giorgio Vasari defined a canon for Italian Renaissance artist,[2] and Karel van Mander did the same for the Low Countries.[3] This intersection of art history and economic interests makes the secondary market both fascinating and perilous. Essentially, art history's epistemological problems are the market's problems. The secondary market's past is littered with cautionary tales reminding us how fragile the structures of knowledge are in the art world.

We call it the secondary art market because it occurs when artworks are sold for a second time (as well as every time afterward). These sales can occur either through galleries (the subject of this chapter) or through auctions (Chapter 3).[4] Furthermore, the resale of applied arts: antique furniture, porcelain, and lighting, is another category which is called the antique market. Secondary market galleries, then, refers to galleries that buy up fine artworks (non-applied, i.e., paintings, works on paper, prints, photography, and sculpture), either directly from collectors or estates, or from other dealers in more

DOI: 10.4324/9781003431756-3

peripheral markets, or at auction, and then resell those artworks. Furthermore, rather than purchasing ownership in the works, dealers may instead enter into a consignment arrangement with collectors discreetly wishing to sell.

In the heyday of Joseph Duveen in the early twentieth century, these sorts of secondary market dealers represented the pinnacle of the business. Duveen scoured Europe for purchasable old master works, especially from impoverished aristocratic families and ecclesiastical institutions and resold them to newly minted American millionaires. This model of buying up artworks in one market and moving them to a higher-value market becomes one of the essential acts of the secondary market dealer. Duveen's endeavors set in motion, one of the greatest transferences of art treasures in history, from Europe to the United States, and reinforced one of the art market's relentless dynamics, which is that art flows to the market where it is most monetarily valued.[5] Creating value, however, remains a complicated process of developing canonical status for an artist, which is the product of the coordinated activities of museums, art historians, and cultural tastemakers.

THE CULT OF A GOLDEN AGE

Inherent to the notion of an art historical canon is the ideal of a golden age, often referred to as an Arcadia, first employed by the Greeks to describe an idyllic age prior to the corruptions of civilization. In art history, this concept is adapted to important periods when a school of art reaches its pinnacle. This term can be used for the high Hellenic period of Periclean Athens (450–430 BCE), for Florence of the fifteenth and sixteenth centuries, Holland of the seventeenth century, Rome of the sixteenth-nineteenth centuries, and Paris of the nineteenth to early twentieth centuries (especially around movements such as Impressionism, Cubism, and other variants of modernism). In recent years, the same golden age association has been applied to the mid-century New York School of abstract-expressionism and pop art. The cult of a golden age establishes a group of elite artists who defined that era, and the market will correspondingly apply greatest value to their works because collectors have been inculcated with an understanding of that hierarchy. A golden age is established through complex indoctrination reinforced over many different cultural platforms, including museum exhibitions, art history courses, books, auction records, and now increasingly cinema, television, and social media.

When a critical mass of homage has been paid to a golden age, then collectors will begin to prize its most characteristic works of its most identified artists. These greatest masters will begin to enter the international universal canon and command the kind of super-prices that the art world is famous for. Furthermore, lesser masters who worked during that golden age will be marketed for their connection to the period. Their careers will be mined for times when they exhibited at seminal shows, and their connections to the great masters will be played up. The golden ages, even if they remain eternally significant, will still go through periods when they fluctuate in degree to which they are fashionable. Often, cultural phenomena, such as a successful film or novel, might catapult an era back in to fashionability in a way that produces a noticeable upturn in sales of art from that period.

EVER-DEPLETING HUNTING GROUNDS

A secondary market gallery's inventory must be gathered on the secondary market. In other words, it must be bought up from willing sellers. Since the guiding value structure is based on art history, this hierarchy can be known to many competitors. Occasionally, a dealer may be able to buy up an under-valued work from an owner who fails to appreciate what they have, but such ignorance rarely lasts for long. Owners are actually much more likely to over-value what they have than under-value it, and the success of the BBC and PBS television programs *Antiques Roadshow* has only further emboldened owners to believe that their heirlooms hold spectacular value. Over time, any œuvre or period gets bought up and the best pieces enter a sort of market dead-end in the form of public collections, and the rest are in the hands of collectors who have no intention of selling. That means, the only way to acquire new inventory is to buy from collectors who do not know what they have (hard to find) or from those who do know what they have (and tend to over-value it). Furthermore, purchasing inventory at auction, which had been the trade's primary sourcing method, has seen the internet make sale prices globally available knowledge. Clients knowing what a dealer paid for a piece makes it very difficult to achieve a 100 percent mark-up on a resale, which is the secondary market's standard profit margin on speculative purchases of inventory. Alternatively, when the dealer works with a collector or an artist's estate to sell their holdings, they might sell pieces on consignment. In this case, the dealer does not need to purchase the work outright, but rather only needs to pay the consignee when the work is sold. In such cases, however, the profit margin will be significantly lower than 100 percent.

"Hunting" remains a very apt metaphor for the act of acquiring inventory on the secondary market. Because over-hunting can easily deplete their stomping grounds, dealers frequently must adjust to the fact that available works by a certain artist have become "hunted-out." Therefore, they must content themselves with lesser works (preparatory works, studies, sketches, and ephemera) or adjust their profile to later periods and find new un-discovered artists. It is worth remembering that the original antique dealers of the Renaissance dealt in antiquities, that is, art objects from the age of classical antiquity (500 BCE–400 CE), until those sorts of things became almost impossible to acquire except through illicit means. Secondary market galleries will frequently specialize in a period but then expand their offerings to a more recent period as it becomes increasingly difficult to find good work from the first period that was their original profile. The period generally called Old Masters is now widely seen as having gone into decline because there simply remain very few major works by the canonical artists still available on the market.[6] A good dealer is watching the process of art history in production, especially in the form of exhibitions at museums with a contemporary and modern profile, and they can use these shows as an indicator for where to speculate next.

ATTRIBUTION AS PRINCIPAL ACT

The knowledge of art history that a secondary market dealer possesses serves as their primary business asset. Essentially, a dealer's principal act is to recognize what an object is and what it can be sold for, when others do not. This ability requires a more in-depth understanding of art history than what is likely to be taught in undergraduate university courses. They will need to become intimately familiar with the core monographs and *catalogues raisonnés* that govern the œuvres they trade in. The secondary market is ultimately about information, and a dealer can only make a profit on the purchase and re-sale of an artwork when they possess more knowledge of a work's attribution and worth than either the seller or anyone else in their market. Good secondary market galleries usually possess many walls shelving art books floor-to-ceiling in a clearly displayed message to collectors that this place knows its business.

The act of attribution becomes not just the source of value, but also the very discourse by which the artwork is marketed to a client. Dealers like to present a painting with a story about how they discovered it. That no one else understood what it was, but with some cleaning, a signature became apparent, and with some research an authorship was established. The mystique of a long-lost discovery is far more likely to capture the imagination of a potential collector than admitting that the painting was bought on speculation at an auction a year earlier. Furthermore, additional research can reveal the importance of a particular work within a given œuvre, and such findings can determine if the work was present at seminal exhibitions, won awards, or is regarded as a representative example of a particular style or period. In general, the more that is known about an artwork (where it was shown, who owned it, what was said or written about it), the more that information can be used in order to market and sell it. For the purposes of the secondary market, art historical research and marketing texts are one and the same thing.

PERILS OF THE SECONDARY ART MARKET

Although the secondary art market generally allows for much greater profit margin than primary market sales, it is also fraught with many more perils that do not exist in contemporary art. Since art history occupies a central role in the functioning of this market, subsequently all of art history's problems are also the problems of the secondary art market. Among a short list of these problems are the following:

1. Art history is written for the benefit of art historians first and foremost, and the concerns of the art market are far from their minds. In fact, many academic art historians consider

entering the market, or even cooperating with the market, is something akin to going over to the "dark side."

2. On many subjects, artists, periods, and genres, there can often be one reigning art historian whom the art market likes to hear from. But when this art historian passes away, the new generation of authority might have radically different ideas about attribution. Such was the case when Bernard Berenson passed from the scene and a new group of Italian Renaissance experts began to revise his opinions.[7]

3. Where high-value artists exist, their estates may organize an artist's foundation, authentication board, or *catalogue raisonné* committee. Those bodies hire art historians to decide on issues of attribution, and their decisions are usually considered authoritative. If this body determines a dealer's artwork to not be by the artist in question, there is little the dealer can do to appeal the decision.

4. Where dealers have sought to appeal a decision, it usually occurs in the form of a lawsuit in a court of law. These lawsuits have become so onerous for some of these committees that they have disbanded (e.g., Andy Warhol, Jean-Michel Basquiat, and Keith Harring), leaving the art market with unclear authority to turn to if a new work is discovered.

5. While certain elite canonical artists, for whom there exists a *catalogue raisonné*, remain almost over-researched, the vast majority of artists remain tragically under-researched. It is no over-statement to say that 99.9 percent of all artists who ever worked receive no mention in any textbook or lecture which an undergraduate art history student is likely to encounter.

6. Art history is itself subject to fashion, especially with shifting notions of a golden age and collectors who follow those trends. These trends are generally set by museums in their temporary exhibitions, or on entirely different cultural platforms such as literature or cinema. In any case, these institutions operate largely independent of the art market, and it is the dealers who must react to these trends.

7. Art history can always be revised as a result of new scientific or archival discoveries, overturning established knowledge paradigms.

All of these problems frequently leave dealers with essentially un-sellable or nearly worthless artworks. The resulting wasted investment (what the dealer spent on the piece) counts as the most frequently cited peril of the secondary market. Furthermore, this pitfall can occur after a sale, when a collector has received a negative opinion about a work's authenticity and now wants the dealer to buy it back.[8] In such cases, a dealer faces a quandary of saving their reputation and returning the money, or standing by their initial attribution, thereby risking alienating an important collector, damaging their reputation, incurring litigation, or all three.

Hunting grounds deplete because all artists had finite œuvres. Furthermore, collectors possessing coveted artists' works have ever more resources to educate themselves on the value of their holdings, and dealers are less and less likely to encounter naïve collectors who are unaware of their artwork's worth. One of the leading causes of the over-informed collector has emerged from the digitalization and online platforming of the auction business. Auction house catalogs are readily available and searchable. Subscription databases can offer even more information, especially on sales results. The greatest threat of all, however, is that auction houses themselves have been able to directly reach those collectors who would have earlier bought works from a secondary market dealer (who would have been acquiring the work at auction) and thereby cut the dealer out of the exchange.

In the absence of good available inventory, a dealer may instead encounter forgeries posing as works by sought-after artists. The stress of financial survival can often delude a dealer into ignoring the obvious signs of a piece's inauthenticity. Among the signs that should have been noticed, but might (intentionally) not receive appropriate due diligence, can be a vague or unlikely provenance, an untrusted source, indications of recent production, material attempts to appear aged or worn, and stylistic inconsistencies. Nonetheless, the number of galleries who have succumbed to the lure of a well-made forgery is sadly numerous. The notorious Knoedler gallery would actually twice succumb to collapse resulting from forgery scandals. The first time was in the late 1960s, as a result of selling forgeries by Elmyr de Hory.[9] Their sudden closure in 2011 directly resulted from a market made scarce by an increasingly transparent auction sector, and a small-time dealer offering access to a previously never-heard-of collection. Knoedler would have gone bankrupt decades earlier had it not been for the frequent injections of immense profits (up to nearly 1,000 percent on some re-sales) on the mid-century works coming from Glafira Rosales.[10] The unlikely profit margins also rank as another sign which a scrupulous dealer would have observed and developed suspicions about the work's authenticity.

SECONDARY MARKET SALES AS A COMPLETE BUSINESS STRATEGY

In the nineteenth century, dealers such as Paul Durand-Ruel and Charles Sedelmeyer would have been simultaneously primary and secondary market dealers,[11] They would have been developing the careers of living artists through dedicated exhibitions. Durand-Ruel was promoting the Impressionist painters such as Monet and Renoir. Sedelmeyer supported artists from the Austro-Hungarian Empire, like Mihály Munkácsy and Hans Makart. Simultaneously, each also pursued activities on the secondary market which helped support their enterprises. Durand-Ruel frequently served as an expert cataloger for auctions held at Drouot.[12] Sedelmeyer acted as the most important dealer in Rembrandt during that period and published the artist's definitive *catalogue raisonné* at that time.[13] New York's art markets, both the primary and secondary, used to be all centered around the vertex of Fifty-Seventh Street and Fifth Avenue.[14] By the 1970s, however, the centers of those markets diverged, with the secondary market moving farther up the East Side along Madison Avenue.[15] The primary market, with its lower profit margins, began to migrate down to the nineteenth-century warehouses of Soho,[16] and from there in the 1990s, again in search of cheaper rents, to the warehouses near the Hudson River adjacent to the meat-packing district, known as Chelsea.[17]

The geographical division between primary and secondary markets would seem to increasingly reinforce this segmentation of markets, but, in fact, there is more crossover than immediately is apparent. Larry Gagosian, as he was developing his contemporary art business, would also pursue a secondary market strategy of arranging high-price private sales between collectors he knew.[18] Eventually Gagosian would have galleries in Chelsea and on the Upper East Side on Madison Avenue in order to have venues that are were specifically focused on one or the other profile. Furthermore, many other Chelsea galleries are beginning to represent the estates of deceased artists as a way to supplement their income from contemporary sales.[19] Antique dealers, because they frequently have wall space above the furniture they sell, will also deal in secondary market sales of works that conform to their general stylistic and period profile. As a rule of thumb, the art business is best pursued through multiple revenue streams, and current-day dealers are frequently discovering that secondary market sales are best employed as part of a larger, diversified income strategy.

CASE STUDY: JOSEPH DUVEEN AND BERNARD BERENSON

The narrative of Duveen and Berenson provides the single most cautionary tale about the perils of collusion between the art market and art history. Duveen was born into an already well-established dynasty of antique dealers, but young Joseph turned the firm toward Old Master paintings in the 1890s by buying up entire collections from impoverished European families.[20] One of the problems in the Old Master's market, though, was that there was little certainty in attributions: everything seemed to claim to be a Rembrandt and a Botticelli, and that was not possible.[21] The Gilded Age collectors in the United States had until then preferred to purchase the leading contemporary names of the Salons.[22]

With the arrival of a system of connoisseurship developed by Giovanni Morelli,[23] and further developed by his most authoritative practitioner Bernard Berenson, a new level of certainty entered the market, causing prices to rise dramatically in the early twentieth century. Berenson's definitive publications on the painters of Italian Renaissance made him the authority on the entire period from 1300–1600 CE.[24] Berenson came from a poor family of Lithuanian Jewish immigrants and had earned a scholarship to Harvard and would subsequently travel around Europe until he had found his calling as Morelli's disciple. He also began to develop a side profession as an art agent and helped Isabella Stewart Gardner acquire some of the most important Italian pieces that hang in her museum in Boston, including Titian's *Rape of Europa*.[25]

By 1912, Berenson and Duveen had entered a secret agreement whereby Berenson helped source and authenticate paintings, and he received a share of the profits.[26] The arrangement proved immensely profitable to Berenson, who was able to purchase a villa, I Tatti, outside of Florence. To understand how much this pair dominated their era: when the Benois family of St. Petersburg claimed in 1913 to have a work by Leonardo da Vinci, Duveen had Berenson study it.[27] Once Berenson had determined it to be by Leonardo, Duveen offered $1 million, a record price for any painting at that time. In the end, the Czar of Russia bought it instead.[28] After all, if Berenson had said it was a Leonardo, then no one at that time would have doubted the attribution. Berenson's reputation, however, suffered precipitously as a result of the trial over the American Leonardo,[29] when he was forced to reveal in court that he had been in the pay of Duveen. Their business relationship ended in 1937 in a dispute over the correct attribution of a painting showing an Adoration of the Shepherds scene referred to as *The Allendale Nativity*. Berenson declared it to be by Titian, while Duveen had been hoping for an attribution to Giorgione, because he had a client in Samuel Kress who wanted a Giorgione but who already had Titians (which were not as rare).[30] Today the painting hangs in the Washington National Gallery of Art as a Giorgione.

SECONDARY ART MARKET—TERMS

Dead art market—a crude term preferred in the business designating the key distinction, which is not so much if the artwork is being sold a second time (hence secondary market), but rather when the artist dies and is no longer available to validate their work.

Canon—an elite category of cultural products which are the best known and most widely studied achievements of the art form. The term derives from the canonical gospels of the bible and the canon of saints. Canons exist for every medium, genre, and sub-genre.

Joseph Duveen—the dominant secondary market dealer of the early twentieth century. He initiated the massive transference of artworks from Europe to the United States. He employed Bernard Berenson as his authenticator for works of Italian Renaissance art.

Bernard Berenson—the leading art historian and connoisseur of Italian Renaissance art in the first half of the twentieth century. Collectors and dealers trusted his opinion and considered it a guarantee of authenticity. Berenson maintained a secret business relationship with Duveen and received a share of profits on the sale of paintings on which he had issued opinions.

Authentication—a process whereby an acknowledged expert or committee of experts issue an opinion on the attribution of an artwork. There currently exists no standard for how this process should be conducted, and consensually acknowledged expertise exists for only a small number of artists.

Catalogue Raisonné—a publication assembled by an individual or committee of art historians which includes all acknowledged artworks in a certain medium by a certain artist. Where a *catalogue raisonné* exists, the market expects an artwork sold as being by the artist to reference its inclusion and index number, or at least present a letter by the author(s) of their intention to include the work in a subsequent addendum.

Old Masters—a category of art generally understood to refer to the artists working in the period of the Renaissance in Italy and Northern Europe, as well as the Baroque period in Italy, Spain, and the Low Countries.

Provenance—is the history of ownership, custody, possession, commercial transactions, location, handling, usage, and exhibition of an art object.

Renaissance—a term only coined in the nineteenth century, but which captured that era's imagination and led to massive price inflation in the market for Italian works from 1400–1600 CE.

Golden Age—a concept that exists in most cultures which involves idealizing an earlier era admired for its cultural and intellectual production. In European civilization, common Golden Ages were Athens 450–430 BCE, Rome 100–200 CE, Italian city-states 1400–1600 CE, and Paris 1890–1930 CE.

Notes

1 Xenocrates of Sicyon is a source that Pliny frequently relied upon, but lost now, and only known through the writings of Pliny. Pliny the Elder. Ed. John Bostock, M.D., F.R.S. H.T. Riley, Esq., B.A. "Book XXXV: An Account of Paintings and Colours, Chapter 8 — At What Period Foreign Paintings Were First Introduced at Rome." In *The Natural History.* London: Taylor and Francis, 1855.

2 Vasari, G. *The Lives of the Artists.* Oxford University Press, 1998.

3 Mander, Karel van. *The Lives of the Illustrious Netherlandish and German Painters, from the First Edition of the Schilder-boeck (1603–1604).* Davaco, 1994.

4 Lynch and Singer refer to this as the Tertiary Market, but this term has never taken on wide usage in the Trade. Singer, L. and Lynch, G. "Public Choice in the Tertiary Art Market." *Journal of Cultural Economics,* vol. 18, no. 3, 1994, pp. 199–216.

5 Joseph Duveen is frequently misattributed the quote: "Europe has a great deal of art, and America has a great deal of money." It is in fact derived from Saul Behrman's profile in *The New Yorker,* "Lord Duveen... noticed that Europe had plenty of art and America had plenty of money." Behrman, S. N. "The Days of Duveen: A Legendary Art Dealer and his Clients." *The New Yorker,* Sep. 22, 1951.

6 Reyburn, S. "Is the Old Masters Market in Terminal Decline?" *The Art Newspaper,* Dec. 7, 2022.

7 Richard, P. "Bernard Berenson — Portrait of a Connoisseur: The Life of a Renaissance Man, the Rewarding Life of a Self-Made Aristocrat." *The Washington Post,* Jan. 21, 1979.

8 Such was the case when the opinion of a Robert Motherwell painting was revised, which set in motion the collapse of the Knoedler Gallery. See: Taylor, J. "The Rise and Fall of the Knoedler, New York's Most Notorious Art Gallery." *The Conversation,* Feb. 5, 2016.

9 Ibid.

10 Miller, M. H. "The Big Fake: Behind the Scenes of Knoedler Gallery's Downfall." *ARTnews*, Apr. 25, 2016.

11 Huemer, C. "Charles Sedelmeyer's Theatricality: Art Speculation in Late Nineteenth Century Paris." In Bakoš, J., ed., *Artwork through the Market: The Past and the Present*. Bratislava: VEDA, 2004.

12 See, for example, the collection of the painter Jean-François Millet: *Catalogue de la vente qui aura lieu par suite du décès de Jean-François Millet*. Expert: Durand-Ruel. Hôtel Drouot, May 10–11, 1875.

13 Bode, W. V. and de Groot, C. H. *The Complete Work of Rembrandt, History, Description and Heliographic Reproduction of all the Master's Pictures, with a Study of His Life and Work*. C. Sedelmeyer, 1897–1906.

14 Scher, R. "'Round 57th Street: New York's First Gallery District Continues (for Now) to Weather Endless Changes in the Art World." *ARTnews*, July 19, 2016.

15 Knoedler moved into their Madison Avenue location between 70th and 71st Street in 1970. See: Gray, C. "When Elegance Sold Art." *The New York Times*, Mar. 8, 2012.

16 Fensterstock, A. *Art on the Block: Tracking the New York Art World from SoHo to the Bowery, Bushwick and Beyond*. St. Martin's Press, 2013.

17 Molotch, H. and Treskon, M. "Changing Art: SoHo, Chelsea and the Dynamic Geography of Galleries in New York City." *International Journal of Urban and Regional Research*, vol. 33, no. 2, June, pp. 517–541.

18 Segal, D. "Pulling Art Sales out of Thinning Air." *The New York Times*, Mar. 7, 2009.

19 Hanson, S. "The Great Artists' Estates Race." *The Art Newspaper*, May 17, 2017.

20 "$2,500,000 Paid for M. Kann Collection." *The New York Times*, Sep. 1, 1909.

21 Brewer, J. *The American Leonardo: A Tale of Obsession, Art and Money*. Oxford: Oxford University, 2009, pp. 10–70.

22 Vottero, M. "To Collect and Conquer: American Collections in the Gilded Age." *Transatlantica*, vol. 1, 2013.

23 These ideas were largely worked out in his pseudonymously authored: Lermolieff, I. *Die Werke Italienischer Meister*. E. A. Seeman, 1880.

24 Berenson, B. *The Venetian Painters of the Renaissance with an Index to Their Works*. Putnam & Sons, 1894. And Berenson, B. *The Florentine Painters of the Renaissance*. Putnam & Sons, 1896.

25 Saltzman, C. *Old Masters New World: America's Raid on Europe's Great Pictures, 1880-World War I*. Viking, 2008, p. 77.

26 Simpson, C. *Artful Partners*. Macmillan, 1986.

27 Samuels, E. and Samuels, J. N. *Bernard Berenson, the Making of a Legend*. Belknap Press, 1987, p. 216.

28 Secrest, M. *Duveen: A Life in Art*. New York: Alfred A. Knopf, 2004.

29 "$500,000 Suit Hangs on da Vinci Fingers: Impressions on Canvas Said to Prove Master Painted Picture Denounced by Duveen." *The New York Times*, Nov. 5, 1921.

30 Samuels, E. and Samuels, J. N. *Bernard Berenson: The Making of a Legend*. Harvard University Press, 1987, pp. 428–439.

Auction Houses

Chapter 3

AUCTIONEERING AS A DISTRIBUTION MODEL

Auctions have existed since ancient times as a means for quickly disposing of goods and converting them into liquid currency. The Romans frequently used the method for selling off booty after a conquest or disposing of the property of a proscribed individual.[1] As well as this is how we hear, for example, of Lucius Mummius and the auction after the sack of Corinth in 146 BCE,[2] which marks the beginnings of the Roman art market. In seventeenth-century Holland, auctions were used as a quick means to sell off cargo arriving from colonial ports.[3] Auctions, as a method for the sale of artworks, however, really developed in Holland, England, and France in the seventeenth century.[4] The method was also adopted for the sale of Renaissance art that was being exported from impoverished Italian collections, as well as for the collection of debts, as was the case with the sale of Rembrandt's collection.[5] In the eighteenth century, most of today's leading auction houses were founded: Christie's, Sotheby's, Phillips, Bonhams, and the Dorotheum of Vienna. In fact, these are some of the oldest, continuously operated businesses in the world.

It should be remembered that the auctioning of fine and applied arts is, in fact, only a small sector of the total global auctioning business, which also sells repossessed automobiles, government bonds, and livestock. In the nineteenth century,

DOI: 10.4324/9781003431756-4

auctions became the primary means by which the assets of large estates would be liquidated and became the primary sourcing method for the secondary art and antique markets. The Hôtel Drouot auction house in Paris has held multiple auctions almost every day since its founding in 1852, and to this day it remains a massive clearing house for the trade in a vast array of art, applied art, collectables, and antiquities. Throughout the twentieth century, auction houses (especially the big two, Christie's and Sotheby's) would absorb greater and greater portions of the trade in art and antiques. The arrival of the internet at the end of the twentieth century brought radical changes to the industry in the form on new players like eBay and also fundamentally altered the way established auction houses marketed, catalogued, and conducted their sales. Above all else, the internet has made participation in auctions much more accessible.

RISE OF THE TWO BIG AUCTION HOUSES

Among the many auction houses being formed in the eighteenth century, two, Sotheby's and Christie's, would rise to global dominance by the end of the twentieth century. They arrived at relatively similar positions through quite different paths. Both were founded in London, but Sotheby's, founded in 1744, served the book trade (which was larger and more important at the time)[6] and only entered the art auction business around the time of the First World War. In the 1950s, it opened an office in New York, and in 1964 acquired the largest U.S. auctioneer, Parke-Bernet.[7] In the 1970s, it became a publicly share-held company in Britain, and in 1988, Sotheby's was listed on the New York Stock Exchange. At this point, New York became the primary base of the firm. In 2019, Sotheby's was taken private by a group of investors led by Patrick Drahi in order to give it the same agility that their rival Christie's enjoyed from not being a publicly traded company.[8]

James Christie conducted his first sales of art in 1766, and Christie's would remain London's dominant auctioneer of art and antiques until Sotheby's began to compete with them in the early twentieth century.[9] Christie's took great advantage of the sales of the collections from French aristocrats fleeing the French Revolution in the 1790s[10] and in the late nineteenth century when British aristocratic collections were sold off because of the Settled Lands Act (1882). Christie's held its first New York sale in 1977 and also, like Sotheby's, was for some time a publicly traded company. At the same time, however, that Sotheby's was being listed on the New York Stock Exchange, Christie's was being de-listed as a result of being bought out entirely by luxury goods businessman, François Pinault.[11] He remains, to this day, essentially the firm's sole proprietor. The Simplicity of this structure was frequently cited as the primary advantage Christie's held over Sotheby's and the primary reason for the latter's decision to also pursue private ownership.[12]

Both auction houses pursued many common strategies during their twentieth-century expansions. They both acquired galleries that gave them access to vast inventory and expertise: Sotheby's acquired Pierre Matisse Gallery in 1990, which had been run by the son of the painter Henri and had amassed over 2,300 works of prime early- and mid-twentieth-century modernism.[13] Christie's acquired the London firms Spink & Son and Leger Gallery at the same time for the same intended acquisition of inventory and expertise.[14] Also in the 1990s, both auction houses acquired luxury real estate arms which operate as somewhat independent entities. Most importantly, at this time the top management of both firms began to collude on setting seller's premiums, agreeing not to compete on this most essential business cost. The result was that the U.S. Department of Justice brought changes of anti-competitive business practices in what became known as the Christie's and Sotheby's Price-Fixing Scandal, and which resulted in jail time for both the chairman and the CEO of Sotheby's.[15]

THE CURRENT DOMINANCE OF CHRISTIE'S AND SOTHEBY'S

The reach and dominance of the two big auction houses has never been greater. The secondary market gallery sector had been atrophying specifically because of the increasing accessibility and transparency that these two firms have brought to the auction business. Clients who had previously bought from secondary market dealers could now buy directly from auctions, and even from the day sales. Sales that go on during the daytime had historically been a place for galleries to acquire their inventory, but they have begun to attract collectors who outbid the trade.

Both firms have workforces that fluctuate around 2,000 paid staff worldwide and have flagship headquarters and sales rooms in both New York and London. Overall, Christie's maintains nine salesrooms worldwide (Amsterdam, Dubai, Geneva, Hong Kong, London, Milan, New York, Paris, Shanghai) and Sotheby's keeps eight (including Hong Kong, Paris, New York, and London). In addition, both have a global network of representative offices, maintaining between 70 and 80 locations worldwide—which serve as places to receive pieces hoping to be auctioned, and where department experts can visit the objects to decide whether to put them in an upcoming sale.

All larger and medium-sized auction houses tend to organize their sales along art historical and medium categorizations. Individual departments are tasked with putting on these sales once or twice a year. The staff of the department should have high-level expertise in the material they sell. The head of the department, who is also often the auctioneer conducting the actual sales, may serve as a sort of celebrity expert in the field. Sotheby's currently maintains 75 distinct departments, and Christie's has 67. Among these departments is the venerable field of antiquities (called Ancient Sculpture and Works of Art at Sotheby's and Ancient Art & Antiquities at Christie's), which refers to objects from the ancient Greek and Roman civilizations, as well as Egyptian, Mesopotamian, Celtic, and other early cultures, until approximately AD 500 (later works and non-Western works have other categories). The large category known broadly as Old Masters (which can include European artists from late Medieval to Baroque periods and tends to be closely associated with the Italian Renaissance and the Dutch Golden Age of the seventeenth century) is divided into different departments for paintings and another for drawings and works on paper. While antiquities and Old Masters used to be the most high-value sectors of the art market, in the latter twentieth century, they have diminished in importance. To some degree, these sectors are not as fashionable as they once were to collectors, but also good-quality material has become ever scarcer as the best pieces have long-ago entered public collections. More rigorous enforcement of cultural heritage regulations by both governments and the auction houses have cut off the flow of works with illicit (theft, plunder, and looting) origins.[16] While Old Masters would have been the most high-value sector of the early twentieth century, the sector has largely faded in terms of significance because of a scarcity of major works by the canonical names,[17] and the debacle of the *Salvator Mundi* may have briefly inflated the sector's records but did little to enhance its reliability.[18] The Impressionist and Modern department has now become the most high-value sector, though it is increasingly challenged by the category of Postwar and Contemporary.[19] In many recent years, in fact, the latter has outsold the former, reflecting the increased interest in mid-century Abstract Expressionism and Pop Art periods, as well as a shortage of highly desirable works from the earlier eras of modernism. Many departments overlap in terms of the material in their purview. The Sotheby's departments of 19th Century European Paintings, Impressionism and Modernism Art, and German, Austrian, and Central European Paintings would all be searching for sellable material from the same periods. The determination over which department will sell a work usually is decided in terms of whether an artist has escaped the gravity of origin. The vast majority of artists remain most coveted in their local market. Lovis Corinth and Franz von Stuck, although extremely important Symbolist painters and founders of the Munich Secession, continue to be most known and sought after in the German world and hence would be sold by the German, Austrian, and Central European Paintings department. Gustav Klimt and Egon Schiele, however, have escaped the gravity of their Central European origins and achieved a global cachet that means that their works are more likely to appear at an Impressionism and Modern sale. The 19th Century European Paintings department tends to take especially French works (because other countries and regions have their own categories) made prior to the onset of Impressionism, genres we term: neo-classicism, romanticism, realism, and the Barbizon school, as well as works made in the later nineteenth century but by artists considered contrary to modernism, such as Ernest Meissonier and William-Adolphe Bouguereau. In general, works move up and down the hierarchy of the department system depending on where they are believed to be best sold for the most money, and within the bigger departments works can appear in either the day sale or the evening sale depending on their perceived importance. Both auction houses have recently added departments for Non-Fungible Tokens (NFTs).

MEDIUM, SMALL, AND REGIONAL AUCTION HOUSES

Many of the leading medium-size auction houses (defined as having between 50 and 1,000 employees) also originated in the eighteenth century: Phillips and Bonhams in London (both now have headquarters in New York) and the Dorotheum in Vienna, Austria. These auction houses very much follow the Christie's/ Sotheby's model with different departments based on period and medium and have sales organized along those categories. They maintain representative offices across the globe and operate sales rooms in multiple cities: Bonhams acquired the California auction house Butterfields in 2002, and this gave them a presence in both San Francisco and Los Angeles.[20] In 2022, they also went on a buying spree, acquiring five auction houses, which could be a strategy of making itself into a global rival to Sotheby's and Christie's, and it could also be a prelude to making the firm more sellable.[21] These relatively smaller competitors to the Big Two can sometimes snare top pieces to sell because they have strong expertise and profiling in certain categories. The Dorotheum, for example, because of its location in Vienna and its clientele, sells some of the most important works of the Vienna Secession, works which might otherwise have gone to Christie's or Sotheby's. One outlier to all these models is the Paris entity known as Hôtel Drouot. Founded in the mid-nineteenth century, this institution functions almost entirely different than all the other auction houses.[22] In fact, it is not really an auction house, but rather more of an auction platform. Its main facility in central Paris can host up to six or more auctions a day, but these are often rapid-fire sales with the exhibition occurring in the morning and the sale in the afternoon or next day. Over 70 different auction syndicates stage these sales and pay Drouot for the use of the sales rooms, and for their storage and payment systems. The fact that most of the sales are conducted over the course of one or two business days means that Hôtel Drouot remains a classic institution that primarily serves the trade.

In the art business, where most enterprises can only be described as micro (one to ten employees), even technically small-size auction houses (ten to fifty employees) are in fact quite complex, intricate entities. Most major cities have at least one, if not three or four, of these types of auction houses serving their market. Many of them have distinct areas of specialization. Wright in Chicago particularly sells twentieth-century design. Swann Galleries in New York focuses on prints and graphics. Heritage Auctions of Dallas built a profile in stamps, coins, and sports and entertainment memorabilia and has grown into a significant enterprise with seven offices worldwide, and markets itself as the largest auctioneer for collectables.

Many of the smaller auction houses choose to focus on what they identify as the most profitable sector where their expertise is most able to elevate values. In Budapest, Hungary, both the Judit Virag Gallery and the Kieselbach Gallery hold auctions that are almost entirely composed of oil on canvas paintings from the Impressionist and Modern eras of Hungarian art. As with the New York art market, this sector represents the highest values in many national art markets. On the other hand, in the same Budapest market, other auction houses, Nagyházy and Bizományi Kereskedőház és Záloghitel (BÁV), pursue generalist strategies. They hold minor and major seasonal (fall and spring) sales that have a mixture of antique furniture, porcelain, silver, jewelry, clocks, architectural pieces, icons, paintings, and oriental carpets. These generalist institutions often hold estate sales containing an entire personal collection. Some regional auctioneers even hold the sales at the collector's original home.

STRUCTURES AND FUNCTIONING OF AUCTIONS

Auctions can happen in many different formats, but most art auctions tend to have relatively standard features. From beginning to end, the process generally happens in something like the following: the owner of an artwork wishes to sell it and contacts an auction house to see if they are interested. Nowadays that usually involves emailing photographs. If the auction house is interested, they look at the piece in person, usually in their own viewing rooms. If they accept a work for auction, they may hold on to the piece in their own storage area for the intervening one or two months until the auction. In the meantime, the work might be conserved, cleaned, or re-framed. It will also be photographed (and Photoshopped) to appear in the catalogue, which will be both printed and placed online with a description of the work. Some descriptions can be very basic: artist, title, medium, and size. In cases of works deemed more important, however, the lot description might include provenance, exhibition history, some description of condition, even miniature art historical essays on a piece, and on rare occasions a supplemental publication might be produced just for that one lot. Such was the case when Christie's sold the painting *Salvator Mundi* in 2017.[23] For a few weeks prior to the auction, the entire sale material will be on exhibition at the auction house's venue, and sales staff will be available to distribute catalogues and discuss the auction lots. On the day before the auction, all the works in the sale are put in a storeroom near the sales room from where they can be carried out and displayed on a special easel or stand when their time comes to be bid upon.

The auction begins at a set day and time as published in the catalogue. Also included in the front or back of the catalogue will be a list of the auction's rules governing what sales commissions or premiums are charged to buyers and sellers. It is from the buyer's and seller's premiums that an auction house earns nearly all of their income. Typical percentages can be 12–25 to buyers, usually with a downward sliding scale as the hammer prices increase. For example, Christie's Fall 2016 Postwar and Contemporary evening sale in London charged 25 percent on the first £100,000, 20 percent on everything over that until £2,000,000, and 12 percent on everything above that. Seller's premiums generally work the same way but might be 2–5 percent lower than the same level of a buyer's premium. That said, seller's premiums on important pieces are highly negotiable and might be waived altogether for a lot capable of selling for a high price, thereby generating good revenue from the buyer's premium alone. Sellers often negotiate between the Big Two for better commission rates. The cause of the Christie's-Sotheby's price-fixing scandal was when, in the 1990s, the two firms secretly agreed to not compete for this crucial fee.[24] Additional fine print in the catalogue will concern the auction house's very carefully worded policy on questions of authenticity or attribution. The levels for bidding price increments are explained, and the rights of the auctioneer to control particular aspects of sale are established.

At the appointed time of the auction, the auctioneer will begin by repeating these essential rules, and then begin the bidding on the first lot. Two different methods for initiating bidding exist: one is the estimate system and the other is the opening bid system. The estimate system is far more prevalent, especially at the upper level of the auction business. In the catalogue, each lot will be listed with a low and a high estimate (in very fine print in the sale rules, estimate is explained to *not* include buyer's premium), and in addition, there will be an undisclosed reserve, which is the amount below which the seller will not sell. The reserve will be somewhat below the low estimate (but known only to the auctioneer), and the starting bid will be somewhat lower than the reserve but will be set by the auctioneer only when bidding on that lot begins. Since bidding usually begins below the reserve, it is possible that the hammer price does not reach the reserve, in which case the auctioneer will use the euphemism that piece has been "bought in." That means that it will be returned to the seller, unsold. Certain pieces might be listed as without reserve, in which case, any hammer price will be accepted by the seller. The other method, widely used for example in Eastern European markets and on internet platforms, is the opening bid system, where the opening bid is clearly indicated in the catalogue and is the only value listed for the lot. The opening bid is also the reserve, and if a single bidder is the only one to bid, and the work is hammered at that opening bid price, it is a valid sale.

When bidding on a lot is competitive, a good auctioneer tries making the process theatrical, sometimes rapidly bouncing between competing bidders, and other times allowing a dramatic pause in the action. The auctioneer will be taking bids from bidders in the audience, who will have small, numbered paddles, for which they have registered prior to the auction. Bids may also come in the form of pre-set bids left by clients who could not be present, but more often they come from telephone bidders, and internet bidders using the auction house's own platform or one of the new auction services such as Invaluable, Artnet, or eBay. An auction may have ten or more people fielding bids and acting as spotters to make sure the auctioneer does not miss a bidder.

The auctioneer will continue to point out who is the current highest bidder and what their bid is at and will also state the next increment that a new bidder would have to offer in order to be the new high bidder. When no new bids come in, the auctioneer will say "going once, going twice, sold" or perhaps their own variation on this notice. Upon the word "sold," the auctioneer should strike their gavel, and that event is referred to as the "hammer." The price that the high bidder offered is referred to as the "hammer price." In other words, it is the base price to which the buyer's premium, will be assessed. Additional costs would include taxes (sales or VAT) and possibly Artist's Resale Right fee. After a lot has been hammered, the high bidder will soon receive a visit from an auction staffer who will take down the buyer's details and also attempt to collect a 10–20 percent deposit to make sure that the buyer returns and pays for the piece in full.

PERILS OF THE AUCTION BUSINESS

The perils of the auction business are numerous: for buyers, sellers, and for the auction houses themselves. Below is a short list of these hazards that occur at nearly every level of the auction business.

PERILS FOR BUYERS

- The buyer did not visually inspect an artwork and failed to notice a significant flaw.
- The buyer fails to understand how not rare the piece is and overpays for it.
- The auctioneer does a technique called "chandelier bidding" where imaginary bids are taken in order to push up the hammer price, and the buyer ends up paying more than necessary.
- The owner of the artwork (or their agents) is in the audience and bid up the lot so that the buyer ends up paying more than necessary.
- The buyer may discover that an artwork purchased at auction was not correctly attributed in the catalogue and would like to return the work and receive a refund, but this might be quite difficult as the auction house may have very high standards to prove a misattribution.

- The buyer has been influenced by corrupt auction records. This happens in markets like China[25] and Eastern Europe, where buyers frequently do not return to actually pay for their purchases (or they never existed as real buyers, but were just plants), but the hammer price is still recorded as a real sale on the auction house's own website. From there, it finds its way into price databases that overall reflect a highly inflated market. In this way, buyers are misled about the real condition of the market and the real value of certain artists and their works.

PERILS FOR SELLERS

- That an auction house may have intentionally undervalued and misattributed a seller's artwork with the intention of purchasing the work themselves and reselling it at a later date with a much more valuable attribution.
- That their object sells, but the buyer never returns to pay for the work, and so the sale essentially is void.
- If their work does not sell because it does not reach the reserve, the work will be returned to them. They will still have to pay a catalogue and photography fee, and their artwork will ever after carry the stigma that it did not sell at auction.
- They set a very low reserve and end up selling their piece very cheaply.

PERILS FOR AUCTION HOUSES

- The greatest peril for an auction house is that they misattribute something and develop a reputation for selling fakes.
- They accept something for sale where there is not good ownership or title. This often happens when competing members of a family with an important collection try to sell off pieces without the others knowing.
- The artwork is stolen, looted, or in some other way does not have good title.
- Buyers do not return to pay for the works they purchased at auction.
- Buyers do not show up and bidding is soft at the auction.

- Among the Big Two, in order to secure very important works, they offer guarantees that the seller will receive a prescribed amount even if the bidding does not reach that amount. This leaves the auction house with a significant loss on a sale if their guarantee is much higher than the actual hammer price. In order to offload that risk, auction houses have increasingly made use of third-party guarantors.[26]

LATEST TRENDS IN AUCTIONS

The auction business has changed dramatically in the last two decades, most significantly because of the influence of the internet on its business model. New players have entered the business by way of online platforms, none bigger than eBay. But eBay's platform has proven more successful for selling used household items and consumer goods than it has for important artwork. While the site successfully sells the lower levels of the antique market, collectables, memorabilia, and mass-market objects, it has difficulty attracting buyers for objects above $1,000. Partially, the reluctance of buyers stems from their unwillingness to trust sellers on works over that value because there are too many authenticity issues to be determined. Furthermore, the listings on eBay are simply far too vast for any supervision, and a cursory search for works by any canonical artist will bring up a long string of dubious items at unlikely prices. Also, the transportation of purchased items can be a not-inconsiderable cost if the objects are of high value and should travel by fine art shipping standard (and this cost would be very difficult to predict until after it is bought). Other platforms such as Artnet, 1stdibs, and Invaluable.com provide services for brick-and-mortar auction houses and galleries in order to capitalize on eBay's inability to capture a significant portion of the online art and antique market.

At the higher end of the market, Christie's has been innovating new methods of organizing sales. Instead of holding auctions according to departments (defined by period and medium), they held an auction in 2015 that was "curated." This meant that works were selected along an intellectual idea and also because these lots would have been the stars of other auctions, and so the sale was meant to be a sort of "All Star Sale."[27] When Christies sold the *Salvator Mundi*, it was not sold at an Old Masters auction, but rather at one of their higher profile Postwar and Contemporary Art sales.[28] In 2021, they held a two-week-long online sale of an NFT, Beeple's *Everyday: The First 5000 Days,* which was sold for $69 million, marking the onset of the brief surge of interest in the medium.[29]

Another significant trend in the auction market has been the increasing presence of collectors at day sales, which had normally been the hunting grounds of the professional dealers. Day sales had usually been composed of smaller works, works on paper, and pieces by lesser masters, and because they happened in the daytime, only the trade would be able to show up. Because the auction market, however, has been made so much more accessible by the internet, collectors can easily view catalogues, check price databases, and bid for items with ease. The secondary market gallery sector has been visibly withering in the face of this competition. In fact, now in terms of volume, though not in terms of value, over 90 percent of Sotheby's bids are now coming through online bidding. With 2022 being one of the best years for auction houses in general, particularly driven by the collectables market.[30]

That said, all is not so well with the big auction houses either; Sotheby's held large-scale layoffs in recent years and also acquired a major art advisory firm in order to boost their private sales.[31] Private sales (i.e., deals done discreetly with no public disclosure, except for carefully planned "leaks") had been a field that Christie's had used extensively to conduct some of the most high-value sales in history (and many others we are not allowed to know about). Most significantly, Sotheby's had been taken private in order to allow it to better compete with its rival but is now already considering listing itself again as a publicly held company[32] following a series of cost-cutting measures.[33] Overall, the auction business in its current internet, turbo-charged version remains one of the most dynamic sectors of the art market.

CASE STUDY: SOTHEBY'S AND CHRISTIE'S PRICE-FIXING SCANDAL

By the 1980s, the current-day auction business was taking shape. The Big Two, Sotheby's and Christie's, had both made the migration to New York, which was now becoming the center of gravity for this sector of the art market, as it had already been for most other sectors already. In 1987, however, the New York market entered one of its frequent crashes, this one brought on by the collapse of Japanese speculative buying of Impressionism. In the early 1990s, the chairman Albert Taubman of Sotheby's and the chairman of Christie's, Sir Anthony Tennant, began secret meetings to agree to no longer compete on their key business pricing which were their seller's and buyer's premiums. Until that point, the two firms had been competing on seller's premiums when they regarded major pieces that were likely to bring significant income from the buyer's premium alone, and with savvy sellers knowing that both auction houses were finding it difficult to turn much of a profit. Significant buyers had also been knuckling down their premiums as well, and both firms were increasingly taking heavy risks in the process of giving sellers guarantees. As a result of those talks, though, quite suddenly in 1995, both firms stopped competing on these fees, declaring them to be non-negotiable.[34]

The U.S. authorities began to take interest and by 1997 had issued subpoenas, but the case seemed to be going nowhere until quite spectacularly, Christie's recently dismissed CEO Christopher Davidage turned over massive amounts of documents in exchange for amnesty.[35] Their chairman, Tennant, escaped prosecution because he could not be extradited from the U.K., but it brought to an ignominious end what had been a very distinguished career in business. Both the chairman of Sotheby's, Taubman, and their CEO, Dede Brooks, however, both did jail time (Brooks managed to do hers through home incarceration). Both firms would end up paying civil damages of $256 million to their victims who were their clients who overpaid on premiums, but Christie's managed to come out the better from it because they confessed first and escaped without incarceration for their leadership. The settlement was in some ways set in motion by the acquisition of Christie's by Francois Pinault in 1998 because his firing of Davidage[36] was what led the former CEO to turn over documents to investigators. One result from the fallout, then, was that Pinault consolidated his more nimble leadership at Christie's, and that has subsequently allowed the firm to continually outmaneuver their rival.

AUCTION HOUSES—TERMS

Estimate—a price range with both a low and high estimate. These prices indicate where the auction house believes the hammer price will be.

Opening bid—the price at which bidding begins. It is usually secret and the auctioneer may set it at their discretion. At some auction houses, an opening bid is listed instead of an estimate.

Reserve—the price below which an artwork will not be sold to a bidding buyer and instead will be "bought in," meaning it will not be sold and will return to the seller.

Hidden reserve—an unethical technique where a seller wants to ensure that an artwork appears to sell for a certain price even if there are no willing bidders to take it to that price. In such cases, the seller and the auction house collude to pack the audience with fake buyers to bid up an artwork to a certain price, where it is hammered. In fact, however, the artwork goes unsold and is returned to the seller, but the market is left believing that the work has sold for an impressive price.

Buyer's premium—the commission paid by the buyer of an artwork, usually a percentage in the range of 10–25 of the hammer price.

Seller's premium—the commission paid by the seller of an artwork, usually a percentage in the range of 8–20 of the hammer price. However, for high-value works that the auction house has a strong interest in selling, the seller's premium might be dropped in order to persuade the seller to choose to work with them rather than a competitor.

Hammer price—the actual amount that the winning seller is offering to pay when the artwork is "hammered," that is, when the auctioneer literally hits their gavel on the podium. The hammer price will then have a buyer's premium added to it on the buyer's invoice. The seller will have the seller's premium deducted from the hammer price when they receive their payment from the auction house.

Chandelier bidding—an unethical tactic where the auctioneer accepts bids from non-existent bidders in an attempt to drive up the price of an artwork.

Guarantee—an offer to buy an artwork coming up at auction at a prearranged price if the lot fails to reach that price at the auction. Guarantees can be given by the auction house or by a third-party guarantor.

Day sale—auctions that take place during the day, featuring less expensive works, either by lesser masters or smaller or less valuable mediums (watercolor, drawings, and prints). Frequented by the trade.

Evening sale—auctions that take place in the evening and include the most high-value works. Generally frequented by collectors or their representatives.

Notes

1   Morcillo, M. G. "Staging Power and Authority at Roman Auctions." *Ancient Society*, vol. 38, 2008, pp. 153–181.

2   We understand this sale to be an auction because of the price to which the painting by Aristides rose, thereby indicating the presence of competing bidders. See: Pliny the Elder. Ed. John Bostock, M.D., F.R.S. H.T. Riley, Esq., B.A. "Book XXXV: An Account of Paintings and Colours, Chapter 8 — At What Period Foreign Paintings Were First Introduced at Rome." *The Natural History*. London: Taylor and Francis, 1855.

3   Boerner, L., van Bochove, C., and Quint, D. "Anglo-Dutch Premium Auctions in Eighteenth-Century Amsterdam." *Modern and Comparative Seminar*, Nov. 22, 2012, London, UK.

4   Montias, J. M. *Art at Auction in 17th Century Amsterdam*. Amsterdam University Press, 2002.

5 Crenshaw, P. *Rembrandt's Bankruptcy: The Artist, His Patrons, and the Art Market in Seventeenth-Century Netherlands*. Cambridge University Press, 2006.

6 Elliott, J. E. "The Cost of Reading in Eighteenth Century England: Auction Sale Catalogues and the Cheap Literature Hypothesis." *ELH*, vol. 77, no. 2, 2010, pp. 353–384.

7 "Sotheby's Acquires 75% of Parke-Bernet." *The New York Times*, July 15, 1964.

8 Kinsella, Eileen. "French Media Tycoon Patrick Drahi Has Acquired Sotheby's for $3.7 Billion, Taking the Publicly Traded Auction House Private." *ARTnet*, June 17, 2019.

9 Bayer, T. M. and Page, J. R. "The Formation of a Nexus: A Story of Christie's." In *The Development of the Art Market in England: Money as Muse, 1730–1900*. London: Pickering and Chatto, 2011, pp. 143–151.

10 De Smet, C. "Marketing the French Revolution? Revolutionary Auction Advertisements in Comparative Perspective (Paris, 1778–1793)." *French History*, vol. 36, no. 1, Mar. 2022, pp. 68–99.

11 Hamilton, A. "Christie's Is Bought Out By the French." June 1, 1998.

12 Reyburn, S. "Why Sotheby's Agreed to Be Bought by a Telecom Executive for $3.7 Billion." *The New York Times*, June 17, 2019.

13 "Sotheby's to Pay $148.8 Million for N.Y. Gallery." *Los Angeles Times*, Apr. 26, 1990.

14 Moncrieff, E. "Christie's Close Down Spink and Take over the Building for Corporate Headquarters." *The Art Newspaper*, Mar. 1, 2000.

15 Osborn, A. and Kennedy, M. "Sotheby's Fined £13m for Price-Fixing Scandal with Christie's." *The Guardian*, Oct. 31, 2002.

16 Alberge, D. "Antiquities for Auction Could Be Illicitly Sourced, Archaeologist Claims." *The Guardian*, Dec. 7, 2021.

17 Reyburn, S. "Is the Old Masters Market in Terminal Decline?" *The Art Newspaper*, Dec. 7, 2022.

18 Brady, A. "What Does a $450m Leonardo Mean for the Old Master Market?" *The Art Newspaper*, Dec. 1, 2017.

19 Kaplan, I. "Why Impressionist and Modern Works Are Losing Ground at the Top End of the Auction Market." *Artsy*, Aug. 8, 2016.

20 "Bonhams Buys Butterfields." *Forbes*, Aug. 6, 2002.

21 Jhala, K. "Bonhams Owner Floats Sale of Auction House at $1bn." *The Art Newspaper*, Feb. 7, 2023.

22 Fuchsgruber, L. "The Hôtel Drouot as the Stock Exchange for Art. Financialization of Art Auctions in the Nineteenth Century." *Journal for Art Market Studies*, vol. 1, no. 1, 2017.

23 *Leonardo da Vinci. Salvator Mundi. Christie's*. Auction catalogue for sale on Nov. 15, 2017.

24 Vogel, C. and Eaton, L. "Sotheby's and Christie's Face Lawsuits from Angry Customers in Antitrust Case." *New York Times*, Feb. 21, 2000.

25 Barboza, D., Bowley, G., and Cox, A. "A Culture of Bidding: Forging an Art Market in China." *The New York Times*, Oct. 28, 2013.

26 Woodham, D. "Common Mistakes of Rookie Auction Guarantors." *The Art Newspaper*, Nov. 12, 2018.

27 Duray, D. "Christie's Nets $705.8 M. at 'Looking Forward' Sale, Led by Picasso and Giacometti Record Setters." *ARTnews*, May 12, 2015.

28 Reyburn, S. "Five Years Since the $450m Salvator Mundi Sale: A First-Hand Account of the Nonsensical Auction." *The Art Newspaper*, Nov. 15, 2022.

29 Jhala, K. "WTAF? Beeple NFT Work Sells for Astonishing $69.3M at Christie's after Flurry of Last-Minute Bids Nearly Crashes Website." *The Art Newspaper*, Mar. 11, 2021.

30 Reyburn, S. "How Online Buyers of Luxury Collectibles Reshaped Auctions in an Economic Slump." *The Art Newspaper*, Feb. 23, 2023.

31 Forbes, A. "Why Sotheby's Just Bought an Art Advisory for $85 Million." *Artsy*, Jan. 12, 2016.

32 Sutton, B. "Sotheby's Owner Patrick Drahi Reportedly Considering Taking Auction House Public." *The Art Newspaper*, Dec. 15, 2021.

33 Sutton, B. "Pensioners Revolt: Patrick Drahi Winds up Sotheby's 'Defined Benefit' Pension Plan, and Former Employees Are Not Happy." *The Art Newspaper*, Feb. 9, 2021.

34 Ashenfelter, O. and Graddy, K. "The Rise and Fall of a Price-Fixing Conspiracy: Auction at Sotheby's and Christie's." *Journal of Competition Law and Economics*, vol. 1, 2005, pp. 3–20.

35 Blumenthal, R. and Vogel, C. "Auction Case Takes Turn to Documents." *The New York Times*, July 11, 2001.

36 Tharp, P. "Auction House Bombshell; Exec's Affair with Socialite Led Scandal to Surface." *New York Post*, Oct. 1, 2000.

Public Collections and Museums

Chapter 4

EARLY MUSEUMS AND CABINETS OF CURIOSITY

The growth of museums, both in the creation of new ones and expansion of older ones, has served as the underpinning for a vast increase in the amount of art consumption that now occurs in the leisure sector. In that sense, museums remain a core anchor to the wider art business, but they maintain an uneasy relationship with the market itself. On the one hand, museums act as a dead-end to the commercial process: where objects go to never be traded again (with notable exceptions). On the other hand, museums can be some of the most important buyers in the market, and what they buy and exhibit can quickly influence tastes and speculative activity. In the nineteenth century, only a few public collections in the model of today's museums existed in Europe and North America. From those beginnings, the current level of expansion can be described as nothing short of exponential. Governmental entities now clearly understand how important public collections are to a thriving cultural tourism industry, and ever more wealthy collectors are establishing private museums to give their artwork a permanent home and a platform by which it can achieve the canonical status that public exhibition provides.

Most of our great Western museums can trace their origins to the nineteenth century, and a few to the eighteenth century: notably the British Museum and the Louvre. The tradition of public

DOI: 10.4324/9781003431756-5

collections, however, derives from institutions already existent in the classical world. The competition between the leading libraries of antiquity, Alexandria and Pergamon, to acquire the oldest and most authoritative texts of important literary works, would set a pattern for the priorities and hierarchies of collectors.[1] It was also in Alexandria where an institution called the *Mouseion* was founded, which would be the origin of the term museum.[2] According to Pausanias, in Athens the building on the left side of the *propylaea* (gateway into Acropolis) was the *pinacotheca*, which had a display of paintings (or frescoes) depicting famous events and characters from Greek history and literature.[3] The Romans would also employ the word *pinacotheca* to describe a building housing artworks, often adjacent to public baths. At this time in the Mediterranean world of antiquity, forms of public collections began to emerge, either in the holdings of sacred institutions,[4] libraries,[5] or public spaces such as the Portico of Philippus in Rome.[6] With the revival in the art market in renaissance Europe, wealthy individuals began assembling collections to impress their peers. These collections contained a vast diversity of objects including visual art objects (paintings, sculpture, and bronze medals), artifacts from ancient Greece and Rome (coins, sculpture, cameos, and inscriptions), applied arts from non-European cultures (porcelain and textiles), natural history objects from exotic locations (precious stones, shells, coral, and taxidermy), and even the occasional embalmed human (Inuit, Inca, and Egyptian). All of these objects would be exhibited in a single room together in a grand expression of wonder. The word in German, *Wunderkabinett*, in English often translated to Cabinet of Curiosities, captures the sensation of awe at the world in the age of discovery. Many of these collections would form the core of our earliest public museums.[7] The Amerbach Cabinet would be acquired by the city of Basel, Switzerland to become the first public collection in 1661.[8] The vast holdings of Sir Hans Sloane would become the foundation of the British Museum;[9] the Ashmolean collection would become the core of the eponymous museum at Oxford University.[10]

MODELS OF MUSEUMS

Our current-day museums have come into existence in many different methods, and each museum's history is a narrative peculiar to itself. That said, there are a number of museum models that prevail around the world, and these models can be quite distinct in terms of the source of their collection, their governance and oversight, and most crucially in terms of their financing. The classic model of a European art museum would have its core holdings derive from the private collection of the historical ruling house: the French royal family, the Bourbon's, collection would become the Louvre in Paris; the Spanish royal family's—the Prado in Madrid; and Habsburg Imperial Family— the *Kunsthistorisches* in Vienna. These transitions from private royal collection to public collection can be either violent, as with the French Revolution resulting in the creation of the Louvre,[11] or quite peaceful, as with the Austro-Hungarian Emperor Franz Joseph's enthusiastic creation of the *Kunsthistorisches*.[12] These museums would then be increasingly identified with the national patrimony, with the state both governing and financing the museums through their Ministries of Culture. Since these museums have not (at least until recently) sought patronage from private sources, their only other revenue source would be earned income from ticket as well as café and gift shop sales. In Britain, the state-run museums do not even charge for admission to their permanent collections (only for temporary exhibitions), but they do actively cultivate giving among private donors much more so than on the continent.

The American model of museum originates quite differently. A typical American example would be the Metropolitan Museum of Art in New York, which was founded by an enthusiastic group of New York-based elites who wished to establish an art museum worthy of their growing city.[13] They had no core collection. Everything in the museum was either donated or purchased with donated funds. Furthermore, the institution operates in the classical American nonprofit business model: it earns income through ticket sales, massive gift shops, and many other revenue-generating methods and then supplements that with a highly sophisticated donated-income strategy. This unearned income comes in the form of six- and seven-figure donations from board members all the way down to the basic membership (giving free admission), which costs around $100 per year. Membership income somewhat straddles the distinction between earned and unearned income since, in theory, it is a tax-deductible donation, but for many of the members, their membership serves more as a volume discount at a museum they visit frequently. The membership system, furthermore, has been picked up by European museums, as well, as way of forming stronger links to their local audience. It should also be emphasized that the great art museums of the United States (with the exception of the Washington National Gallery) do not serve as national museums (though the Whitney does profile itself as the leading collection of American art). The Metropolitan, the Boston Museum of Fine Arts, the Art Institute of Chicago all were set up and intended to serve their city and act as anchors to their city's cultural landscape. Their service is civic not national.

A third model would be that of the private museum. Although most museums were built on donated collections, the private museum is one that essentially remains entirely composed of the collection of its original founder. This kind of museum remained relatively rare until the late twentieth century when a new wave of private museums began to appear. The three great early examples in the United States all derived from the collections of American gilded age millionaires: the Frick Collection in New York, the Isabella Stewart Gardner Museum in Boston, and the Barnes Collection in Philadelphia. The museums were intended to be left an endowment which (although still supplemented by latter-day donors and ticket sales) insures the institutions long-term survival. In the case of the first two, the founder's distinct palatial home and original curation largely remain intact. The Barnes, however, ran into difficulties in the 1990s and eventually, through a highly controversial process, has become an orphan, and saw its collection move to a new facility near the city's other museums and installed in a structure that reproduced the original configuration of Barnes' house so that his personal curation could be re-created.[14] In the mid-twentieth century, Solomon Guggenheim had Frank Lloyd Wright design his iconic spiral building for his collection of non-objective (abstract) art.[15] After his death, however, the museum leadership pursued a broader approach to Modernism, and today few people have ever even seen Guggenheim's core collection of abstract art.[16] John Paul Getty established a museum in a building modeled on a Roman villa located in

Malibu, California. When Getty died, the museum was less of a collection than it was a massive endowment for acquiring one. The Getty expanded its profile to many sectors but continued to grow its leading profile in works from classical antiquity. However, acquisitions of first-rate works came with cultural heritage issues which resulted in a significant scandal for the museum in 2006.[17] London has the Wallace Collection and Paris has the Musée Jacquemart-André, which also follow the model of a world-class collection still installed in the collector's home. Recent years have seen many more private museums established across the globe: the Louis Vuitton Foundation in Paris, the Thyssen-Bornemisza in Madrid, and The Broad in Los Angeles. The latest edition would be the completion of Bourse de Commerce located in Paris' former stock exchange (to add to his two in Venice, Palazzo Grassi and Punta della Dogana) to hold the collection of François Pinault.[18]

ART MUSEUMS

In terms of museum collections, four distinct profiles can be identified: Art Museums, History and Material Culture Museums, Natural History Museums, and University Museums. The first, art museums, are the ones that most directly participate in the art world. Within that designation, there exist still further divisions: comprehensive museums, such as the Metropolitan Museum of Art, that aim to show the entire history of both fine and applied arts, across the globe and throughout time; modern museums, such as the Museum of Modern Art (MoMA) in New York or the Centre Pompidou in Paris, which have permanent collections covering twentieth-century art, and temporary exhibits focused on living or recently deceased artists; applied arts museums, that focus exclusively on design objects with functional purposes, such as the Victoria and Albert in London or the Austrian *Museum für angewandte Kunst* (MAK) in Vienna; and artist or genre museums, which focus on a single artist, like the Salvador Dalí Museum in St. Petersburg, Florida or group, like the Brücke Museum in Berlin, which features artists of the early twentieth-century expressionist movement. In addition to these models, there are a growing number of non-collecting museums that have no permanent collection, like the Aspen Art Museum, which hold curated temporary exhibitions of contemporary art, and this model is referred to with the nineteenth-century German word for salon buildings: *kunsthalle*, and in fact many in Europe are functioning in those same buildings today, like the Műcsarnok in Budapest, and the Künstlerhaus in Vienna.

Art museums all draw their mission from an aesthetic purpose: namely, to show beautiful things. In addition, many national art museums, like the National Galleries of Austria, Hungary, and Czech Republic, all have very similar goals of telling the story of their national school of art, and particularly to impart a narrative that demonstrates that their artists were participating in the wider progression of international art history. The curation in these museums, therefore, endeavors to show that their national artists were doing impressionist painting at nearly the same time as French ones (Monet, Renoir, and Pissarro), and they were doing modernism (Cubism, Fauvism) concurrent with the internationally canonical practitioners in Paris (Picasso, Matisse). Most art museums are usually simultaneously showing their permanent collection and also holding a number of temporary exhibitions. The permanent collection will be drawn from the museum's own holdings as well as from long-term loans, and its curators will periodically rearrange the display pulling out unseen works from the storage. Many long-established museums may have stored collections equaling nearly ten times what is out on the museum floor, hence the importance of rotating the permanent exhibition. Temporary exhibitions are usually composed of some pieces from the museum's own collection which are combined with pieces borrowed from other museums and private collectors. These exhibitions usually remain at one location for three to four months and then possibly move to another museum (often one of the other primary lenders of material). These exhibitions will usually have lead curators, for whom the show can be a very personal aesthetic and intellectual vision and the pinnacle of their career. For museums, these temporary exhibitions can be a key source of revenue since they usually require a supplemental entry ticket, and they can attract local audiences who already know the permanent collection quite well and need something new to pull them back in.

HISTORY AND MATERIAL CULTURE MUSEUMS

Although history and material culture museums may include art objects very similar to those found in art museums, their profile and how they present these objects can be quite different. The key difference is that while art museums collect objects based on their aesthetic importance, history and material culture museums collect objects based on their historical importance. In other words, an art museum would acquire a painting based on who painted it. A historical museum would collect a painting based who or what the painting depicts (a portrait, an important battle scene). Many countries have such museums to represent a national history with an express purpose to inculcate patriotism among its citizens. In time, many of these national collections will be subdivided into more focused museums: military history museum, ethnographic (folk culture) museum, and ancient history museums that deal with civilizations that predate the arrival of the current dominant nation in that locality, for example, museums to Roman civilization found throughout today's modern European and Mediterranean nations. Open-air ethnographic museums exist in many countries and are modelled on (and named after) the Skansen that was opened on an island in Stockholm harbor in 1891 to conserve rural architecture and regional practices that were disappearing in Sweden in the face of industrialization and modernity.

In addition to these broad profile museums with national perspective, a vast array of more narrowly defined collections also falls into this category including museums devoted to toys, cars, airplanes, trains, catering, postal service, as well as those devoted to other sectors of the arts, such as theater, cinema, literature, and music. Important historical characters may warrant their own museum, for example, political leaders, cultural producers, economic actors. In many cases, these institutions will be located in the subject's former home. History and material culture museums necessitate much more didactic material than art museums. While the aesthetic value of an object may speak for itself, its historic importance does not and requires interpretation and contextualization. An appropriate example would be one of the star attractions of the world's foremost museum of this type, the British Museum, and the Rosetta Stone which sits at the entrance to the Egyptian section.

The stone itself is nothing pretty. It is a large, engraved stele with text in Ancient Greek, Demotic, and Hieroglyphics. Despite the fact of its lack of beauty and the fact that virtually none of the museum's visitors can read any of the languages on it, the object remains the institution's most visited object. It is an artifact in an archaeological meaning and a relic in a metaphorical religious meaning. The Rosetta Stone was the very tool by which Hieroglyphics were translated, and it is for this reason that it attracts visitors to make a pilgrimage to see it for themselves.

NATURAL HISTORY MUSEUMS

Natural history museums have historically pursued two profiles: presenting the geological, zoological, and botanical history of the Earth (and the Cosmos) and providing an anthropological survey of pre-urban civilization peoples. The latter role has become increasingly problematic as first-nations peoples raise numerous protests to the way in which their ancestors and their material culture are exhibited like natural history specimens. Many museums have moved away from anthropological exhibits altogether because of the inherent problematics of grouping some peoples in a museum that otherwise shows non-human species and runs the danger of appearing to class the exhibited peoples as somehow sub-human. The process of de-accessioning and restituting human remains has gathered pace as a result of the landmark 1990 Native American Graves Protection and Repatriation Act, but thousands of remains still reside in museum collections.[19]

Although natural history museums will rely on authentic objects to form the core of their collection, they must also work very hard to provide a contextualization that communicates to the visitor what the object is, and how it functions in nature. Furthermore, many objects, such as dinosaur fossils, are fragmentary and must be painstakingly and scientifically extrapolated with modern materials in order for the viewer to see the full-size skeleton. Natural history museums must devote inordinate attention to the creation and curation of didactic materials to bring their objects to life. In fact, the costs of acquiring objects may be relatively modest compared to the costs of creating unique, highly engaging multimedia immersion experiences. Unlike art museums, which have to work very hard to develop educational programs to interest children in their artworks, natural history museums are generally designed with children as their core audience. On any given Saturday in the American Museum of Natural History in New York, nearly all the visitors are families with children. The dinosaur collection (always by far the most popular section of any natural history museum), which is essentially composed of fossils that in isolation would be of little meaning to the viewers, is expanded with animatronic life-sized simulations of dinosaurs, as well as models, visual renderings, and many electronic interactive features.

UNIVERSITY MUSEUMS

Museums located on the campuses of many universities may have any of the above-listed profiles and may include holdings that could fall into any of the categories: art, history and material culture, and natural history. The defining feature of this type is that the museum is, in some way, attached to a university and its holdings are regarded as a teaching collection. Although a museum may have received its real estate from the university and possibly some of its operating financing, they also usually maintain a somewhat distinct fundraising and governance structure from that of the university itself. These museums generally have received their core collection as bequests from alumni or local benefactors, but archaeological or scientific collections may also have originated from the research activities of the school's own faculty and students. Because of the peculiarities of these sorts of collections, university museums rarely have a comprehensive profile, but more often serve as concentrated studies in objects in their collection. That said, certain high-profile collections rise above the category of "university museum" and really act as world-class attractions that happen to be based on a campus. These include the Ashmolean at Oxford, the Fitzwilliam at Cambridge, the Fogg at Harvard, the Yale Art Gallery, the Clark Art Institute at Williams, and the Allen Memorial at Oberlin. All these collections contain canonical artworks that frequently can be found in art history textbooks, and these works are often lent for temporary exhibitions at high-profile venues. Many museums complement their collections by also staging temporary exhibitions of contemporary artists. University museums, however, can frequently become a burden if the institution's profile becomes muddled. Furthermore, since university museums rarely charge for entry, they generate almost no earned income and can quickly become a money hole for the university.

THE ROLE OF MUSEUMS IN THE ART MARKET

Art museums may hold the market at arm's length but, in fact, they are very active players in the trade. Although most collections were built on the donation of artworks, wealthier museums also have acquisition budgets and spend it to get pieces that their curators believe will help fill the gaps in their holdings. Chief curators, since it is widely known that they have acquisition budgets, try to keep a low profile since otherwise they would be besieged with offers to purchase artworks. They usually buy from dealers they trust, as well as at auctions, art fairs like TEFAF in Maastricht, and collectors who are not so generous as to donate the work. For museums that have a modern and contemporary profile, the purchasing can often take place at art fairs like Art Basel, Armory, or Frieze. In these cases, elite museums like the MoMA, Whitney, Centre Pompidou, and Tate Modern know the cachet attached with being able to claim that an artist's work is in their collection and leverage that to be able to buy works and expect to pay less than what a private collector would pay.[20] Dealers are usually more than happy to oblige because the increasingly sophisticated means of tracking values in the art market, instruments such as *Kunstkompass*, that treat artists like financial securities, will count inclusion and exhibition at major public collections as the most important indicator of rising valuation.[21]

Although inclusion in a public collection is considered to be a dead-end in an artwork's commercial history, that is, it will never be bought or sold again, in fact, notable exceptions exist where museum holdings do end up back on the market. One cause is the process known as "deaccessioning," which means selling off works from the collection. These decisions can be highly controversial, and the museum leadership must make a strong case for this action. The justification will usually be that the collection is rich in a certain subject (perhaps a certain artist) and cannot show all the works and would benefit from selling off some of the lesser pieces and using the income to diversify and fill gaps in the holdings. The financial crisis brought on by Covid has led the museum sector to reconsider what would have been unconscionable only a few years earlier.[22] Another cause for museum works returning to the market is the Second-World-War-era restitution cases. Many important Jewish art collections were plundered by the Nazis, and these works often ended up in European museums after the war. In the last two decades, heirs of these families have been pursuing restitution claims in the U.S. and European courts, eventually winning back title to the works and then placing them on the market. The most spectacular instance of recent years involved Gustav Klimt's *Portrait of Adele Bloch-Bauer I*, which had been in the possession of the Austrian National Gallery and had hung in the Belvedere Palace next to one of the world's absolutely most iconic paintings, *The Kiss*. When the heir of Bloch-Bauer acquired title to the work (and four other Klimts) as a result of a ruling by the U.S. Supreme Court, Christie's arranged a private sale of the piece to Ronald Lauder (and currently hangs in his Neue Galerie museum in New York) for what was at the time a record price of $135 million.[23] This demonstrated the value to an artwork in having been seen by millions of museum-goers and being associated with (by having been hung next to) one of the world's best known artworks.

CURRENT TRENDS IN THE MUSEUM WORLD

New museums seem to be going up in nearly every corner of the globe. Some are being built by states and cities, and many more are being erected by private individuals to enshrine their holdings as a public collection. Museums are now recognized by governments as absolutely essential anchors to a vibrant tourism industry. The building of museums has become to architecture what building cathedrals had been to the Middle Ages: the highest calling and supreme opportunity of artistic expression. All of our best-known architects, the ones who are truly household names, achieved that status through the building of museums: Renzo Piano, Frank Gehry, Zaha Hadid. In fact, Gehry's Bilbao Guggenheim structure has become so iconic that it has become the leading engine of the tourism industry in northwest Spain.[24] As a result, all major new museum constructions attempt to turn their building into the most important object in the entire collection.

With the ongoing process of restitution producing so much turmoil in the museum world, some institutions, such as the Museum of Fine Arts in Boston, have taken the step of appointing a curator for provenance, whose sole mandate is to investigate the ownership and title of objects in the museum collection, as well as works being considered for acquisition. Because of the searing scandal of the archaeological works coming through Giacomo Medici's warehouse in the Freeport of Geneva, museums have been much more careful about only acquiring works with a believable and verifiable pre-1970 (date of landmark UNESCO Cultural Heritage treaty) provenance.[25] Otherwise, the work is (likely) assumed to be stolen or resulting from illicit archaeology, and if the museum purchased the work, they would have been supporting that illegal industry.

Museums have also reluctantly begun to divest themselves of toxic trustees and donors. Leon Black had only recently ascended to the chairmanship of the MoMA when he was forced to leave the position because of his dealings with Jeffrey Epstein.[26] The Sackler family, who made their fortune from OxyContin which led directly to the opioid crisis in the United States, have seen their name removed from the Louvre, the British Museum, and the Met's glassed wing that held the cherished *Temple of Dendur.*[27]

CASE STUDY: THE MUSEUM OF JURASSIC TECHNOLOGY

Culver City, California, a working-class neighborhood of Los Angeles, is the last place one would imagine finding one of the most influential museums in the world for curators, and yet that is what the Museum of Jurassic Technology has become. Few people, however, would know of it if not for a 1995 book by Lawrence Weschler, *Mr. Wilson's Cabinet of Wonder: Pronged Ants, Horned Humans, Mice on Toast, and Other Marvels of Jurassic Technology.* The museum is the creation of David and Diana Wilson as a meditation upon the very idea of museums and

---

particularly on the concept of wonder. Everything about the presentation is entirely deadpan, and as the visitor enters what appears to be a musty out-of-the-way museum of material culture/natural history, one is pulled into a wormhole of didactic dioramas where the visitor is never certain when the departure from reality has occurred.

The exhibits include an expansive Delani/Sonnabend section which details an intertwined narrative of an early twentieth-century opera singer, Madalena Delani, and a neurologist, Geoffrey Sonnabend, who constructed a vast theory of Obliscence: Theories of Forgetting and the Problem of Matter. Diagrams give full explication to Sonnabend's concepts with authoritative-sounding names such as Cone of Confabulation and Spealean Ring Disparity.[28] In fact, everything about the Museum of Jurassic Technology speaks with great authority, an authority that museum-goers have learned from a lifetime of going to museums. And it is exactly that inclination that the Wilsons are constantly toying with, because everything is stated so convincingly one does not know when to stop believing. Furthermore, as Weschler's writing aptly expresses, the more one explores, the more one finds there is in fact a much larger grain of truth in the exhibits than one initially suspected.

Among the other attractions are ones devoted to bats that can penetrate lead, a horn that had grown out of a woman's head, and tropical ants who become infected with fungus that causes them to impale themselves at the tops of tall trees (a phenomenon that serves as the origin for the hit HBO series *The Last of Us*)[29]. Much of the inspiration for the Museum of Jurassic Technology came from the early proto-museums that we would call a *Wunderkabinett* (cabinet of curiosities). It is this experience of wonder, finding that our world is more complex and in some ways beyond our comprehension, that inspired those early collections, and it is what now brings hordes of jaded curators to the Museum of Jurassic Technology to learn how they can recover that experience.

PUBLIC COLLECTIONS AND MUSEUMS—TERMS

Museum curator—primarily concerned with the care, conservation, exhibition, and contextualization of the museum's collection. At larger museums they will be assigned to specific periods and mediums within the collection.

Registrar—primarily concerned with the storage, security, and transportation of the museum's collection, as well as any works currently having been lent to the museum and therefore under its custody.

Wunderkabinett (Cabinet of Curiosities)—an early form of collecting in Europe from the fifteenth to the eighteenth centuries, involving artworks, archaeological artifacts, natural history, botany, geology, and other mediums all organized around the principle of wonder.

Didactic—an informational text posted in a museum near to the objects it discusses. This can include factual information such as title, artist, medium, size, accession date, and source (donor) of the object. This can also include longer aesthetic or contextualizing commentary to help the museum-goer to better appreciate the object.

Permanent collection—the objects possessed by the museum which have been chosen to be exhibited in the public areas in a format that does not change frequently. It will include the museum's most prized and celebrated objects, though the permanent collection on display may represent only a tiny percentage (sometimes as little as 10 percent) of total holdings.

Temporary exhibition—a short-term exhibition lasting generally around three to five months, which will then often travel on to another museum. The material for a temporary exhibition is usually partially drawn from the museum's own collection, but the rest will come from loans from other collections. These exhibitions usually have a theme or concept that connects the objects on display.

Retrospective—a temporary exhibition about the career of one artist providing a comprehensive overview of their work. Generally done only for a late-career or deceased artist.

Deaccessioning—a controversial process whereby a museum sells off parts of their permanent collection. The justification for such an action is usually because the museum possesses large holdings in a certain artist and cannot display all the works and would use the proceeds of the sale to diversify the collection.

Bequest—a donation given upon the death of the donor. Museums often acquire high-value artworks as bequests. The tax deduction accorded the donation often helps heirs to offset their tax liabilities.

Docent—an employee or volunteer of the museum who gives guided tours of the museum's exhibitions.

Notes

1 Young, L. "The Fierce, Forgotten Library Wars of the Ancient World: The Dark Trade of Collecting Books Used to Get Really Messy." *Atlas Obscura*, Aug. 26, 2016.

2 The etymology of the *Mouseion* meant something operating under the protection of the muses, but its exact usage remains unclear because of a paucity of sources describing its functioning clearly. It may have been more of a symposium of scholars than a public collection. Jochum, Uwe. "The Alexandrian Library and its Aftermath." *Library History*, vol. 15, no. 1, 1999, pp. 5–12.

3 Pausanias. *Description of Greece*. Trans. Jones, W. H. S. and Omerod, H. A. Cambridge, MA: Harvard University Press; London: William Heinemann Ltd. Book I, xxii. 6–7, 1918.

4 Pausanias, in *Description of Greece*, enumerates the holdings of many of the most important temples and holy places, for example in Thespiae. 9.27.1–4.

5 The library at Pergamon was known to contain a copy of Phidias' sculpture of *Athena Parthenos*. See: Hill, D. K., "A Copy of the Athena Parthenos," *The Art Bulletin*, vol. 18, no. 2, June 1936, pp. 150–167.

6 Heslin, P. *The Museum of Augustus: The Temple of Apollo in Pompeii, the Portico of Philippus in Rome, and Latin Poetry*. J. Paul Getty Museum, 2015.

7 See: Impey, O. R. and MacGregor, A. *The Origins of Museums: The Cabinet of Curiosities in Sixteenth- and Seventeenth-century Europe*. House of Stratus, 2001.

8 Merian, W. "Bonifacius Amerbach." *Basler Zeitschrift für Geschichte und Altertumskunde*, vol. 16, 1917, pp. 144–162.

9 De Beer, G. *Sir Hans Sloane and the British Museum*. Oxford University Press, 1953.

10 Ovenell, R. F. *The Ashmolean Museum, 1683–1894*. Clarendon Press, 1986.

11 McClellan, A. *Inventing the Louvre: Art, Politics, and the Origins of the Modern Museum*. University of California Press, 1999.

12 Schellenberg, R. "Museums and Museality." *Journal of Austrian Studies*, vol. 51, no. 2, Summer 2018, pp. 31–50.

13 Tompkins, C. *Merchants & Masterpieces: The Story of the Metropolitan Museum of Art*. E. P. Dutton & Co., 1970, pp. 15–94.

14 *Art of the Steal*. Documentary film. Maj Productions, 9.14 Pictures. Sep. 12, 2009.

15 Bashkoff, T. R., Hanhardt, J., and Quaintance, D. *The Museum of Non-Objective Painting: Hilla Rebay and the Origins of the Solomon R. Guggenheim Museum.* Guggenheim Museum, 2009.

16 Knöfel, U. "The German Artist Who Inspired the Museum Gets Her Due in New Show." *Spiegel*, Mar. 21, 2005.

17 Felch, J. and Frammolino, R. *Chasing Aphrodite: The Hunt for Looted Antiquities at the World's Richest Museum.* Boston and New York: Houghton Mifflin Harcourt, 2011, pp. 265–266.

18 Berning Sawa, D. "Bourse de Commerce: Opening of Pinault's Long-Awaited Paris Museum Is — Pandemic Permitting — Finally around the Corner." *The Art Newspaper*, Jan. 5, 2021.

19 Small, Z. "Push to Return 116,000 Native American Remains Is Long-Awaited." *The New York Times*, Aug. 6, 2021.

20 Louie Sussman, A. "The Strategies Art Dealers Use to Discount Artists' Work." *Artsy*, Aug. 21, 2018.

21 Adam, G. "Show and Sell: The Added Value of a Museum Exhibition." *The Art Newspaper*, June 12, 2018.

22 Goldstein, C. "In a Major Shift, Museums Can Now Use the Proceeds From Deaccessioning for More Than Just Buying Art." *Artnet*, Oct. 3, 2022.

23 Vogel, C. "Lauder Pays $135 Million, a Record, for a Klimt Portrait." *The New York Times*, June 19, 2006.

24 Moore, R. "The Bilbao Effect: How Frank Gehry's Guggenheim Started a Global Craze." *The Guardian*, Oct. 1, 2017.

25 Noce, V. "Wanted in the US, Lebanese Antiquities Collector Maintains His Innocence, Says His 'Big Mistake' Was Trusting New York Art Crime Official." *The Art Newspaper*, Sep. 9, 2022.

26 Kenney, N. "Philanthropist Marie-Josée Kravis Will Replace the Embattled Leon Black as MoMA's Board Chairman." *The Art Newspaper*, Apr. 28, 2021.

27 Seymour, T. "Tainted Gifts: As British Museum and the Met Disavow the Sackler Name, Museums Rethink Donation Deals." *The Art Newspaper*, Mar. 28, 2022.

28 Weschler, L. *Mr. Wilson's Cabinet of Wonder.* New York: Vintage Books, 1995.

29 Some of the exhibits turn out to be entirely truthful, such as the fungus afflicting carpenter ants. See: Lu, Jennifer, "How a Parasitic Fungus Turns Ants into 'Zombies.'" *National Geographic*, Apr. 18, 2019.

Business Models:

For-Profit, Nonprofit, Government-Supported, and Others

Chapter 5

BASIC BUSINESS FUNCTIONS COMMON TO ALL GALLERIES

All galleries do certain universal activities that earn them the designation of "gallery." The most primary activity is the exhibiting of artworks, and all galleries aspire to show art in the best possible presentation that allows the audience to most fully appreciate the works' aesthetic merits. In addition to this most basic role, all galleries also wish to remain an open, operating institution, and this requires adequate finances to meet the gallery's costs. Therefore, galleries require revenue streams to ensure adequate operating funds, and although that revenue may come from profits on sales, government funding, or donations, the essential imperative remains: the gallery must generate income if it intends to survive. All galleries must, in a literal sense or metaphorical sense, *sell* their artwork. Commercial galleries are selling ownership of an artwork,

DOI: 10.4324/9781003431756-6

but non-commercial galleries and museums are trading in an art experience. Even if the venue has no entrance fee, its stakeholders and funders expect enthusiastic attendance to justify their patronage.

Other activities common to all galleries include marketing and promoting their artists and exhibitions. In fact, second to selling artworks, this would represent the most essential act a gallery engages in. The publicity a gallery generates for an artist will produce significant beneficial outcomes for their long-term career. The exhibition will provide an entry on the artist's CV and the digital platforms of gallery websites and social media provide an enduring record of the event having taken place. The print advertisements a gallery takes out, especially full-page ads in important trade journals, can transmit images of an artist's work well beyond the exhibition's immediate local orbit. All of the word-of-mouth and social media buzz that an exhibition generates also further facilitates recognition among art consumers. The combination of all these activities contributes to an overall goal of audience building, which is an endeavor common to all types of galleries.

FOR-PROFIT GALLERIES

Galleries with a profile in selling ownership of artworks are most likely to be for-profit galleries, and the income from these sales will be the primary source of revenue that sustains these entities. This is not to say that there are no nonprofit and state-funded institutions that also transact sales of artworks, but such an activity is not nearly so central to their very economic survival. In fact, the primary distinction between for-profit and nonprofit cultural institutions is the role played by earned income, which is revenue produced from doing the entity's primary activity and being paid for it. For a theater, this means selling tickets to their productions. For a pop music band, this would be the sale of their recordings, as well as touring income. In the art world, earned income can either be the profits from sales of artworks, or from the sale of entry tickets. For-profit institutions will rely on the former, while nonprofits are sustained by the latter. Both models generate earned income, but for-profits must survive from it alone, while nonprofits will have sources of unearned or donated income to assist in covering their operating costs.

For-profit galleries can primarily earn profits on sales in two methods: sales of wholly owned artworks and sales of artworks placed with the gallery on consignment. The former offers greater profit potential but incurs more risk because it places greater demand on the firm's cash flow. The consignment option will not produce as much profit (usually the gallery receives only 40–60 percent of the sale price), but the venture does not require the gallery to sink its own funds into acquiring the object with all the incurred risks of having precious capital being tied up. Wholly acquiring works tend to be a more common practice in the secondary market, where dealers purchase inventory at auctions catering to the trade and from collectors eager to get cash from their collection. When a seller clearly does not understand what they have, then a dealer may want to quickly buy up the piece before the owner becomes more knowledgeable about its market value. This strategy would be advisable when the offered price is low enough (possibly because of a misattribution) that the dealer could earn profits many times over the purchase price once the work is correctly attributed. Secondary market galleries can also earn income from the following activities: for renting out their inventory for photo shoots, film sets, and real estate marketing purposes; by doing appraisals (if the dealer is an accredited appraiser); by doing interior design work; and by acting as an art advisor assisting clients in buying at auction (for which the dealer might earn a commission of approximately 5–15 percent of the hammer price).

Primary market galleries rarely buy artworks outrightly. One major dealer known to pursue this strategy was Ambroise Vollard [see the case study in Chapter 1].[1] Although a high-risk, cash-intensive strategy, it allowed him to monopolize the œuvres of Cezanne and Gauguin, as well as many important early works from Picasso. Then he could sell off his holdings slowly over decades while pushing prices up. Most primary market dealers, however, follow a simple process of accepting works from exhibiting artists on a consignment method, with the gallery keeping between 40 and 60 percent of the sale price. Many galleries maintain a stable of artists and often control the sale of their artworks through exclusivity contracts that prohibit sales through any other avenue than the gallery. A few Chelsea galleries pursue more complex business arrangements with their artists and offer contracts that provide guaranteed monthly stipends that can be counted against future sales. It is, however, only a very tiny elite of galleries who offer these contracts, and an even relatively smaller elite of artists who enjoy them.

In the United States, the business structure for most for-profit art enterprises is the Limited Liability Company (LLC), and most commercial galleries will be the sole-proprietorship variant. The art business can be catastrophically unpredictable, and does not lend itself to conforming to standard accounting practices. Therefore, even the simplest of partnerships can prove contentious and unstable. Even Christie's functions as essentially a sole-proprietorship, and this fact is frequently cited as a reason for its ability to outmaneuver Sotheby's. With the exception of Sotheby's, until it too was taken private,[2] the art business is virtually absent of publicly traded, share-held corporations. U.S.-based for-profit LLCs should plan that they will need to be registered in a state and will need to pay both federal and state corporate income tax (sole-proprietorships, however, should file through their personal income tax),[3] federal and state payroll taxes, as well as state and local sales and property taxes. European firms will need to plan on national corporate income tax, significant payroll taxes (which will include national health care insurance), and a 16–27 percent Value-Added Tax (VAT) on sales.

NONPROFIT GALLERIES

Galleries with a nonprofit business structure can be frequently found operating under the umbrella of a larger nonprofit community arts center. The gallery may be only one of many core activities the institution pursues, alongside activities in performing arts events and educational offerings. For many nonprofit arts organizations, their educational profile and the income earned from the sale of classes represent their core activity. The gallery then functions more as a facility serving local artists for whom little opportunity exists for representation in commercial galleries. Very often the art center will rotate through a series of exhibition types. The gallery will fund curated exhibitions which will be put on with the institution's own modest resources as well as those from sponsors, but these endeavors might only be possible once or twice a year. Other times the gallery may be rented by artists who self-stage their own exhibition and incur all costs. In this case, the rental of the gallery can actually be a source of income for the institution but earning the reputation of being a "rental gallery" can, over time, degrade the prestige of holding exhibitions there.

Nonprofit galleries may, in fact, engage in sales, but usually in a far less aggressive manner than commercial galleries. Enthusiastic salespeople are not normally present in the gallery. Rather, if a client wished to make a purchase, they would search out the institution's receptionist who might be able to accept payment for the work but would be unlikely to play any active role in creating the sale. Accordingly, nonprofit galleries tend to ask lower sales commissions (around 20–30 percent) than commercial galleries, and they also generally produce fewer sales. Nonprofit galleries tend to look upon gallery sales as a bonus that might come from holding an exhibition, but not a planned-for revenue stream.

In the United States, nonprofit galleries or their parent institution will be registered as a 501(c)(3). This is the term from the U.S. Tax Code, and it covers a vast array of nonprofit organizations. These include universities, hospitals, churches, and social welfare and environmental organizations. In fact, arts organizations make up only about 5 percent of the entire U.S. nonprofit sector.[4] The key characteristic of a 501(c)(3) is that it may receive donations and in exchange offer the donor a deduction on their income tax. By being a nonprofit, this does not imply that the organization does not seek to generate profits, but rather that if profits occur, they are ploughed back in to the organization or set aside in an endowment for later capital investments. A 501(c)(3) will not pay corporate income tax because in principle there is not a notion of profit in the way that it applies in the for-profit world. A nonprofit institution will, however, still pay payroll taxes and sales tax or VAT (in Europe) on most commercial transactions.

The nonprofit organization does not have owners who receive a share of profits; rather there is a governing board whose members serve as volunteers (and very often donate considerable amounts of money for the honor of doing so). Most other Western countries have adopted similar tax-reducing incentives to promote charitable giving. For example, many European nations allow a small percentage of people's income tax refund to be devoted to a registered nonprofit of their choice. Museums all over the world have used memberships as a way to attract small giving, and these memberships in some way straddle the designation of earned and donated income. For many avid museum-goers, these memberships act as a volume discount on entry tickets (since the primary attraction of the membership is free entry), but usually counts as a tax-deductible donation.

Attracting nonprofit donations, however, is always its own form of sales, and what is being sold by the development office is the institution's success. In other words, to receive donated income, an institution must trumpet its success in its earned income activities (such as selling tickets). Donors like to feel like they are on a winning team, and, on the contrary, donors are not interested in propping up a failing enterprise.

GOVERNMENT-SUPPORTED GALLERIES

Government-supported galleries are more likely to be found in European countries, and only relatively rarely in the United States. In so far as the U.S. Federal Government supports visual arts, it tends to come through the relatively meager budget of the National Endowment for the Arts. There exist a few high-profile exceptions: the Washington National Gallery of Art and the art-exhibiting entities of the Smithsonian network, all located on the National Mall in Washington, D.C., and these institutions do receive over $1 billion in funding from the federal government budget.[5] In addition, local institutions like a public library may also maintain a gallery, and this could be an example of a local, publicly-funded art venue. Otherwise, government support (whether federal, state, or local) in the United States tends to be received as grants to promote specific projects as well some operational support but would not be considered direct governmental funding or control.

In Europe, however, central governmental budget-funded arts venues are frequently encountered. In addition to an extensive museum sector, which the state will largely support directly from the Ministry of Culture budget, most larger cities will also have an art hall [*kunsthalle* in German], a vestige from the nineteenth-century salon system of exhibiting art. These impressive venues have mutated over the twentieth century from being the site of massive shows of hundreds or thousands of paintings, to being prestigious platforms for leading contemporary artists to hold high-profile solo and travelling exhibitions. While some of these entities persist in putting on current-day salons, such events no longer command much attention or do much service to an artist's career. Instead, these venues have moved toward the twenty-first century's versions of the salon: art fairs and biennales and hold these as their signature annual events.

In addition to large art halls in the biggest cities, most smaller towns in Europe will have a culture house of some sort. These institutions mirror the American nonprofit arts center in terms of profile: offering classes in music, art, dance; providing a performance space for traveling groups; and maintaining a small gallery where local artists may hold exhibitions. The primary difference in the two models is that the European culture house will be funded by a state budget (central or local), and the American arts center will raise its funds from the area's donor base. But much like American nonprofits, these culture houses might sell the art they exhibit, but they will not aggressively pursue sales because they have neither specialized staff nor do they rely on that income for their operations.

UNIVERSITY GALLERIES

Institutions of higher education very often have a campus gallery, sometimes many. These galleries can be combined with a university museum or can be a distinct entity. The primary role of a university gallery will be to show the work of their students and faculty. To give the gallery more prestige and standing within the art world, these institutions often have one or two curated exhibitions a year where outside artists show work. University galleries tend to be almost exclusively non-commercial (with the exception of fundraiser sales), and the lack of a need to sell pieces allows them the freedom to feature installations, conceptual art, and video and media. In fact, in the United States, the university gallery network provides one of the primary venues for art forms that cannot exist in the commercial sector.

With large numbers of graduating students each year needing exhibition space, university galleries can have great demands placed on their space. Some schools will have multiple galleries: a less prestigious one for undergraduates, and more prestigious one for graduate students and faculty. Even relatively minor exhibition spaces can face an overwhelming wave of applicants to use them (from alumni, from friends of faculty) and the entity's management will need a clear and fair method for deciding programming. In the commercial sector, the gallery proprietor does not need to justify their decisions on whom they show. But at a university or nonprofit gallery, where ownership and decision-making are not as clear, battles over exhibition opportunities can lead to friction if the process is not deemed fair.

University galleries tend not to be their own incorporated entity but rather have a legal status by way of their governing institution. In the United States, most private universities exist as a 501(c)(3), and state universities have various charters from their founding state. European universities will usually receive their status from a Ministry of Culture or Education. The gallery will then be one of many businesses or activities going on under the university's umbrella. Like a nonprofit, there is not likely to be any corporate income tax, but the gallery may have a payroll and subsequent taxes. If the gallery has a large enough profile, such as a university museum, it may have a separate 501(c)(3) status, distinct from that of the university, and raise money through tax-deductible donations.

OTHER BUSINESS MODELS

In addition to these legally incorporated models, many gallery configurations exist that avoid formal legal status. Emerging artists will often pursue these strategies in the absence of gallery representation. One model is called a pop-up gallery and involves using an improvised location for a limited amount of time. In such instances, the landlord has usually made an informal agreement with the artists to use the location until such time as a paying renter emerges or a planned renovation begins.

Many forms of artist collectives exist that largely operate on informal agreements between themselves, and casual payment systems of cash or direct payments to the artists. The collective generally does not incorporate either as a for-profit or nonprofit entity and will have an informal decision-making process.

Not incorporating will have disadvantages in that there will be no entity to enter into formal contracts, and, in the case where a contract must be signed, usually one of the artists must sign in their own name.

A very recent model is that of the crowd-source-funded project. These internet-based platforms such as Kickstarter and GoFundMe are popular with large-scale installation and public art projects. The advantage of the crowd-source-funded model is that it also does not require incorporation, but in that case, the funded monies go to one person, and this will be counted as personal income for income tax purposes. The flexibility of the model means that projects can be quickly proposed and funded; furthermore, no requirement for post-facto accounting exists. Subsequently, if a project fails to achieve its stated goals, no formal repercussions will occur (other than damage to reputation). Overall, crowd-sourced funding has opened up enormous possibilities for art forms that do not otherwise fit easily into the commercial art sector. The mediums that have used crowd-source models include: video and projection art, public art works, book-making, and digital mediums. Artists have also used the platform to raise funds in order for them to rent an exhibition venue (in Chelsea: often referred to as project spaces) which can give the appearance of a gallery exhibition, but one which was in fact self-funded and self-staged.

Many artists continue to choose to operate as their own business independent of the gallery system, and use other means, including operating their own website, selling on artist market platforms like Etsy, and making use of Instagram to reach collectors directly.[6] A recent revival of the open studio method has provided another means of circumventing galleries. Former industrial areas, for example parts of Brooklyn and Jersey City, NJ, have seen repurposed buildings, usually warehouses or factories, being converted to artists' studios. The concentration of many studios together, and the fact that these are often larger spaces (more than $50m^2$ or $500ft^2$), means that they can be converted into gallery-like venues if the building hosts an open studio event. These one-day or weekend events usually combine music, performing arts, and cuisine and beverage to create a total aesthetic leisure experience that can attract an urban intelligentsia audience as well as, of course, collectors.

CASE STUDY: THE FIRST IMPRESSIONIST EXHIBITION, 1874

Of all the secessions that would break up the monopolistic salon system, the most important of all would be the one that became known as a movement. In fact, Impressionism can be regarded as the single most successful brand in the history of culture. Its leading members, Monet, Renoir, Degas, and Cezanne, have œuvres in market value in billions of dollars. Yet it began as something very different, not a movement, but simply an alternative salon, a secession from the official Salon of 1874 (where they risked being refused).[7] The idea was developed especially by Camille Pissarro who was often the great connector and organizer among the group. They took as their location the unused, magnificent third floor studio of Paris's leading photographer Nadar, which was located at 35 Boulevard des Capucines.[8]

The name they chose for themselves, *Société Anonyme des Artistes, Peintres, Sculpteurs, Graveurs, etc.*[9] (which might translate to Corporation for Artists, Painters, Sculptors, Engravers, etc.) said nothing about an aesthetic agenda, and the organization featured over 30 members. Most of the names would go unremembered, but the canonical figures of the movement were present: Monet, Renoir, Degas, Pissarro, Sisley, Morisot, and Cezanne, but one was not: Édouard Manet. He would not bring himself to show alongside Cezanne, whose work he did not admire, and Manet chose instead to attempt to show at the official Salon in 1874.[10] Manet would be frequently identified as the leader of this group, though he never showed in any of their exhibitions, and this can cause some problem for students of art history that he should be so closely identified with a movement to which he did not belong.

The show opened ahead of the official Salon and ran for four weeks. It attracted a good deal of hostile press and some that was sympathetic. One early derisive review by Louis Leroy appeared in the satirical journal *Le Charivari* with the title "The Exhibition of the Impressionists," and this would be the source of their movement's name. The article took the form of an imaginary conversation between the author Leroy and a distinguished painter, where they visit the exhibition and comment on the works. The painter grows exasperated with the overuse of the term "impression," and particularly so when he sees a work Monet had painted at the harbor of l'Havre.[11] The title *Impression, soleil levant* [Impression, Sunrise] had actually been given by Edmond Renoir (the painter's brother) who had been assembling the catalogue for the show. A recent conference at the Musée Marmottan, where that work currently hangs, closely examined it and how it could have been set in the harbor at l'Havre, and an especially long-running dispute as to whether it showed a sunrise or a sunset and determined that it was indeed a sunrise.[12]

BUSINESS MODELS: FOR-PROFIT, NONPROFIT, GOVERNMENT- SUPPORTED, AND OTHERS—TERMS

Nonprofit—corporation which operates with the purpose of achieving its mission statement. If the corporation earns a profit through its earned income, that profit is reinvested into the entity as it does not have owners, but rather trustees or board members.

501(c)(3)—the U.S. tax code entry for a nonprofit corporation, and essentially the byword for an American nonprofit. Entities with this status have the benefit of offering a tax deduction in exchange for donations.

Unincorporated entity—a collective of artists and managers who have not taken the step to incorporate legally either as a nonprofit or for-profit. Therefore, their entity is not a legal person and has no official status.

Earned income—a term used in the nonprofit sector designating income derived from the sale of the organization's primary products: that is, entry tickets to an exhibition, tickets to a performance, educational programming, and sales at a gift/book shop.

Donated income—a term used in the nonprofit sector designating income derived from donations to the organization. In principle, nothing of value has been exchanged for that donation. The donation is tax-deductible (in the United States) for the donor.

Government support—can be given to nonprofit arts organizations in many ways: direct financial support, sponsorship, real estate and infrastructure grants, and special tax deferments.

Open studios—a strategy for turning artists' studios into temporary galleries. Usually done in coordination with other artists working in the same building or area.

Self-staged exhibition—an exhibition curated and organized by the artist, without assistance from a gallery or dealer.

Educational programming—is an important revenue source for nonprofit arts organizations. It also helps to build community support and nurture a new generation of art lovers.

Repurposed building—is a formerly industrial, commercial, or educational structure that has now been reoriented for use as an arts institution. These buildings have been a leading source of new physical capacity for the art world.

Notes

1 Dumas, A. "Ambroise Vollard Patron of the Avant-Garde." In Rabinow, R., ed., *Cézanne to Picasso: Ambroise Vollard, Patron of the Avant-Garde*. New York: Metropolitan Museum of Art, 2006, pp. 3–27.

2 Kinsella, E. "French Media Tycoon Patrick Drahi Has Acquired Sotheby's for $3.7 Billion, Taking the Publicly Traded Auction House Private." *ARTnet*, June 17, 2019.

3 irs.gov *Sole proprietorships*. 2018, www.irs.gov/businesses/ small-businesses-self-employed/sole-proprietorships.

4 In 2018, $19.5 billion was given to arts organizations (which include all types of arts, such as performing arts sectors of dance, theatre, and music, in addition to the visual arts) out of a total of $410 billion in charitable donations. See: *Giving USA 2018*. Giving USA Foundation, 2018.

5 "Smithsonian Fiscal Year 2022 Federal Budget Tops $1 Billion." si.edu [Smithsonian website]. Mar. 29, 2022.

6 Fleming, O. "Why the World's Most Talked-About New Art Dealer Is Instagram." *Vogue*, May 13, 2014.

7 Galenson, D. and Jensen, R. "Careers and Canvases: The Rise of the Market for Modern Art in the Nineteenth Century." Van Gogh Studies: Current Issues in nineteenth-century Art. Van Gogh Museum, Waanders Publishers, 2007, pp. 146–147.

8   Tucker, P. "The First Impressionist Exhibition in Context." In Moffett, C., ed., *The New Painting: Impressionism*. San Francisco, CA: The Fine Arts Museum of San Francisco, 1986.

9   *Premiere Exposition 1874, 35 Boulevard des Capucines. Catalogue*. Société Anonyme des Artistes, Peintres, Sculpteurs, Graveurs, etc., 1874.

10 Rewald, J. *The History of Impressionism*. New York: Metropolitan Museum of Art, 1961, p. 314.

11 Leroy, L. "L'Exposition des Impressionnistes." *Le Charivari*, Apr. 25, 1874.

12 Olson, D. "Dating Impression, Sunrise." *Monet's Impression, Sunrise: A Biography of a Painting*. Paris: Musée Marmottan Monet, 2014, pp. 11–15.

Antiques

Chapter 6

THE ART MARKET IN APPLIED ARTS

A commerce in used objects has always existed in so far as
humans made items of value and had a means of exchange
by which to purchase them. Before industrialization, usable
objects such as furniture, ceramics, weapons, and textiles were
extremely expensive investments (either in money or labor)
and would be handed down through the family. If defective,
the object would be repaired rather than replaced. Since such
objects were a type of property that could be moved, the term
for furniture in many languages is a variation of *mobile*. It is
because of their mobility that these objects were often used
as collateral to secure loans, and the pawn shop became our
earliest form of antique dealer.[1]

With time, all objects become obsolete, either because newer
items could serve their function better, or their stylistic features
had gone out of fashion. Obsolescence is an essential feature
of the antiques world, and many of the items collected on
the antiques market are essentially obsolete in their original
function, that is, something newer and cheaper will perform
the task better, for example, antique cars, weapons, scientific
instruments, jukeboxes, peasant butter-churns. These kinds of
items are not collected to be used for their primary function, but
rather for the aesthetic and historical properties these objects
possess.

DOI: 10.4324/9781003431756-7

As one of the eight by-products of art,[2] a market in antiques occurs when a generation of collectors has learned the principles of rarity and developed an admiration for the aesthetic achievements of craftspeople from earlier eras. Like the market in visual arts, the market in antiques follows a guiding principle of rarity, for which there are seven sub-variants:

1   Age: in general, the older the better.
2   Genre/period: applied arts have periods, genres, and movements. Some are more prized than others. Many European periods have a first period to which the name is applied (more valuable), and then the period is revived again later, known as a revival period (less valuable).
3   Maker: if the maker or designer is known, this is superior to anonymous works. This can be the name of the firm, or individuals, the more precise, the better. These makers conform to the hierarchies of art historical canons.
4   Condition: an object in pristine, unrestored condition will be more highly valued.
5   Integrity: a variant of condition refers specifically to the component parts being original—particularly important among mechanical antiques: clocks, firearms, automobiles.
6   Size: this variable can go both ways, a bigger object is generally more highly valued over a comparable smaller one, until that object becomes too big to place, and then its size works as a detriment driving down its value relative to a smaller more easily placed piece.
7   Provenance: the origin or previous owner or usage of an object can give value over what a similar object with no information would have. For the memorabilia market, provenance (in terms of its prior usage) provides almost entirely the sole source of value.

The antique market and the art market tend to seamlessly mix with one another. Both antique shops and art galleries can be found side-by-side in the same art and design districts of most cities. Furthermore, antique dealers are frequently also players in the market for fine art, that is, paintings, graphics, and sculpture. The obvious reason for this is because furniture and applied arts generally sit on the floor or shelves (or hang from the ceiling), but this usually leaves a good deal of wall space to be filled. Some dealers fill the space with mirrors, but many dealers of furniture and applied arts frequently fill the space with pictures from the same era as their other wares. The problem, however, lies in being unspecialized in secondary art sales, which means that these paintings, that demand investments of capital, can go unsold for a long time. Some antique dealers choose to exhibit contemporary art on their walls, and essentially be a dealer of older furniture mixed with contemporary art.[3] This strategy has the advantage of contemporary artworks being placed on consignment by the artist and thereby not requiring up-front purchase, saving valuable capital. But this approach also runs the risk of a confused profile, and one which fails to do either successfully. Furthermore, contemporary art dealers will not take them seriously as an important gallery as long as the dealer also sells antique furniture. For better or worse, the contemporary art world expects a white cube for a gallery to be considered "serious." The antique dealers who do make this strategy work are usually selling more their own "look" and are less identified as specialized in a certain period.

SECTORS OF THE ANTIQUE BUSINESS

The antique trade probably exceeds the art market in terms of merchants involved, though not necessarily in terms of money involved. The realm of objects that are traded along the rules of the antique market is vast, almost exceeding categorization. Some antique pieces can still sustain their intended use and will be valued for their ability to be simultaneously old, beautiful, and functional. Furniture, chandeliers, and porcelain dinnerware are some examples of these sorts of functional, operational antiques. Other types, however, have become antiques because they managed to survive the oblivion faced by most obsolete objects. Objects in this category can be automobiles, 1980s' computers, firearms, and peasant farm equipment. In the sector called antiquities, meaning objects from before the Middle Ages, such as items from Greek and Roman antiquity, the fact that these items survived at all would be their primary source of value, and anything that survives from those eras, no matter how functional and not-beautiful, will be valued. Furthermore, the enormous sector of religious objects: icons, tabernacles, masks, Judaica, has generally been divorced from their original use in sacred practice and has now become decorative art objects.

A short list of all the largest sectors that can be traded as antiques would be the following:

Furniture: tables, chairs, wardrobes, settees, commodes, from all regions and all periods, generally at least 50 years old. Furniture less than 50 years old tends to be sold under the category of vintage.

Lighting: chandeliers, sconces, table lamps, and these can be from crystal, bronze, brass, and chrome. Many lights that were originally gas or even candle-illuminated are often retrofitted to work with either 120 volts (North America) or 230 volts (Europe).

Textiles: pile carpets and flat-woven textiles in wool, cotton, goats' hair, or silk from the historical carpet producing regions of Anatolia, Persia, Caucasus, Central Asia, and China. Tapestries from Flemish and French production are highly prized. Fashionware from all historical periods.

Ceramics: porcelain, majolica, faience stoneware, and other techniques. Nearly every corner of the Earth produced ceramics, and often these objects produced trade between distant civilizations. This is why so much Chinese and Japanese porcelain can be found in Europe and United States, and why Greek pottery is dug up in Etruscan sites in Italy. Ceramics can be functional objects for eating and drinking or purely decorative objects.

Glass: blown glass, stained glass, crystal, mirrors, etched and beveled glass. Glass is often included in other objects, such as crystal chandeliers, stained glass lamps, and beveled glass doors on cabinetry. But it also exists in individual self-standing works created by glass artists.

Timepieces: longcase (colloquially known as grandfather) clocks, mantel clocks, cuckoo clocks, painting clocks, and Swiss watches. Mechanical integrity and functionality remain as important to this sector as the aesthetic features of the object.

Weapons: melee weapons (armor, helmets, shields, swords, polearms, maces), missile weapons (bows, crossbows, arrows, javelins), and firearms (blunderbusses, dueling pistols, muskets, rifles, handguns). These can also be from any era and virtually any civilization. If the weapon is associated with a certain military leader or celebrity outlaw, value can be added through a memorabilia/provenance factor.

Automobiles: luxury cars and sports cars tend to have most value, though all forms of automobiles are collected. Condition, functionality, and mechanical integrity guide valuations. Automobiles usually become obsolete after 20 years and often scrapped. Most collected cars tend to be at least 30 years old. For an automobile to become an antique, it must survive that ten-year span between obsolescence and collectability. Few do survive and this creates the phenomenon of rarity.

Geological and Paleontological material: geodes, fossils, dinosaur bones, and extraterrestrial objects. Unlike every other sector of the antique world, these objects were not made by humans, but were found by them, and are often cut, prepared, and framed by them. Otherwise, the same principles of rarity apply to this sector as to all the others. Integrity can also be important with these objects. Christie's had to remove a Tyrannosaurus rex skeleton from an auction because of concerns as to how few of the fossils were original.[4]

Architectural salvage: wrought iron fences and gates, paving stones, fireplaces, sculptural elements from buildings, garden objects. To trade in these items, a dealer needs a large amount of outdoor and indoor space and may have to assist clients in preparing and installing these objects so that they can be installed in a new construction.

Furthermore, there are two additional sectors which are also traded by the same structure of the antique world: collectibles and memorabilia.

COLLECTIBLES

This sector covers mass-produced objects that are traded and collected in much the same way as antiques are. These include stamps, coinage, paper currency, sports cards, and many types of toys. A few key differences, however, distinguish the collectable market. In an ironic twist on the fact that the antique market values quality and craftsmanship, certain collectibles, particularly coins and stamps, will be valued for flaws and imperfections. In principle, these standardized, mechanically manufactured manifestations of monetary value should be identical within a series. When an imperfection occurs, the problem in the production is corrected, but a few of the flawed pieces enter circulation. Following the rule of rarity, these flawed pieces become the most sought-after pieces in the trade.[5] The sub-sector of collectable toys tends to focus on those lines manufactured on license agreements with film or television productions, especially action hero figurines. In this field, the importance of obsolescence is extended to the full life of the object, and value is placed on it never having been used. Therefore, collectors prize figurines that have never even been taken out of the original box. In this way, commercial packaging is regarded as an integral part of the object.

MEMORABILIA

Like the market in collectibles, the memorabilia market also features generally mass-produced items, which in themselves carry little aesthetic distinction. The memorabilia market derives almost all its value from the provenance of the objects: who possesed them and how they were used. Two of the largest sub-sectors of memorabilia are entertainment memorabilia and sports memorabilia. Entertainment memorabilia can be costumes, props, sets, and musical instruments. Such objects have museums that collect these objects, such as the Rock and Roll Hall of Fame and the Popular Entertainment section of the Smithsonian's National Museum of American History. Sports memorabilia generally features athletic equipment worn (jerseys, helmets, hats, shoes) or used (balls, gloves, bats, skis) in important sporting events and by elite athletes. Since nearly all the value in these objects lies in their provenance, that is, that this item was used by a certain person at a certain time, then the essential act of the memorabilia dealer is to validate this provenance, but in reality, such claims can often be virtually impossible to prove.

BUSINESS MODELS FOR ANTIQUE DEALERS

Antique dealers pursue a variety of business models that they believe best suit their profile and their market. Most dealers try to give themselves a profile and limit their inventory to a circumscribed group of sectors and periods, so that their venue projects a consistent "look." Furthermore, because of the enormity of sectors, mediums, and periods, specialization becomes an essential strategy so that collectors of those items can become aware of the dealer. An antique shop, in order to be successful, must exhibit an advanced degree of knowledge in what they sell, and that kind of expertise and experience can only realistically be developed in objects that can be acquired reliably in either the local market or one which the dealer is intimately familiar with. A taxonomy of different business models within antique markets is the following:

Prime retail antique shops: these venues will be found in prime retail real estate, which would be a street-frontage space with visible window display capacity and ideally located in a city's gallery or design district. These dealers will be selling their inventory at the highest prices the market will bear and will generally be selling to collectors because the trade (other dealers) would struggle to make money off reselling these objects. These dealers will often acquire their inventory at auctions, especially estate auctions. They may also acquire from wholesalers, restorers, and collectors. In addition, these dealers might conserve on spending their own capital and take works on consignment from these same sources. They often will purchase large quantities of their inventory on foreign buying trips where they purchase in a cheaper market. Generally, the works these dealers sell will be in a highly restored condition, and their investments in restoration will be one of their most significant costs.

Wholesale dealers: these venues will be located in subprime real estate, without an orientation toward attracting walk-in shoppers. The location can often be a warehouse located in a low-rent periphery to an important urban market. As opposed to prime retail detailers who will arrange their space as an interior designer would, a wholesale dealer arranges their wares in a highly functional manner designed for large scale purchasing.

These businesses will rely on interior designers to bring clients to their location, and they also sell up to prime retail dealers.

Flea market dealers: these merchants might maintain a stand, a permanent shop-like structure, at the flea market and open on the days the market does, which might be three to five days a week, but usually always Saturdays (generally the main day for any flea market) or Sundays. They may also trade as anitinerant dealer, who rents display space for setting up their wares on the prime market days.

Interior designers: much like art advisors for fine art, designers negotiate purchases between their clients (collectors) and antique dealers. Designers with a specialization in certain antique looks are expected to maintain a list of wholesale locations for buying below retail prices, which would be unknown to someone outside the trade. They may also expect some sort of remuneration from the dealers to whom they bring their clients.

Restorers: especially in the furniture business, restorers are frequently the source of a lot of material entering the market. Restorer is the appropriate term (not conservator) because these people take pieces that are unsalable in their current condition and make them whole with a finished appearance. They will often speculatively purchase pieces in poor condition, and after restoration, sell them to or place them on consignment with dealers.

SOURCING METHODS FOR ANTIQUES

Antique dealers acquire their inventory in ways like that of the secondary art market. They particularly buy up material at auction, but antique dealers usually prefer estate sales where a large mix of poorly understood objects are being quickly sold. In these situations, the dealer's expertise in a certain field allows them to spot bargains at these sales. Furthermore, applied arts do not usually have a known artist associated with them, and so smart collectors would have a harder time tracking the source and purchase price of an object the way they frequently do in the secondary fine art market. With the increasing ease of buying at even small auctions scattered around the world, the sourcing possibilities for dealers have increased enormously. With antique furniture, however, the significant cost of shipping must be considered, which may make a single purchase from far away unprofitable when transport is factored in.

Purchasing from collectors would also be a traditional means of acquiring inventory, but the recent increase in the amount of information available to collectors causes them to frequently demand prices that would not be profitable for the dealer. Sellers often see list prices for similar pieces at other shops or auction estimates and expect to receive a similar amount of money. Such collectors/sellers fail to understand the stage in the commercial process at which they stand, and that the prices asked by dealers reflect the cost of maintaining a retail establishment, which the collector does not. The Antiques Roadshow television programs on the BBC and PBS have added to the phenomenon of emboldened private sellers. Because of the high cost of acquiring from collectors, a dealer will often propose a consignment arrangement. In such cases, the dealer may keep 30–40 percent of the sales price once the object has sold.

The antique market resembles a food chain starting with restorers, flea market dealers, travelling Romani (Gypsy) pickers,[6] and wholesalers. These people sell up to retail dealers, who then sell up to collectors. At each stage of this commercial process, the new purchaser will usually double the price of the object for the next sale. In order to achieve those kinds of mark-ups, objects are frequently moved to markets where they can achieve higher prices. Central European furniture is transported to New York and sold there. Venetian chandeliers are taken to Paris and sold in the flea market there. When a certain product exists in large numbers in its region of origin, it is often profitable to move pieces to wealthier markets where higher prices can be asked. If, however, many of the best pieces have been shipped out of a region, then wealthy collectors there might hold a patriotic passion to collect these items and, in such cases, these collectors will pay the highest prices. This would be the case with Chinese porcelains that were transported to Europe 200–300 years ago; now those pieces are being resold, and the buyers are usually the new rich from Mainland China.[7]

KNOWLEDGE AND AUTHENTICITY FOR ANTIQUES

Given that the antique market is another type of secondary market, it will follow the same principles as the one for art. This means that knowledge remains the essential value-added ingredient that any dealer brings to an antique sale. The art history in objects is in fact surprisingly vast, with books having been written on virtually every field of the trade. Fine art, however, follows the governing organizational structure of artists and their names. Most applied arts have far fewer works with signatures and known masters. Instead, there are often industrial firms, names of designers and craftspeople, but much less of a clear-cut notion of an artwork that can be identified with a singular artist. With some objects, if the firm is still in existence, it or its museum might preside as the reigning monopolistic authority on the authenticity of objects purporting to be from earlier eras of production, but in most cases, there are no clear undisputed experts. This absence of monopoly expertise means that disputes on the authenticity of a piece can go unresolved.

Given the prevalence of restoration in the applied arts, especially furniture, many pieces can contain such a high quantity of new material that the overall authenticity of the item is called into question. The fact is, there exists no clear standard for when an unacceptable level of restoration renders something no longer a true period piece. Furthermore, good furniture restorers keep a stockpile of cannibalized furniture that can be used as a source of period material, making the act of distinguishing between the original and later cabinetry challenging.

PERILS OF THE ANTIQUE BUSINESS

The antique trade contains essentially all the perils of the secondary art market, and then it contains some more. All the same threats of forgeries lurk in the antique business, even at the lowest price levels. To complicate things, so little undisputed authority exists in the field that forgeries can never be officially dismissed the way a fake painting can be refused by a *catalogue raisonné* committee. For that reason, dealers who shamelessly sell fakes can get away with the practice for decades with little threat of legal repercussions. When French antique dealers were arrested in 2016 for selling fake chairs for placement at Versailles, it came as a great surprise for a sector generally known for its impunity.[8]

Most every sought-after item has a second- and third-rate version, and the difference between them might be difficult to determine by the non-expert. Most brands that become cult collector items usually have a lower-cost competitor whose pieces will look similar but should be sold for much less. Because of the lack of artists' names to give reference points, it is much more difficult for buyers to know how rare or not-so-rare a thing is and therefore would have uncertainty about what is an appropriate price to pay.

Other perils can be more mundane: the large size of many antiques, especially furniture, means that dealers must rent larger spaces, and get smaller profit per square foot/meter than the picture dealer. Furthermore, furniture can be extremely expensive to transport safely, and this is true for both long-distance shipping and local delivery. Clients can quickly lose interest in a piece once they understand what it will ultimately cost to be installed in their home. Finally, tastes in antiques change and evolve. In recent decades, numerous antique shops have gone out of business because the type of furniture being sold simply went out of fashion with collectors. The repercussions of the so-called Brown Furniture Market Collapse are still being felt in today's market.

CASE STUDY: BROWN FURNITURE MARKET COLLAPSE

The global art and antique markets were both going strong in 2001, prior to the double blow of the September 11 attacks and the Dot-Com Crash. The art market recovered after a few years, but the antique market never really did. By 2006, dealers and designers in New York had begun to derisively refer to all periods of antique furniture as simply Brown Furniture. Rather than recover, the market for old furniture has only continued to soften in the subsequent decade.[9] The collapse of values in this sector can teach us much about how these markets function.

The principle of rarity that guides all commerce in art and things like art only becomes viable when a critical mass of buyers enters the market, and if even a few of them exit the market, prices can quickly collapse. Art markets are different particularly because of the relatively few participants involved relative to mass markets, and pricing can be thought of as something like a slow-motion auction with the dealer getting feedback on interest in their pieces and forming opinions about what the market is willing to pay. Like a real auction, however, if a few of those bidders are removed, the lot will not climb nearly so high without their competitive bidding.

Explaining why prices fell, though, does not help understand why buyers lost interest in old furniture. To explain that wider change in taste, a number of cultural forces can be cited, from the aesthetic to the mundane.[10] Pop culture certainly played a role. The Antiques Roadshow programs on the BBC and PBS produced a number of contradictory forces: one, it ignited a boom in antiques collecting in the 1990s and also began to convince collectors that they possessed valuable pieces which they would not part with cheaply. But to younger home owners, the show closely aligned nineteenth century and earlier styles with the show's elderly viewership. Styles as diverse as George III, Louis XV, and Victorian were all lumped together as having a "Grandma Look," and regardless of whether they were mahogany, walnut, or oak, they would all be collectively called "Brown Furniture."[11] More recent periods have started to displace older styles. The Mid-century Modern look received a great boost from the Mad Men show, and due to the fact that those pieces had only been scorned a few years earlier, meant they presented good profit margins for dealers.[12]

A few prescient designers have started to take advantage of the drop in prices and are using highly ornate pieces such as gilded mirrors and consoles in otherwise industrial loft interiors. When these kinds of pieces are squeezed into rooms crowded with other similarly ornate pieces, they can seem stuffy, but in a more spaced-out setting, given room to "breathe," these objects can blossom. Newer waves of dealers are increasingly pursuing a joint profile in a similar vein to the designer, in order to sell their look, and place interesting antique pieces based on an overall aesthetic concept, and less on the old concepts of the item's value as an art object alone. Because of antiques' far-higher level of craftsmanship and low price points relative to new furniture, a revival in the market has been predicted to occur in new generations of collectors.[13]

ANTIQUES—TERMS

Period—a chronological categorization for applied arts. In many national traditions, period names are derived from the name of the ruling monarch. Periods might have revivals at later points where the stylistic characteristics are once again employed.

Style—similar to a period, but with its name drawn from art historical terminology rather than monarchs, but also progresses in a chronological structure.

Collectable—mass-manufactured consumer objects which are collected in a similar fashion to art and antiques. Particular emphasis can be placed on flaws (stamps, currency) or on the object being unused and in its original packaging.

Memorabilia—objects used in entertainment (such as instruments or costumes) or sports (such as equipment or uniforms) which have value because of the famous person who used them.

Integrity—a quality of being intact and having its original component parts. This is extremely important for mechanical applied arts such as clocks, firearms, or antique automobiles.

Flea Market—a temporary market filled with itinerant merchants who often serve as the lowest level of the antiques, collectable, and memorabilia trade.

Picker—a person employed by an antique dealer to find inventory by traveling throughout the countryside visiting distant flea markets and estate sales.

Interior designer—a professional employed to design interior spaces, including choosing the furniture and furnishings. Many collectors only purchase high-value antiques in consultation or at the recommendation of their interior designer. The profession was formerly referred to as interior decorator. That term is now very much out of fashion.

Retail—businesses located in high-rent arts and antiques districts with street-front exposure. The clientele will primarily be collectors, that is, end-users.

Wholesale—businesses located in low-rent industrial or ex-urban areas with large amounts of storage space, but little effort given to creating a designed sales room. Their clientele will primarily be the trade: that is, other dealers or interior designers who will sell the objects on to collectors.

Notes

1 De Roover, R. "The Three Golden Balls of the Pawnbrokers." *Bulletin of the Business Historical Society*, vol. 20, no. 4, Oct. 1946, pp. 117–124.

2 Alsop, J. *The Rare Art Traditions: The History of Art Collecting and Its Linked Phenomena Wherever These Have Appeared*. New York: Harper & Row, 1987, pp. 28–29.

3 Abrams, A.-R. 'Why Are Antiques Fairs Showcasing Contemporary Art?" *Artnet*, Aug. 3, 2016.

4 Dafoe, T. "Christie's Pulled a $25 Million T-Rex Skeleton from Auction After Experts Pointed Out That Most of Its Bones Are Replicas." *Artnet*, Nov. 21, 2022.

5 Kettles, N. "Mistakes That Will Earn You a Small Fortune: Look out for Stamps with Errors in Them if You Want to Make a Really Lucrative Investment in Philately." *The Guardian*, Nov. 30, 2003.

6 Quarmby, K. "Meet the Gypsy Entrepreneurs: Travelling People Are Putting Their Business Skills to Increasingly Impressive Use." *The Spectator*, Aug. 24, 2013.

7 Reyburn, S. "Market for Chinese Art Is Increasingly in China." *The New York Times*, Mar. 25, 2016.

8 Noce, V. "Leading Parisian Antiques Dealers Arrested for Forgery: Ministry of Culture Is Investigating Authenticity of Furniture Bought by Versailles since 2008." *The Art Newspaper*, July 1, 2016.

9 Arkell, R. "Furniture Index Falls Another 7%: Hopes of a Recovery in the Value of Antique Furniture Have Been Dealt a Blow after the Antiques Collectors' Club's Annual Furniture Index (AFI) Saw Prices Fall by Seven Per cent during 2009." *Antiques Trade Gazette*, Jan. 25, 2010.

10 Seal, T. "The Recline and Fall of Antique Furniture." *Financial Times*, Mar. 10, 2016.

11 Tarmy, J. "Your Unloved Heirlooms Might Mean Serious Money: The Market for Fine Antiques and Decorative Arts Is Still Well Below Former Highs, Which—for Some—Is a $100 Million Opportunity." *Bloomberg*, July 1, 2021.

12 Fenton, L. "Why the World Is Obsessed with Midcentury Modern Design: The Story behind the Ubiquity." *Curbed*, Apr 8, 2015.

13 Koncius, J. "Antique and Vintage Sales Have Soared, Thanks to Supply Chain Issues: Consumers Are Finding That Secondhand Furniture Is Both Sustainable and Available." *The Washington Post*, Jan. 26, 2022.

Art Fairs

Chapter 7

EARLY FAIRS AND THE PARIS SALON

Occasional and itinerant forms of commerce usually predate the models of fixed retail commerce such as shops and galleries, and that would largely be the case as European trade emerged from the Dark Ages.[1] Fairs would be held on occasional and seasonal gatherings, often associated with holy-days-related to prized saints relics that would also be driving forms of pilgrimage.[2] Markets would happen on a more regular weekly or monthly schedule. In either case, the merchants consolidated goods in a specific place and time. Their associated costs would be the security, packaging, transport, and temporary display of their wares.

In the later fifteenth century, a market for pictures emerged in in Flanders (Belgium). The Pand market took place in the courtyard of the Church of Our Lady in Antwerp.[3] This fair is understood to have focused on the new, very entrepreneurial sector of printing devotional images. These printed works, especially woodcuts, were popular with the private piety movement of the fifteenth century, which emerged as an alternative to an institutional Catholic church that had been riven by competing papacies.[4] As that religious movement gathered pace throughout Northern Europe, printers began a speculative production of popular motifs and sending prints to multiple locations.

DOI: 10.4324/9781003431756-8

The production of one-of-a-kind oil painting, however, remained a far more controlled trade, generally governed by the municipal Guilds of St. Luke, which would try to restrict the production of paintings to their own membership.[5] The creation of the French Royal Academy was, in many ways, an attempt to circumvent the power of the guilds through the protection of the king.[6] When the Academy began holding shows in the late seventeenth century of the latest works by the teachers and their students, it formed the basis for the dominant model of art commerce up until the beginning of the twentieth century.

The Paris Salon, named for the *Salon Carré* [Square Room], would evolve over the centuries into the primary platform for the exhibition and sale of contemporary art. The other art centers of the West would imitate the model: the Royal Academy Summer Exhibitions in London,[7] the Glaspalast exhibitions in Munich,[8] as well as the Art Unions [*Kunstverein* in German] that were based in serving a particular city's art market.[9] During the later nineteenth and early twentieth century some of those municipal organizations would aspire toward holding a national profile, such as the attempt by the National Academy of Design in New York to take on this status, that triggered the 1913 Armory Show.[10] These salons would face a phenomenon of secessions [alternative exhibition societies] as these salons were overwhelmed by waves of artist-proletariat in the late nineteenth century. These new competing secessions might promote a far more egalitarian approach to selecting entries,[11] others might favor a more restrictive exhibition policy providing greater focus on fewer artists.[12] Neither approach, however, ultimately proved satisfactory.[13] The model began to fade into irrelevance in the twentieth century as the sole-proprietor entrepreneurial dealer became the dominant model.[14] Right before the First World War, two of the these secessions, one on each side of the Atlantic: the Cologne *Sonderbund* exhibition of 1912,[15] and then the 1913 Armory Show in New York,[16] would point toward a new accommodation where the artworks for an exhibition were selected and provided by dealers. The salon model would then be revived in the later twentieth century with the innovation of the contemporary art fair. The distinct difference between the nineteenth century salon and the current twenty-first century art fair is that the salon juried artists, while the art fair juries dealers.

NON-COMMERCIAL ART FAIRS

In addition to the national salons that began appearing in nearly every major metropolis in the Western world by the later nineteenth century, there were also an ever-increasing number of world expositions taking place in older and newer cities across the globe. These events usually always had both a fine art and an applied art component.[17] Although the applied arts suppliers like furniture-makers and ceramics factories might fully intend to secure orders from international distributors, the fine art halls may have given off a decidedly non-commercial appearance. Prices were usually not posted, and the primary income for artist came in the form of cash awards that came with medals, but purchases could indeed be made, and many times these were made by the host national government.

A new model was established in 1895 in the form of the Venice Biennale,[18] though it would only emerge into its current non-commercial format after reforms made between 1968 and 1973.[19] For much of its early years, it functioned in much the same way as the Paris Salon, intending to provide a new market held every other year where the working painters of the *Fin de Siècle* could sell their artworks to collectors. With a few notable exceptions (Klimt and Renoir), the Biennale showed little of future canonical modernism before the First World War (during which the event was not held). In the 1920s and 1930s, the exhibitions did finally begin to address some of the most important developments in art, including Impressionism, Post-Impressionism, and Expressionism. In 1942, the Biennale was again suspended, and only resumed in 1948. This would be the first year that Picasso ever showed (one of his works was removed from the exhibition in 1910).[20] It was also at this time that Peggy Guggenheim moved her collection to Venice, which had been housed in New York at a venue called Art of This Century. She made use of the abandoned Greek pavilion in order to exhibit the works and then installed them in a palazzo on the Grand Canal, where they have been ever since.[21]

The Biennale of 1968 did not go unaffected by the upheavals of that year, and by 1973, reforms had made the event entirely non-commercial, with no works for sale. Increasingly, the orientation of exhibits moved away from paintings and toward everything else. The event began to resemble a sort of Olympics of the art world and is often referred to as such. Since 1907, individual nations have built pavilions in the Giardini section of Venice surrounding the original exhibition hall structure. In recent years, those pavilions tend to be dominated by a few large-scale installations by a single artist or collective, for example, the 2011 U.S. exhibit by Allora and Calzadilla featured an upside-down tank converted to a treadmill and an enormous pipe organ operated by a cash-dispensing ATM.[22] At the 2022 Biennale, sculptor Simone Leigh's project *Sovereignty* saw the pavilion covered with a thatched roof (*Façade*, 2022),[23] for which she would win a Golden Lion,[24]. Nations which achieved statehood later in the century no longer have the opportunity to build a permanent structure in the Giardini and instead make do by renting an unused church, monastery, or palazzo as their temporary pavilion. The Biennale generally runs from early May until late November, and although the works on exhibit are not for sale, inquiries can still be made about them (or they have already been sold).[25] Furthermore, those artists who do well and win awards will almost surely sell well at Art Basel which usually opens in June.

Biennales have become common throughout the world in the last three decades, being held in metropolises like Berlin, Shanghai, Moscow, Sao Paulo, and Istanbul, and some have been held in less-likely locations: Gwanju, Havana, and Marrakech. These more recent biennales have international profiles but do not draw representatives from the vast array of nations like Venice does. Rather they serve as a grand, organizing principle for a city's art scene to all prepare events for this period. As with other fairs, Covid made these events impossible in the earlier format[26] and forced their organizers to reconsider the very nature of their format.[27] These events are only now beginning to recover, and some still have not.

Perhaps an even more influential event in the canonization process would the non-commercial fair, Documenta, occurs only every five years, for 100 days, in the German city of Kassel. Its origins derive from the pervasive destruction to Germany's cultural heritage as a result of the Second World War. In 1955, marking ten years since the end of the war, West Germany held a nationwide flower festival. An art teacher in Kassel, Arnold Bode, suggested an exhibition of modern art be held at that same time, since Germans had largely missed out on the previous 20 years in artistic developments. The first exhibition held in 1955 attempted to reintroduce those artists (e.g., Klee, Chagall, and Kandinsky) who appeared at the notorious *Entartete Kunst* [Degenerate Art] exhibition held by the Nazis in 1937.[28] The subsequent Documenta was held four years later in 1959 and heavily featured American abstract artists selected with the guidance of the Museum of Modern Art and probably funding from the CIA. The Cold War remained eminently present in these early exhibitions, which draws uncomfortable attention to Bode's co-organizer for these exhibitions, the former Nazi, Werner Haftmann.[29] From 1964 on, the exhibition would be held every five years for a hundred days making use of the entire area of the city of Kassel, including its historic museum, the Fridericianum, the reconstructed palaces of the Elector of the Palatinate, their gardens, as well as the train station and warehouses. It became the event where many postwar figures, such as Joseph Beuys, Ed Ruscha, and Claes Oldenburg, secured their international celebrity status. In 2012, documenta 13 made an art star of Theaster Gates, who rebuilt, reconverted, and repurposed an entire derelict structure in Kassel known as the Huguenot House.[30] The curatorial team for Documenta 15, the Jakarta-based artist collective *ruangrupa* successfully navigated some initial outrage at anti-Semitic images in the exhibition[31] and now subsequently rank as the number one most influential entity in the art world.[32] Both Documenta and the Venice Biennale have modified the most contentious part of the salon model: the jury. For the Venice Biennale, individual nations select their own entries, and the general exhibition is curated by a single curator. The same system follows for Documenta: a large committee selects a single curator (or in the case of 15, an artist collective) who will make that Documenta their own personal *Gesamtkunstwerk*, and that one curator selects each participating artist personally. In this way, the non-commercial art fair adopted the lessons of the commercial market: that a single despot can more effectively organize a coherent exhibition than a committee, (i.e., jury).

COMMERCIAL ART FAIRS

In so far as the jury survives in the current day, its most significant variation would be those those juries that select participants for commercial art fairs. As mentioned earlier, the difference between the nineteenth century salon and today's art fairs is that the salon had a jury of artists jurying other artists. The contemporary art fair has a jury of dealers jurying other dealers. The model for these events was Art Basel, organized by the dealer Ernst Beyeler, in Basel, Switzerland. This fair was first held in 1970 at exactly the time that the Venice Biennale was shifting toward its non-commercial structure. The format established by Art Basel, which generally occurs in June of each year, operates on a short run of four days plus a VIP vernissage (compared to the Biennale which runs for nearly half a year, and Documenta for 100 days). The event selects 300 exhibitors (out of thousands of applicants) based on the prestige and reputation of the gallery, as well as the strength of their curatorial plan.[33] Most exhibitors take stands of approximately 30–50 m^2 (300–500 ft^2) and will have to largely construct the entire space and complete the installation in a few short frantic days prior to the fair's opening. Even if the goal is to sell art, some leading dealers choose to mount some complex (and not very sellable) conceptual pieces, electing instead to make a statement of the gallery's aesthetic commitment. Art Basel, although very much a for-profit entity, still secures significant sponsorship for the event from Switzerland's leading bank, Union Bank of Switzerland (UBS), giving their private banking staff access to the super-rich who attend the event.[34] The success of the summertime fair in Basel led them to expand to the United States and hold a wintertime fair in Miami in early December. Their parent company, MCH Swiss Exhibition Ltd., acquired their Hong Kong fair in 2014, thereby insuring the dominance of their brand, and for the time, anointing Hong Kong as the leading art center in Asia.[35]

This model has been adapted to most major metropolises for their signature art fair. New York started holding the Armory Show in 1994, which was not in an armory, but rather a pier over the Hudson River. That was until 2022, and in a post-Covid reset, the fair was moved to New York's cavernous Javits Center.[36] The name is an attempt to reference the legendary 1913 Armory Show. To further add to the confusion, New York does have an armory, the Park Avenue Armory, which does hold art events, including the Art Dealers Association of America's (ADAA) annual The Art Show, which used to occur simultaneously as the Armory Show in March during New York Art Week, but post-Covid re-alignment has seen the fairs move to different times in the Fall.[37] London has the Frieze Art Fair and then expanded to hold a Frieze in New York in May in a tent on Randall's Island, but they now hold a more intimate event (just 65 dealers) in the newly built Shed near Chelsea on the Hudson River.[38] Most European capitals have at least one major fair, but recent years have also seen upheaval: Berlin no longer holds Art Berlin,[39] and Cosmoscow is no longer international in that there are no longer any foreign galleries.[40] Paris had traditionally held FIAC in the Grand Palais (same location as the nineteenth-century Salon), but when the building underwent renovations, Art Basel swooped in to claim Paris as another in their franchise of art fairs with their 2022 Paris+.[41] Other arts centers are again challenging Hong Kong's pre-eminence in Asia with Frieze now expanding to Seoul.[42] The Covid pandemic forced nearly all art fairs to construct virtual viewing rooms in lieu of in-person gatherings, which quickly came to be seen as just another webpage.[43]

In most cases, these fairs focus on contemporary art, and some, like Armory, may have two sections: a Contemporary and a Modern Section. Modern, in this case, tends to mean late-career, living artists, and deceased artists who worked in the twentieth century. Most cities may also have an antiques fair that features secondary market dealers selling nineteenth-century and earlier artworks, but the only major art fair to be specifically devoted to the secondary market is TEFAF, held in the Dutch city of Maastricht (and the fair had often just referred to as "Maastricht" in the trade). This event remains the leading opportunity to immediately purchase an old master or a Louis XIV piece of furniture outside of a major auction. In 2016, TEFAF expanded into holding a fair in New York, in the Park Avenue Armory building in fact.[44]

SATELLITE ART FAIRS

Whenever significant amounts of collectors gather in a certain location, gallerists will want to take advantage of the opportunity to try to catch their attention. Therefore, whenever a major art fair is going on, such as Art Basel or Art Basel Miami Beach, there will also be six to ten satellite fairs also going on at the same time.

For example, when the Armory Show previously was being held in mid-March, the entire week was called New York Art Week, featuring Armory's own emerging artist fair: Volta, as well as the following other fairs going on throughout the city: Art Dealers Association of America, Pulse, Volta, Independent New York, Art on Paper, and Spring/Break Art Show. Many of those synergies were undone by Covid and so now the satellite fairs are realigning to the new main fair scheduling, Volta (which acquired Pulse) occurred in New York in May 2022 to coincide with Frieze (not Armory) and in Basel in June for Art Basel.[45] A satellite fair will usually profile itself as featuring emerging galleries and artists. Its jury is relatively more open to newcomers than the main fairs, and the costs of having a stand will also be considerably lower. By attending one of the many satellite fairs concurrent with Art Basel Miami Beach, a dealer can still say, "We'll be down in Miami," and therefore allow them to feel part of the big art party going on there, even if they have neither the prestige nor finances to be able to have a stand at the main fair. It is also at satellite fairs that dealers earn their reputation and eventually hope to acquire the clout to get into the main fair.

A satellite fair may try to locate itself as close to the main fair as possible, but they may also seek out less refined locations, as well. A disused industrial structure may house a satellite fair because, with its emerging art profile, highly polished interiors are also not required. In Miami, some fairs have been known to be located in Art Deco hotels along the beach. The dealer rents the hotel room and, during the day, converts the room into their exhibition stand, and at night the dealer sleeps in the room. In general, these smaller fairs serve to help even out some of the elitism prevalent in the art fair system and allow new galleries a chance to participate.

ARTIST-LED ART FAIRS

Despite the preponderance in attention that the leading commercial art fairs command, with their dominant structure of stands rented to established galleries, there also exist significant networks operating in alternative formats. Smaller, and less prestigious, art fairs may waive the restriction that the gallery must have a physical, permanent home venue and may rent stands to virtual galleries, art agents, or directly to artists themselves. All art fairs usually have some component which does not belong to galleries, but rather directly exhibits art works, installations, and sculpture that have been curated by the art fair's own artistic directors.

For the vast numbers of artists working with either no gallery representation or not being represented by a Chelsea-type gallery, they often turn toward directly marketing themselves through the vast system of artist-led fairs that serve as alternatives to the Art Basel-type gallery-led model.[46] For a large part of the United States, these art fairs, or often branded as arts festivals, serve as the best means for essentially a two-agent model of direct commerce with collectors. They often involve a jury who select artists across a broad range of mediums including paintings, sculpture, furniture, jewelry, and fashion. The artists pay a modest fee of $1–2,000 for a stand over a three- to four-day weekend run. Since these events usually take place in regional touristic centers in the outdoors, many artists follow a circuit of arts festivals over the summer season.

THE CURRENT OVER-SUPPLY OF ART FAIRS

In 2005, there were 68 international art fairs. By 2016, that number had grown to 270.[47] Over approximately a decade, the number of art fairs had grown nearly fourfold. That growth can be explained by the fact that galleries have also proliferated at a shocking rate, as have art scenes in many cities worldwide where previously there had not really been one of any significance. Furthermore, many types of art fairs exist with very distinct profiles appealing to very specific groups of collectors. These variations include antiques fairs, print fairs, affordable art fairs, secondary market-oriented, as well as both the artist-led type fair and the Art Basel model of gallery-led contemporary art fair. The most compelling explanation for their rapid growth in the gallery-led fair model derives from the fact that attendance has become an essential activity for any Chelsea-type art gallery. Most cities in the United States have long had multiple formats of the artist-led art fair/ festival model but having a gallery-led fair on the Art Basel model is seen as signalling a city's arrival as a global art metropolis. Given the saturation in the market for art fairs and the difficulty of competing for collectors' attention, many question whether the sector is bound for a contraction and consolidation.[48]

COST-BENEFIT ANALYSIS OF ATTENDING ART FAIRS

With the cost of attendance at a major fair easily costing up $150,000 for a stand,[49] Art Basel began in 2018 to offer a graduated pricing structure so that the largest galleries paid a slight premium, and smaller galleries received a small discount on the basic per/square meter rate for stand space.[50] Given the high costs incurred to be at a fair, galleries will often attempt to quietly pre-sell their most significant works they are bringing, so as to guarantee a return on the investment in attending the fair.[51] The opportunity to pre-purchase works destined for a major fair derives from alpha galleries providing "primary access" to only their most esteemed collectors.[52] In this way, though, much of the initial rush to purchase at the VIP openings have been rendered superfluous. What the event remains, however, is a complex web of marketing in order to transmit perceived hierarchies to current and potential collectors. In fact, Chelsea-type gallerists will claim that they can spend nearly an equal amount on art fair appearances as they do on rent for their gallery, and they look upon their art fair stand as essentially a second venue they must maintain in order to be taken seriously. Sales at fairs can also account for half or more of a gallery's revenue, as well as be a chance to meet new collectors, and the prestige of being seen provides a good deal in intangible benefits beyond strictly income. Attendance at fairs can represent significant gambles, however, and if the art brought does not sell, it can seem like a costly mistake.

CASE STUDY: ERNST BEYELER

No other person shaped the postwar art market quite so much as Ernst Beyeler, and his most lasting achievement was helping in the creation of Art Basel, the model for today's art fair system. Like earlier eras of dealers, he came to art by way of the book trade. He began working for Oskar Schloss, an antiquarian book and print dealer. Upon Schloss' death, Beyeler took over the shop at the age of 24 and began dealing more and more in paintings and sculpture. His big coup in the market occurred in the early 1960s when he managed to acquire the G. David

---

Thompson collection from Pittsburgh, PA, which included 100 works by Paul Klee, 90 by Alberto Giacometti and hundreds by Cézanne, Monet, Picasso, Braque, Matisse, Miró, and others.[53] By this time, he was emerging as one of the dominant players in an increasingly global art market. He became a close confidant of the elderly Picasso, which allowed him access to the artist's horde of paintings from which he was notoriously reluctant to sell. Beyeler often acted as intermediary to help some of the leading museums secure the works they coveted for their collection.

The museum he and his wife Hilda founded, the Fondation Beyeler, designed by leading museum architect, Renzo Piano (Pompidou, new Whitney), stands as one of the most outstanding single private collection museums anywhere in the world. Ironically, many of its star attractions, especially its Klee and Giacometti holdings, were acquired from Thompson, who had hoped to have a wing at Pittsburgh's Carnegie Museum with his name to house the collection. That offer was rejected, and so he sold it to Beyeler, and now those works are exhibited as Beyeler's collection in Basel.[54]

An earlier art fair, Kunstmarkt Köln (now called Art Cologne), had already opened by 1967 and was visited by three Basel dealers: Beyeler, Trudi Bruckner, and Balz Hilt.[55] They saw the potential in such a commercial conception and attempted to reproduce it in Basel in 1970. The location, on the borders of France, Germany, and Switzerland, provided an international platform for the global demand for modern art. The idea of so much art gathered in one place in such blatant commercialism, with gallerists quickly throwing up improvised stands led *New York Times* critic Hilton Kramer to describe it as a "mammoth indoor 'flea market' of twentieth-century art."[56] The fair grew quickly from 90 galleries exhibiting in 1970 to 300 by 1975. In 2002, the fair branched out to hold Art Basel Miami Beach, which has become so important in its own right that many Americans think the Miami fair is *the* Art Basel, and are unaware of the one in Basel, Switzerland.

ART FAIRS—TERMS

Jury—a committee designated to select entrants to an art fair. For the nineteenth-century salons, jurors would be artists. For the twenty-first century art fairs, jurors tend to be art dealers.

Stand—the individual spaces allotted to dealers within the art fair. These stands will serve as their retail space for the duration of the art fair.

Satellite fair—art fairs organized to occur simultaneous to a major art fair going on in that city. Satellite fairs have a less restrictive jury and are generally where younger dealers will first make their appearance before eventually moving up to a main art fair.

Biennale—a massive, city-wide art exhibition held every two years, based on the model of the Venice Biennale. These are generally noncommercial exhibitions.

Paris Salon—the leading nineteenth-century, state-sponsored, annual exhibition of art. The Paris Salon created the business model that most art centers imitated for much of that century.

VIP event—an exclusive gathering held during the period of an art fair intended to allow dealers and sponsors close contact with wealthy collectors.

Red dot—a red circular sticker placed next to an object at an art fair which indicates that the object has been sold. Dealers often use these red dots strategically, sometimes placing them next to unsold artworks in order to give the appearance of sales.

Exhibition of degenerate art—an exhibition of modernist art shown by the Nazis in Munich in 1937, intended to show the German public what was bad, or degenerate [*Entartete*] art. The first Documenta in 1955 intended to re-acquaint the German public with these artists.

Documenta—an art exhibition now held every five years in the city of Kassel, Germany. Considered to be the most prestigious venue for an artist to be exhibited.

Notes

1 Casson, M. and Lee, J. S. "The Origin and Development of Markets: A Business History Perspective." *Business History Review,* vol. 85, no. 1, 2011, pp. 9–37.

2 Bell, A. R. and Dale, R. S. "The Medieval Pilgrimage Business." *Enterprise & Society,* vol. 12, no. 3, 2011, pp. 601–627.

3 Ewing, D. "Marketing Art in Antwerp, 1460–1560: Our Lady's Pand." *Art Bulletin,* vol. 72, no. 4, 1990, pp. 558–584.

4 Suykerbuyk, R. "Chapter 2 The Image of Piety at the Dawn of Iconoclasm." *The Matter of Piety.* Series: Studies in Netherlandish Art and Cultural History, vol. 16. Brill. July 17, 2020, pp. 74–107.

5 Prak, M. "Guilds and the Development of the Art Market during the Dutch Golden Age." *Simiolus: Netherlands Quarterly for the History of Art,* vol. 30, no. 3/4, 2003, pp. 236–251.

6 Landois, P. *Academy of Painting.* 1751. In *The Encyclopedia of Diderot & d'Alembert Collaborative Translation Project.* Trans. Benhamou, R. and Arbor, A. Michigan Publishing, 2003.

7 See: Earlom, R. *The Exhibition at the Royal Academy in Pall Mall in 1771,* May 20, 1772. Mezzotint. Collection of the Royal Academy.

8 See: Kunstausstellungen im Münchner Glaspalast. Catalogues 1869–1931. www. arthistoricum.net/themen/textquellen/glaspalast

9 Romain, L. "Zur Geschichte des deutschen Kunstvereins. In: Arbeitsgemeinschaft deutscher Kunstvereine" in: *Kunstlandschaft Bundesrepublik.* Stuttgart: Klett-Cotta, 1984, pp. 11–37.

10 "May Oppose Building on Site of Arsenal; Secretary Watrous of Academy of Design Says No Offer Has Been Made and No Vote Taken. Some of the Members Might Object -- Bill in Legislature Permits the Arrangement." *The New York Times,* Feb. 17, 1909.

11 For the *Salon des Indépendants,* see: Brauer, F. *Rivals and Conspirators: The Paris Salons and the Modern Art Centre.* Cambridge Scholars Publishing, 2013, pp. 83–86.

12 For the *Münchener Secession,* see: Maakela, M. *The Munich Secession: Art and Artists in Turn-of-the-Century Munich.* Princeton University Press, 1990, pp. 58–60.

13 Taylor, J. *In Search of the Budapest Secession: The Artist Proletariat and the Modernism's Rise in the Hungarian Art Market, 1800–1914.* Helena History Press, 2014, pp. 185–192.

14 Boime, A. "Entrepreneurial Patronage in Nineteenth-Century France." In Carter II, E. C., Forster, R., and Moody, J. N., eds., *Enterprise and Entrepreneurs in Nineteenth- and Twentieth-Century France.* Johns Hopkins University Press, 1976, pp. 137–207.

15 Schaefer, B. "1912 – Mission Moderne." In Schaefer, B., ed., *1912 – Mission Moderne. Die Jahrhundertschau des Sonderbunds.* Wienand, 2012, p. 21.

16 Brown, M. *The Story of the Armory Show.* Abbeville Press, 1988, pp. 244–327.

17 Gilmore Holt, E. *The Expanding World of Art, 1874–1902.* Yale University Press, 1988.

18 Russeth, A. "The Venice Biennale: Everything You Could Ever Want to Know." *ARTnews.* April 17, 2019.

19 Martini, V. and Collicelli Cagol, S. "The Venice Biennale at Its Turning Points: 1948 and the Aftermath of 1968." In de Haro García, N., et al., eds., *Making Art History in Europe After 1945.* Routledge, 2020, pp. 90–97.

20 labiennale.org *Biennale Arte history.* The Beginning of the 20th Century. www. labiennale.org/en/history-biennale-arte

21 Mackrell, J. "Sex and Art by the Grand Canal: How Peggy Guggenheim Took Venice." *The Guardian,* May 10, 2017.

22 Smith, R. "Art Review: Combining People and Machines in Venice." *The New York Times,* July 8, 2011.

23 Baumgardner, J. "At the Venice Biennale, Simone Leigh Embraces Sovereignty." Hyperallergic, May 1, 2022.

24 Greenberger, A. "Black Women Reign Victorious at Venice Biennale as Simone Leigh, Sonia Boyce Win Top Awards." *ARTnews,* Apr. 23, 2022.

25 Russeth, A.

26 Mitter, S. "Art Biennials Were Testing Grounds. Now They Are Being Tested." *The New York Times*, May 1, 2020.

27 Morton, E. "An Art Biennial in a Pandemic? How Latvia's RIBOCA2 Embraced COVID-19 as Its Co-curator." *The Calvert Journal*, Sep. 3, 2020.

28 *"Entartete" Kunst: Digital reproduction of a typescript inventory prepared by the Reichsministerium für Volksaufklärung und Propoganda*, ca. 1941/42. (V&A NAL MSL/1996/7), vol. 1–2. Victoria & Albert Museum, 2014.

29 Brown, K. "A Startling Exhibition on the History of Documenta Reveals the Political Moves—and Nazi Ties—of Its First Curators." *Artnet News*, June 25, 2021.

30 Koerner von Gustorf, O. "Theaster Gates: Inner City Blues." *ArtMag*, vol. 76, June 14, 2013.

31 Greenberger, A. "Documenta's Anti-Semitism Controversy, Explained: How a German Art Show Became the Year's Most Contentious Exhibition." *ARTnews*, July 22, 2022.

32 *Art Review Power 100: The Annual Ranking of the Most Influential People in Art, 2022*. Dec. 5, 2022.

33 Kerr, D. "How to Get Your Gallery into Art Basel in 5 Not-So-Easy Steps." *Artspace*, June16, 2015.

34 Chow, J. "UBS Secures Global Art Basel Sponsorship." *The Wall Street Journal*, May 26, 2013.

35 Cascone, S. "Art Basel Completes Hong Kong Art Fair Buy-Out." *Artnet News*, Oct. 28, 2014.

36 Cassady, D. "The Armory Show, 'New York's Art Fair,' Is an Increasingly Global Juggernaut." *The Art Newspaper*, Sep. 9, 2022.

37 Ghassemitari, S. "The 2022 ADAA Art Show Is Back at New York's Park Avenue Armory." *Hypebeast*, Nov. 4, 2022.

38 Loos, T. "Frieze New York Sticks with a Winning Formula: The Art Fair, To Be Held Again at the Shed, Will Have "More of an International Feel" This Year — And at Least One Surprise." *The New York Times*, May 17, 2022.

39 Brown, K. "The Organizers of Berlin's Most Important Art Fair Have Canceled All Future Editions Due to Financial Shortfalls." *Artnet News*, Dec. 11, 2019.

40 Kishkovsky, S. "First Cosmoscow Fair since Russian Invasion of Ukraine to Open with No Foreign Galleries and Internal Complaints of Censorship." *The Art Newspaper*, Sep. 13, 2022.

41 Sansom, A. "After the Arrival of Paris+, Is There a Future for FIAC? Its New Director Is Plotting a Return." *Artnet News*, Nov. 21, 2022.

42 Movius, L. "Seoul's Art Market Ascent Reaches New High with First Frieze Fair." *The Art Newspaper*, Aug. 29, 2022.

43 Schneider, T. "Virtual Art Fairs Were Seen as a Lifeline in the Lockdown Era. A New Study Shows They Are Failing New York's Art Market." *Artnet*, Nov. 18, 2020.

44 Cassady, D. "Tefaf, Back in New York after Years of Cancellations, Takes Visitors Outside of Time." *The Art Newspaper*, May 7, 2022.

45 Batycka, D. "Volta Finds Its Niche in Basel, Offering Exciting New Work by Emerging Artists at Affordable Price Points." *Artnet News*, June 16, 2022.

46 Benzine, V. "Highlights from the Other Art Fair: The Bright and Boozy Arts Bonanza Returned to Brooklyn This Weekend, Allowing Artists and Their (Potential) Customers to Rub Elbows." *Brooklyn Magazine*, Nov 7, 2022.

47 Stromberg, M. "Are Art Fairs Necessary?" *KCET*, Feb. 4, 2016.

48 Thaddeus-Johns, J. "Can New York Have Too Many Art Fairs?" *Artsy*, May 11, 2022.

49 Salz, J. "A Modest Proposal: Break the Art Fair." *New York Magazine*, May 1, 2018.

50 Shaw, A. "Art Basel Introduces New Booth Pricing Structure to Subsidise Younger Galleries." *The Art Newspaper*, Sep. 3, 2018.

51 Ng, B. "Why Everything at Major Art Fairs Seems to Be Pre-Sold." *Artsy*, Nov. 18.

52 Eckardt, S. "Hilde Lynn Helphenstein Wants to Be the Art World's Anthony Bourdain." *W Magazine*, Sep. 20, 2022.

53 Grimes, W. "Ernst Beyeler, Top Dealer of Modern Art, Dies at 88." *The New York Times*, Feb. 26, 2010.

54 Karakatsanis, C. G. "G. David Thompson: A Pittsburgh Art Patron and His Collection." *Storyboard*. Carnegie Museum of Art, Apr. 7, 2015.

55 Zarobell, J. *Art and the Global Economy.* Oakland: University of California Press, 2013, p. 143.

56 Kramer, H. "3-Year-Old Basel Art Fair Lures Some Top Dealers." *The New York Times*, June 27, 1972.

Curatorship

Chapter 8

EVOLUTION OF THE ROLE OF CURATOR

Originally, the term had meant the person assigned to the care of objects, and early curators did just that. Over the last two centuries, that role has expanded to include the study of objects under their care, the display of the objects with a visiting public in mind, and the contextualization and explanation of these objects to that public. In larger museums, curators belong to departments designated by period and medium, and they will make decisions about which works from their department's collection will appear on the floor of the permanent exhibition. These decisions can often be complex for larger museums, such as the Metropolitan or the Louvre, which have ratios of over ten to one for objects in storage to objects on display.[1] Those objects that make it on to the floor often conform to the expertise and predilections of a department's head curator. Within the construction of a permanent exhibition section, a curator can find countless opportunities for creative expression. Among many possibilities are concentrated ensembles of works by a certain school or star of the era, locating works in prestige positions like at the head of stairs or at the far end of a prominent entry area, or simply deciding to include an outstanding piece by a little known artist in the hope of elevating visitors' familiarity with their work. In many small ways, museums' permanent collections will bear the intellectual imprint of its curatorial staff.

DOI: 10.4324/9781003431756-9

With the medium of the traveling temporary exhibition, however, the full evolution of the curator began to take shape, especially in terms of their ability to shape the writing of art history. That continues to this day, as is the case with the blockbuster shows that are often co-productions of major museums such as the Musée d'Orsay, the Washington National Gallery, and the Art Institute of Chicago. In addition to the revenue generating possibilities these events represent, they also provide the pinnacle achievement for which a museum curator might aspire. Works that have never been seen side-by-side can be gathered from across the globe, and a new insight into a beloved era or artist can be presented to a massive public. For contemporary art curators, the networks of biennales and major *kunsthalle* installations represent their premier league in which they aspire to compete. Being named as the curator for Documenta or for a national Venice Biennale pavilion would be the ultimate achievement a contemporary art curator could attain. In the same way that museum curators can shape the art history of more distant eras with high-profile traveling temporary shows, contemporary art curators can essentially canonize living artists by selecting them for these events.

THE GESAMTKUNSTWERK

The current cult of the curator-as-artist has much to do with the evolving medium of the *Gesamtkunstwerk*. The term means "total work of art" in German. It first came to prominence as a way to describe the operas of Richard Wagner, which acted as a combination of narrative, sung theater combined with classical orchestral music. The libretti themselves represented probing explorations of ancient Germanic mythology and Romantic sensibility. The staging of these productions furthermore provided opportunities for artistic expression in the set, lighting, and costume design.[2] The essential feature of a *Gesamtkunstwerk* is the combination of art forms across medium and even bridging the sectors of literary, visual, and performing arts. In fact, the techniques of working across medium were already being explored in the Renaissance period and achieved its early perfection in Gian Lorenzo Bernini's *Ecstasy of St. Teresa* in the Cornaro Chapel of the church of Santa Maria della Vittoria in Rome (1647–1652). The chapel was designed to coherently portray the moment of spiritual ecstasy when the saint is about to be pierced by the spear of an angel. Sculptural representations of members of the Cornaro family (the chapel was intended to be a burial chapel of the Venetian Cardinal Federico Cornaro) are arrayed along theater boxes to observe the miracle.[3]

In the late nineteenth century, this concept of merging the arts corresponded to a wider appreciation of the non-fine arts, that is, the applied arts, which began to take root with the Arts and Crafts Movement coming from Britain. With the onset of the architectural and design movements that would subsequently be called Art Nouveau (in French and English) and Secession (in Central European languages), architects in the 1890s began to rebel against the tired-out regime of recycled historical European motifs and yearned to create something new (as the French name would indicate). These architects often had the benefit of generous and adventurous patrons, and they began to seek out other sources of inspiration, such as non-Western art, folk art, and botany. Early practitioners such as Henry van de Velde and Victor Horta in Brussels[4] and Louis Sullivan in the American Midwest began to experiment with excesses and extremes of floral-inspired decoration.[5] The whimsical works by Antoni Gaudí in Barcelona[6] and Ödön Lechner in Budapest made innovative use of ceramics both for structural and decorative features.[7] Frank Lloyd Wright emphasized an organic style tied to the American prairie. The Glasgow Four (Charles Rennie Mackintosh, Margaret Macdonald, Frances Macdonald, and James Herbert MacNair) brought a more geometric severity to design, and their exhibitions at the Vienna Secession at the *fin de siècle* would point toward a much less decorative future.[8] Specifically, it was there in Vienna that this influence would be most greatly felt in the works of Otto Wagner, Josef Hoffmann, Koloman Moser, and Adolf Loos, and lead in a straight trajectory to the Bauhaus, international style, mid-century modernism, and an un- ornamented twentieth century.[9] What all these architects had in common, however, was that they did not just design the building. They had furniture constructed to specifically work with the interior concept. The wrought iron, lighting fixtures, windows, elevator doors, and radiator grills were all coordinated to a unified aesthetic program.

THE INSTALLATION AS WORK OF ART

The works of these turn of the century architects, especially those of the Vienna Secession, elevated this concept of the *Gesamtkunstwerk* into a cult of art, a sort of aesthetic, walled garden in which they hoped to ensconce themselves as the Austro-Hungarian Empire unraveled.[10] From this inclination emerged some outstanding achievements in the merging of art forms. In 1902, Josef Hoffmann curated the Beethoven Exhibition, which featured a large, symbolist sculpture by Max Klinger and a three-wall mural by Gustav Klimt dramatizing Beethoven's 9th Symphony.[11] Gustav Mahler even arranged and conducted an abbreviated version of the piece, because to this generation of Viennese, Beethoven represented the ultimate embodiment of the heroic artist [see this chapter' Case Study: Vienna Secession 1902 Beethoven Exhibition].[12] Subsequently, Klimt would be expelled from the Secession and would curate his own *Gesamtkunstwerk* in the form of the 1908 *Kunstschau* to celebrate the sixtieth anniversary of Franz Joseph's reign, where he showed his landmark piece, *The Kiss*. He had Hoffmann design the pavilion and invited the leading designers of the *Wiener Werkstätte* to exhibit their works.[13] In Paris in 1909, Sergei Diaghilev founded the *Ballets Russes* and began staging groundbreaking performances that merged modernism with dance, classical music, and costume and set design. Some of the most important composers of twentieth century, for example, Igor Stravinsky, Claude Debussy, Sergei Prokofiev, Erik Satie, and Maurice Ravel, wrote pieces that were choreographed by Michel Fokine and Vaslav Nijinsky, with sets and costumes designed by Léon Bakst, Alexandre Benois, as well as Picasso and Matisse.[14] At the 1912 *Salon d'Automne* in 1912, Raymond Duchamp-Villon and André Mare constructed the *La Maison Cubiste* (decorated with Cubist paintings),[15] which would lead to a whole genre of Cubist architecture and design that especially blossomed in Prague in the teens and twenties.[16] Raymond's half-brother, Marcel Duchamp, would stage two seminal Surrealist exhibitions—first in Paris in 1938, which included an unlit exhibition chamber hung with coal sacks (smelling of coal dust) and visitors used flashlights to view the works.[17] Later, in New York in 1942 (having fled the Nazis), for the exhibition First Papers of Surrealism, Duchamp filled a room with string, like cobwebs, and had children playing in the corners.[18] The Surrealists were quite keen to bring their totality of art out into the world, no more so than in the Spanish Civil War when Republicans constructed a Surrealist prison in which to intern captured Francoist troops.[19]

Out of that *Gesamtkunstwerk* milieu in Vienna would emerge the most influential curator of the twentieth century in the installation artist variant of the profession, Frederick Kiesler. He was originally a stage set designer, an artform which was a frequent point of crossover in the early twentieth century, for example, the *Ballets Russes*. He designed the Austrian pavilion for the 1925 *Exposition Internationale des Arts Décoratifs et Industriels Moderne* (from which the period name Art Deco is derived), entitled "City in Space," which featured hanging panels unattached to walls. In 1942, Peggy Guggenheim asked him to design the rooms for her short-lived museum/gallery, Art of This Century. He created distinctive rooms for each of the different orientations of Peggy Guggenheim's collection. The room for abstract art had paintings hanging in space from floor to ceiling straps. Visitors could sit on Miró-style blob furniture. The Surrealist room had concave walls, lights that flashed on and off, and the sound of a locomotive passing through the gallery.[20] The paintings were mounted on baseball bats and could be moved to emphasize there being no fixed point of perspective. Although the institution would only last a couple of years before being dismantled, it remained legendary enough in curatorial circles that the Los Angeles County Museum of Art recreated the Surrealist room in 1989.[21]

THE MUNDANE ESSENTIALS OF CURATING

Regardless of the type of exhibition being undertaken, there are certain tasks curators are always going to have to do. As the name originally indicated, they have a mandate to look after the artworks under their care. If the exhibition being prepared involves a temporary loan of pieces, then several logistical tasks need to be undertaken. If the curator works at a larger institution like a museum or a large gallery or auction house, then they might have the assistance of a registrar to perform many of these tasks. In that case, the curator will work closely with the registrar on these highly detailed processes. In these activities,

Curatorship

the role of the curator resembles less that of the theater director and more that of the stage manager. A short list of these essential tasks would be the following:

- Preparing the checklist of artworks that will be exhibited. This task can become quite complicated when it is a group show with limited exhibition space, and each artist would like to submit more pieces than can be accommodated. Many other working parts need to be accounted for here. For example, will lenders be willing to lend? Will the artworks be available at the time of the exhibition (or will they be on show somewhere else)? At this stage, many types of cost estimates are going to need to be made, the most important of which are the transportation and logistics expenses. For this reason, the ultimate checklist is in flux at this point because certain artworks might come with prohibitive shipping costs and therefore have to be removed from the list.

- Drafting a budget that will include all the relevant costs to the exhibition needs to be done at this planning stage. These costs will likely include transportation, insurance, installation, marketing, and didactic costs. In addition, a larger scale undertaking might also include an honorarium for the artists or for an outside curator, as well as travel expenses for them to be present for the installation and opening. One of the important questions for a gallery to consider for how it accounts for exhibition costs is: which costs are apportioned to programming (i.e., holding an exhibition), and which are covered in the general operating budget. The checklist and budget preparation have to essentially be done simultaneously because one constantly informs the other. These processes will usually begin at least two to three years before (if not many more) a major traveling museum exhibition because of the need to fundraise based on budget projections.

- Once the checklist has been prepared, loan agreements can be prepared, and logistics can begin to be arranged in earnest. At this stage, a curator may have to make significant changes because certain key works had to be scratched from the exhibition, forcing intellectual and aesthetic alterations to the general concept. The loan agreements can take on many specifications as to the means of transport and packaging, and some high value works (usually above $1 million) may require a courier throughout the transportation process.

- Two to eight weeks (and earlier if special preparations are required) prior to the exhibition's opening, the pieces should be arriving at the staging venue, which could be a storage area or just the gallery's backroom. At this location, works will need to have a condition report taken as they are unpacked and compared with the one completed prior to the work having been shipped. At this point, pieces may require preparation before they are ready for installation. They may need to be matted, framed, or even quickly conserved. At a larger institution, the curator may again have the assistance of a registrar to process the reception of deliveries. Many museums will have an entire team of trained preparators and installers who, in fact, are legally the only ones allowed to move or install artworks. At any smaller institution, however, these tasks will fall almost entirely on the curator.

- Prior to the arrival of the artworks, the curator should have already prepared an exhibition plan to show where each piece will be placed. In the past, curators often constructed models of the gallery spaces and then printed out scale examples of the works so that different configurations could be considered in proportion. Newer, computer-aided design platforms have increasingly made this process easier to perform.

- When the installation begins, many changes will need to be made to the original plan as the realities of artworks' relationships with one another become apparent in ways that were not in the mock-up. In some cases, hangings "don't work" or alternatively, the curator recognizes possibilities not previously seen until all the work was present in situ.

- Marketing actions need to be taken at least six to eight weeks prior to the kind of solo exhibition that occurs on a monthly basis at a commercial gallery. For a major museum show, marketing will need to begin planning and preparing at least six months prior to opening.

- All exhibitions will provide some amount of didactic or informative material about the artworks on display. Chelsea galleries are notorious for providing only printed checklists/pricelists and no wall labels or wall texts. This has something to do with their quick turnover of exhibitions. Museum exhibitions may require months of preparation for hundreds of labels that each contain detailed contextualizing information, as well as large wall texts, audio guides, and multimedia materials.
- Once the exhibition closes, pieces will need to be quickly condition-reported, packed, and then returned to their lenders or on to the next exhibition venue.

KEY DECISIONS A CURATOR MUST MAKE

For some curators, the above tasks are the lion's share of their duties and provide little creative outlet, but most exhibitions will provide opportunities for a certain amount of artistic input in terms of placement and arrangement of works. In many cases, however, curators have enormous aesthetic and intellectual control over an exhibition and do indeed look upon the production as their own *Gesamtkunstwerk*. The following decisions are the ones the curator makes that really shape the exhibition and make it the art experience that it is for visitors.

Which Artists to Include?

If the exhibition is a group show, inclusion can have huge ramifications on an artist's career, especially if the exhibition starts to subsequently act as a defining event in the formation of an artistic grouping. For example, Impressionism would be quite a different movement if Edgar Degas were not part of the group.

Which Artworks to Include?

Even if the artists to be included are quite set, the works are usually more variable, but again they play a large role in defining the scope of an exhibition. Furthermore, if careful cataloguing of the works exhibited has been retained, then, almost certainly, those works that have been shown will be ultimately worth more money on the secondary market because

of that provenance reference point than similar works from the
œuvre that were not shown.

What Is the Narrative of the Exhibition?

This is really the single most important decision a curator
will be making about an exhibition, and this is because so
many different types of narratives can be employed. The show
can emphasize a narrative of discovery and revelation. The
exhibition can create a tone of solemn reverence or playful
exuberance. The narrative can be presented as an exercise in
art historical documentation, or one that moves along aesthetic
concepts.

How Can the Installation Emphasize That Narrative?

Installation arrangements can be surprisingly communicative in
terms of relaying the show's primary themes. In order to achieve
expression in the placement of artworks, the curator must make
careful use of their spaces' built-in features: sight lines, places
for revelation, and points of prestige (tops of staircases, entry
points, and privileged sight lines).

How Can Didactic Materials Emphasize That Narrative?

Didactic materials (labels, wall texts, audio guides, and
multimedia) can easily veer into the realm of being "too much"
and distract the visitor from experiencing the artworks, which
should always be kept front-and-center as the core attraction.
A good curator will first produce an overflow of didactic material
and then carefully edit back until only the most key phrases
remain, the ones that truly heighten the visitors' overall aesthetic
experience.

CASE STUDY: VIENNA SECESSION 1902 BEETHOVEN EXHIBITION

The Vienna Secession began when Gustav Klimt and some
of his followers abandoned the Austrian capital's version
of the Salon, the *Künstlerhaus*, and formed a competing
exhibition society composed mostly of younger artists.[22]

The rebels were dismayed by the treatment of landscapists and, in particular, by the *Künstlerhaus*'s unwillingness to hold a retrospective of the plein air painters Theodor von Hörmann and Josef Engelhardt.[23] At the same time, though, similar to the Munich and Berlin versions, the Vienna Secession expressly declared their aim for greater internationalism and receptivity to foreign exhibitors. The Vienna Secession would also proceed along the pattern of repeated rupture, with the first one occurring in 1905, along the familiar lines of egalitarian versus elitist. This dispute began with a question about sending of works to the St. Louis World Fair, but the tensions ultimately surrounded the role of a dealer, Gallery Mietke, and its involvement with the Vienna Secession. The result was that the "Klimt Group" departed, leaving the organization in the hands of its lesser masters.[24] Gustav Klimt's new incarnation in the form of the *Kunstschau* of 1908 was not a permanent exhibition society but rather a one-off event and in that way more resembles the 1913 Armory Show.[25]

Vienna's Secession was fortunate to almost immediately acquire a permanent venue (1898), an asset Munich and Berlin also would come to have, but which many other like-minded alternative salons would never secure, severely impeding their longevity.[26] The steel magnate Karl Wittgenstein (father of the philosopher Ludwig) helped finance the construction of their iconic Joseph Maria Olbrich-designed building just on the other side of the Karlsplatz from their competitor, the *Künstlerhaus*. Having a permanent venue gave the institution the possibility to hold exhibitions year-round and opened up more adventurous curatorial possibilities than a rented space would have. Among the many seminal shows staged at the Vienna Secession, the 1900 appearance of the Glasgow Four would have a dramatic influence on the development of twentieth-century architecture and design.[27] The 1903 presentation of French Impressionism spread familiarity with the movement deep into Central Europe.[28] The achievement, however, that most completely embodied the institution's

Gesamtkunstwerk aesthetic would be the 1902 Beethoven Exhibition.

To this generation, Beethoven, who brought classical music into the Romantic era, embodied the supreme artist.[29] The core attraction of the exhibition was a monumental statue by Max Klinger of the composer seated like a god on an Olympus-like throne. The architect Josef Hoffmann curated the exhibition and organized 21 other artists to all produce works based around Beethoven, and he designed the interior to resemble an ancient temple with Klinger's sculpture in the role of votive statue. The most memorable work from the show would be one that was meant to be only an ephemeral decoration at the entrance to the sanctuary area of the interior.[30] Gustav Klimt painted three enormous murals directly on to the Secession building's walls, which depicted a dramatization of Beethoven's 9th Symphonies. This is the last of Beethoven's symphonies, and the one that features a chorus singing its last movement set to a poem by Schiller and the piece now features as the European Union's anthem.

Klimt's work, titled *This Kiss to the Whole World* (from the text of Schiller's poem),had never been intended to be permanent but was subsequently sawn out of the walls and preserved. The murals have been reassembled in the basement of the Secession building and form a core pilgrimage to fans of the artist. Painted in 1901–1902, the narrative scrolls across 34 meters (112 ft.) and shows humanity's quest for happiness, in which a knight figure must confront an array of hostile forces but eventually finds consolation in art and concludes with an embracing couple. That motif would be reused in a slightly different format for his iconic 1907 work, *The Kiss*. Furthermore, the widespread use of gold (Klimt's father and brother were goldsmiths) in the Beethoven Frieze began his work in a style we call his "gold period" or the "mosaic period." Essentially, this is when Klimt began to resemble that Klimt who has become one of the world's best-loved artists.

CURATORSHIP—TERMS

Gesamtkunstwerk—a German word meaning a "total work of art"; an artwork that combines many media to create a coherent aesthetic totality. First applied to the operas of Richard Wagner, the term became popular in the art and design world of the Central European Secessions.

Installation—an arrangement of artworks in an exhibition space. A curator's primary act is to create a meaningful installation that heightens the audience's aesthetic and intellectual appreciation of the artworks.

Salon-style hanging—a method of hanging 2D artworks intending to maximize usage of the limited wall space. Artworks generally cover most of the wall with little organization by theme, medium, or artist.

On-the-line hanging—a method of hanging 2D artworks, which hangs one object at eye level, progressing around the space horizontally.

White cube—an exhibition interior characterized by white walls with no ornamentation or interior features other than the artworks on display.

Concept—a unifying intellectual conceit that binds all the artworks at an exhibition. The concept is the responsibility of the exhibition's curator.

Hans-Ulrich *Obrist*—the leading example of the contemporary art curator who might almost be regarded as an artist in their own right.

Change-over—the period between the closing of one exhibition and the opening of the next one. During this time, the closing exhibition works will be brought down and packaged for transport or storage, and the new artworks will be received, unpacked, and installed.

Gatekeeper—a person who controls access to the metaphorical "playing field" of a cultural industry. In the visual arts, a curator is an important gatekeeper for artists.

Conversation (between Artworks)—a relationship between installed artworks where component parts (colors, materials, and themes) seem to be having a metaphorical conversation with one another.

Notes

1 Fabrikant, G. "The Good Stuff in the Back Room." *The New York Times*, Mar. 12, 2009.

2 Rehn Wolfman, U. "Richard Wagner's Concept of the 'Gesamtkunstwerk.'" *Interlude*, Mar. 12, 2013.

3 Fahrner, R. and Kleb, W. "The Theatrical Activity of Gianlorenzo Bernini." *Educational Theatre Journal*, vol. 25, no. 1, Mar. 1973, pp. 5–14.

4 Eidelberg, M. and Henrion-Giele, S. "Horta and Bing: An Unwritten Episode of L'Art Nouveau." *The Burlington Magazine*, vol. 119, no. 896, Special Issue Devoted to European Art Since 1890, Nov. 1977, pp. 747–752.

5 Roche, J. F. "Louis Sullivan's Architectural Principles and the Organicist Aesthetic of Friedrich Schelling and S. T. Coleridge." *Nineteenth Century Studies*, vol. 7, 1993, pp. 29–55.

6 Calvera, A. "The Influence of English Design Reform in Catalonia: An Attempt at Comparative History." *Journal of Design History*, vol. 15, no. 2, 2002, pp. 83–100.

7 Sisa, J. *Motherland and Progress: Hungarian Architecture and Design 1800–1900*. Birkhäuser, 2016.

8 Billcliffe, R. and Vergo, P. "Charles Rennie Mackintosh and the Austrian Art Revival." *The Burlington Magazine*, vol. 119, no. 896, Special Issue Devoted to European Art Since 1890, Nov. 1977, pp. 739–746.

9 Koss, J. *Modernism after Wagner*. University of Minnesota Press, 2009.

10 Karnes, K. C. "'All of Vienna Has Become Secessionistic:' Longings of an Organization." *A Kingdom Not of This World: Wagner, the Arts, and Utopian Visions in Fin-de-Siecle Vienna*. Oxford Academic, 2013, pp. 66–92.

11 Schorske, C. E. *Fin-de-siècle Vienna: Politics and Culture*. New York: Vintage Books, 1981, pp. 208–278.

12 Harwell Celenza, A. "Music and the Vienna Secession: 1897–1902." *Music in Art*, vol. 29, no. 1/2, Music in Art: Iconography as a Source for Music History Volume I, Spring–Fall 2004, pp. 203–212.

13 Husslein-Arco, A. and Weidinger, A. *Gustav Klimt und die Kunstschau 1908*. Vienna: Prestel, 2008.

14 Bowlt, J. E. "Stage Design and the Ballets Russes." *The Journal of Decorative and Propaganda Arts*, Vol. 5, Russian/Soviet Theme Issue (Summer, 1987), pp. 28-45.

15 Brauer, F. *Rivals and Conspirators: The Paris Salons and the Modern Art Centre*. Newcastle upon Tyne: Cambridge Scholars Publishing, 2013, pp. 138–157, 347–348.

16 von Vegesack, A., ed. *Czech Cubism: Architecture, Furniture, and Decorative Arts, 1910–1925*. Princeton Architectural Press, 1992.

17 Ricci, B. "The Shows That Made Contemporary Art History: The International Surrealist Exhibition of 1938." *Artland Magazine*.

18 Kachur, L. *Displaying the Marvelous*. MIT Press, 2001, pp. 195–197.

19 Tremlett, G. "Anarchists and the Fine Art of Torture." *The Guardian*, Jan. 27, 2003.

20 Bogner, D. *Peggy Guggenheim & Frederick Kiesler: The Story of Art of This Century*. Guggenheim Museum Publications, 2004.

21 Martin-Gropius-Bau "Frederick Kiesler: Architect, Artist, Visionary at Martin-Gropius-Bau Berlin." *Bigmat International Architecture Agenda*, Mar. 22, 2017.

22 Vergo, P. *Art in Vienna, 1898–1918*. Ithaca, NY: Cornell University Press, 1975, p. 23.

23 Hevesi, L. *Acht Jahre Secession.* Vienna: Carl Koregen, 1906, pp. 120–121.

24 Ibid., p. 504.

25 *Gustav Klimt und die Kunstschau 1908.* Munich: Prestel Verlag, 2008.

26 Taylor, J. *In Search of the Budapest Secession: The Artist Proletariat and Modernism's Rise on the Hungarian Art Market, 1800–1914.* Helena History Press, 2014, pp. 166–178, 185–192.

27 Billcliffe, R. and Vergo, P. "Charles Rennie Mackintosh and the Austrian Art Revival." *The Burlington Magazine,* (special issue devoted to European art since 1890), vol. 119, no. 896, Nov. 1977, pp. 739–746.

28 Huemer, C. "Historicizing the Avant-Garde: The 1903 Impressionist Exhibition at the Vienna Secession." Database of Modern Exhibitions (DoME), European Paintings and Drawings 1905–1915, July 9, 2018.

29 Harwell Celenza, pp. 203–212.

30 Schorske, C. E. *Fin-de-siècle Vienna: Politics and Culture.* New York: Vintage Books, 1981, pp. 208–278.

Venue Management

Chapter 9

RENT AS RELENTLESS FORCE IN THE ART MARKET

The single most powerful force in the shaping of the physical landscape of the art market remains the constant quest for cheaper rents. This is because the sale of art is rarely capable of providing income adequate to pay market-rate rents. If a gallery fails, almost invariably its failure can be traced back to an inability to afford its rent. The commercial art market is one of those industries where the firms almost never own their venues and must pay retail rates to lease premises equal to those paid by the restaurants, cafes, shops, and other services located next door. Art sales tend to not come regularly, but rather in seasonal spurts and occasional high-profit deals, but that does not help with rent, which remains a relentless monthly phenomenon. In fact, choosing a retail location and balancing the need for good location at an affordable cost will always be one of the most important strategic decisions a gallerist can make.

Nonprofit institutions and public collections can often escape this consideration by receiving their venue largely rent-free. They can either own the deed to their property outright, or they might receive the building from their local government authority at a representational rent of $1 per year. These organizations generally benefit from these favorable real estate opportunities because of the social and cultural good they bring to the community, and because they are not a private individual or firm

DOI: 10.4324/9781003431756-10

which would profit from the location. In fact, nonprofit entities that do not secure a long-term, low-cost residence frequently will fail. Cities often use the placement of important nonprofit public art collections to provide an anchor to a wider arts and leisure district. If the strategy works well, then agglomeration of commercial galleries will sprout off this core institution, and other culturally oriented leisure activities such as theaters and music venues will join in to form an arts district. For both good and bad, this sets in motion a process referred to as gentrification where previously neglected areas with low property values become fashionable, usually through leveraging the cultural economy, and quickly rents escalate.[1] In fact, galleries might have been some of the first brave businesses to venture into the region, driven by their constant quest for cheaper rents, and they are often the first to be pushed out.

PRIME RETAIL LOCATIONS

The preferred venue for a gallery can be described as prime retail location, which for galleries would mean a street-front entrance on the ground floor with well-placed display windows. Furthermore, the ideal street would be one that has excellent foot traffic and muted vehicle noise but with convenient parking opportunities. One peculiarity about cultural industries is that they welcome concentration, whereas other retail businesses prefer isolation and to have a mini-monopoly for their trade in that neighborhood. Theater districts welcome more theaters, and similarly gallery districts welcome more galleries. This is particularly true for the art market because of the vast diversity of the kinds of art that galleries could show. Therefore, galleries are less likely to perceive their neighbors as selling a directly competing product.

The advantages of such a location are numerous; being located in the city's leading gallery district will have the benefits of foot traffic, which would be much more infrequent anywhere else in the city. Gallery districts usually coordinate and market their openings to all occur on the same evening, on Thursdays in Chelsea, and in many other cities on the first Friday of the month. The close concentration of galleries means that when art-goers come to see an exhibition at one venue, they often spill over into other locations and view those exhibitions as well. The district acts as a magnet for collectors, especially those from out-of-town and who wish to see what the city's art scene is like. Having such a location holds many of the attractions it would for any retail business: the convenient access from the street ensures that customers find the location easily. The street-level windows give the gallery an opportunity to display a signature piece that could attract buyers in off the sidewalk.

The downside of the location is usually going to be its high rent, and concurrently, its small size. Therefore, the location may lack good backroom space or storage, which is, in fact, essential infrastructure for a successful Chelsea-type gallery. Even more of a difficulty may be the restrictions on truck deliveries, and if the location has limited parking (they usually do) then trucks may have a hard time even stopping long enough to drop off or pick up. These kinds of locations are unlikely to have loading docks and may even have additional obstructions such as stairs or awkward entrances. All of these problems, in theory, should be countered by the much higher revenue potential, which the location promises through better exposure to collectors and greater possibilities for walk-in clients. Many gallerists, however, complain that, in fact, the location does not justify the rent, and therefore they seek out other venue solutions.

SUB-PRIME RETAIL ALTERNATIVES

The first alternative to prime retail that a gallerist will consider will be something that can be termed "sub-prime retail." Venues that can be broadly categorized as such would be either because they are located in a less-than-ideal neighborhood, or because they are not on a street-front. Gallerists choose these locations for various strategic reasons, calculating that the loss of prominence will be compensated by the lower rent. Commercial galleries know that the people who really pay their bills are collectors, and often a few collectors will essentially sustain an entire enterprise. Therefore, if a dealer is confident that those who actually buy their art will still find their way over to their new venue, they may take the risk of moving to a less visible location. Emerging galleries establishing their first venue may also choose a sub-prime spot because they can afford nothing else, and with lower rent, the stakes are lower, allowing for a larger learning curve. Another reason for choosing a sub-prime location would be the need for more space, and a gallerist could calculate that they would sell pieces better if they could show more of them in better installations. Furthermore, a larger space would provide more backroom storage, and so thus the possibility of stocking more inventory to show prospective collectors when they visit.

A location that is in a street-front, shop-like space can still be considered sub-prime if it is not in a gallery district, and not in a high-end shopping street with other luxury goods retailers (jewelry, haute couture, wine, and confectionary). Antique shops may survive in isolation, at least on the lower end, but art galleries rarely do without the company of other galleries. Therefore, it is a brave dealer who decides to open their gallery in a part of town with no existing art scene and would only do so in the hope of attracting others to the neighborhood. The first movers in such colonization processes tend to be galleries with a pre-existing clientele moving down-market for the rent-saving opportunity (possibly even purchasing a property), as well as the prospect of a much larger venue. They can then provide the anchor for emerging galleries to join them, given that they can themselves guarantee a certain amount of buying capacity being brought into the area. However, creating a mature art district may take many years and also a lot of organizing, marketing, and branding.

The other common sub-prime retail solution would be an off-street location. This usually means the gallery is located on the second floor or higher, and so their windows are of no use for advertising wares. Galleries are rarely located inside of shopping centers or malls, and if they are, then they tend to be of the suspect print dealer type and are not taken seriously in the art world. The idea of not having a street-front presence most often works where galleries exist in such concentration that art-goers expect to go inside buildings and upstairs to visit places. The Chelsea district of New York particularly fits this description. Only the most elite and deep-pocketed dealers such as Larry Gagosian, David Zwirner, and other alpha galleries have street-level locations, and all the other 300 galleries are located on the second to ninth floors of buildings that were former warehouses and office buildings.[2] This system works because nearly all of these galleries exist in buildings with almost nothing else but other galleries and so in some ways serve as art gallery malls (this concept is already widespread in the American countryside in the form of antique malls). Given the rents Chelsea gallerists pay, it would be difficult to call these spaces sub-prime. In other metropolitan markets or any other part New York, such above-street solutions, however, would be sub-prime.

If the above-street gallery is in a building with other similar businesses, and especially if it is directly above street-level venues in the city's gallery district, then it can hope to attract walk-in visitors during the scheduled art walks. Some of the most important galleries in the history of the art market in fact functioned in just such a way. Ambroise Vollard operated his initial business out of a seventh-floor apartment.[3] Alfred Stieglitz's gallery 291 (originally called the Little Galleries of the Photo-Secession) was located on the fifth floor of 291 Fifth Avenue, across the hall from an apartment rented by Edward Steichen (who suggested the space).[4] When it opened, virtually no one visited, but during its 12 years of operation (1905–1917), it would be the first gallery in the United States to host exhibitions of Henri Matisse, Auguste Rodin, Henri Rousseau, Paul Cézanne, Pablo Picasso, Constantin Brâncuşi, Francis Picabia, and Marcel Duchamp.

SPLIT LOCATIONS

A partial solution to the high rent cost can be to split locations. This will usually involve a very small place on the street-front where walk-ins can be sized up, and if they appear to be serious clients, they can be sent over to a much larger low-cost location. That second space can be an apartment located near the primary gallery, since generally residential real estate rents for much less than commercial retail properties. Antique dealers frequently employ this strategy because of the large amount of floor space demanded by furniture and the setting of an apartment can also allow for interior arrangements that show off the objects. Cost conscious dealers may even discreetly use that apartment as their private residence. These kinds of locations essentially split the two parts of a Chelsea-type gallery: the street-front venue serves at the exhibition space (albeit small), and the upstairs space functions as the backroom where the gallery's full stable of represented artists can be exhibited and sold.

The other variation of a split location can also be a small space in the primary gallery district and a larger street-front gallery in a new emerging arts district. This second solution has the advantage of keeping the gallery anchored in the old art scene but able to point clients toward the new emerging one. In this case, the business may profile its two venues with the up-market one showing late-career artists, and the down-market one featuring emerging work. The key problem with both solutions is that, although they may generate rent savings by keeping the prime-retail location small, labor costs increase because at least one person is required to staff each space. Furthermore, the dealer can only be present at one location and so must constantly move between them in order to be able to provide their personal selling prowess.

GENTRIFICATION

Galleries are often the first to be priced-out of a gentrifying area because, as mentioned before, the sale of art can rarely pay prime-retail commercial rents. Therefore, the galleries are forced to seek out some other more affordable solution, many of which are discussed above, but the most common solution is to seek out a new area with below-market rents which could become the new emerging arts district. When looking back at the last 100 years of the New York art market, the driving force of every major migration in the contemporary art commercial center, from 57th Street to Soho, from Soho to Chelsea, and now from Chelsea to the Lower East Side, Brooklyn, Long Island City, or New Jersey), has been the constant search for cheaper rents. In some cases, dealers can even profit from this migration; those dealers who had been smart enough to purchase their buildings in Soho in the 1980s were able to sell them and move to Chelsea in the late 1990s. After much searching for an alternative to Chelsea's unaffordability, Tribeca is emerging as the next concentration with critical gravity to possibly dislodge the latter's dominance, but the same associated gentrification costs may be unavoidable.[5]

Emerging art scenes face significant obstacles to overcome, the first being the public's perception that the neighborhood lacks good public safety. In fact, the explosions of new arts districts in cities across the United States in the last 20 years have nearly all occurred in areas that had previously been regarded as low-income, unsafe areas, or, in common parlance, ghettos. As public safety rose and crime rates fell, these arts districts were usually on the front line of urban rehabilitation.[6] The galleries that lined the streets often coexisted with artist studio spaces in repurposed industrial structures. Bars, cafes, and restaurants would set up in the district to take advantage of the low rents and a newfound clientele who are were looking for complete cultural experiences involving both art and the consumption of high-quality food and beverages. If the area is well located in regards to the places where many people work, like a downtown business district, then it can also become desirable as a place to live. This type of development would conform to the fashionable trends of new urbanism and mixed use. Some jurisdictions, however, saddle commercial real estate with the bulk of the property tax burden, and a rise in residential real estate values pushes the commercial tax rates that galleries (or their landlords) pay to a level that prices them out of that neighborhood.[7]

Up until 2010, gentrification had not become a bad word. It was associated with urban rehabilitation, rescuing great architecture from oblivion, and creating liveable cities.[8] As the recovery from the 2009 recession began to take hold, especially in the highest-value real estate markets (which bounced back very fast), increasingly a flip side of this process began to be discussed. In the biggest cultural production centers in the world, New York, Los Angeles, and London, resentment was emerging at the process of displacement of earlier residents,[9] and creatives and artists were complaining that there was simply nowhere in the entire metropolitan area where they could afford to live anymore. Instead of colonizing new neighborhoods, artists are moving to rural locations in relative proximity to the center, for example, moving upstate from New York City to places along the Hudson River.[10] Others alternatives were being found in colonizing cities that were mostly associated with industrial decline such as Buffalo, Cleveland, and Detroit.

OTHER OPTIONS: POP-UPS, STUDIO GALLERY, BORROWED SPACE, AND VIRTUAL GALLERY

The history of the art market is essentially the history of artists, dealers, and other impresarios attempting to solve the crushing problem of the rent and somehow still manage to show and sell art. Some gallerists completely forgo the retail gallery (prime or sub-prime) and essentially operate an office with artworks. In this case, they might have become more of an art agent than a gallerist. They may still maintain a website that presents them as something like a brick-and-mortar gallery, and the artists they represent would still prefer to say they are represented by a gallery. The gallerist may still hold shows in spaces that are rented, often called project spaces, and might also appear at art fairs, though more serious art fairs often accept only galleries with a brick-and-mortar presence. The Covid pandemic, however, forced nearly every dealer to in some way temporarily create a virtual gallery of themselves.[11]

Gallerists and curators hoping to put on a show with minimal overhead may attempt a pop-up gallery. This term covers a wide array of conceptions that essentially avoid taking on a long-term lease on a space. A typical arrangement may involve a location slated for renovation or demolition, but which will not take place for a few more months. Therefore, the landlord makes an arrangement with a pop-up gallerist to put on art exhibitions until the construction work begins. A landlord might consider such an arrangement because they already want to start attracting attention and goodwill for the location. These kinds of spaces can often lack basic infrastructure such as electricity, Wi-Fi, plumbing, or heat, and so staffing them over a long period can become quite burdensome. For curators who just want to start putting up exhibitions, however, the opportunity can provide a chance to build their resumes with bold emerging art in distinctive settings.

One of the attractions to artists who rent studios in large industrial buildings that can be found in the Williamsburg and Bushwick sections of Brooklyn is that these places often hold open studio days. During these events, hundreds of visitors pour through the buildings to enjoy the street festival atmosphere and see art and get to know the artists. The artists will rearrange their studios to become improvised exhibition spaces, and in this way they can serve as their own gallerist. They can possibly even meet collectors and sell directly to them and circumvent the gallery dealer system entirely.

Artists who have no gallery representation usually face poor options for holding exhibitions. They can apply to their local nonprofit arts center for one of their exhibition slots and may do the same at their public library. The problem with holding shows in non-art-oriented locations such as a library or other public building is that these shows do not look very impressive on an artist's resume. Artists may also use other borrowed or non-art-specific locations like the walls of a café or restaurant, but, again, these venues are hardly considered prestigious locations to show one's art.

The internet is filled with various types of online galleries where artists can show. As mentioned above, many gallerists abandon brick-and-mortar galleries and essentially operate a virtual gallery. Artists themselves usually create their own websites, which can also function to market their works. Furthermore, many large-scale operations have emerged in recent years offering to sell artists' works. The same problem with the internet auction market also exists here: collectors are unwilling to buy anything significant (above $1,000) without seeing it in person or otherwise knowing the dealer and artist already.

CASE STUDY: ART OF THIS CENTURY

Peggy Guggenheim's collection is frequently confused with that of her uncle Solomon's. Part of that confusion can be explained by the fact that both are now under the umbrella of the global Guggenheim Museum brand. The two collections, however, were assembled with very different narratives. Solomon's branch of the Guggenheim dynasty was much wealthier, which made his collecting much easier, and allowed him to afford the iconic Frank Lloyd Wright building on Fifth Avenue.[12] Peggy's own father drowned with the *Titanic*, and her inheritance was relatively modest, which made her own achievement all the more impressive.[13]

In the 1930s, Peggy made an attempt at running a gallery called Guggenheim Jeune (making a play upon an important Paris gallery Bernheim-Jeune) in a second-floor, sub-prime location in Cork Street in London's gallery

Venue Management

district. Although the venture ultimately did not work out and lost money, she formed strong connections to some of Europe's leading avant-garde figures such as Marcel Duchamp and managed to exhibit some of the most important abstract, surrealist, and expressionist artists: Cocteau, Kandinsky, Dalí, Ernst, Magritte, Miró, Moore, and Kokoschka. She also made a point of always buying one piece from each exhibition, and this way started assembling her own collection.[14]

She decided to found instead a museum of modern art, which London did not have, and set to acquire a collection in Paris. She had the good fortune of making her purchases just as the German army had invaded France in 1939, and the market was in utter panic and her dollars went a long way. She purchased 90 major works of Modernism for approximately $40,000.[15] Unable to return to the U.K., she instead managed to escape to the United States with her new fiancé, Surrealist Max Ernst, and take the collection back as well. After considering other cities, she settled on New York, and rented a seventh-floor location on 57th Street. She had already had her collection cataloged and published under the title, *Art of This Century*,[16] and so used that name again for the venue.

The most important decision she made was hiring the Austrian expatriate set designer, Frederick Kiesler, to construct the interior. His Surrealist room featured curving walls, intermittent lighting, and paintings mounted on swiveling baseball bats, and the Abstract room held paintings hung from straps in the middle of the room like sculpture. Peggy was not pleased about what she saw as gross extravagance on the part of her designer.[17] Despite charging a 25¢ entry fee, she knew the enterprise needed another source of income so she set aside one room for a changing rotation of group and solo shows. She managed to give many of the core figures of abstract expressionism their first exhibition opportunities. She gave Jackson Pollock four shows and even sustained him with a regular stipend.[18]

Art of This Century operated for only five years, 1942–1947. Then Peggy decamped to Venice with her collection, first to show it at the Biennale, and eventually to install it in a palazzo on the Grand Canal.[19] It serves as Venice's premier modern art attraction and operates now as part of the Solomon R. Guggenheim Foundation network of museums.

VENUE MANAGEMENT—TERMS

Prime retail location—a commercial location in a city's leading arts and antiques district. The venue is at street level with street-facing, display windows.

Sub-prime retail location—a commercial location that in some way is less than ideal. It can be located in a city's leading arts and antiques district, but the venue, would not be located at street-level, but rather above (or below), and will not have any visual presence or display windows to attract the attention of passers-by. Alternatively, the location will be street-front, but not in a good retailing location.

Split location—a venue solution that involves a small prime retail location, and a second lower-cost storage location, to which serious buyers can be brought to by appointment.

Gentrification—a process of rising property values brought on by improvements in public safety and expansion of retail offerings that make neighborhoods desirable. Art galleries, by seeking out lower-rent districts, often play a crucial role in this process.

Repurposed industrial building—a frequent location choice for art galleries and studio artists looking for lower rents in neighborhoods that might gentrify in the future.

Studio gallery—a gallery temporarily placed inside an artist's studio, usually in conjunction with other studios in the same building.

Pop-up—a gallery temporarily occupying a space in exchange for little or no rent. The gallerist will be taking advantage of a short-term opportunity at a location that would have otherwise been empty.

Virtual gallery—essentially a website, also referred to as a viewing room, that provides something of a virtual reality simulation of seeing an artwork in a gallery space, perhaps with restricted access. These solutions became briefly essential for galleries and art fairs during the Covid pandemic.

Wall-space—the actual exhibitable space at a venue as defined by the amount of wall area on which pictures can be hung.

Storage—an area of a gallery for storing works not on exhibition. This location is important because many sales will be of works drawn from the storage. Some gallerists opt to locate the storage in a second location in a lower-rent district.

Notes

1 Deutsche, R. and Ryan, C. G. "The Fine Art of Gentrification." *October*, vol. 31, 1984, pp. 91–111.

2 Artsy Editorial, "What It Costs to Have a Gallery in New York City." *Artsy*, Mar. 1, 2017.

3 Dumas, A. "Ambroise Vollard patron of the avant-garde." In R. Rabinow, ed., *Cézanne to Picasso: Ambroise Vollard, Patron of the Avant-Garde*. New York: Metropolitan Museum of Art, 2006, p. 6.

4 Mintz Messinger, L. ed., *Stieglitz and His Artists: Matisse to O'Keefe*, New York: The Metropolitan Museum of Art, 2011.

5 Chen, X. "Can Tribeca Avoid Repeating the Boom-And-Bust Cycle of Previous New York City Gallery Districts? *The Art Newspaper*, Sep. 23, 2022.

6 Cole, D. B. "Artists and Urban Redevelopment." *Geographical Review*, vol. 77, no. 4, Oct. 1987, pp. 391–407.

7 Alvarez, A. "Santa Fe Arts District Faces an Uncertain Future." *Axios Denver*, Oct 11, 2021.

8 Ley, D. "Artists, Aestheticisation and the Field of Gentrification." *Urban Studies*, vol. 40, no. 12, special issue: The Gentry in the City: Upward Neighbourhood Trajectories and Gentrification, November 2003, pp. 2527–2544.

9 DeVerteuil, G. "Evidence of Gentrification-Induced Displacement among Social Services in London and Los Angeles." *Urban Studies*, vol. 48, no. 8, June 2011, pp. 1563–1580.

10 Newell-Hanson, A. "Why New York's Young Artists Are Leaving the City and Moving Upstate." *i-D [Vice]*, June 12, 2016.

11 Feinstein, L. "'Beginning of a New Era': How Culture Went Virtual in the Face of Crisis." *The Guardian*, Apr. 8, 2020.

12 Barnett, V., Rosenblum, R., Salmen, B. *Art of Tomorrow: Hilla Rebay and Solomon R. Guggenheim*. Guggenheim Museum, 2005.

13 Davis, J. H. *The Guggenheims: An American Epic.* William Morrow, 1978, pp. 238–239.

14 Goldstein, M. *Landscape with Figures: A History of Art Dealing in the United States.* Oxford: Oxford University Press, 2000, pp. 218–219.

15 Dortch, V., ed. *Peggy Guggenheim and Her Friends.* Berenice Art Books, 1994, p. 11.

16 Arp, J., Mondrian, P., Guggenheim, P., Breton, A. *Art of This Century.* Art of This Century & Art Aid Corporation, 1942.

17 See: O'Connor, F., Quaintance, D., Sharp, J. *Peggy Guggenheim & Frederick Kiesler: The Story of Art of This Century.* Guggenheim Museum, 2005.

18 Goldstein, p. 230.

19 Mackrell, J. "Sex and art by the Grand Canal: How Peggy Guggenheim Took Venice." *The Guardian*, May 10, 2017.

Marketing

Chapter 10

PRINT MEDIA MARKETING

If marketing in the art business represents the actions taken to cultivate demand for artworks, then virtually everything a dealer does all working day (and beyond) should be considered some form of marketing. The most obvious form of marketing remains the traditional realm of print advertisements. Despite the general collapse of the magazine publishing industry and its advertising revenue-generating model, the art press has managed to remain resilient, primarily due to the sustained importance that the full-page ad holds relative to the art criticism system. It is always worth restating, however, that the elite art press covers only a very tiny percentage of all working artists (probably less than 0.1 percent). For all other artists and their gallerists, the press means general publications such as newspapers and arts and culture weeklies that cover their city.

The largest share of print marketing will always come from the museum and public collections sector. This is because the art business has two forms of consumption: experiential consumption, that is, purchasing a ticket to see a museum's collection, and ownership consumption, that is, purchasing ownership of an artwork. The experiential market will always be vastly larger than the ownership market, because there are so few people who have disposable income adequate to become collectors of even moderately priced pieces. Purchasing a museum exhibition ticket

DOI: 10.4324/9781003431756-11

falls into a price category comparable to a movie ticket or the entry cover to see a local pop-music act. In other words, museum entries are one more type of cultural leisure product in a vast marketplace for competing experiences. Therefore, the museum world advertises to a mass market because to make their business model successful, they must rely on thousands of visitors purchasing tickets, especially for their big, temporary shows. It will be these three- to four-month traveling temporary exhibitions which will account for a large part of their marketing expenditures because that is what will bring in the local visitors who are already quite familiar with the museum's permanent collection. In addition to purchasing large advertisements in the local press, a museum may engage in outdoor advertising in the form of streetlamp hangings and billboards in locations where they might be seen by potential visitors.

Advertising for the art market, that is, galleries who sell artworks as their primary source of revenue, is anything but a mass-market sector. In fact, when one considers how much a painting sells for in the kind of gallery that can afford to purchase print advertisements (generally above $20,000), then their clientele can truly be termed "The One Percent." The art press that these galleries concern themselves with are a handful of elite magazines: *Art Forum*, *Art in America*, and a few others. These journals' business model relies heavily on the sale of full-page advertisements which routinely cost at least $5,000–8,000 for publication in a single monthly edition.[1] In fact, these ads could hardly be considered advertising in its traditional understanding; that is, a retailer promoting goods to a potential consumer. It is rare for a collector to purchase an artwork based on a print advertisement they saw in a magazine. Rather, the role these ads play is similar to the role they play in fashion publications. The ads are, in fact, more than marketing. They represent a large part of the magazine's actual content, and to some degree readers view them as content. The full-page ads placed in the elite art press allow other players in the business to know which artists other galleries are showing and hopefully embed the name of the artist in the reader's memory.

Beyond the visual impression an advertisement makes, galleries also believe it improves the likelihood of being reviewed by the journal.[2] In many ways, making these ad buys act as a testament to a gallery's financial power, which should concurrently attest to its art-dealing prowess. Since status in the art world largely comes as a result of second- and third-party validation, the fact that a gallery would sink thousands of dollars to publicize an image of their artist's work would serve to communicate to readers that this artist must be important. The same group of galleries that can afford to advertise in *Art Forum* are almost exactly the same ones with stands at Art Basel.

The galleries that do not advertise in the elite art press may still take out ads in their local papers, arts and culture weeklies, or even tourism marketing materials such as maps or guides. A Chelsea-type gallery may promote their new exhibitions, and a regional gallery or antique shop might have a static ad that has a recurring run. Static ads tend to alert potential clientele of the business's offerings, with terms such as: local artists and artisans, plein air painters, Mid-century Modern, and vintage furniture, estate appraisals and consignment opportunities. Regional auction houses will also make frequent use of the local newspapers to promote their auctions and encourage people to contact them with estates needing to be valued and liquidated.

FACE-TO-FACE MARKETING

For those in the art market, print advertising can really seem like just the first step in creating demand for an artist because still much more needs to be done in order to actually sell artworks. The dealer must ultimately locate the most precious commodity from their perspective: collectors with enough disposable income that they can afford to buy the gallery's pieces. To truly excite buyers about a certain artwork they must receive a marketing spiel from the dealer themselves, ideally in a face-to-face setting with the artwork present. Despite the high level of erudition and training of the gallery staff, people buying an object that costs as much as an automobile (with none of its functionality) want to receive the sales pitch from the director of the enterprise. What the dealer says will be a combination of placing the artist in the wider stream of art history and also explaining why the individual work being considered for purchase stands out as an exceptional example from the oeuvre. Essentially, this is salesmanship but with the discourse being a blend of aesthetics, personal testimony to the work's power, factual listings of the artist's verifiable achievements, and speculation as to where this artwork will end up relative to the great canon of art.

Even long before concluding a sale, the dealer must be constantly talking up their artists, using every opportunity to highlight their latest successes. The really top dealers essentially seem to be permanently locked into their salesperson role, and even their leisure time, such as appearing at swank events, are essentially more opportunities to hunt for clients. Larry Gagosian reportedly would only take vacations in locations where he might meet new collectors.[3] This kind of marketing ideally should not seem like marketing to the person receiving it. It may sound like art world gossip but should in fact be a veiled attempt to cultivate curiosity and eventually a desire to possess works of a certain artist. Much of the activity at an art fair resembles this variety: talking to collectors, critics, other dealers, artists, students, and the general art-loving public.

In fact, dealers must spend a great deal of effort marketing to people who cannot afford to shop at their gallery. The process of creating demand for an artist remains a complicated, long-term strategy, perhaps as long as the lifetime of the dealer. Some reasons why they will talk up an artist to young people who do not appear to have the means to buy the work are because: 1. In New York (and other celebrity-laden cities), you cannot know if someone has money just based on how they are dressed; 2. these people could very possibly significantly raise their earning potential in ensuing years; and 3. they can serve as influencers and create "buzz" around this artist. It is also important to remember that the two forms of consumption in the art business—experience and ownership—influence each other significantly. A successful exhibition at a museum can create cultural capital for an artist, which will quickly convert into financial capital, that is, high prices for their works.

INTERNET AND SOCIAL MEDIA

Despite being a very new phenomena, the internet and social media have become indispensable platforms for a venue's marketing strategy. In its early stages (1990s-2005), internet marketing largely meant that most galleries would build a static website which would standardly have announcements about exhibition openings, an archive of former shows, a list of represented artists with sample images of their work, location, opening hours, and contact information. Internet advertising largely meant banner advertisements for large-scale museum exhibitions. Since 2005, websites themselves have improved dramatically, with website-builder services making sleek professional sites available to any gallery, and now virtually every professional artist has some kind of site unless they have gallery representation that stipulates that the gallery has exclusive right to market their work online. The content found on websites, however, has not changed much, but the ability to deliver different types of media, especially video, has become dramatically more reliable because of services such as YouTube.

Museums have continued to expand what they offer on their websites. Increasingly, the ethos of open access has taken hold among the museum community, and some of the world's leading institutions have begun posting high-quality digital images of their entire collection, which can be used for any purpose as long as proper credit and attribution is given.[4] In this way, and many others, museums have been looking to the internet to broaden their mission and reach, and be able to make their collection (and their knowledge about it) available to a much wider audience. Websites are also proving useful in streamlining many functions, from downloadable audio guides (instead of having to rent physical devices), pre-purchased tickets, but perhaps the most important improvement brought on by web presence comes in the field of fundraising. Nearly all museums have some kind of pull-down tab on their site called something like "Donate," where a host of membership and patronage options can be presented together with easy electronic payment methods. This infrastructure has vastly increased the success rate on pledges becoming donations by making automatic recurring payment systems effortless for even the computer unsavvy.

Social media, in its early years of Myspace and Facebook, was not seen as something important to the art world, at least for serious galleries. But it became a classic example of low culture influencing high culture, first with artists using Facebook to promote their latest works, and then with emerging galleries employing the platform to emphasize how fun their openings were. Eventually even the most elite galleries grudgingly acknowledged that they might need a social media presence. Twitter never emerged as a tool of any importance in the art world, but Instagram very much has. Its usefulness might be similar to a dealer talking to young people who cannot afford the art but might become influencers who talk up the artist.

As compared with a static website, social media poses problems on a number of fronts, which may require a dedicated staff person to look after. First of all, social media by definition requires interaction with other actors on a publicly visible domain. Comments are welcomed until they become unflattering to the gallery or its artists, and, keeping a social media presence positive and clear of trolling, in fact, may require a lot of work. On the other hand, if employed effectively, a well-managed social media strategy can create a feeling of dynamism that websites can never achieve. If openings are well documented in images and video, then this can serve as a sort of society page to flatter collectors, and a reference point for the artist to be able to prove that their exhibition took place and people came to see it. Likes and comments afterward can serve as additional validation and hopefully also generate buzz.

SYNERGY IN MARKETING

Multiple actors can join forces to collectively promote themselves with a strategy of synergy in marketing. The most common form of this strategy would be monthly art walks in gallery districts. In these cases, the galleries collectively organize and share marketing costs in the form of published advertisements promoting the event and listing participants, as well as published maps of the district. Furthermore, the art trade might reach out to the local restaurants and bars to encourage them to offer promotions and events in a further expansion of the synergetic circle. These businesses all willingly pool their resources because they understand the importance of being an identified arts district. Since districts acquire gravity as more venues appear in the area, these mutual promotion endeavors will help to attract more businesses to migrate from other areas. As cities come to recognize the importance of creative industries, the organizing of mutually beneficial arts events may increasingly be done by municipal administrators for cultural activities, or employees of the local nonprofit arts center, who see it as part of their profile to help network the wider art scene. In addition to monthly art walks, a municipality may organize an art fair of some sort. These events can range from a flea market atmosphere where artists and gallerists erect their own venue, to highly professional, juried, vetted events that are modelled on the major international fairs. Larger metropolises might even hold a biennale, which, although not as centralized as the Venice role model, will essentially encourage every art-exhibiting venue to participate and create a city-wide spectacle.

NON-TRADITIONAL MARKETING TECHNIQUES

In the arts, marketing can be achieved through many other means than simply purchasing advertisements, and, in fact, the accidental, unintended, and even ironic will become the most effective means to creating mass audiences. Among the many examples that could be cited to demonstrate these forces could, first of all, be the 1874 Impressionist exhibition, which was not named such but rather earned the name through a derisive review.[5] The group would ultimately embrace the name, and Impressionism would, by the twentieth century, become the most successful brand in cultural history. Scandal, if successfully navigated, has proven, time and time again, to be an essential ingredient in the modernist paradigm: a short list would include Édouard Manet's *Olympia*,[6] the Fauves at the 1905 Salon d'Automne, the 1913 Armory Show, Marcel Duchamp's *Fountain*,[7] and Damion Hirst's Shark [*The Physical Impossibility of Death in the Mind of Someone Living*].[8] Sometimes a temporary setback, like the demolition of Richard Serra's *Tilted Arc*[9] or Andres Serrano's *Piss Christ* controversy,[10] actually elevates an artist's fame and can reap dividends later. For example, Christie's auctioned an NFT of the *Piss Christ* in December 2022 as part of its Next Wave: the Miami Edit sale.[11] Originally, the Guerrilla Girls were protesting sexism and racism in the art world in the 1980s. The unintended consequence was that they in turn made themselves famous, and many of the members would take off their masks and work in their own name. The group's 2016 retrospective at the Whitney Museum showed how these outsiders had now moved to one of the primary canonizing vehicles and in that way could almost now be regarded as insiders.[12] The Jean Freeman Gallery placed advertisements in leading art journals for their exhibitions at 26 West 57th Street in the early 1970s, but in fact neither the gallery nor its artists actually existed. They were the conceptual work of Terry Fugate-Wilcox.[13]

The modernist paradigm holds that rejection by the majority and appreciation by only a small brave minority to be a central experience for an artist who drives the history of art forward. Therefore, these setbacks and humiliations only serve as validation for later generations. Sometimes artists have been known to embellish these details. Igor Stravinsky claimed that people threw tomatoes at the *Ballets Russes* opening of his *Rite of Spring*, and this anecdote has become a widely reported feature of the work's history. Contemporary press reports, however, do not to support the idea of a riot occurring at the ballet performance.[14] Nonetheless, this piece of apocrypha has become a central event in the cultural history of the avant-garde.

CASE STUDY: MANA CONTEMPORARY

With New York's overheated real estate market squeezing many artists and art-related operations out of the five boroughs completely, expansion over to the other side of the Hudson River in New Jersey was being seen as one of the best hopes to sustain the region's complex cultural economy. An art storage facility, however, would not be the first place one would expect to find this new hub across the river. The facility known as Mana Contemporary, in fact, does just that by leveraging a complex hybridity of for-profit and nonprofit-type activities to synergize disparate sectors of the art business. The concept originated with the moving magnate Moishe Mana and his business partner Eugene Lemay. They had been doing household moving and storage long before entering art handling and did so when they noticed the substandard conditions at which some of the world's leading artworks were being stored.

Mana is located in Jersey City, New Jersey, right across the Holland Tunnel from Manhattan, and a short walk from

---

a PATH train station. In other words, it is ideally suited to anchor the cross-Hudson migration of New York's art world. The facility is based at a former factory and warehouse and actually houses two entities: Mana Fine Arts and Mana Contemporary. Mana Fine Arts is the for-profit firm that provides high-end art handling, shipping, and storage facilities. Their massive storage facility provides museum-caliber, climate-controlled spaces with viewing rooms where pieces and can be visited and transactions discreetly arranged. They market their offerings as Art Collection Management, which provides a full range of services including digital tracking, framing, and installation.[15]

Although Mana Contemporary is a for-profit company, it serves as a base to a number of nonprofit arts entities, and its operation would more resemble the activity of an arts center or culture house. It provides a full-scale arts campus that features artists' studios, a resident dance company, and holds large-scale temporary exhibitions in its massive spaces that can hold the sort of installations that could never be staged in Manhattan. For example, the International Center for Photography opened a 15,000-sq. ft. space there in 2015. Mana Contemporary hold open studio events that feature new exhibitions and the resident artists open up their studio spaces to the public. The studios are all large and allow for reconfiguring to make them serve as impromptu galleries. These events allow the artists to connect directly to collectors and possibly even circumvent the gallery system completely, and to further this kind of 2-agent commerce, in 2019, they launched the Mana Decentralized sales platform.[16] In addition to performances of dance, theater, and music, children's programs are also provided in recognition that contemporary cultural consumption is increasingly a family activity, especially for the urban intelligentsia. Overall, Mana represents a highly sophisticated blending of art-related activities that cross-market each other through the mix of audiences brought over to their Jersey City campus, and now they have reproduced their model in Chicago and are also expanding into Miami.

MARKETING—TERMS

Press release—a document to be sent out to press outlets. A press release should be composed in a journalistic format as if it were the article you would wish to be written. This can be useful because smaller publications often print them in whole or in part largely as written.

Studio visit—an opportunity for a gallerist to bring collectors directly into the studio of an artist. Ideally, these events forge close bonds and help the collector to better understand the artist's work—which leads to sales.

Gallery event—usually occurs in the evening when the gallery would not otherwise be open. It is an attempt to draw in a wider public and create a social entertainment experience, centered around the gallery's exhibited artworks.

Finissage (Closing)—an adaptation of the French *vernissage* (opening) but occurs on the night before an exhibition is to be taken down. It provides one last opportunity to get collectors and visitors in to see the artwork.

Artist conversation—a type of gallery event that may occur at an opening, a finissage, or at any other point in an exhibition's run. The artist is normally interviewed by a curator or the gallerist and will also take questions from the audience.

Synergy—the capacity of different businesses and stakeholders to work in concert to create localities and events that draw the public.

Gallery district event—an evening or weekend event that draws the public to a gallery district, often happening on a recurring timetable, for example, monthly.

Trade journal—a publication that has a specific profile focused on an industry or sectors of an industry. In the art world, there are journals focused on auctions, antiques, contemporary art, and the secondary market.

Full-page ad—an advertisement that occupies one complete print page in a trade journal. In many art journals, these advertisements serve to inform collectors and other art world actors about a gallery's latest exhibition. Because they are expensive, they serve as a statement of prestige. Taking out such an advertisement might be perceived as enhancing a gallery's chances of being reviewed.

Hype—an intangible form of marketing that moves along word-of-mouth and newer social media platforms. A key feature of hype is that the promotion should seem authentic and voluntary, not purchased.

Notes

1   Salz, J. "2 Big Things Wrong with the Art World as Demonstrated by the September Issue of Artforum." *New York Magazine*, Sep. 2, 2014.
2   Boman, D. and Fusselman, A. "On Writing and Criticism: An Interview with Jerry Saltz." *Ohio Edit*, Sep. 8, 2016.
3   Segal, D. "Pulling Art Sales Out of Thinning Air." *New York Times*, Mar. 7, 2009.
4   McCarthy, D. and Wallace, A. "Open Access to Collections Is a No-Brainer – It's a Clear-Cut Extension of any Museum's Mission." *Apollo*, June 1, 2020.
5   Leroy, L. "L'Exposition des impressionnistes." *Le Charivari*, Apr. 25, 1874.
6   Takac, B. "The Controversy behind Edouard Manet's Olympia Masterpiece." *Wide Walls*, Oct. 28, 2018.
7   Mann, J. "How Duchamp's Urinal Changed Art Forever." *Artsy*, May 9, 2017.
8   Thompson, D. *The $12 Million Stuffed Shark: The Curious Economics of Contemporary Art*. Macmillan, 2010, pp. 1–3.
9   Gaie, S. Dilemmas of Public Art: (strolling around Richard Serra's Tilted Arc*). Cultura. International Journal of Philosophy of Culture and Axiology*, vol. VII, no. 2, 2010, pp. 21–37.
10 Chrisafis, A. "Attack on 'Blasphemous' Art Work Fires Debate on Role of Religion in France." *The Guradian*, Apr. 18, 2011.
11 Markowitz, D. "Is Nothing Sacred? Andres Serrano's Piss Christ Becomes NFT." *Miami New Times*. December 2, 2022.
12 Sayej, N. "The Guerrilla Girls: 'We Upend the Art World's Notion of What's Good and What's Right.'" *The Guardian*, Oct. 19, 2020.
13 See: Howard, C. *The Jean Freeman Gallery Does Not Exist*. MIT Press, 2018.
14 Hewett, I. "Did the Rite of Spring Really Spark a Riot?" *BBC*, May 29, 2013.
15 Kozinn, A. "From a Moving Van to an Arts Complex." *The New York Times*, May 16, 2013.
16 Duron, M. "Mana Contemporary Launches 'Decentralized' Platform for Artists to Sell Work Directly to Collectors." *ARTnews*, Apr. 26, 2019.

Art History, Art Criticism, and the Art Press

Chapter 11

ORIGINS OF ART HISTORY

A concept of art history remains an essential precondition
for a market in art to come into existence. Without a historic
perspective, there will not be much of a concept of art at all,
and the production of visual and material culture will largely be
regarded as constructing the trappings of religious and cultural
practice, as well as projecting political power. Only when a
society sees their production of visual arts through a historical
lens does that allow for the charting of evolution in style and
technique. The first recorded instances of cultures doing this
were Hellenistic Greece and Han Dynasty China.[1] An essential
feature of describing any historical process in art would the
fact that it inevitably engenders brevity and simplification, and
only certain masters can be mentioned. This binary distinction
between the mentioned and the unmentioned sets in motion art
history's primary contribution to the art market: the creation
of a canon. Collectors' obsession with possessing works by
this small group of canonical producers provides the driving
dynamic for the commerce in artworks.

The Roman historian Pliny the Elder told the story of the
Aphrodite of Cnidus in his *Natural History*, and this narrative

DOI: 10.4324/9781003431756-12

demonstrates the fundamental features of art history and how this phenomenon influences valuations in the art market. Originally, Praxiteles had sculpted two statues for the island of Cos for their temple to the goddess Aphrodite, one which was clothed and one nude.[2] For what was regarded as the first instance in Greek art, Praxiteles had represented the goddess nude. The scandalized people of Cos refused the nude statue and chose the clothed version, but the smaller, poorer city of Cnidus offered to buy the statue. Subsequently, this statue, this first rendering of a nude Aphrodite, would become one of the most famous artworks of the ancient world, as it would set the trend of always showing Aphrodite in the nude. Three hundred years after its creation, the King of Bithynia offered to pay off the entire municipal debt of Cnidus in exchange for the statue, but was refused. Within this short anecdote can be found all the essential characteristics of an art historical narrative: a canonical master risks opprobrium to push his medium forward toward a paradigm shift. To subsequent generations, this ground-breaking work takes on cult status that will be reflected in cultural and financial capital.

Giorgio Vasari might be rightly referred to as the father of art history because his *Lives of the Most Excellent Painters, Sculptors, and Architects* set forth a comprehensive historical retelling of the production and producers from over two centuries of what we now call the Italian Renaissance. His book was one of the first bestsellers of the early era of printing, and it also established a clearly defined canon of the most important masters from Giotto through to the High Renaissance triumvirate of greatest artists: Leonardo, Michelangelo, and Raphael.[3] The hierarchy of great, greater, and greatest masters that Vasari established still very much holds true today. Karel van Mander produced a similar study for Northern European painters.[4] From this point, the discipline progressed little until the nineteenth century, when historians Jules Michelet and Jacob Burckhardt[5] created the notion of a historical era called the Renaissance, [6] and the first modern art historian Heinrich Wölfflin (a disciple of Jacob Burckhardt) created the idea of two distinct periods: the Renaissance followed by the Baroque.[7] This concept of periodization will provide another essential intellectual construct of the field. A Viennese school of art history would emphasize formalist characteristics of artists, and Edwin Panofsky[8] and Aby Warburg[9] laid the foundations for studying art based on its iconology. From this point, art history would develop rapidly with tendencies that followed all the major intellectual trends of the twentieth century: Psychoanalysis, Marxism, Feminism, Structuralism, and Post-colonialism. Although there were virtually no designated art history academics at the beginning of the twentieth century, by the end of the century, it has become a widely taught subject at universities worldwide.

As a professional field, art historians largely exist in the university and public collection sector. They may also earn income from writing, curating, and possibly serving as a connoisseur on a subject in which they have particular expertise. The production of art historical knowledge can rarely be anyone's full-time profession. Academics must juggle their research with teaching and administrative commitments, and museum curators must look after their collections. When art historians do produce new knowledge, they generally either publish it as an article or book, or they use it to support a new exhibition. These discoveries may also be presented at an academic conference such as the CAA (formerly College Art Association), which is the main U.S. academic organization for art historians and studio art faculty, or the Association for Art History, which is the main organization for the field worldwide, as well as any of the numerous discipline and period-specific conferences. Other points of distribution of new knowledge would be peer-reviewed journals of art history, either general ones or publications with a more tightly focused profile like nineteenth-century American art or Central European architecture and design. In any other academic discipline, these revelations would be greeted with disinterest from the general public, and such would be the same for the art history field, except for the fact that it coexists with the art market, and frequently significant financial valuations can be dictated by the work of the humble art historian.

ORIGINS OF THE ART CRITIC

Art critics arrive much later in history than art historians. The delayed development of their role is reflected in the fact that secondary markets for art develop earlier than primary markets.

Art history more heavily influences the secondary market, and art criticism influences the primary or contemporary art market. The Englishman Jonathan Richardson founded the idea of art criticism with his *An Essay on the Whole Art of Criticism as it Relates to Painting* (1719),[10] which offered a highly objective methodology for evaluating the quality of a work. At the same time in France, the Paris Salon, when combined with the emerging medium of newspapers, was producing a new class of art critics. Denis Diderot (most famous for his *Encyclopédie*) cultivated the notion of passing judgment on the aesthetic merits of a work,[11] and this sets in motion a vast industry that would coexist with the yearly Salon. By the nineteenth century, the dozens of dailies of Paris would be publishing reviews of the Salon with boldly stated pronouncements intended to rile up their readership. These relationships would be replayed across the Western world in its emerging art markets, which patterned themselves on the French capital. Newspapers and their art critics would provide the same highly anticipated commentary to the exhibitions that a sports writer gave to an important athletic competition.

Many of the leading critics of the nineteenth century had roles as poets or writers in other genres. John Ruskin, one of the founders of the Arts and Crafts movement in Britain, was also famously the defendant in a libel suit brought by James Abbott McNeill Whistler because his critique of the artist's exhibition accused him of "flinging a pot of paint."[12] The writer Émile Zola was one of Manet's first defenders,[13] and Apollinaire was spokesperson for the Cubists in the early twentieth century.[14] Time and again critics would be the ones to coin the name of a movement that will define an era. Furthermore, many of these names (Impressionism, Fauves) were given in derision, but the branding was embraced by derided artists and would subsequently enter the art historical canon. Most movements had a critic who was considered their defender. Clement Greenberg, for example, served that purpose for the Abstract-Expressionist group.

CRITICISM AS ROUGH DRAFT OF ART HISTORY

Art criticism serves two purposes: one, it provides taste-making functions for the current-day market, and, two, it serves as a document by which latter-day art historians will be able to reconstruct the career of an artist and their period. If one reads well-researched art history publications on periods from the eighteenth century onward, one will notice that a large percentage of the footnotes will be referencing period art criticism. Furthermore, from the onset of modernism, some of the most useful reviews are ones written by reviewers who were quite hostile to the art on exhibition. In the process of describing the outrages of this gone-too-far exhibition, a derisive reviewer will often provide more precise and insightful details than the very sympathetic pro-modernism reviewer. Especially for very important exhibitions in the development of a period, a thorough art historian will track down every review of a show because each one might give away key clues about which works were shown and how. Even for very famous artists, it remains shocking how many of their early works cannot be located. Therefore, trying to ascertain which works were shown and what they might have looked like is an example of how an art historian employs reviews from the past.

Art criticism from a certain era also provides a snapshot of the milieu in which an artist worked. One can see what the canon would have looked like at that moment, from the names that are dropped and comparisons made. Furthermore, the artists on the scene working contemporaneously might be referenced, which gives a better sense of with whom an artist would have seen themselves in competition, and how did the direction of art appear to observers at that time. What also can become apparent from studying art criticism from a certain period is how often self-assured critics were wrong about which artists would be remembered by subsequent generations. The annals of art criticism are littered with current-day superstars who become forgotten soon after their deaths.

THE ART PRESS

The art press, as a term, relates primarily to journals devoted solely to writing on visual arts. In addition, there are a few generalist publications that also do actual art criticism: *The New York Times*, *The Wall Street Journal*, *Financial Times*, and *Time Out*, for example. Otherwise, the art press means visual arts-oriented publications that do reviews of exhibitions, and this sector has shrunk to a shockingly small number given the outsized influence they have on the upper echelons of the art world. Many other publications (newspapers, art and culture weeklies, magazines) write about art, but almost none of them publish proper reviews, where a writer visits the exhibition and writes an aesthetic evaluation on the merits of the art. In most cases, these other publications are printing press releases or other kinds of overtly positive pieces. The number of journals that do actual critical reviews of art could be best described as a handful, at most. Furthermore, nearly half of all the genuine reviews being published these days will be about museum exhibitions showing the works of artists who may already be dead. Museum reviews in fact count for most of the reviews being done by the abovementioned daily newspapers.

Once museum reviews are set aside, the actual amount of reviewing done of gallery exhibitions for living artists becomes shockingly small. The two current leading titles in the field of reviewing contemporary art exhibitions by living artists are *Art Forum* and *Art in America*. Less than one in a thousand working, professional artists can ever hope for a review in these journals. Gallerists often take out full-page advertisements in the journals under the hopes that this might earn a review for one of their exhibitions. Even within these journals, there exists a hierarchy of coverage. It is already an immense achievement to be reviewed at all, but many reviews can be only 200–300 words. Preceding these basic-level reviews will be more in-depth ones closer to 1,000 words. The ultimate achievement, however, would be to have a feature article written on the artist's entire œuvre, and usually with the hook of the story being around an important upcoming or current exhibition.

In addition to those two print journals, the online platform Hyperallergic also produces a large number of reviews, but overall the review sector has shrunk dramatically from the days when Paris might have had seen dozens of reviews published daily. Within different media—ceramics, metallurgy, textiles, and print-making—one can find specialist journals which also will publish a certain number of reviews a year. The same forces, however, that have pushed print publications into decline, have also produced a negative effect on art criticism, with reduced art coverage budgets for newspapers, and, in some cases, abandoning writing critically on art altogether.[15]

LEADING, CURRENT TASTEMAKERS

The leading art journals, *Art Forum* and *Art in America*, continue to exercise immense taste-making power, as do the few other genuinely reviewing publications. What is interesting to note, however, is how rare negative reviews occur. While in the nineteenth century, reviews might have provided an aesthetic blood sport for the readers of dailies covering the big salon exhibitions, today, that penchant for boldly and artfully dismissing a work is becoming a lost skill. One can search the art press now and rarely encounter a single outrightly negative review. The article might contain a few caveats or asides that are not positive, but the overall tone of these journals' reviews is nearly always positive. Much of the loss of more critical reviewing has to do with changes in the publishing industry, and editors' reluctance to waste precious print space on a negative review. Essentially what was a trinary system in the nineteenth century, that is, a journal could publish a positive review, a negative review, or simply nothing at all, has now been reduced to a binary system: a journal publishes a positive review, or it publishes nothing at all.

Star curators themselves have begun to fill the taste-making role that the current-day anemic art press has left under-fulfilled. Hans-Ulrich Obrist provides a good example of a curator who can anoint a new art world star through involving them in one of his projects or featuring them on his social media platforms. The major art market events such as Art Basel, Frieze, and Armory Show also provide a chance for fame to be earned in situ rather than in a publication. Above all, the leading non-commercial events, Documenta and the Venice Biennale, are the platforms on which the future canon receives its rough draft. The curators making those selections, then, are more often leading the taste-making process, and the art press is simply reacting to their choices.

Despite the emergence of some online publications willing to publish reviews in greater concentration, such as Hyperallergic, the vast, vast majority of working artists and their galleries, especially those outside New York, will never be reviewed in the current system. Increasingly, however, the frustration of the under-served and under-covered of the art world continues to drive innovation and adaptive use of electronic platforms that may provide a more equitable and egalitarian measure of taste-making function. Among the many promises made by the Non-Fungible Token phenomenon was that its data-driven market-oriented blockchain would better reflect the public's approval.[16]

CASE STUDY: CLEMENT GREENBERG

Most art movements have their defining critic, and for Abstract-Expressionism it was Clement Greenberg. He did not actually coin the term. That honor goes to Robert Coates who fused the general term "abstract" with a genre name mostly associated with the Central European art centers of Munich, Berlin, and Vienna. Greenberg's role was to defend abstraction as the core achievement of avant-garde. He also would serve as Jackson Pollock's first critical proponent.

Few essays in art criticism have achieved the legendary status as his "Avant-Garde and Kitsch." The article, which appeared in the Marxist journal *Partisan Review* in 1939, established a dichotomy between academic art, which is kitsch, and he gave the realist Russian painter Ilya Repin as an example, and the avant-garde, using a Picasso as a counter-example. Most likely Greenberg actually knew little of Repin's work since his Wanderers [*Peredvizsniki*] movement was formed as challenge to the Imperial Academy. Nonetheless, Greenberg used Repin as an embodiment of kitch, whereas he saw the future of art as being about itself and not directly reflecting lived experience. In other words, the future was abstract, non-objective art. He employed a German word, "kitch," which had been previously used to describe the lowbrow, popular-appeal paintings sold in Munich in the late nineteenth century and expanded it to essentially include all representational art:

> Kitsch, using for raw material the debased and academicized simulacra of genuine culture, welcomes and cultivates this insensibility. It is the source of its

---

profits. Kitsch is mechanical and operates by formulas. Kitsch is vicarious experience and faked sensations. Kitsch changes according to style but remains always the same. Kitsch is the epitome of all that is spurious in the life of our times. Kitsch pretends to demand nothing of its customers except their money—not even their time.[17]

In this way, Greenberg lays an end goal for modernism as the drive toward total non-objectivity, which he saw as the most advanced form of art. He was particularly enthusiastic about Jackson Pollock because of his capacity to be an "all-over" artist.

Greenberg would coin a number of terms still widely used today in art circles, for example: Post-Painterly Abstraction, which he coined for a 1964 exhibition to apply to hard-edged abstract artists such as Ellsworth Kelly and Frank Stella.

Greenberg would then become bewildered by the arrival of pop art two decades later, which was, in essence, a celebration of kitsch. He saw abstraction as the culmination of modernism, and we still continue to view this mid-century abstract expressionist period as the last hurrah of the great mega-genre of modernism. What Greenberg failed to understand was that there would be something that would come after, which we call post-modernism.

ART HISTORY, ART CRITICISM, AND THE ART PRESS—TERMS

Taste maker—a person whose aesthetic judgments can drive large audiences toward a cultural product. In the past, these would have been, for example, the critics who wrote for metropolitan daily newspapers and important journals. In many other fields, taste making has become aggregated through the opinions of large numbers of amateur critics: Amazon, Rotten Tomatoes, and Yelp.

Art Forum—the leading high-brow art journal. Being written up in this publication means an artist has arrived.

Art in America—the leading journal on American art and reviews a large number of exhibitions.

Burlington Magazine—the leading journal on connoisseurship issues, where new discoveries are announced.

Review—a format of journalism critiquing a given exhibition. The artist, the artworks, and the curatorship may all be discussed. The review should provide an overall judgment on the aesthetic value of the art on display.

Feature article—a format of journalism devoted to an artist or an art movement. Articles are longer than reviews and discuss more than a single exhibition and would rather focus on an artist's career and the evolution of a movement.

Payola—the paying for airplay, or in the art world—paying for coverage in a certain journal. This phenomenon, though illegal in broadcasting if not declared, often exists in informal arrangements in most cultural industries.

Genre—a multi-faceted term that can either be used to denote something like periods in both fine and applied arts. It can also mean paintings that focus on particular subjects, like landscapes, seascapes, or interiors.

Movement—an art historical term, similar to genre, but with an emphasis on the stylistic direction being set by a heroic avant-garde. It tends to have more application with genres from the nineteenth and twentieth centuries, such as the Impressionist movement, Cubist movement, and Surrealist movement.

Art history—a selective chronicle of the workings and production of artists in the past. Art criticism can often serve as some of the crucial original primary source material.

Notes

1 Alsop, J. *The Rare Art Traditions: The History of Art Collecting and Its Linked Phenomena Wherever These Have Appeared.* Harper & Row, 1987, pp. 28–31.

2 Pliny the Elder. Ed. John Bostock, M. D., F.R.S. H. T. Riley, Esq., B.A. Book XXXVI: The Natural History of Stones, Chapter 4. (4.)—The First Artists Who Excelled in the Sculpture of Marble, and the Various Periods at Which They Flourished. *The Natural History.* London: Taylor and Francis, 1855.

3 Vasari, G. *Lives of the Most Eminent Painters Sculptors & Architects.* Trans. G. D. C. De Vere. Macmillan and Co. & the Medici Society. 1912–1914.

4 See: Melion, W. S. *Shaping the Netherlandish Canon: Karel Van Mander's Schilder-Boeck.* University of Chicago Press, 1991.

5 Burckhardt, J. *The Civilisation of the Period of the Renaissance in Italy* [Die Kultur der Renaissance in Italien]. Trans. S. G. C. Middlemore. C. K. Paul & Co., 1878 (1860).

6 Tollebeek, J. "'Renaissance' and 'fossilization': Michelet, Burckhardt, and Huizinga." *Renaissance Studies*, vol. 15, no. 3, 2001, pp. 354–366.

7 Wölfflin, H. *Renaissance und Barock: eine Untersuchung über Wesen und Entstehung des Barockstils in Italien.* Theodor Ackermann, 1888.

8 Moxey, K. "Panofsky's Concept of "Iconology" and the Problem of Interpretation in the History of Art." *New Literary History*, vol. 17, no. 2, Interpretation and Culture, Winter, 1986, pp. 265–274.

9 Warburg, A. *Bilderatlas Mnemosyne – The Original.* Ed. H. D. K. der Welt and The Warburg Institute; R. Ohrt, A. Heil. Hatje Cantz, 2020.

10 Richardson, J. *Two Discourses: I. an Essay on the Whole Art of Criticism, as it Relates to Painting. Ii. An Argument in Behalf of the Science of a Connoisseur: Certainty, Pleasure, and Advantage of It.* HardPress Publishing, 2020.

11 Topazio, V. W, and May, G. Diderot's Art Criticism: A Controversy. *The French Review*, Oct., 1963, Vol. 37, No. 1, Part 1 (Oct., 1963), pp. 3-21.

12 Jones, J. "Artists v Critics, Round One." *The Guardian*, June 26, 2003.

13 Hemmings, F. W. J. "Zola, Manet, and the Impressionists (1875–80)." *PMLA*, vol. 73, no. 4, 1958, pp. 407–417.

14 Apollinaire, G. *Les peintres cubistes, méditations esthétiques.* Paris: Eugène Figuière Éditeurs, 1913.

15 Gerard, J. "New York Times & Wall Street Journal Prepare to Slash Entertainment Coverage and Staff as Print Ads Vanish." *Deadline Hollywood*, Nov. 9, 2016.

16 For the most recent patterns in the relatively short development of NFTs, see: Vasan, K., Janosov, M. & Barabási, AL. "Quantifying NFT-Driven Networks in Crypto Art." *Scientific Reports*, vol. 12, no. 2769, 2022.

17 Greenberg, "Avant-Garde and Kitsch." *Partisan Review*, vol. 6, no. 5, 1939, pp. 34–49.

Cultural Heritage Compliance

Chapter 12

EARLY FORMS OF CULTURAL HERITAGE PROTECTION

Art objects and their predecessors, treasure, represent some of the earliest types of trade goods. One of the continuing dynamics of the art market is that objects inexorably move toward the markets that value them most in monetary terms. That this flow should happen for treasure is unsurprising. Wealthier societies will also be able to pay the highest prices for the things they consider luxuries. Art objects may also travel great distances to other markets and new owners, but only once an appreciation for the artists of the source region has developed in the target market. A highly developed art history is required for such a trade to even exist, and, furthermore, this art history would have had to have spread to another region which had become wealthier than the areas where those objects were originally produced. The classic example for such trade would be that of the Romans' taste for Greek art in the late Republican and Imperial periods. Works that had been created in the Hellenic and Hellenistic regions of the Eastern Mediterranean were removed from their in-situ historical setting and relocated to the Imperial capital of Rome,[1] or later to the Eastern capital of Constantinople.[2] Those same patterns would be repeated in the sixteenth century when the Italian peninsula sank into endless war and economic stagnation as a result of new routes to the East. By the end of the century, Giorgio Vasari's *Lives of the Most*

DOI: 10.4324/9781003431756-13

Excellent Painters, Sculptors, and Architects had provided a canon to the period we would now call the Italian Renaissance,[3] and that hierarchy could become widely known to Northern European monarchs who began to compete with one another to collect leading works from that period.[4]

The combination of those forces, superior purchasing power north of the Alps and an art historical hierarchy to guide collectors, would set in motion one of the great transferences of cultural heritage. Over the next three centuries, Italy would be emptied out of its art treasures, going first to powerful individuals (monarchs, nobility, and later new industrial elites) and then usually being transferred to a public collection in France, Germany, Russia, Austria, Britain, and the United States. It is, therefore, not surprising that Italy also developed some of the earliest cultural heritage protection laws. The first law resembling something like cultural heritage was the Papal Bull *Cum almam nostram urbem* issued in 1462 by Pope Pius II in the form of protecting the archaeological remnants from Roman culture within the Papal States.[5] In some sense, these instructions were intended to give the State (in that case, the Vatican) priority in claiming archaeological relics on its territories.[6] That idea would be adapted in the nineteenth century to the belief that the State was acting on behalf of "The Nation," that is, the people of the country, but the role of the State acting as enforcer and ultimately title-holder to objects dug up from the past would essentially remain the same. In 1474, the Pope Sixtus IV promulgated *Cum provida sanctorum patrum decreta* to ensure that religious artworks were not removed from the churches where the piece had been in-situ.[7] It would be of little help in 1527, when the devastating *Sacco di Roma* [Sack of Rome] would destroy or remove so many of those protected works. Many Italian city states would institute various legislative attempts to stem the flow of artworks northward and westward, but they proved to be relatively ineffective to prevent such powerful economic forces.

The Pope's librarian in the 1760s, Johann Joachim Winckelmann, would begin the process of systematic, scientific archaeology when he also became Clement XIII's Prefect of Antiquities and began to impose order on the excavations at Pompeii and Herculaneum. It would be more than another century, however, before the field really evolved beyond the profession of treasure hunter. Archaeology and the extraction of art objects, or more correctly termed "cultural property," as a practice, generally spread apace with European colonization of the non-Western world. These objects would fill museums in London, Berlin, Madrid, and Paris, as the archaeological expeditions were usually launched and financed from these imperial capitals, as well as increasingly from the United States. The process of decolonization, first politically and subsequently culturally, would lead to landmark treaties in the 1970s that continue to shape the cultural heritage compliance landscape today. The other significant force leading to the current structures would be the traumatic experience of the Second World War in both the outright destruction of cultural treasures, and the widespread looting of artworks, the legacy of which is still being dealt with today.

The United Nations Educational, Scientific, and Cultural Organization (UNESCO) was one of a number of United Nations entities formed in 1945, immediately following the conclusion of the Second World War. Among the many profiles the organization has in promoting education, science, and freedom of the press, UNESCO is widely known as the chief advocate for cultural heritage protection in the world. It should be remembered, however, that its role is primarily that of advocate. Like many other UN agencies, such as Interpol or the UNHCR, it has no enforcement authority or mechanisms. For the protection of important locations for immovable cultural property, that is, archaeological sites as well built and natural environments, UNESCO has developed a designation of World Heritage Site. Most countries have at least one, and these entities are almost always its leading tourist attraction, especially given that the site is widely advertised to be a UNESCO World Heritage Site. Working with UNESCO, member countries began to exert much more control over cultural heritage compliance in the second half of the twentieth century through the development of administrative structures that attempted to better supervise, control, and restrict the export of art and cultural property.

THE MAJOR TREATIES OF THE 1970s

The most important treaty from the perspective of cultural heritage compliance would be the landmark UNESCO 1970 *Convention on the Means of Prohibiting and Preventing the Illicit Import, Export and Transfer of Ownership of Cultural Property.* Article 1 of the Convention provides the following list of the types of Cultural Property it is meant to cover:

a. rare collections and specimens of fauna, flora, minerals and anatomy, and objects of paleontological interest;
b. property relating to history, including the history of science and technology and military and social history, to the life of national leaders, thinkers, scientists, and artist and to events of national importance;
c. products of archeological excavations (including regular and clandestine) or of archeological discoveries;
d. elements of artistic or historical monuments or archeological sites which have been dismembered;
e. antiquities more than 100 years old, such as inscriptions, coins, and engraved seals;
f. objects of ethnological interest;
g. property of artistic interest, such as:
   i. pictures, paintings, and drawings produced entirely by hand on any support and in any material (excluding industrial designs and manufactured articles decorated by hand);
   ii. original works of statuary art and sculpture in any material;
   iii. original engravings, prints, and lithographs;
   iv. original artistic assemblages and montages in any material;
h. rare manuscripts and incunabula, old books, documents, and publications of special interest (historical, artistic, scientific, literary, etc.) singly or in collections;
i. postage, revenue, and similar stamps, singly or in collections;

j. archives, including sound, photographic and cinematographic archives;

k. articles of furniture more than 100 years old and old musical instruments.[8]

What is important to remember about this treaty and others subsequently arranged by UNESCO, is that they are umbrella treaties. They provide a framework for signatory nations to then conclude bilateral treaties on particular areas of cooperation. It is then these bilateral treaties that provide the enforcement framework whereby actions can be taken to bring about cultural heritage compliance. The United States has concluded treaties with many countries that are significant sources of illegally excavated archaeological relics.

CURRENT ENFORCEMENT PRACTICES

The primary enforcement of cultural heritage compliance occurs when objects cross borders, and most of the bad actors usually get caught during the process of attempting to transport illicit goods internationally. Most countries have export and import controls built into their customs process to ensure that shippers are compliant with cultural heritage regulations. European Union countries usually follow a common practice of developing an inventory of certain objects that are prohibited for export and those that may receive export permits. Generally, countries proscribe an era before which everything is declared "ancient" and thereby default protected, and non-exportable. Many European nations place this dateline around the era of the Late Middle Ages or Renaissance. Though it should also be stressed that the nations of the European Union do not have remotely consistent or compatible designations, and those also shift quite frequently over time. For works that might be potentially exportable, there remains no clear standard as to how decisions are made. The European Union has, however, developed initiatives to combat illicit trafficking in recent years that signal a more unified approach to the problem.[9] Some national frameworks only consider works above a certain value and will only restrict its export if enough funds can be found to purchase the work "for the Nation." This would be the case in the U.K.[10] Other countries may restrict the export of an item but not offer to compensate the owner. In these cases, the current owner is allowed to continue to own the piece but must keep it at a registered location within the country's borders. Enforcing these rulings, however, has become increasingly difficult with the Schengen area's open borders within the European Union. The United States does not have much of an export customs regime as regards cultural heritage, and largely no controls on the flow of art objects, except for those from Native American-Pre-Columbian cultures, which are protected, but the actual application of those restrictions can be difficult given the ease with which goods can be exported out of the United States.

Each country will have its own process for applying for a cultural heritage export permit. Very often, different types of objects will need to be viewed by curators from a relevant state museum to determine that the piece to be exported is not of such a quality that it must be "protected," that is, not allowed to be exported. If the object is determined to be allowed to leave the country, then it is documented carefully with photographs and given an official export permit that will be included in the customs filing when the shipment is cleared to leave the country. That same export permit very often may be required by the importing country's customs process. Furthermore, the leading auction houses have started to be much more rigorous in only accepting works that have been legally exported (with valid export permits) from their country of origin, but nonetheless looted works continue to find their way into sales.[11] The same can be said of museums: they will only acquire pieces that have full legal export documentation from their country of origin. Museums are especially leery about accessioning antiquities that do not have a provenance, proven through some kind of record or receipt that precedes the ratification date of the bilateral agreement governing the trade in such type of cultural property. That said, carefully crafted false provenances can still deceive vetting processes, as was the case with a Metropolitan Museum acquisition of a looted Egyptian coffin in 2017.[12]

DOMESTIC ENFORCEMENT ENTITIES

The entities that enforce cultural heritage compliance domestically will most often originate in a Ministry of Culture and may even be called something like a cultural heritage

Cultural Heritage Compliance

office, overseeing the upkeep of the nation's immovable cultural property (archaeological sites and historic buildings) and also supervising the export of movable cultural property. The United States, again, would be different in this case, in that the country has no corresponding entity filling this kind of role, with states more often looking after immovable cultural property, and no agency particularly tasked with regulating movable cultural property. In all countries, the key enforcement opportunity occurs at customs when goods cross international borders. Therefore, it is the Customs and Border Protection in the United States and similar entities in most countries, where goods can be inspected to see if they conform to their descriptions in their customs declarations. Many times, smugglers try to ship goods under one description, perhaps as newly made touristic copies (therefore not requiring an export permit), when in fact they are authentic historic pieces. The Hobby Lobby art supply store chain and their owners who were acquiring the collection for their Museum of the Bible became embroiled in such a scandal when they were caught using this practice when knowingly importing Mesopotamian cuneiform tablets.[13] It would, in fact, be the first of many missteps by the museum and its founders, which would result in the restitution of looted objects.[14] Customs officers may often find themselves, as a result, in the position of acting as connoisseurs in order to determine whether regulations are being flouted.

In most countries, the key players in a successful cultural heritage compliance regime would be the national cultural administration, museums, state-employed archaeologists, customs authority, and, of course, law enforcement. All of these entities need to be working cooperatively and be immune to corruption. In many countries, the latter may seem a vain hope, but nonetheless, recent years have seen significant improvement in enforcement and cooperation both at national and international levels. Some of the improvement can be attributed to better technological tools, such as easily searchable databases, which can help to make illicit cultural property difficult to sell. Part of the explanation, however, has to be the reverberations of complex scandals, particularly the Medici Conspiracy [see the Case Study below], which caused considerable embarrassment to some of the world's leading museums, among them the Metropolitan and the Getty.[15]

INTERNATIONAL COORDINATION ENTITIES

On the international level, enforcement entities, per se, do not really exist. Organizations do operate, however, that pursue a coordinating role for national agencies which will have law-enforcement capabilities. First of all, UNESCO executes many functions in this capacity: through its World Heritage designations and through providing umbrella convention frameworks for bilateral treaties. Furthermore, the organization can stage high-profile press conferences about looting crises related to conflicts, such as those in Syria and Iraq.[16] They also provide a host of model legislation and best-practices regulatory sample documents. Most importantly, the organization can provide a great deal of positive marketing for a nation's cultural heritage, which will help drive its tourism industry. Demonstrating the positive economic outcomes from a robust cultural heritage protection regime may be the strongest message that UNESCO can send to emerging economies. Finally, the Director-General of the UNESCO serves as a leading spokesperson worldwide for the concept of cultural heritage and the importance of its preservation.

In addition to UNESCO, Interpol, the international police organization, connects national law-enforcement bodies when one is requesting action in another nation's jurisdiction. In fact, this is the formal protocol for national police forces to connect one another: through Interpol. For example, when Giacomo Medici's warehouse was raided in the Freeport of Geneva, it was the result of an unprecedented cooperation between Italy's Carabinieri Art Squad providing leads to Swiss police with assistance from Interpol.[17] In addition, certain international organizations, such as the International Foundation for Art Research and the Art Loss Register and others relating to theft or looting, may maintain databases that can be searched by auction houses and appraisers in order to determine if a work has issues with its provenance or title.

RESTITUTION

One of the most dramatic developments in the field of cultural heritage activity has been the process known as "restitution." This term applies when a piece of cultural property has been deemed to have improper title (ownership) and is then legally returned to a prior owner or heir of that owner. This process can take many different forms. For example, 142 looted antiquities from Italy, including ones that were discovered in the collection of Michael Steinhardt, were returned to a newly created Museum of Rescued Art established in Rome to display recovered objects.[18] In a most stunning development in a process that seemed to have long been at an impasse, the U.K. government has entered into talks with the Greek government concerning the possibility of returning the sculptures of the Parthenon frieze known as the Elgin Marbles, currently held in the British Museum.[19] A different example would be the return of bodily remains of native aboriginals from museums of natural history where they had been displayed like scientific specimens and given reburials according to traditional customs by their ancestral peoples. This process, however, remains only at its beginnings with tens of thousands of remains still needing reburial.[20]

The most high-profile activity in this sector would be the restitution of artworks owned by Jewish collectors prior to the Nazi era, whose heirs had begun demanding the return of these works in the 1990s. Prior owners or their heirs had often been demanding the return of these works as soon as the cessation of hostilities in 1945, but the separation of Europe between East and West, as well as the lack of means for sharing information (internet, email, and digital photographs), meant that critical momentum really only began to occur with the 1998 Washington Conference on Holocaust-Era Assets, which was co-hosted by the U.S. Department of State and the U.S. Holocaust Memorial Museum. The conference provided a framework, called the Washington Principles on Nazi-Confiscated Art, that ultimately led to the most dramatic case of recent years: the 2006 return of five works by Gustav Klimt, which had been in the Austrian Gallery Belvedere, to Maria Altmann. The story would be subject of the book *The Lady in Gold* and film *Woman in Gold* which were translations of the German name given to the first of two portraits painted of Viennese socialite Adele Bloch-Bauer (and Altmann's aunt). This most famous of the group of pictures, *Portrait of*

Adele Bloch-Bauer I, would briefly become the world's most expensive artwork when Ronald Lauder reputedly purchased it for $135 million.[21] It currently serves as an almost Mona Lisa-category attraction for his small museum devoted to Central European modernism in New York. The painting that this work had hung next to in the Belvedere, Klimt's *The Kiss,* has subsequently become one of the world's absolutely most recognizable works, and the *Portrait of Adele Bloch-Bauer, I* in Lauder's Neue Galerie on Fifth Avenue, just opposite the Metropolitan, cannot be close behind. Klimt, for certain, has benefited enormously from the notoriety. In the 1950s, he was an outlier in art history and has now become a central beloved figure of modernism.

At the current moment, the discovery of the Gurlitt collection in Munich in 2012 will keep provenance researchers busy for some time to come sorting out which pre-War owners may have title to some of these works that had been considered lost.[22] The heirs of the leading dealer of Dutch Old Masters, Jacques Goudstikker, continue to seek out the inventory illegally seized from him (purchased at a fraction of its value) by Hitler's henchman, Hermann Göring, in Amsterdam in 1940.[23] The greatest volume of Second-World-War-era loot remaining to be restituted, however, lies in Russia, much of it taken from Hungarian bank vaults. Ironically, though, most of the artworks that the Soviets appropriated as reparations (Hungary had been part of the Nazi-led invasion of the Soviet Union), in fact came from Jewish collectors, themselves victims of fascism.[24] The Russian government shows no current inclination toward restituting these works or those nationalized from the collections of pre-1917 Revolution collectors such as Sergei Shchukin or Mikhail and Ivan Morozov. Wherever restituted works emerge from public collections, especially some of the world's most prestigious museums (as was the case with the *Portrait of Adele Bloch-Bauer I*), and have made it to market, they often set record prices. This phenomenon essentially proves one of the basic foundations of art valuation: art is valued by the number of eyes that have seen it.

CASE STUDY: GIACOMO MEDICI

If one performs an internet image search for "Giacomo Medici," one is likely to immediately find two pictures, both featuring a distinguished Italian gentleman standing in front of museum cases, one with a Greek vase, and the other with a sculpture of winged griffins. The Greek vase is referred to as the *Euphronios Krater* and is considered the masterpiece of the early classical Athenian vase painter, Euphronios, who is one the first artists in history to have signed his own work. It was purchased in 1972 for $1 million by the Metropolitan Museum of Art.[25] The griffin sculpture was in the collection of the J. Paul Getty Museum, which purchased the piece in 1985 for over $6 million.[26] Both of them were looted, that is, illegally excavated, and came through the hands of Giacomo Medici. We know this because when the Swiss and Italian police raided his warehouse in the Free Port of Geneva, they found Polaroids of the griffins in their original condition with the dirt still on them. The police also found the pictures of Medici brazenly posing next to these works now installed at these world-famous museums.

The book by Peter Watson and Cecilia Todeschini, *The Medici Conspiracy: The Illicit Journey of Looted Antiquities: From Italy's Tomb Raiders to the World's Greatest Museums*, recounts the case with the drama of a fast-paced thriller. The strands of the story converged as a result of some apparently unrelated events in Italy that produced a fascinating hand-drawn organogram (a diagram of organization) showing a pyramid with the *tombaroli* (tomb raiders in Italian) at the bottom. These gangs would find out about archaeological sites that had been located by construction crews and loot them in the middle of the night, extracting saleable items, but otherwise destroying the archaeological context and losing the provenience (the exact location of its excavation). These pieces would be sold up through a network of organized criminals, until they reached the main dealers, the most important of which was Giacomo Medici. He, however, did not sell directly to the leading museums of the world. Rather he used what is called in criminal networks a "fence," a respectable business that can then pass illicit goods in to the legitimate economy. That role was filled by the Paris-based American dealer, Robert Hecht, whose gallery would actually sell to the museums. He features at the very top of the organogram.[27]

Medici probably assumed he was quite safe with his warehouse in the Free Port of Geneva, given the Swiss authorities' traditional hands-off approach to the banking sector. The preponderance of evidence, however, provided by Italy's Carabinieri Art Squad forced the Swiss into an unprecedented raid in 1995 that yielded a shocking trail of polaroids documenting the process from looting, smuggling, sale, and eventual installation in a public collection. The case proceeded quite slowly, with Marion True, the Getty's curator for antiquities being charged in Italy and Greece in 2005. She would eventually have charges dropped because of statute of limitations, and the fact that the Getty restituted a large number of artworks. Medici received a ten-year sentence, but charges were dropped against Robert Hecht in 2012, also because of statute of limitations.[28] Some interesting patterns became apparent in the investigations. Illicit archaeology often comes with fake export permits from Lebanon, which by the 1990s was an utterly failed state, and hence it would be very difficult to validate the authenticity of those documents. The other observation is that the shadiest dealings, still to this day, seem to continue to go through the Free Port of Geneva [see Chapter 14 Case Study: Free ports].

CULTURAL HERITAGE COMPLIANCE—TERMS

Plunder—items of value, including artworks and cultural heritage objects, removed during a state of war. Plunder is often justified under claims of reparations, but those claims are rarely accepted by the international community in the case of artworks or cultural heritage objects.

Looting—the act of removing items of value, including artworks and cultural heritage objects, during a state of anarchy or otherwise in the absence of the state power.

Illegal archaeology—the excavation of archaeological sites without proper cultural heritage permission from the authorized state entity for the purpose of quickly extracting items of saleable value, often to the detriment of the site context and the archaeological provenience, which will be lost.

Smuggling—the act of moving goods across customs borders without the proper customs clearance and permits or without paying appropriate duties and taxes.

Restitution—a process of returning plundered artworks and cultural material objects to their rightful title-holders. In recent years, important trends have been the return of Second-World-War-era plunder, colonial era looting of the Global South, and the repatriation of human remains to indigenous peoples.

Export permit—is a document used for customs procedures which ensures that a transported artwork or cultural heritage object has been authorized to leave the country by the appropriate cultural heritage authorities.

National treasure—an artwork or cultural heritage object that a county's cultural heritage authorities have determined to be of particular importance, and therefore that object cannot leave the country. It might be able to be owned by a private collector but must be kept at a registered location within the country.

Provenience—a word of similar origin to provenance, but with a very precise meaning in the archaeological world. It means the exact location of an object's discovery and excavation. This is information is lost if the object is looted from the site.

Pre-1970 Provenance—essential for the sale and acquisition of archaeological objects, especially by museums. Such a provenance would show that the object had been privately owned prior to the 1970-era UNESCO treaties that banned the sale of illegal archaeological material from signatory countries.

Endangered species—animal and plant species that are designated by government and supra-governmental agencies as "endangered." Artworks and cultural heritage objects that contain material from these species must have special CITES permits in order to travel internationally.

Notes

1   Pliny the Elder. Ed. John Bostock, M.D., F.R.S. H.T. Riley, Esq., B.A. "Book XXXV: An Account of Paintings and Colours, Chapter 8 — At What Period Foreign Paintings Were First Introduced at Rome." In *The Natural History*. London: Taylor and Francis, 1855.

2   Dawkins, R. M. "Ancient Statues in Mediaeval Constantinople." *Folklore*, vol. 35, no. 3, Sep. 30, 1924, pp. 209–248.

3   Vasari, G. *Lives of the Most Eminent Painters Sculptors & Architects*. Trans. G. D. C. De Vere. Macmillan and Co. & the Medici Society, 1912–1914.

4   Whitaker, L. and Clayton, M. "'Art Becomes a Piece of State': Italian Paintings and Drawings and the Royal Collection." *The Art of Italy in the Royal Collection: Renaissance & Baroque*. Royal Collection Publications, 2007, pp. 11–41.

5   Karmon, D. *The Ruin of the Eternal City: Antiquity and Preservation in Renaissance Rome*. Oxford University Press, 2011, p. 69.

6   Rubinstein, R. "Pius II and Roman Ruins." *Renaissance Studies*, vol. 2, no. 2, 1988, pp. 197–203.

7   Blondin, J. E. "Power Made Visible: Pope Sixtus IV as 'Urbis Restaurator' in Quattrocento Rome." *The Catholic Historical Review*, vol. 91, no. 1, 2005, pp. 1–25.

8   UNESCO *Convention on the Means of Prohibiting and Preventing the Illicit Import, Export and Transfer of Ownership of Cultural Property*. Paris: UNESCO, 1970.

9   European Commission. *Communication from the Commission to the European Parliament, the Council, the European Economic and Social Committee and the Committee of the Regions on the EU Action Plan against Trafficking in Cultural Goods*. Dec. 13, 2022.

10 Jacobs, H. and Villa, A. "U.K.'s National Portrait Gallery Is Raising Funds to Purchase $58 M. Joshua Reynolds Portrait." *Artnews*, Aug. 31, 2022.

11 Alberge, D. "Antiquities for Auction Could Be Illicitly Sourced, Archaeologist Claims. *The Guardian*, Dec. 7, 2021.

12 Stapley-Brown, V. and Kenney, N. "Met Hands over an Egyptian Coffin That It Says Was Looted." *The Art Newspaper*, Feb. 15, 2019.

13 Moss, C. and Baden, J. "Feds Investigate Hobby Lobby Boss for Illicit Artifacts." *The Daily Beast*, July 12, 2017.

14 Goldstein, C. "The Museum of the Bible Must Once Again Return Artifacts, This Time an Entire Warehouse of 5,000 Egyptian Objects." *Artnet*, Jan. 29, 2021.

15 Watson, P. and Todeschini, C. *The Medici Conspiracy: The Illicit Journey of Looted Antiquities: From Italy's Tomb Raiders to the World's Greatest Museums*. New York: Public Affairs, 2006.

16 Charbonneau, L. "UNESCO Sounds Alarm about Illicit Syria Archeology Digs." *Reuters*, Dec. 14, 2013.

17 Ibid.

18 Dafoe, T. "New York City Has Returned $14 Million in Stolen Antiquities to Italy, Including Dozens Recovered from a Hedge-Fund Billionaire." *Artnet*, July 21, 2022.

19 Addley, E. and Smith, H. "British Museum in Talks with Greece over Return of Parthenon Marbles." *The Guardian*, Jan. 4, 2023.

20 Small, Z. "Push to Return 116,000 Native American Remains Is Long-Awaited." *The New York Times*, Aug. 6, 2021.

21 Vogel, C. "Lauder pays $135 million, a Record, for a Klimt Portrait." *The New York Times*, June 19, 2006.

22 Perlson, H. "Hildebrand Gurlitt Built a Brilliant Trove of Art Under the Nazis. Two New Exhibitions Show His Taste, and His Duplicity." *ARTnews*, Nov. 3, 2017.

23 Riding, A. "Dutch to Return Art Seized by Nazis." *The New York Times*, Feb. 7, 2006.

24 Mravik, L. *The "Sacco Di Budapest" and Depredation of Hungary, 1938–1949: Works of Art Missing from Hungary as a Result of the Second World War*. Hungarian National Gallery, 1998.

25 Nagin, C. "First the 'Hotpot'- Now, the Uncup." *New York Magazine*, Dec. 7, 1981, pp. 61–74.

26 Povoledo, E. "Photographs of Getty Griffins Shown at Antiquities Trial in Rome." *The New York Times*, June 1, 2006.

27 Watson, P. and Todeschini, C. *The Medici Conspiracy: The Illicit Journey of Looted Antiquities: From Italy's Tomb Raiders to the World's Greatest Museums*. New York: Public Affairs, 2006.

28 Weber, B. "Robert Hecht, Antiquities Dealer, Dies at 92." *The New York Times*, Feb. 9, 2012.

Taxation

Chapter 13

CORPORATE INCOME TAX

Most countries have some kind of tax assessed on the profits earned by for-profit corporations. This rate can vary widely from 10 to 30 percent, and in some offshore tax-haven locations, it can be virtually negligible. In the United States, it will be assessed on both the federal and state levels, though some states have very low state-level corporate income tax as an incentive to base the corporation there. Most corporations, both big and small, usually become quite good at minimizing their taxable profits. Art enterprises of the small or micro size will usually immediately reinvest any sizable profits from a successful venture much the same way real estate speculators will quickly invest in a new property. Furthermore, the sad reality is that many art-related businesses really do not operate profitability. Therefore, it is not surprising that most pay very little in the way of corporate income tax.

Smart dealers who earn profits usually do reinvest it promptly in new inventory, updated infrastructure, or better real estate, and all of these activities might legitimately reduce the tax burden. Dealers with an inclination toward tax avoidance will often try to keep some transactions in cash or with reduced invoices. Those working on a global scale may use international transactions, free ports, and offshore companies to reduce their

DOI: 10.4324/9781003431756-14

declared profits. It must also be noted that given the small size of most art businesses, and the fact that they are usually sole-proprietorship enterprises, there often exists little difference between corporate profits and the owner's personal income. Furthermore, the gallery may incur a number of expenses which are in reality some form of compensation to the gallery owner: for example, renting an office that is in fact a home, international business travel that is in fact leisure, and lunch meetings that are entirely social. Sole-proprietor dealers tend to live through their business, and for all intents and purposes, the personal and professional are one and the same, and in the United States, they should file through their personal income tax.[1] For this reason, they tend to make corporate expenditures that are in fact for their own personal benefit. These are deducted as expenses, and so minimize the overall corporate income tax burden. The case of Mary Boone's conviction for tax fraud should, however, serve as a caution against excessive deductions for personal expenses.[2]

PAYROLL TAXES

The group of taxes that a corporation must pay when it disperses payroll to its employees can be called "payroll taxes." They include, first of all, the withholding contribution made by both the employer and the employee on the employee's personal income tax. Most countries (again except for certain tax havens such as Monaco) have some form of personal income tax, but rates vary significantly from country to country, and even from year to year, as different governments can radically alter tax rates for ideological and political purposes. In the United States, income tax will be assessed on both the federal and the state levels. As with corporate income taxes, states frequently compete with one another to attract residents by offering lower state income tax levels. In addition to personal income tax, payroll taxes frequently also can contain contributions for unemployment insurance, disability insurance, and some sort of a state pension (in the United States, this is Social Security). In most Western countries, a national healthcare premium is also paid, giving the employee access to the state healthcare system. The exception here is the United States, where healthcare insurance is generally provided by an employer, and smaller firms, like galleries, frequently do not provide it at all. The passage of the Affordable Care Act in 2010 required individuals to secure their own healthcare, either from their employer or purchasing it from an exchange (for which they receive some compensation from their employer and in a federal tax deduction), but the individual mandate was then repealed in 2017.[3]

Dealers will often try to avoid the high payroll taxes that come with full-time employees by relying on unpaid interns or informally paid part-time workers. If the gallery is located anywhere near a university with an art history department, then it can expect a reliable stream of interns looking for experience in the art business. These kinds of casual workers can be excellent for sitting the gallery while the proprietor is out attending to other tasks. The problem with this solution is that artworks do not sell themselves, and uninvested staff are unlikely to sell them either. Only highly motivated, very knowledgeable employees will ever be able to sell works for any significant money, and they will expect the benefits commensurate with full-time employment if they have such capabilities. Employees may, however, receive a large portion of their salary in the form of commissions based on a percentage of sales they conclude, which is perfectly consistent with compensation structures for salespeople in other high-price sectors, like automobiles. In many countries with high payroll taxes, a culture of subcontracting exists, where almost everyone working in a small enterprise like a gallery will themselves be a separate sole-proprietorship business and will bill their employer each month for their services. This gallery staff person's own business officially employs themself and pays themself a small salary, on which they pay their payroll taxes and earn their access to welfare state services.

The proprietor of a gallery might also keep themselves on the payroll, usually at a modest salary, on which their payroll taxes are paid. This will allow the proprietor to also receive the benefits of the welfare state, especially the healthcare. As mentioned before, though, a large part of their actual income will come from in-kind compensation through the gallery: rental of residence, use of the company car, payment of travel, and/ or deduction for meals. In this way, a dealer's real income is frequently larger than actually reported. From a wealth or taxation perspective, separating the dealer from their gallery becomes almost impossible.

SALES TAX OR VALUE-ADDED TAX (VAT)

Most countries have some sort of sales tax (as it is called in the United States) or VAT (as it is called in most European countries). These taxes are assessed on goods and services at the point of sale by the business conducting the transaction. In the United States, sales tax is determined at both the state and municipal levels. Some states have no sales tax as an incentive to shop there, and municipalities throughout America compete with one another to attract merchants by offering lower local sales tax. New York City, where a vast majority of high-value transactions are conducted, has a sales tax of 8.875 percent, which is composed of a 4.5 percent assessment to New York City, 4.0 percent for New York State, and 0.375 percent for the Metropolitan Commuter Transportation District. On million-dollar sales, this kind of a tax begins to add up to significant amounts money in itself. Much like a sovereign nation, states will not assess the sales tax if the item is shipped to another state. The shipment and placement of the artwork outside of New York State, however, must be well documented with shipping bills. The lack of such documentation (because the works were never shipped outside of Manhattan) was what would bring about the downfall of the tycoon Dennis Kozlowski [see this chapter's Case Study: Dennis Kozlowski].

European countries usually only assess VAT at the national level, but the countries of the European Union do very much compete with one another in their VAT rates, with variance between 16 and 27 percent. Most countries offer some kind of VAT refund if goods are taken or shipped out of the country, but they often only extend it to newly manufactured goods, and not to used items.

When sales tax or VAT on an art sale represents a significant enough amount to justify shipping an artwork through a low-tax jurisdiction, then dealers and collectors will frequently pursue this strategy. For example, many of the high-value sales that are agreed upon in oral contract at the major secondary market art fair, The European Fine Art Fair (TEFAF) in Maastricht, Netherlands, could be in fact legally concluded in the Free Port of Geneva after the fair is finished. The dealer and the collector can in this way avoid Dutch VAT. A free port has opened in the state of Delaware that can also be used by collectors to avoid the sales tax in New York City.[4]

When artworks travel into a new jurisdiction, depending on the type of entry document used, VAT may be immediately assessed by the importing country. The huge variance in VAT rates across Europe frequently leads dealers and auction houses to vocally complain that they are being placed at a disadvantage relative to their competitors in neighboring countries or relative to U.S.-based businesses. In 2014, Germany raised the VAT on art transactions to 19 percent, but only on the profits realized after the resale, provoking large-scale protest from the dealers and auction houses.[5] The Paris art market had recently begun to reassert its former status following London's Brexit-driven decline, but their pre-eminence was also not in a small way promoted by their 5.5 percent import VAT tax on imported artworks, and only a 20 percent VAT rate applying to profits made from secondary sales. In 2022, the European Commission quietly adopted a directive to set the import sales tax of goods, including works of art, at 20 percent for all EU members.[6] French dealers have been vocally complaining that this will cause the loss of their competitive advantage and drive their business back to non-EU jurisdictions.

TAXES AND FEES SPECIFIC TO THE ART BUSINESS

In Germany, there exists a tax on art transactions for the *Künstlersozialkasse*, which funds welfare-state services for cultural producers. Taxes like this can be found in other European countries which try to establish a professional designation for freelance working artists together with the benefits associated with full-time employment, but which also requires that in some way or other those costs are paid into state coffers.[7]

In the late nineteenth century in France, outrage grew over the fact that the painting *Angelus* by Jean François Millet was resold at auction for over 550,000 francs while his widow and children lived in poverty.[8] This would ultimately lead to the creation in France in 1920 of something called *droit de suite* meaning "right to follow," and in English it is usually referred to as Artist's Resale

Right (ARR). Other countries would follow this pattern, and now approximately 70 nations have some kind of resale royalty system for artists. In 2001, the European Union issued a directive to harmonize the legislation across the common market.[9] The implementation of ARR in the United Kingdom in 2006 provoked widespread protest from their gallery and auction sector, claiming that it would put it at a competitive disadvantage relative to the United States.[10] Since the program went into effect, many galleries continue to flout the voluntary-based contribution system, but nonetheless the two U.K. artist registry organizations still manage to collect and redistribute millions of pounds every year.

The United States has never implemented any sort of ARR system on a national level, and because one does not exist, American artists are not eligible for royalties collected on their behalf in countries with an active ARR structure. California, however, had a 35-year experiment with its own system called the California Resale Royalty Act (CRRA), which mandated that a 5 percent royalty must be paid on any resale over $1,000 if the artist is a U.S. citizen or a resident of California and is living and or has been deceased for less than 20 years (in which case royalties go to heirs). It applied to any artwork sold in California or if the seller lived in California. The legislation emerged from a well-documented incident in 1973, when Robert Rauschenberg confronted the collector Robert Scull who had purchased a work from the artist for $900 in 1958 and had just resold it at auction for $85,000.[11] The event led Rauschenberg to team up with Jim Dine to promote the passage of CRRA in the California legislature. It would stand from 1976 to 2012, but with the onset of the internet and the auction world having become so much more fluid, the royalties became more and more difficult to collect. Finally, in 2011, Chuck Close and a few other high-value artists and estates brought suit against Christie's, Sotheby's, and eBay. The strategy backfired, however, when in 2012, a federal judge argued that the law violated the Interstate Commerce Clause and was therefore unconstitutional. As a result of the ruling, CRRA has been essentially struck down and is no longer in effect.[12] Attention has now turned toward the passage of a national ARR structure, but for the moment, heavy lobbying by Christie's, Sotheby's, and eBay has ensured than the current proposed legislation has little support in Congress.

THE ART MARKET AS VEHICLE OF TAX EVASION
AND MONEY LAUNDERING

If gallerists have a bad reputation for being tax evaders, then the art market itself has an even worse reputation as a vehicle for tax evasion and money laundering by all sorts of bad actors. Artworks became tools of these practices because they possessed unique characteristics that allowed them to hold and transfer wealth in an opaque manner. To begin with, art can be purchased in a number of different ways that can suit the collector's ulterior motive: with cash, with barter, with financial securities, with wire transfers from offshore banks, or through a shell company. Dealers and auction houses do not ask many questions of either buyers or sellers, just as long as they get paid. Once in the possession of the collector, ownership can be transferred to any number of other entities: spouses, children, offshore companies, and trusts. In this way, large amounts of wealth can be stashed in plain sight. At a later date, the collector can redeem the monetary wealth of the artwork and again direct it to where they wish to move their wealth next. Many less-than-savvy collectors hoping to use their collection this way may be sadly disappointed when they attempt to redeem their artworks and find that they did not hold their redeemable value nearly so well as planned. Nonetheless, the art market continues to be polluted with many actors buying and selling with no aesthetic intention whatsoever. The only purpose is to exploit art's peculiar ability to hold and transfer wealth opaquely. The two primary and related activities for using art in this way are tax evasion and money laundering. Since artworks can be used to conceal wealth, it is not surprising they would be used to mask the true income earned by a collector and thereby reduce their tax burden.

A closely related activity, money laundering, involves moving illegal money (earned by illicit activity) through a process that "launders" it and makes it available for use in the legal economy. High-value artworks are particularly useful, in that they can be paid for with illicit money, then the artwork can be resold at a later date, with the proceeds being received as legitimate income for the collector. There are too many incidences in recent years to cite, but perhaps the most spectacular involved the Helly Nahmad Gallery, located on the ground floor of the Carlyle Hotel on Madison Avenue. For years, the gallery and the Nahmad family were considered geniuses in the buying and selling of Impressionist and Modernist masterpieces at auction. In 2013, Helly Nahmad was indicted for holding illegal high-stake poker games involving celebrities and people connected with Russian organized crime in his residence on the 51st floor of Trump Tower on Fifth Avenue.[13] He would eventually cop a plea and serve only about five months in prison. The Nahmads' supposedly savvy purchases at auctions now appear to be not so much brilliant market maneuvers as they were strategic attempts to launder their proceeds from acting as the House for unlicensed gambling. Their example goes a long way toward explaining the disruptive effect of tax evasion and money laundering on the art market. Legitimate actors who play by the rules must compete against nefarious actors who appear to be playing by the same rules but are in fact propped up by the constant infusion of cash to be laundered. These firms have an inherent unfair advantage over the fair players and are not a minor cause for the fact that so many small galleries fail when they try to play by the rules. The problem has become so grave, especially now that art transactions have become a vehicle for evading sanctions on Russian oligarchs, that the US Senate held an investigation on the problem in 2020.[14]

CASE STUDY: DENNIS KOZLOWSKI

In 2001, Dennis Kozlowski was one of the highest-paid CEOs in the United States, running Tyco, a conglomerate employing over 200,000 people across the globe and $40 billion in revenue. He was not someone who would be expected to be particularly concerned about the sales tax on his art purchases, but he was, and it cost him everything. Around that time, he and his wife began collecting paintings for the Fifth Avenue apartment Tyco had purchased for their CEO. They first purchased three paintings in London and had those works trucked to Tyco's headquarters in New Hampshire in order to get a signature from an employee that they were delivered. Then the paintings were taken to Kozlowski's Fifth Avenue apartment.

The point of the maneuver was to avoid New York sales tax, which at that time was 8.25 percent, and would have been assessed on the London purchases, but since they had, in theory, been delivered to Tyco's New Hampshire office, no tax was paid. Since the scheme worked once, they pursued it again. When the Kozlowski began collecting art they purchased in New York, they did the same, except they became sloppier. When they bought a Monet for over $3 million, Kozlowski signed a document asserting that the painting would be sent to New Hampshire, but it never was. In another case, rather than send five paintings on a round trip, Kozlowski had his art advisor ship empty boxes up to the Tyco corporate office.[15]

It took New York State a very short time to figure out what was happening. Within six months, a grand jury issued a multi-count indictment for conspiracy to commit tax fraud.[16] A few days before the indictment was issued, Kozlowski had to resign as the CEO of Tyco. The investigation into his art collecting and tax evasion had brought to the attention of his Board of Directors that some of the works had been acquired as Tyco's assets. Furthermore, the Board became aware of excessive spending and compensation by Kozlowski and his CFO Mark Swartz. Both would eventually be convicted of multiple counts of grand larceny and conspiracy, and Kozlowski would serve eight years in prison.[17]

Kozlowski had been earning over $100 million a year in annual compensation, but because he was too cheap to pay around $1 million in New York sales tax, he lost his career, his entire fortune, and would spend eight years in prison.

TAXATION—TERMS

Corporate income tax—tax paid to federal, and state authorities on the profits earned by a corporation.

Payroll tax—a set of taxes paid by an employer relative to their employees' salaries. These can include personal income tax, state pension (in the United States—Social Security), and national healthcare insurance (or private insurance in the United States).

Sales tax—a consumption tax in the United States paid on the value of a good or service at the point of sale. Each state sets its own sales taxes and determines on what items and services it is assessed. State sales tax ranges from 2.9 to 7.25 percent, but some states have no sales tax. Local authorities can assess their own sales tax as well on top of that rate.

Value-added tax (VAT)—a consumption tax on sales and services in European countries that functions similarly to U.S. sales tax but tends to be higher: 15–27 percent, and is assessed on the value added to goods and services.

Cash—means ready currency in a bank account that can be transferred immediately. It can also mean currency in its paper form. In the lower levels of the art and antiques business, cash (paper money) is preferred because it allows sales and corporate income tax to be avoided.

Offshore—a corporation that is founded and pays taxes in a jurisdiction other than the one in which it does its business. Offshore corporations often are used to hold assets and minimize taxes on those assets.

Money laundering—a process giving money earned through illicit means the appearance of having been acquired through legitimate legal means.

Tax avoidance—the concerted attempt to avoid payment of taxes to a jurisdiction's tax regime.

Write-off— is an expense that can reduce the amount of taxable income.

Shell company—a corporation that owns other corporations. Its primary purpose is the ownership of other corporations which actually produce goods and services, and possibly also to conceal the true ownership of the enterprise

Notes

1   irs.gov *Sole Proprietorships*. 2018, www.irs.gov/businesses/small-businesses-self-employed/sole-proprietorships.
2   Carrigan, M. "Dealer Mary Boone Pleads Guilty to $1.6m in Tax Fraud." *The Art Newspaper*, Sep. 5, 2018.

3   Scott, D. and Kliff, S. "Republicans Have Finally Repealed a Crucial Piece of Obamacare." *Vox*, Dec. 20, 2017.

4   Bowley, G. "Art Collectors Find Safe Harbor in Delaware's Tax Laws." *The New York Times*, Oct. 25, 2015.

5   Forbes, A. "German Dealers Forced to Make Up Tax Law." *Artnet*, July 21, 2014.

6   Jhala, K. "'Fatal for the French Art Market': Dealers Decry New EU Sales Tax that Could Wipe Out Paris's Booming Commercial Scene." *The Art Newspaper*, Feb. 24, 2023.

7   Parker, K. "An Introduction to the Künstlersozialkasse (KSK)." *Redtape Translation*, Aug. 2, 2017.

8   Fratello, B. "France Embraces Millet: The Intertwined Fates of 'The Gleaners' and 'The Angelus.'" *The Art Bulletin*, vol. 85, no. 4, Dec. 2003, pp. 685–701.

9   "Directive 2001/84/EC of the European Parliament and of the Council of 27 September 2001 on the Resale Right for the Benefit of the Author of an Original Work of Art." *Official Journal L*, vol. 272, Oct, 13, 2001, pp. 0032–0036.

10 Davies, C. and Addley, E. "Art Dealers Claim Droit de Suite Levy Threatens London's Art Trade." *The Guardian*, Dec. 22, 2011.

11 Sussman, A. L. "How the Scull Sale Changed the Art Market." *Artsy*, Apr. 26, 2017.

12 Kinsella, E. "Ending a Seven-Year Dispute, a US Court Rules That Artists Aren't Entitled to Royalties for Artworks Resold at Auction." *ARTnews*, July 9, 2018.

13 Luhn, A. "Billionaire US Art Dealer Hillel "Helly" Nahmad Admits to Running $100M Global Gambling Ring." *The Independent*, Nov. 14, 2013.

14 Egan, M. "The Art World Has a Money Laundering Problem." *CNN*, July 29, 2020.

15 Berenson, A. and Vogel, C. "Ex-Tyco Chief Is Indicted in Tax Case." *The New York Times*, June 5, 2002.

16 Morgenthau, R. *Supreme Court of the State of New York—Grand Jury Indictment for Dennis Kozlowski*. ind. no. 3418/02.

17 Freifeld, K. "Ex-Tyco CEO Kozlowski Says He Stole Out of Pure Greed." *Reuters*, Dec. 5, 2013.

Customs

Chapter 14

CUSTOMS, TARIFFS, AND INTERNATIONAL TRADE ORGANIZATIONS

Governments have always tried to control their international trade. Relatively free-flowing trade has been a very recent phenomenon, and not the norm. Early forms of customs, such as it was practiced along the Silk Road across Asia and the Incense Trade along the Indian Ocean and Red Sea, could have more resembled a form of tribute demanded by a ruler in exchange for safe passage or safe harbor. Merchants usually would leave a percentage of their trade goods, which would enrich the sovereign and serve as a reminder to the merchant as to how precarious their position was. In the Early Modern Period (c. 1500–1800 CE), a political-economic theory prevailed, referred to as Mercantilism, which sought to maximize exports and minimize imports through erecting tariff barriers against competing nations' products. In the nineteenth century, however, the philosophy of Free Trade emerged and promised that all nations would benefit from finding their competitive advantage and otherwise enjoying low-cost foodstuffs and goods. The supporters of Free Trade have been locked in a battle with Protectionists (who would raise tariff barriers) from that point to the present. Despite a prevailing trend toward free-trade agreements and a general lowering of trade barriers in the late twentieth and early twenty-first centuries, recent developments

DOI: 10.4324/9781003431756-15

have seen a significant resurgence in protectionist tendencies in the West.

In recognition of the role that protectionism had played in exacerbating the Great Depression and the ensuing Second World War, the postwar period saw international organizations work toward creating more harmonious conditions for world trade. The General Agreement on Tariffs and Trade (GATT) came into effect in 1948 and immediately led to concessions on lowering thousands of tariff barriers among the initial signatory countries. In 1995, after decades of negotiating rounds, GATT became the World Trade Organization, a fully fledged standing body dedicated to promoting free and fair trade across the globe. The International Chamber of Commerce (ICC) has been in existence since 1919 and has bureaus devoted to fighting counterfeiting and copyright infringement as well as forms of fraud, all of which can touch on the art world. The World Customs Organization (WCO) came into existence in 1952 and successfully concluded numerous treaties that have greatly simplified the process of customs clearance worldwide. Of particular importance is the Harmonized System (HS) Convention which came into force in 1988, creating HS codes with a six-digit tariff nomenclature globally recognized among the over 200 participating countries. The ATA Convention of 1961 provided a universally recognized document, the ATA Carnet, for the Temporary Admission of Goods, which is jointly administered by the ICC and the WCO.

On a regional level, the customs landscape has changed dramatically in the last 30 years.[1] The North American Free Trade Agreement (NAFTA) created a free trade zone between Mexico, the United States, and Canada in 1994, allowing goods to move largely unhindered between their shared borders. The most important development, though, from the perspective of the art business, is certainly the completion of the European Union's customs and borderless entity known as the Schengen Area (named for the town where the original agreement was signed). Between 1995 and 2007, the area was expanded until it included nearly all of the EU except for the U.K. (who subsequently left the EU altogether) and Ireland (who opted out), and Romania, Bulgaria, Cyprus. Croatia only just joined the group on January 1,

2023.[2] Between neighboring Schengen countries, there essentially exists no fixed customs or border control, though weigh stations and other spot-checking roadside controls may exist for commercial traffic. This means that nations within the European Union often have a difficult time enforcing their cultural heritage regulations within the Schengen Area when there are no border crossings or customs officers to enforce them.[3]

EXPORT REGIMES

In order for any good to be exported out of its country of origin, it must be legally customs cleared. To do anything less than observe correct procedures would be smuggling, and the same would be true on the import side. Goods officially leave the country when a government official called a customs officer has stamped a customs declaration and then sealed the shipment in some way. For example, traditionally a customs officer would close a shipping container, put wire through the doors, and bind them with a piece of lead, which would then be squeezed between a hand press with government seals that would impress into the lead. This lead seal, referred to as a plomb (French for the element lead), would only be broken by a customs officer (or with their authorization) in the importing country. Any sign of tampering with the plomb is considered a serious offence and a sign of possible theft, smuggling, or some other type of illicit activity. Having that seal would also allow the freight to travel through transit countries without having to be opened up for intermediary customs authorities to inspect the goods. The fact that the freight remains sealed assures them that it would not be offloaded at some point inside their country without going through the proper import procedures. The 1975 Convention on International Transport of Goods Under Cover of TIR Carnets (TIR Convention) established a generalized method of creating TIR Carnets.[4] These documents allow goods to travel under seal through transit countries. It had been widely used throughout Europe before the implementation of Schengen. Now, the system is largely still active in the parts of Eastern Europe that are not in the European Union. Carnet is a French term for a binder or group of papers. It is frequently used to describe documents that function as a sort of "merchandise passport" that allow goods to travel without being immediately subject to customs duties. One type is the TIR Carnet used for the transport of goods through transit countries. The most important to the art world, though, would certainly be the ATA Carnet, which is used to temporarily import an object into a country without paying taxes, customs duties, or posting a customs bond. This ATA Carnet system is a central feature of the global museum exhibition industry, and the explosive growth of blockbuster shows would be inconceivable without it. Problems occur, though, when an artwork has been sent to a country on an ATA Carnet for an ostensibly non-commercial exhibition, but the owner then decides to sell the work to a buyer in this new jurisdiction. Changing the import status of something that arrived on an ATA Carnet can range from impossible to extremely difficult. In such cases, it can frequently be easier and less expensive to send it back to the home country as planned and re-export it with paperwork appropriate to a permanent import into the buyer's country.

In the United States, the Department of Homeland Security, through its Transportation Security Administration (TSA) and the Customs and Border Protection, has significantly increased its security procedures for air cargo shipments as a result of changes brought about by the attacks on September 11, 2001. The requirement that 100 percent of all air cargo be screened means that TSA authorizes facilities around the country, through the Certified Cargo Screening Program, to act in its place and verify that a shipment is properly screened. The facility with such a status must then maintain a rigorous chain of custody over the freight from the point it is screened and closed, to when it is delivered to the airport and turned over to the airline. Most major art shippers or their subcontractors have access to a Certified Cargo Screening facility, and that can greatly speed the export clearance process.

Most countries do not assess any export duties on the export of artworks or cultural property. The primary point of interest in export customs from an art business perspective is that it is at this point that cultural heritage export permits are presented and stamped. The United States does not have a system of export permits as regards cultural heritage but, like most countries, it does restrict the transportation of materials derived from an endangered species. If an antique involves ivory or feathers from tropical birds, then one can expect a very demanding approval process, and in the case of elephant ivory, the international community is moving increasingly toward prohibiting its transport in nearly all circumstances.[5] Most countries in the European Union have some system of restrictions on the export of cultural property, for which a shipper must obtain an export permit to validate that the cultural heritage office of the Ministry of Culture, and its relevant museums with expertise in this sort of object, do not consider it to be a protected national treasure and can be allowed to leave the country. A customs officer will view this document and its attached photographs and verify that the actual freight and the customs declaration all conform to one another. It is at this point that most smugglers of cultural property get caught, most often because they are disguising or describing their freight as something else. It is for this reason that a country's customs authority needs to remain uncorrupted and not susceptible to bribery. Otherwise, it will have a difficult time enforcing its cultural heritage protection policies.

In addition to customs officers who work for the government, there are customs brokers who work directly with the client and help determine the best customs-clearance method for their needs. Most art shippers have an in-house customs broker, and that service is usually part of the larger invoice. If budgets are tight, however, many galleries will try to do as much of the shipping process themselves, including packing, crating, and preparing customs documents. The problem here is that a layperson may need advice on how to fill out the declaration, and generally the only people with that expertise are customs brokers, who are not keen to give out advice without being paid. One standard feature of the customs declaration is giving the freight its six-digit HS code. There are only a few which tend to be important to the art world. For example, 9701.10 is the code for "Paintings, e.g. oil paintings, watercolors and pastels, and drawings executed entirely by hand." The code for original sculpture and statuary is 9703.00. A very important category for which art shippers frequently categorize many different items is 9706.00: "Antiques of an age exceeding one hundred years." Another important piece of information that must be declared is the country of origin, which can be something quite different from the country from which an object was exported. Because treaties for both tariffs and cultural heritage protection are concluded bilaterally, knowing the country of origin will be necessary at the import side to determine rates and procedures.

IMPORT REGIMES

Importing artworks can be some of the most challenging experiences a gallerist ever faces. It is at this moment that many first-time shippers learn what they face in the way of import duties and taxes, and they often discover an unpleasant surprise. At the point of entry, customs duties may be assessed according to the tariffs set out in the bilateral trade agreement with the freight's country of origin (not necessarily the same as the country it was shipped from). Customs duties should not be confused with normal taxes, which may also be assessed. Frequently, laypeople shippers learn that art and antiques can be imported duty-free, which is true. But they fail to understand that in addition to duties, consumptions taxes like sales tax and Value-Added Tax (VAT) are frequently assessed on the declared value. For this reason, art is frequently shipped at a declared value that is a fraction of its actual value, with the purpose being to minimize those taxes. One unpleasant reality faced by people sending an artwork for auction in a foreign country is that if it does not sell, and they try to repatriate it, they will likely face a new VAT charge upon reimport. This is because the original export was permanent, and so the national customs authority treats it as a new work entering the country. This would not be the case of ATA Carnet goods, which would return without any duty or tax assessment.

In the last decades, the French share of the global art market had grown, especially recently, as Paris has begun to reassert its former continental dominance, in no small way as a result of London's Brexit-driven decline. That revival was also aided by their 5.5 percent import VAT tax on imported artworks, with only a 20 percent VAT rate applying to profits made from secondary sales. In 2022, the European Commission, however, adopted a directive to harmonize the import sales tax of goods, including works of art, at 20 percent for all EU members.[6] French dealers worry that this will result in a loss of their competitive advantage and push the market to non-EU jurisdictions.

For a major museum to consider a piece for acquisition or for a major auction house to accept something for a sale, they will now expect that the piece has been correctly exported and imported with all proper documentation. This is particularly important to verify in terms of cultural heritage compliance, which has been an area where leading museums and auction houses have sometimes been less than always scrupulous until recent years. In the same way that exporters try to evade controls, importers also try to receive goods categorized as something distinctly different than what they are. The founders of the Museum of the Bible (also owners of the Hobby Lobby chain of craft stores) were found to have been importing cuneiform tablets, and had attempted to import them as samples of "hand-crafted clay tiles"[7] and thereby avoid the near total prohibition in the trade and transport of archaeological material from this region, so as not to give funding to the Islamic State (ISIS) which was the primary source of looted objects.

CASE STUDY: FREE PORTS

Free ports occupy an odd role, in that they are simultaneously within a country's borders, but in some way seen as not actually in the country. The original purpose of free ports was, in the field of maritime commerce, to provide a warehouse where goods could be temporarily kept while they have their customs duties assessed and paid, and then the goods could be taken out of the warehouse into the importing country's economy. Most freight harbors have areas where their shipping containers are stacked until customs clearance, and international airports usually have areas referred to as bonded warehouses. These facilities are meant, however, to be short-term storage locations, not least because airport bonded warehouse fees can be prohibitively expensive.

The location of a free port in Geneva, Switzerland, a landlocked country, would then seem peculiar if one was not familiar with the country's leading industry, which has been discreet banking services. The facility exists in a peculiar legal no-man's land. Although it is technically located on the territory of Switzerland, from a customs' perspective, the goods stored there have not entered the country, and so, in

---

many ways, the free port was meant to provide no-questions-asked art storage. It is for this reason that Giacomo Medici located his warehouse of illegally looted archaeological relics there. He assumed no authority would ever claim jurisdiction, let alone raid his building. In fact, his scandal is one of many that swirl around this unassuming collection of warehouses, earning it the unofficial name "sleaziest place in the art world." One of the central players in the creation of the Free Port of Geneva is Yves Bouvier, a Swiss art shipper and dealer, who has himself been mired in a number of controversies. Most recently, he built and then subsequently sold at a significant loss a Free Port in Singapore.[8] In the past, he has been associated with dealing in the works of art forger Wolfgang Beltracchi,[9] and he's most recently been embroiled in controversies with his former leading client, the Russian billionaire Dmitry Rybolovlev, who has complained of being dramatically overcharged for works he bought through Bouvier, including being overcharged by $47 million on the *Salvator Mundi*.[10]

The Nahmad family also maintains a warehouse where they keep an estimated 1,000 plus paintings. David Nahmad was accused of being the real owner of a Modigliani painting belonging to a Jewish family who lost it during the War. Only with the revelations of the Panama Papers was it revealed that indeed the International Art Center, the ostensible owner of the Modigliani, was in fact a Nahmad shell company. Swiss police raided the Free Port of Geneva in 2016 to retrieve the 1918 work, *Seated Man with a Cane*, and litigation continues[11] with new information to support the heir's claim.[12]

The primary benefit to most free port users is that their property can be stored safely, out of the observing eyes of their own country's tax authority. Therefore, one of the primary purposes for transporting something into the facility is so that a sales transaction can be conducted and the relevant VAT, that would have been incurred, can be avoided. A free port has now opened in the state of Delaware with the same possibility for avoiding New York City's 8.875 percent sales tax.[13]

CUSTOMS—TERMS

Carnet—a customs document that ensures an object entering a jurisdiction will also leave it at some point in the future.

Customs officer—a government employee tasked with overseeing and processing the goods entering and leaving the country. They ensure that paperwork is properly filed and that duties and taxes are paid.

Customs broker—a private-sector professional who prepares customs documents and understands the intricate category systems used in declarations. The broker usually brings the paperwork to a customs officer for it to be stamped and the shipment can proceed in transit.

Customs declaration—a description of goods being transported with correct identifying categorization according to a country's customs taxonomy.

Pro-forma invoice—an invoice produced only for the sake of customs clearance, not an actual document of a commercial transaction.

Bond—an amount of money held as insurance against customs duties or tax liabilities for an importer of goods.

Bonded warehouse—a warehouse that functions as an in-bond customs warehouse, meaning that the goods stored in the warehouse are technically in transit between two customs jurisdictions.

Free Port—a designated zone within a country that is considered to be still technically on "the High Seas," meaning that the goods stored there are not inside any country's current jurisdiction.

Duties—a tariff or tax imposed on goods when transported across international borders.

Smuggling—the act of moving goods across customs borders without the proper customs clearance and permits or without paying appropriate duties and taxes.

Notes

1 Fisman, R. and Wei, S-J. "The Smuggling of Art, and the Art of Smuggling: Uncovering the Illicit Trade in Cultural Property and Antiques." *American Economic Journal: Applied Economics*, American Economic Association, vol. 1, no. 3, 2009, pp. 82–96.

2 Bennet, C. and Gus, C. "Croatia to Join Schengen Free-Travel Zone In 2023; But Romania and Bulgaria Were Left Out as Austria Objects to Their Inclusion." *Politico*, Dec. 8, 2022.

3 Roodt, C. *Private International Law, Art and Cultural Heritage*. Cheltenham: Edward Elgar Publishing, 2015, pp. 293–297.

4 *Customs Convention on the International Transport of Goods under Cover of Tir Carnets (TIR CONVENTION, 1975)*. Tenth Revised Edition. UNITED NATIONS, 2013.

5 Actman, J. "U.S. Adopts Near-Total Ivory Ban." *National Geographic*, June 3, 2016.

6 Jhala, K. "'Fatal for the French Art Market': Dealers Decry New EU Sales Tax that Could Wipe Out Paris's Booming Commercial Scene." *The Art Newspaper*, Feb. 24, 2023.

7 Moss, C. and Baden, J. "Feds Investigate Hobby Lobby Boss for Illicit Artifacts." *Daily Beast*, Oct. 26, 2015.

8 Pakiam, R., Chanjaroen, C., and Huang, Z. "Chinese Crypto Tycoon-Backed Bitdeer Buys Asia's 'Fort Knox:' Le Freeport Sold to Jihan Wu's Company for S$40 Million. Wu Is One of the Most Influential People in Crypto Market." *Bloomberg*, Sep. 19, 2022.

9 Sennewald, J. E. and Timm, T. "Im Bunker der Schönheit." *Zeit Online*, Apr. 25, 2013.

10 Bowley, G. and Rashbaum, W. "Sotheby's Tries to Block Suit over a Leonardo Sold and Resold at a Big Markup." *The New York Times*, Nov. 28, 2016.

11 Gilbert, L. "Legal Battle over Modigliani Painting Rumbles On." *The Art Newspaper*, Apr. 20, 2018.

12 Hickley, C. "New Evidence Cited in Restitution Claim for Panama Papers Modigliani." *The Art Newspaper*, Jan. 9, 2020.

13 Bowley, G. "Art Collectors Find Safe Harbor in Delaware's Tax Laws." *The New York Times*, Oct. 25, 2015.

Insurance

Chapter 15

VENUE INSURANCE

Depending on the type of venue being operated, many different forms of insurance policies can be considered. Galleries just starting out will certainly need to take out a small business insurance policy. The primary purpose of this kind of coverage is more for liabilities that your physical venue may incur. Even if avenue is only operating as a pop-up gallery for a few weeks or months, most landlords will still insist on a general liability policy. From the landlord's perspective, this covers the eventuality that the tenant's activity may cause damage to their property. This kind of policy can cover a great number of risks. The most basic coverage will insure against risks that your business may incur, particularly in the form of physical accidents occurring on the gallery's property. These kinds of liabilities tend to be of great importance in the United States where tort law is particularly robust. Outside of the United States, insuring against risks to your clientele may be less of a prevailing obsession. The other risks a gallery should insure against will be are fire, storm, and flood damage. Galleries have a tendency to congregate near water, since so many of them are located in beach towns or picturesque waterfront locations in cities. In the cases of Chelsea in Manhattan or Williamsburg in Brooklyn, galleries have taken over obsolete warehouse locations close to port facilities. The result is that flood risk can

DOI: 10.4324/9781003431756-16

be a serious consideration and, in some locations, a very difficult and expensive type of insurance to procure.

The gallery's infrastructure—computers, furniture, display structures—can also be insured, but this may usually require a valuation on those items. Furthermore, the gallery's inventory may be able to be insured up to a default point, for example, up to $30,000. For that coverage to be valid, a gallery inventory listing all pieces on the premises must be constantly maintained. This task itself can be quite challenging to keep up with when the artworks and exhibitions are constantly changing. As the business grows and begins handling larger value pieces, the maximum coverage can be raised. In the event of a short-term show with exceptionally expensive inventory, a rider (a supplement to the basic policy) can be obtained for temporary coverage of a higher value. For the business insurance to cover the possibility of theft, the insurer will probably require certain security features to be in place. At a minimum, this would include deadbolt locks on the doors and a basic motion-sensor alarm. With the rapid drop in price for security technology, currently most galleries can afford a system of surveillance cameras that can record all activity in view, 24/7. This kind of a system will certainly be necessary for an insurer to consider covering higher-value inventory. Furthermore, such a surveillance system can also be extremely useful in handling all sorts of questions about who took what where, even if no malfeasance is in question. A basic insurance policy can cost less than $100 per month and provide an opportunity to begin working with a local insurance broker who can provide advice about securing the facility against greater risk, which will come if the business prospers. More mature galleries can have very complex policies tailored to the exact needs of a global operation. In addition to basic inventory coverage for pieces on the premises, the policy can extend to any artwork the dealer buys worldwide, from the moment of purchase and through its transportation process to the gallery. If the gallery lends out works to a museum exhibition or gives pieces on consideration to an interior designer, the policy can cover these activities as well. These global policies can be very useful in that the gallery does not need to purchase transportation insurance from the art shipper when they ship pieces; their coverage is automatic.

Most established galleries will usually migrate to one of these kinds of policies as their business becomes more complex and long-distance.

COLLECTION INSURANCE

Collection insurance can cover the long-term possession of pieces in relatively stable, secure locations. For collectors, this kind of insurance can be a basic homeowner's policy adapted with riders for their particularly large and valuable art collection. If the collection, however, begins to reach valuations in the higher six figures, an insurer may recommend a tailored policy for the collection. There are also many insurers, as well as branches of larger firms, that specifically focus on the needs of insuring high-value private art collections. In particular, these specialized brokers will help assess the risks and devise a policy that accounts for those risks relative to the collection's appraised value.

If the collector intends to store the works in open display in their residence, then the broker can review the property and advise on the most secure way to exhibit works. In addition to reviewing the collection's threats from flood, earthquake, or other natural disasters that a region may be prone to, the broker should assess the risk of theft relative to the home security system. Different types of works represent different theft risks. Lower value works might represent more work for the thief to resell and so are unlikely to be stolen. Extremely important works, however, can often be so famous that they would be difficult to exchange on the open market, and they would be quickly listed on stolen art databases. In such cases, the theft is more a sort of "kidnapping," where the insurance company will eventually pay a type of ransom for the return of the work. The kinds of works that most often get stolen are excellent pieces, but not necessarily by a particularly famous master, which makes them much more difficult to trace on databases. Art collection insurance specialists can also recommend certain types of hanging and installation hardware, such as security hangers (hooks that make it difficult to remove a painting from the wall) and protective museum glass. For works that are susceptible to moisture, they may require a museum-quality HVAC system.

Many collectors have already amassed collections that exceed all the wall space in their homes, and so they store a large part of the collection in art storage facilities. Overall, art storage has grown exponentially as an industry, and so has the business in insuring all of this stored artwork. Many of the leading art storage facilities also serve the museums in their vicinity, since museums usually have vastly more works in storage than they can display in the permanent collection. Therefore, these locations usually observe museum standards in how works are stored. The New York art world learned a painful lesson in 2012, when Hurricane Sandy caused widespread flooding in the galleries of Chelsea and in the warehouses of Brooklyn. The galleries which suffered the most were those able to afford a ground-floor retail location. The less prestigious galleries that were on the upper floors were largely spared. The worst damage occurred in the Red Hook area of Brooklyn, and for the art storage businesses and their insurers, it raised a much-debated question: when does a work of art cease to exist? As a result of the flooding many works had been saturated, and once they dried, they often looked quite different. Artists wanted to declare the works destroyed, but their dealers often tried to salvage and restore them.[1] The insurance adjusters faced many new cases of determining when the artwork should no longer be considered viable, and when a settlement should be made.

TRANSPORTATION INSURANCE

The best insurance for safe transportation of artworks is good packing. Numerous incompetent individuals may handle the freight in a less-than-ideal manner, and still the artwork will arrive intact because superior quality packaging takes into account this eventuality. Nonetheless, when shipping valuable art objects, one should always have it insured. If the gallery has a global policy, then the shipment would be automatically covered. Otherwise, insurance can usually be purchased from the art shipper. The rates for this type of insurance can vary in terms of the amount of coverage. Antique dealers shipping whole containers of relatively low-value furniture will opt for a low-cost coverage called "total loss." The rate for this kind of policy can be around 0.7 percent of insured value, but it only covers the eventuality of the freight being completely lost (e.g., the freight sinks), with nothing else, such as damage, being insured. This strategy makes sense for their business because the furniture can be restored when it arrives, and that will be easier and cheaper than trying to get a damage settlement out of the insurance company. A policy that covers all risks, that is, damage to the goods while in-transit, will be a much higher rate, and will depend on the quality of the packaging, and can range from 2 to 4 percent of insurable value.

The problem with insuring goods for transport is that if one (or one's art shipper) does not maintain a good chain of custody and take notice of the condition of the works and immediately file a damage report, then insurance can be essentially worthless. For transport insurance to be actually valid, the work should be documented in a condition report prior to packing. The packing must also be constructed to standards, which include proper soft and hard pack (crates). The local transport and handling will need to have been done by competent art handlers. Insurers do not like paying out claims, and they will definitely investigate if there is any indication that incompetence on the part of the shipper was the cause. Also, higher-quality art shipping crates come equipped with shock sensors (which go off if the crate receives a sudden blow, e.g. if it is dropped) and humidity sensors (that indicate if high levels of moisture have gotten in the crate). If either of these has gone off, it necessitates at least filing a damage report. The artwork might still be fine, but it needs to be documented immediately.

Insurers may often have stern instructions for how highly fragile or high-value items must travel in order for the coverage to be valid. They often insist on airport supervision, courier service, and armed escort [see Chapter 16: Transportation] depending on the value of the shipment. They will even put upper limits on the amount of risk they will allow on one plane at a time. Blockbuster mega shows for canonical art can easily feature works with a total insurable value of over $1 billion. Insurers will frequently refuse to allow any more than $200 million in value on any one plane, and in such cases as these, shipments must travel in multiple phases.

CASE STUDIES: TITLE INSURANCE

Home buyers will be familiar with the term "title insurance." This type of insurance guarantees the owners the value of their property if, at a later date, the title to the property (i.e., ownership) ever comes in to question. In most jurisdictions, property title insurers know where to look to find out where the deed is deposited, and if there are any liens against it or if the ownership has been in any way divided. Real estate also has the benefit of being immovable, and therefore much more difficult to steal than movable property.

Title insurance for movable property, specifically art, is a relatively new concept, and one that is intended to directly address the perils of improper title, and specifically improper title because of some earlier theft or appropriation. The need has arisen particularly because of the phenomenon of Second-World-War-era-related restitution claims. It is important to note that an important legal underpinning to the restitution process is the notion that one cannot hold legal title to any object if it is stolen property, even if it has been bought in good faith at a public auction. This would be the case in the United States, but in some jurisdictions, for example, Switzerland, one can have good title as long as one has bought it in good faith.[2] The fact that some owners have found that their artworks now being claimed by heirs of former owners as a result of the restitution process has led to the creation of the title insurance industry.

The new product of "art title protection insurance" insures against the risks of bad title arising from theft (either recent or historical, such as during the War), as well from either illegal import or export (such as not having correct export permits). The policy also insures against another set of risks, which is that the most recent seller might not have had clear title. Frequently now, owners use their artworks as collateral for loans, and so there could be a lien against the piece. Another common issue is that the piece was partially owned by other family members, but the seller had presented themself as the sole owner and solely collected the sale payment.[3] The case of the fraudster Inigo Philbrick, however, demonstrated how the art world's methods of title verification can easily be manipulated, especially if the fraud is conducted with the confidence of a well-connected insider.[4]

Other new innovations in the field include work by a couple of firms trying to find ways to register paintings, using microtagging and employing blockchain. These technologies could be useful in defending against future theft, appropriation, or simply loss of attribution information or documentation as to what the artwork is. Creating a public blockchain record of title, however, seems unlikely given the art market's preference for opacity. Furthermore, figuring out the past of an artwork: as to what is what and who owned what, still requires the same time-tested methods of research, connoisseurship, and art forensics techniques. The innovation of Non-Fungible Tokens and their blockchain lineage were supposed to provide both a platform where title was clear and theft impossible, but that has not proven to be the case.[5]

INSURANCE—TERMS

Policy—a contract between an insurer and an insured party stating the terms of coverage, premiums to be paid, and the amount of settlements possible in the case of a incident.

Risk—an intellectual concept insurers use to evaluate the costs of coverage and the likelihood of an incident resulting in loss or damage.

Premium—the fee to be paid by the insured party in order to receive coverage from an insurer.

Deductible—the amount of a claim that an insurer does not cover and which must be borne by the insured party.

All Risks—a type of transportation insurance that covers all forms of loss, theft, and any level of damage incurred in transit.

Total Loss—lower cost type of transportation insurance that covers only the total loss, that is, disappearance or theft of the cargo. It does not cover damage to the cargo. This form of insurance is favored by antiques dealers when shipping full containers of furniture and art objects.

Force majeure—an event of great catastrophic force for which insurance policies often contain clauses denying coverage. These can be natural disasters, terrorism, and acts of war.

Adjuster—an insurance professional who investigates claims and determines the appropriate settlement.

Insurance appraiser—an appraiser who specifically examines damage and loss of artworks for the purpose of determining the appropriate settlement.

Settlement—the amount an insurer agrees to pay out to an insured party as compensation for loss or damage of their insured object.

Notes

1 Stowe, S. "Storm Leaves Residue of Questions." *The New York Times*, May 9, 2013.
2 Laird, M. "No Easy Solutions for Swiss Museums." *Swissinfo.ch*, Nov. 7, 2013.
3 Brodie, S. "The Case for Title Insurance." *Art and Advocacy*, vol. 15, Spring/Summer 2013.pp. 1–11.
4 Alberge, D. 'He's Sabotaged His Entire Life for Greed': The $86M Rise and Fall of Inigo Philbrick." *The Guardian*, May 25, 2022.
5 Hern, A. "More Than $100M Worth of NFTs Stolen since July 2021, Data Shows." *The Guardian*, Aug. 24, 2022.

Transportation

Chapter 16

AIR CARGO

Air cargo is the method by which most of the world's art travels. This is because air cargo provides the fastest, most secure, and most trackable means to get artworks to their destinations. "Air cargo" means the cargo service offered by most passenger airlines, as well as by specialized cargo-only airlines. Air cargo is not the baggage service that accompanies a passenger's air ticket, though many cost-conscious dealers will try to carry some of their smaller purchases in their luggage when returning from a buying trip. Passengers' luggage and the air cargo on a plane both travel in the cargo hold, but they will be on different pallets and they will be handled quite differently. Furthermore, air cargo is something distinct from the courier delivery services such as UPS, DHL, and FedEx. Although dealers will use them for transport for lower-end goods and for inland transport of small goods, they are generally not used for higher-end goods or things of even modestly large size (which tends to make their shipping costs prohibitive). Air cargo shipments are generally booked through a certified IATA air cargo broker, and most larger art shippers will have this status. However, if one wants to avoid the costs of working with an art shipper, then one can take the crate directly to an air cargo broker. One cannot, however, take their freight straight to the airlines. Airlines only sell air cargo space to certified IATA brokers. If the shipment is leaving the country or a free trade zone (North American

DOI: 10.4324/9781003431756-17

Free Trade Agreement [NAFTA] and EU), then export customs clearance will be needed. The air cargo broker can often offer customs clearance services, or one can have the export customs clearance done by a designated customs broker.

The air cargo broker issues an air waybill (AWB). This document contains the 11-digit AWB number, which is unique to this shipment, and the shipment can be tracked with this number. A copy of the AWB will also accompany the import customs clearance papers. On the AWB, one can also find the name and address of the consigner (sender), and the name and address of the consignee (receiver). There will also be a contact for the shipment, which might be the consignee's customs broker, who will be able to quickly process the import customs clearance. The AWB will also briefly list the contents of the freight, although an additional packing list with more specific information will be necessary for the customs clearance. Finally, it will designate the dimensions (in cm) and the weight (in kg) for use in applying charges. Since an air cargo shipment can be completed in two to three days, it is imperative that the exporting shipper send the AWB promptly to the receiving party. The consignee who presents the AWB and identifies themself as that person (with an ID), will be the one entitled to receive the freight.

For air cargo, space is just as important as weight. Although air cargo brokers may cite a per-kilogram rate for the air shipment, one should be aware that air cargo is always assessed twice in order to determine its price. The freight (in its packing) is first weighed for how many kilograms its true weight is. Then the dimensions are measured and those are given a space-displacement weight. The international air cargo system usually assesses one cubic meter of freight as equaling 167 kg. When shipping paintings and antique furniture, the space-displacement weight will usually be significantly higher. It is not unusual for a large painting in a crate to be 20 kg in its true weight, but 100 kg in its space-displacement weight. Therefore, the freight will be billed as if it were 100 kg. When planning for an exhibition that will involve a lot of air cargo, it will be extremely important to be able to accurately predict how big the crates will be, because only by knowing that will one be able to plan how much transportation costs will be. Air cargo rates between most major airports range between

$3 – 6 per kg, with a sliding scale that sees rates drop as volume increases (a standard feature of all transport pricing structures). Therefore, for example, a 1-cubic-meter shipment, which would equal 167 kg in space displacement, might be charged $4 per kg for sending that crate from Paris (CDG) to Chicago (ORD), and so the freight costs the air cargo broker would invoice for would be $668 (in addition to other service charges like customs clearance and local transport).

SEA AND CONTAINER CARGO

The most significant recent paradigm shift in the global transportation system occurred around the 1970s with the acceptance and standardization of the intermodal container, widely known as the shipping container, and by the 1980s, it became the basis for "just-in-time" commercial shipping.[1] Previously, freighter ships just had open hulls where crates were packed in and hauled out by winches and set down one-by-one on the docks to be handled by hundreds of longshoremen. A large ship could take weeks to unload, but with the innovation of the shipping container, the job could be completed in less than a day. The key feature of the container is that it is of a uniform size. There are two main sizes: 20 foot and 40 foot (reflecting their length, and these terms are used worldwide, even in metric countries), as well as a high cube 40 foot (slightly higher capacity), and refrigerated versions on all these types (for perishable foodstuffs). Containers are immensely useful because giant special cranes can lift the containers on and off truck beds or railcars and then stack them for temporary storage until they can load them on to ocean-going freighter ships that carry thousands of these containers at a time. The ports equipped for loading containers are now relatively few because the infrastructure necessary to have these cranes and loading facilities represent enormous capital investments. A huge percentage of European container trade goes through three ports: Hamburg, Antwerp, and Rotterdam. In the United States, on the East Coast, there are only a few major container ports: Boston, New York (actually located in NJ), Baltimore, Charleston, and Fort Lauderdale. Upon arrival in these ports, containers are off-loaded, customs-cleared, and placed on road or rail connections to continue the freight onto its destination.

Containers are, without a doubt, the most cost-effective method for shipping large amounts of goods efficiently. Transit times for most containers are eight to twelve days at sea for most routes, and a total of three to six weeks in-transit total can be normal, from door to door. Containers are generally safe and watertight, but these steel boxes are used over and over again, and so they might develop small holes that can let in moisture. For this reason, everything in there must be wrapped in airtight packaging. Also, the heat inside a container traveling through the Panama Canal can become quite intense and pose other threats to artworks in the form of heat and humidity. Therefore, the container method is not widely used by higher-end art dealers. Rather, it is the preferred method for antique dealers, who routinely purchase a whole container's worth of inventory in Europe and then send it back to the United States to their shop, but they, too, must be aware that if they intend to ship newly refinished furniture, they need to definitely wait until the lacquers are dry before wrapping and shipping them. One advantage of container shipping is that most things will not need to be crated unless they are extremely fragile. The furniture, in general, can travel in soft-packing, and this will save a lot on packaging expenses. A good-sized antiques shop can keep itself stocked with two containers a year from Europe because a 40-foot container can easily contain 100 pieces of furniture. Containers can also be the best methods for transporting statuary heavier than 1 ton. Containers can often have a payload weight of up to 8 tons before any weight surcharge gets added. Therefore, it is definitely the best method for shipping very heavy objects, such as sculpture and architectural antiques.

Container costs are vastly cheaper than air cargo. For the same price that one could send 5 cubic meters from Paris to Chicago by air cargo, one could have instead sent an entire 40-foot container with a payload of about 60 cubic meters. The basic container fee that one pays to the freight forwarder who handles the combined services of rail transport to the harbor, storage, crane loading, sea shipping, and unloading at arrival port can be approximately $2,500 for a 20-foot and $3,500 for a 40-foot to be sent from Europe to North America. These prices can vary, however, depending on demand and trade flows. If one sends a container in the direction of which there is already a lot of container traffic flowing that way, then a "repositioning fee" might appear on the invoice, which is essentially the sea freight company charging the client for sending the container back empty. However, if one is fortunate enough to be sending a container in the opposite direction of prevailing trends, such as from the United States to China, then the container fee itself might be virtually free (though port handling fees will always be assessed).

Similar to an AWB for air cargo, container shipments will receive a bill of lading. This document entitles the bearer to receive the freight at the arrival port. In addition, the bill of lading should have a packing list attached, to be presented for the purpose of customs clearance. Keep in mind that it is quite likely that the containers of first-time shippers into the United States (e.g., if an antique dealer sends a container from France to the United States for the first time) will be searched by Customs and Border Protection (CBP). One should be prepared to promptly show up at the appointed time with trained packers to do the unpacking and repacking, because one does not want the CBP doing that. Once a container arrives at port and is customs cleared, then a truck will transport it to the door of wherever it is to be unloaded. Since the container will be sitting on a semi-truck bed about 4–5 feet (1–1.5 m) off the ground, it is a huge help to have a loading dock which the container doors can be backed up to and easily unloaded.

In the case where one wants to ship just a few cubic meters, for example, one or two pieces of furniture, then consolidated container freight service is a good solution. In most major cities, there are companies who consolidate many different clients' shipments into a single container, which is sent to a certain port. In some cases, these containers are sent from one location, for example, Vienna, and when the container arrives at Hamburg (one of Europe's largest ports), the different crates are removed and then reconsolidated in containers going to many different destinations: Baltimore, Houston, Hong Kong, etc. This solution, especially for a few big pieces of furniture, can be vastly cheaper than air cargo, but one needs to be sure that the pieces are carefully packed and crated because they will be picked up and moved around by forklift many times. These kinds of shipments also take much longer than air cargo and might arrive at their destination six to eight weeks after sending.

SURFACE AND ROAD TRANSPORT

Within the European Union, NAFTA, and within countries, surface transport will be the most affordable and convenient method. Surface, as a term, can mean any shipment moving along solid ground and, therefore, can mean the shipment of shipping containers on rail or on truck beds, though this method would be more likely used for mass-manufactured goods, and not for the art business. Trucks, however, are widely used in all sizes and at different levels of professionalism. When one has a larger shipment, the easiest solution is a truck that is exclusively engaged for that transport and is loaded at the point of departure and unloaded when it arrives at its destination. This solution is secure, and avoids the hazards of multiple loadings and unloadings, which elevate the risk of damage through mishandling. Even for shipments of relatively small size, a sole truck can be the most secure solution, and possibly the only solution, if the destination is an out-of-the-way location. For shipments where the freight is not considered too high value, a road consolidator can pick up freight, even at the door, and drop it off at its destination, although this only works well if one can load the freight easily because it is light or one has access to a loading dock or forklift. Do not expect these drivers to help with loading or offloading. These firms expect that they are working with other professionals who are prepared to load and unload promptly.

For higher-end art shipments, there are regular art shuttles that move across the United States from coast to coast in a regular pattern, stopping at any pickup location roughly along their route. Because these shuttles consolidate across the country, they cannot necessarily do the pickup and delivery immediately, and it is advisable to allot a window of at least six to eight weeks to be sure the shipment will arrive on time. Within Europe, the same services can be provided, but if the truck leaves the European Union, then the customs clearance and potential for duties and Value-Added Tax assessments can become quite problematic. For that reason, although it might have been quite easy to send truckloads of art and antiques to the oligarchs in Moscow, the customs and taxes that might be capriciously charged by Russian customs officers essentially prevented that trade route from being fully developed.

LOCAL TRANSPORT

Local transport, or as it can be frequently referred to in the transport industry, "The Last Mile," can be the most challenging and expensive part of the art shipping process. This step can be done at many different levels of professionalism, standards, and costs. For many galleries, this will be their primary experience in transportation: having artworks brought into their gallery and delivered to local collectors. For this reason, a gallery will quickly develop a relationship with a couple of local truckers whom they consider to be affordable, reliable, trustworthy, and capable of delivering a level of service commensurate with the gallery's own profile. Local transport generally involves three activities: one, having handlers (one who might also be the driver) enter the facility (airport warehouse, gallery, storage unit, or collector's home) and pick up the artwork (either packed or unpacked) and put it on the truck and safely secure it; two, driving the pieces over to the destination; and, three, taking the artwork into the destination location (gallery, collector's home, freight forwarder's warehouse) and possibly removing and hauling away the packaging.

At the lowest level of professionalism are the casual transporters who have a truck or van and do work for cash on an oral contract. For many artists trying to get a large group of canvases over to their gallery, this can definitely be their most viable option. It does not, however, guarantee any protection or liability for damage that might occur in transit, and it is an implicit acknowledgment that the values at stake would not merit any in a cost-benefit analysis. At the next level are professional truckers who handle furniture, moving, and other forms of deliveries where good handling and proper documentation are standard. These firms can be quite adequate, especially if the artwork has already been effectively packaged. For transportation for museums and elite galleries who follow museum standards, however, a climatized truck is a mandatory piece of equipment. A climatized truck will have a heating and refrigeration unit built onto the closed-box payload area. This will ensure that the freight payload area can always be kept at around 20–22° Celsius or 68–72° Fahrenheit, which are considered ideal temperatures for art storage of paintings.[2] A truck designed for art transport will also have special secure locking mechanisms, air shocks, and GPS tracking. In a trans-Atlantic art shipment from, for example, London to New York, it is not at all unusual for the local delivery in the Manhattan portion of the invoice to be larger than everything else on the bill combined. There are two reasons for the high cost of professional local delivery in Manhattan. One, in Manhattan and other high-density art centers (where the most elite galleries and collectors tend to congregate) parking can be virtually impossible for a larger truck. Therefore, the vehicle will most likely need to double-park, and the driver will need to remain with it for the whole duration. In other words, the driver will not be able to help with the delivery of the freight out from its point of origin nor with taking it into its final destination. Two other handlers will need to be on the job, meaning that three people, at minimum, will be engaged for at least three to four hours given Manhattan's slow-moving traffic. The second reason for the high cost is due to the fact that professional art handlers carry very expensive liability insurance, because it is in the process of local delivery that the majority of mistakes happen that lead to damage to artworks.

SUPERVISION AND COURIER

For shipments of artworks above the $100,000 range, it is not unusual for the shipper to provide airport supervision, and, for very important works, there might be a courier. Airport supervision is provided by firms that also provide security services for high-value deliveries. The airport supervisor will be present when the freight is dropped off at the air cargo facility at the airport. Supervisors have authorization to be in the restricted areas of an airport, and will remain physically present with the freight through the customs clearance, palletization (placing the crate onto pallet and securing it) and loading it into the airplane. For arrivals, the supervisor observes the offloading from the airplane, de-palletization, and loading on to the local delivery truck. At all stages, the supervisor is present to observe and document any mishandling or damage to the crate and immediately report it.

At the highest end of the art business, there are people who act as couriers and accompany an artwork from the point of departure to the point of delivery and through the unpacking and condition reporting process. The most frequent reason for using a courier is when a museum sends one of its star artworks for a temporary exhibition. The courier will usually be a curator or registrar from the lending museum, and although the trip may involve a lot of sitting on trucks and in warehouses, it also provides a business- or first-class ticket to an interesting city. There they will be permitted a few days to adjust before returning, and therefore, curators and registrars often find courier work to be a hidden perk of their jobs.

STORAGE

Art very often must be stored, either because it is in transit or because it is being stored rather than being displayed. Most art shippers or their subcontractors provide short-term storage services while they complete the tasks they have been engaged for. But if the client decides they do not want to ship just yet, and hopes to store the work in the shipper's facility for a few weeks or months, then the shipper will often assess punitive storage fees to encourage the client to move the shipment along. Other firms, however, specialize in long-term storage for the art world and offer competitive rates and services. These facilities can be found in the outskirts of major art centers such as New York, as well as in free ports, like the one in Geneva. These firms cater to the large museums and galleries which cannot display any more than a tiny fraction of the works in their possession. They also serve the mega-private collectors who also have much more art than they can display.

These art storage facilities will generally offer good access for trucks with loading docks and flat floors for easy rolling of the crates. They will also need a freight elevator capable of lifting many tons if the facility exists on multiple floors. Since the lessons learned from the flooding caused by Hurricane Sandy, the art world has learned that higher-up storage is superior to storage at lower levels, and therefore a reliable freight elevator is mandatory. The warehouse should also be kept at ideal temperature and humidity, essentially the same standards the museum would demand for its permanent collection out on display (20–22° Celsius or 68–72° Fahrenheit).[3] Like rentable storage units, art storage facilities should provide individualized storage spaces so that different clients' items do not risk being mixed up. Also, many higher-end art storage firms offer a range of registrar-like services to track the works and arrange for other needs such as conservation or framing. Some even offer viewing rooms and opportunities for exhibitions [see the marketing case study in Chapter 10: Mana Contemporary].

PACKING

Along with local transportation, packing can easily be one of the most expensive items on an art shipper's invoice. That is because it is the quality of the packing, more than anything else, that separates the art handler's trade from that of the household-goods mover. Like the other features of the transportation process, this can also be done at many levels of professionalism. At the lowest level would be what can be called the "guerrilla standard," that is, what is necessary to more-or-less safely transport something in a van or a car for a one-time shipment, such as an artist delivering a work to their gallery. For this purpose, blankets, cardboard, and newspaper can be more than adequate to ensure that no damage occurs on the short trip.

Commercial galleries and antique dealers tend to be very cost conscious and so will demand the lowest possible prices that can be provided by their art shipper and still achieve a safe delivery. Therefore, they will prefer to have their artworks and antiques in soft wrap, which can be layers of silk paper, butcher's paper, corrugated paper, and finally, bubble wrap (which, being plastic, gives a watertight, airtight seal). The soft wrapped pieces are put into commercial-standard crates. These are crates designed for one-time use (though dealers are definitely known to reuse them). The frame will be constructed of pine boards (with stamps for certified treated wood) and particle board for the walls, and nailed together. This construction will generally be durable for any risk other than a forklift driving its forks through the walls. Crates of this quality can generally be commissioned for $200–300 per cubic meter (100 cubic feet).

The museum standard for crating is significantly higher than the commercial standard, and significantly more expensive. First of all, the paper that touches the art object must always be acid-free paper. The crates should be constructed of at least ten-ply plywood for both the frames and the walls. At least one panel should be removable using large screws or some other easy opening method. The edges of the crate should be beveled to remove edges that could catch on a door frame, and it should be painted because bare wood can quickly look dirty. When a museum commissions a crate, they intend to use it for many years for that particular artwork. The highest caliber crates will have either foam cast interiors that are molded exactly to the shape of the artwork, or they will have an interior frame crate that slides into the exo-crate. The painting would be affixed to that interior crate much the same way as it would be fixed to a wall and will hang in air untouched by anything inside the crate. These crates will have shock sensors that will go off if the crate is dropped. They will also have humidity control devices built into their walls to regulate the interior moisture levels. Crates of this quality can easily cost about $1,000 per cubic meter (100 cubic feet), and galleries who commission such crates for the works they take to a high-end art fair are known to then use the crates as furniture in their stand at the fair.

CASE STUDY: THE GOLD TRAIN

Few shipments in the history of transport could rival the value that was traveling on the Gold Train when it departed Budapest in late 1944 as the Soviet Red Army was close to encircling the Hungarian capital. It was reported to be 52 cars long and carrying approximately $350 million (over $2 billion now) in gold, silver, jewelry, carpets, and 200 paintings which had been seized from Hungary's Jewish population. Adolf Eichmann, one of the chief architects of the Holocaust and who personally oversaw deportations out of Hungary, had hoped to retreat with this valuable haul back to the German capital of Berlin.

As the train departed across the Hungarian countryside, the commandant frequently bought off marauding gangs of soldiers with smaller amounts of the loot. The train made very slow progress, traveling only about 100 miles in three months. When it reached Austrian territory, the train was stopped short of Salzburg, because Allies had bombed the rail bridge at Brixlegg, and could proceed no further. Its troops and passengers helped themselves to what they could carry and disappeared into the countryside.[4]

The American 3rd Infantry Division, 15th Regiment, found the train in the Tauern Tunnel, near Salzburg-abandoned. Despite the valuables that had already been removed, the train still probably carried hundreds of millions of dollars, even at 1945 values. It would eventually be moved to a depot, with Allied soldiers helping themselves to its contents all the way along the process.[5] Because the pieces had no reference to whom they had belonged, and the train was found in Austria, the Americans had no reason to believe that it had belonged to Hungary or Hungarian Jews, though this should have been the logical conclusion. In time, the entire collection of untraceable valuables slowly disappeared in the slush of wartime looting. Not all U.S. soldiers behaved like Monuments Men (the Allied soldiers responsible for saving artwork).

In 2005, the U.S. government reached a settlement with Hungarian Holocaust survivors for $25.5 million to be distributed through Hungarian social services agencies.[6] The Hungarian Gold Train was not the only train laden with valuables to leave Hungary at that time. After the war, Soviet troops systematically emptied all the bank vaults in Budapest of their gold, jewels, cash, and artworks. This was where Hungary's wealthiest Jews (who were the country's leading collectors) stashed their collections. All of these contents were taken to the Soviet Union as reparations because Hungary had participated in Hitler's invasion of the U.S.S.R. To the best of our knowledge, those works are still in Russia today.[7] In 2015, much attention was turned to the Polish town of Walbrzych when local treasure hunters had claimed to have found the Polish Gold Train. It turned out not to exist, but the hype served to boost the local tourist economy.[8]

TRANSPORTATION—TERMS

Bill of lading—a shipping document that entitles the holder of the document to receive cargo that has been shipped.

Packing list—a shipping document that provides a complete list of the cargo being transported.

Air waybill—a transport document used in the air cargo industry. A shipment can be tracked by way of the air waybill number, and the consignee on the air waybill is entitled to receive the freight.

True weight—a measurement of the actual weight of a shipment.

Space-displacement weight—a calculated weight based on the three dimensional space occupied by a shipment. A formula of 1 cubic meter = 167 kg is frequently used in the air cargo business. The air cargo industry always assesses both the true weight and the space-displacement weight, and in the case of artworks, the latter is usually more and so will be billed on the space-displacement weight.

Soft-wrap—packaging involving only wrapping in paper and bubble wrap. Often used for moving objects across town to a crating facility.

Acid-free paper—artworks moved at museum transport standard will need to be wrapped in acid-free paper. This paper is produced through processes that allow it to maintain a neutral or basic pH level and therefore avoids the problem of acid leaching into the artwork, as can happen with normal paper.

Climatized vehicle—artworks moved at museum transport standard must always travel in a climate-controlled vehicle.

Condition report—when artworks are shipped at museum transport standard, condition reports will be filled out both prior to packaging and upon unpacking at the destination.

Notes

1 Levinson, M. *The Box: How the Shipping Container Made the World Smaller and the World Economy Bigger.* Princeton University Press, 2006.

2 Shelley, M. *The Care and Handling of Art Objects: Practices in the Metropolitan Museum of Art.* New York: The Metropolitan Museum of Art, 1987, pp. 68–69.

3 Ibid.

4 Zweig, R. W. *The Gold Train: The Destruction of the Jews and the Looting of Hungary.* William Morrow & Co., 2002, pp. 99–118.

5 Art Research Staff. "The Mystery of the Hungarian 'Gold Train,'" *Presidential Advisory Commission on Holocaust Assets in the United States*, Oct. 14, 1999.

6 The Associated Press. "Federal Court Approves Deal with U.S. in Nazi 'Gold Train' Case: A Federal Judge Approved a $25.5 Million Settlement between the U.S. And Hungarian Jews Dispossessed during WWII." *Haaretz*, Sep. 27, 2005.

7 Mravik, L. and Bereczky, L. *The "Sacco Di Budapest" and Depredation of Hungary, 1938–1949: Works of Art Missing from Hungary as a Result of the Second World War: Looted, Smuggled, Captured, Lost and Destroyed Art Works, Books and Archival Documents: Preliminary and Provisional Catalogue.* Hungarian National Gallery for the Joint Restitution Committee at the Hungarian Ministry of Culture and Education, 1998.

8 Rębała, M. and Miller Llana, S. "Legend Realized? Discovery of Lost Nazi 'Gold Train' Invigorates Polish Town." *The Christian Science Monitor*, Sep. 4, 2015.

Appraising

Chapter 17

THE ROLE OF THE APPRAISER

Appraisers fill a very important professional niche in the art business. They are the ones who give legally recognizable values for artworks in order that they can be insured, donated, taxed, or divided up in a court settlement or inheritance. There are appraisers for many different parts of the economic world. Anyone who has bought or sold a home will be familiar with real estate appraisers. There are also appraisers for businesses, farm equipment, and even bridges. The people who appraise artworks are referred to as "personal property appraisers." They are the complement to real estate appraisers, who appraise immovable property. In fact, in many European languages, the words for real estate and furniture are essentially the words for immovable and movable, respectively. The vast majority of personal property that gets appraised would fall into the categories of art, antiques, jewelry, books, collectables, memorabilia, archives, and wine.

Each country will have its own system of designating what is a qualified appraiser. Some countries such as France have a process of licensing appraisers. The United States has no such system and do not believe a U.S.-based personal property appraiser who says they are licensed. The United States does, however, have the Appraisal Foundation that was set up in the aftermath of the 1980s' savings and loan crisis, to ensure

DOI: 10.4324/9781003431756-18

that accurate appraisals are carried out, primarily in the real estate business, the area which caused the crisis. The system has further been refined in the wake of the 2009 sub-prime mortgage crisis, which also stemmed partially from wildly inaccurate appraising in the real estate business. The art world did not cause either of these crises, but reforms instituted would directly affect the workings of personal property appraising. The Appraisal Foundation created something called Uniform Standards of Professional Appraisal Practice (USPAP), which applies to all categories of appraisers, but definitely applies to personal property appraisers. The standards are updated every two years, and therefore appraisers are expected to take a refresher course every two years to remain USPAP-compliant. Qualified art appraisers in the United States should not refer to themselves as "licensed appraisers" because no such qualification exists. They should refer to themselves as "USPAP-compliant."

There are three main organizations that are recognized in the United States by the Appraisal Foundation that represent personal property appraisers. These are the American Society of Appraisers (ASA), the International Society of Appraisers (ISA), and the Appraisers Association of America (AAA), and all of these organizations expect their members to remain USPAP-compliant. The first two, ASA and ISA, are much larger organizations and represent all types of appraisers. The latter, the AAA, represents only personal property appraisers and so therefore is known as the association for art appraisers. In fact, many people mistakenly think that the word "art" features in their acronym because the organization is associated with the trade. Their yearly, two-day conference, together with a concurrent Art Law Day, serves as an annual art business jamboree in New York in November.

The AAA offers a training program for appraisers that emphasizes a study of the art market, appraising methodology, and advanced study in their fields of specialization. Once a candidate completes their study and serves an apprenticeship and completes the requirements (submitting a series of sample appraisals), they become an accredited appraiser. After five years of experience, they may apply to become a certified appraiser and are then required to take a day-long exam in their field of specialization. The current fields offered by the AAA form quite a long list and gives one a glimpse of the full gamut of all the things that trade along similar lines to art, or along its same principles: African Art; Islamic Art: Miniature and Manuscript Painting and Works of Art; Native American Art; Natural History; Near East, Egyptian, Greek, Roman; Oceanic Art; Pre-Columbian Art; Antique and Period Gems and Jewelry; Diamonds; Gems and Jewelry Generalist; Gemstones; Modern Gems and Jewelry; Watches; Asian Art Generalist; Asian Textiles; Chinese Fine Art; Chinese Pre-Modern Painting, Prints and Calligraphy; Indian, Himalayan, and Southeast Asian Pre-Modern Art; Japanese Fine Art; Japanese Pre-Modern Painting, and Calligraphy; Japanese Prints; Korean Fine Art; Household Contents; Aeronautical Items Vintage; Modern Automobiles Vintage; Vehicles, Contemporary; Vehicles Machinery and Equipment; Israeli Art; Judaica Books and Manuscripts; Judaica Ceremonial and Ritual Objects; Judaica Textiles and Fine Art; Architectural Drawings; Fine Maps and Atlases; Livres d'artiste; Manuscripts; Historical Documents and Autographs; Press and Illustrated Books; Rare and Antiquarian Printed Books; Percussion; Pianos; Stringed Instruments; Woodwinds and Brass; Advertising; Antique Tools; Arms and Armor: American Arms; European Arms and Armor; Chess Sets; Collectibles: Banks (mechanical, still); Collectibles: Ephemera (including postcards); Collectibles: General (including Kitchenware and Holi-day Decorations); Collectibles: Military Miniatures; Collectibles: Music Boxes and Automata; Collectibles: Railroad Memorabilia; Collectibles: Toys, Games, Model Trains; Couture: Twentieth-Century Couture; Designer Vintage Clothing and Accessories; Dolls and Doll Houses; Hunting and Fishing Maritime Art and Maritime Decorative Art; Military Items (including Civil War Memorabilia); Numismatics: Ancient; Numismatics: Coins of the World; Numismatics: Medals; Numismatics: U.S. Coins and Paper Currency; Scientific Instruments; Sports Memorabilia; Stamps and Postal History; Nineteenth-Century Photography; Twentieth-Century Photography; Cased Images; Commercial Photography; Contemporary Art Photography; Digital Images, that is, Original Media Negatives; Photography Generalist; Transparencies; Nineteenth-Century European Paintings, Drawings and Sculpture; African-American Art; American Paintings, Drawings and Sculpture; Australian Art (including Aboriginal); California and Western Art; Canadian Art; Fine Art Generalist; Fine Art: Contemporary; Asian Art; Impressionist and Modern Paintings, Drawings and Sculpture; Latin American Paintings, Drawings and Sculpture; Old Master Paintings and Drawings; Outsider/Self-Taught Art; Period Frames; Post War, Contemporary, and Emerging Art Prints; Russian Art (i.e., Icons, Fine Art, Works of Art and Faberge); Sporting and Animal Art—Paintings, Works on Paper and Sculpture; Theatre Material (Original Opera and Ballet Set/Costume Design Sketches); Wine.

A frequent problem that occurs within the appraisal business is individuals presenting themselves as appraisers with little qualification or inclination to follow proper appraisal practice. In addition to the ASA, ISA, and AAA, there exist other organizations that claim to certify art appraisers, but demand little more than a membership fee, and do not require their members to remain USPAP-compliant. Furthermore, it is the members of these organizations whose appraisals most often accompany suspicious prints on the online marketplace. An appraisal should always be understood to be an opinion of value. It should not be taken as a certificate of authenticity. Many online merchants try to pass off suspect appraisals as something like a guarantee of authenticity of the work being sold. That is not the purpose of appraisals, and such a document would be of little value should the object turn out to be less than authentic.

TYPES OF APPRAISALS

Appraisals have three primary purposes, and each of these have somewhat different features relative to the requirements of the purpose. An insurance appraisal will be the one most collectors will be familiar with because it is required by insurance brokers in order to insure artworks. The insurance appraisal is also the simplest one to complete. Insurers, furthermore, do not necessarily require the insertion of comparables into the appraisal and essentially accept the appraiser's word as to the insurable value. For higher value works (e.g., great than $5,000), insurers usually, however, expect comparables. Each type of appraisal works with a method of value which will determine what valuation the appraiser sets relative to the market information they have acquired. For an insurance appraisal,

Retail Replacement Value (RRV) should be used, which is defined as:

> the highest amount in terms of US dollars that would be required to replace a property with another of similar age, quality, origin, appearance, provenance, and condition within a reasonable length of time in an appropriate and relevant market. When applicable, sales and/or import tax, commissions, advisement fees, and/or premiums are included in this amount.[1]

Insurers have in the past not been as vigilant as they should have been when accepting appraisals for policies of works that might have been fake and were used for purposes of staging a "theft" in order to claim the compensation pay-out. In recent years, they have become much more attuned to the need for taking only legitimate appraisals from USPAP-compliant appraisers.

In the event of a death and subsequent inheritance, an estate appraisal format is used. This type of appraisal would also be employed for dividing an estate in the event of a divorce or bankruptcy proceedings. Estate appraisals use the Fair Market Value (FMV) method which is defined by the Internal Revenue Service (IRS) as:

> The price at which the property would change hands between a willing buyer and a willing seller, neither being under any compulsion to buy or to sell and both having reasonable knowledge of relevant facts. The fair market value of an item of property includible in the decedents' gross estate is not to be determined by a forced sale price. Nor is the fair market value of an item of property to be determined by the sale price of the item in a market other than that in which such item is most commonly sold to the public, taking into account the location of the item wherever appropriate.[2]

In addition, according to Technical Advice Memorandum 9235005 (May 27, 1992), FMV *should* include the buyer's premium. Estate appraisals should usually always contain comparables for the pieces above $3,000 in FMV, and these documents are held to a higher standard because they are intended to go before a probate court judge, and also because on their value, inheritance tax might be assessed.

The most rigorous type of appraisal is the donation appraisal, and the IRS expects appraisers to only do higher-value appraisals for these purposes in their area of expertise. Donations of art and other valuable objects to museums and public collections is the means by which these institutions acquire some of their best pieces. Collectors or their heirs do this because it provides them with a tax deduction similar to if they gave the same cash amount to the institution. The recipient must be a registered 501(c)(3), and the work must fit within the institution's profile and mission. In other words, you cannot donate a Louis XV table to a museum of contemporary photography. Donation appraisals will also use the FMV method, and all appraisals for objects valued over $50,000 will be reviewed by a special committee of the IRS.

THE PROCESS OF WRITING AN APPRAISAL

Before starting work, it is very important that the appraiser has agreed upon a fixed fee or an hourly rate prior to beginning the work, usually through doing a client-intake form that can serve as a contract for the services that will be provided. USPAP regards it as highly unethical to agree upon a fee that is either based on a percentage of the appraised values or a fee that is based upon a pre-determined outcome. In either case, it is believed that such an arrangement might influence the appraiser's decision-making.

The process of producing an appraisal report involves two steps before writing. The first step is documentation during a site visit or otherwise viewing the objects to be appraised. This process involves closely observing the art objects on all sides, and possibly the use of optical assistance such as a loupe (small magnifying glass) or an ultraviolet light. The works should be carefully photographed in high-quality images with additional images of signatures or the verso (back) if there is useful information in these locations. Then the appraiser would fill in a list of 14 identifiers that reference the work:

Artist/maker: the name of the artist, country of origin, birth/death years. If not known, then the best possible description, for example, Greek vase painter, c. 300 BCE.

Origin/country: the current day nation-state that exists where the work was most likely created.

Medium: for example, Oil on Canvas; or for a piece of furniture: Walnut Veneer on Pine Base.

Style/form: designations such as "Impressionist" or "Louis XV" can be inserted here.

Dimensions: always: Height × Width × Depth. This follows from the standard with 2D works like paintings of always listing Height × Width. Also, this should indicate measurements preferably with both in-frame and without-frame measurements.

Date/period: an exact date if the work has been clearly dated. Otherwise, the best circa date that can be given.

Item description: a brief description of the item.

Signature/markings: this can be a traditional artist's signature or can be stamps or other notations that verify the maker or manufacturer. The location of the marking should always be noted.

Frame: applicable to 2D works, and a brief description is useful as good frames can add significant value.

Edition #: this is important to note in serial works.

Condition: Should describe how intact the piece is and what are its flaws and conservation issues.

Provenance/acquisition cost/date/source: if the collector has this information, it can be extremely helpful in finding comparables and arriving at a value.

Publications/literary references/catalogue raisonné: most artworks may not have any of these, but if they exist, they significantly elevate values.

Exhibition history: similar to publications, past exhibitions validate authenticity and importance, and therefore also significantly elevate values.

With the documentation stage completed, the appraiser would move on to the research stage of the process. The primary activity at this stage will generally involve consulting art market databases, such as Artnet and Invaluable, to seek out the best possible comparables from which an opinion of value can be formed about the piece in question. Ideal comparables are similar to the piece in question in terms of author, medium, size, and subject. Also, it is hoped that they should be recently sold a public auction. If the comparable was placed at auction, but went unsold, then the appraiser should calculate down from the estimate. If no auction comparables can be found, then the appraiser would turn to the retail market of dealers and even the online marketplace. These are less-than-ideal solutions, but the appraiser must turn to them in the absence of reliable auction data. With comparables assembled, ideally at least three, the appraiser would form an opinion of value relative to the method of value being used in that appraisal report, that is, RRV or FMV. The values of all the appraised items in the report would also be totaled.

The completed and signed appraisal is then turned over to the client and their designated users (lawyers, accountants). A properly prepared appraisal report should indicate its designated users, and otherwise note that the document should not be used for any other purpose or users. Also, appraisers usually put in clauses that the document may not be used as a certificate of authenticity. The appraisal can be used in legal proceedings in a court of law, and therefore, an appraiser has to be ready to defend their work. However, a court-room appearance should be accompanied by legal counsel and that can be quite expensive. Therefore, appraisers often put in clauses in their reports that they will be prepared to defend the report in court, but the client should be prepared to meet the costs of their legal representation should that eventuality occur.

CASE STUDY: ROBERT RAUSCHENBERG'S CANYON

Given his canonical status as one of the founders of the Pop Art movement, one would expect a well-documented piece by Robert Rauschenberg to have significant market value. In fact, this piece had been owned by the legendary dealer of Pop artists, Ileana Sonnabend, and it had been shown on-and-off at the Museum of Modern Art (MoMA) for years. The 1959 work, *Canyon*, came from Rauschenberg's period when he began making "combines." In this case, his friend, artist Sari Dienes offered him a taxidermied eagle she had fished out from the junk heap of a recently deceased neighbor, one of Teddy Roosevelt's Rough Riders.[3]

The problem lay with the eagle. Bald and golden eagles are protected species. The Migratory Bird Treaty Act of 1918 and the Bald and Golden Eagle Protection Act of 1940 make it illegal to buy, sell, barter, or possess bald or golden eagles in the United States. One of the reasons *Canyon* was allowed to remain in Sonnabend's collection was because Rauschenberg had provided a notarized statement saying the bird had been stuffed by one of Roosevelt's Rough Riders before the laws' passage.

When Ileana Sonnabend's heirs inherited it with her passing in 2007, they argued that because it could not be sold, the family's appraisers had valued it at zero, and so it should have no inheritance tax. The IRS did not concur and ruled that the work had a FMV of $65 million, assessing estate tax and penalties on the heirs.[4] A resolution was finally reached that allowed the family to donate the work to a U.S. institution in exchange for dropping the tax assement. It now hangs again in MoMA, where it had before.

APPRAISING—TERMS

Appraisal—is the act or process of developing an opinion of value.

USPAP—the Uniform Standards of Professional Appraisal Practice requires appraisers to pass their 15-hour course followed by an exam. All appraisers must take the refresher 7-hour course every two years to remain USPAP-compliant.

Donation appraisal—the most exacting form of appraisal as it is written for the charitable donation of artwork to a public collection which also must be a nonprofit 501(c)(3) (in the United States). The value of the donated artwork may be deducted on the donor's taxable income.

Comparable—an object which has been sold at auction and is similar to the one being appraised. If an auction sale is not available, then the appraiser might turn to dealers or the online marketplace instead. The sale price (or advertised price) of the comparable will be used in setting the appraised value of the object in question.

Method of valuation—an intellectual approach to setting an appraised value that takes into consideration various imagined market settings.

Fair market value—a method of valuation that imagines an equal meeting of buyer and seller without coercion or urgency with both parties having reasonable knowledge of relevant facts.

Retail replacement value—a method of value that imagines the cost of replacing a piece of personal property at the retail cost that would be paid by a purchaser, including relevant taxes, commissions, and fees.

Liquidation value—a method of value that imagines an immediate forced sale, and the value that could be redeemed in the event of such a sale.

Specialization—appraisers usually have general qualifications in all categories of personal property, but they also have a specialization, a category of property, where they have advanced expertise. These specializations often conform to categories used by auction houses to organize their sales: Postwar/Contemporary, Impressionism/Modern, Old Masters.

Appraisers associations—in the United States there are three appraisers associations that represent personal property appraisers and require their members to be USPAP-compliant. These are the AAA, the ASA, and the ISA.

Notes

1 https://www.art-appraisals.net/value-definitions.
2 Internal Revenue Service (IRS), Treasury Regulation. §20.2031 (b).
3 Kim, H. "Diving into Rauschenberg's Canyon." *Inside/Out: A MoMA/MoMA PS1 Blog*, Jan. 24, 2014.
4 Cohen, P. "Art's Sale Value? Zero. The Tax Bill? $29 Million." *The New York Times*, July 22, 2012.

Conservation

Chapter 18

CONSERVATION VERSUS RESTORATION

Art works have been restored and conserved long before they were even considered art or such a concept of art even existed. The Budapest Museum of Fine Arts has in their collection an *apotropaion* which may be described by Egyptologists as a "magic knife" or "magic wand." At some point, it had been broken, and small copper bands can be seen binding the piece together so it would remain intact, repairs made millennia ago.[1] Especially when these objects more often had a religious function, the most important principle was that they should remain intact, otherwise they would not serve their function very successfully. Frescos in a medieval church that were no longer visible could no longer educate an illiterate laity and would need to be redone. Little thought would have been given to the earlier master whose works would now be lost forever if they were painted over. Even with the re-emergence of the cult of art and a concept of art-as-end-in-itself, which began to take hold in Renaissance-era Italy, there was still a great premium placed on something being intact. When fragments of classical-era (500 BCE–300 CE) sculpture were dug up in the vicinity of Rome, contemporary sculptors might be commissioned to fill in the lost pieces and return it to a complete work. Such was the case of the *Laocoön*, discovered in 1506, which needed an arm replaced, and the positioning of the arm would be the subject of great debate, then and still now.[2] What emerged from that

DOI: 10.4324/9781003431756-19

discourse was the concept of artist's original intent, and also the question of what role should latter-day restorers or artists have inserting themselves into the artwork.

The principle that non-intact artworks should be returned to their best possible complete presentation would remain preeminent until the later twentieth century. At that point, a new generation of scholars began to question earlier restorations of works and draw attention to how much the restorer had altered the piece, and sadly how little of the original work remained. As a result of this discourse, two distinct terms began to emerge: restoration and conservation. "Restoration" has come to mean a process of profound intervention that attempts to return an artwork to the closest possible resemblance of its original state, even if that means significant amounts of reconstruction or inpainting in order to achieve that goal. The newer term, "conservation," embodies the emerging ethos that artworks should be stabilized but not added to, and ethical conservators do not desire to insert themselves or their aesthetic visions into the works. Now in the higher levels of the English-speaking art world, one only hears the word "conservation" and not "restoration," which is now somewhat of a bad word. Many other European languages, however, continue to use a variant of "restoration" and make no such semantic distinction.

Furniture, however, might be the one medium in which restorer remains the preferred term over conservator. This may reflect the grudging recognition that furniture is simply too functional of an applied art, and if it is not more-or-less intact, then it is essentially worthless. Furniture restorers frequently find themselves presented with heavily degraded pieces that will never be of any use to anyone without significant amounts of intervention and reconstruction. Furthermore, furniture operates in forms and patterns. So, if one leg of a table is missing, its shape can be inferred from the other three remaining legs. Still, some purists insist that original condition is preferable, and so dealers and auction houses will usually sell important pieces in unrestored condition so that the decision about how, if at all, the restoration should be done can be left up to the new owner. Furthermore, seating often has upholstery which inevitably gets worn out and must be replaced. Antique dealer may, however, stop short of re-upholstering chairs and just restore the wood portion of the piece and have all of the structural parts of the seat (springs, canvas straps, Algerian fiber or horsehair stuffing, and a thin layer of muslin fabric) constructed, with the final layer of patterned upholstery usually left to the taste of the new collector, or more likely their interior designer.

Another related trade is that of the framer. Framers in smaller markets very frequently double as lower-end painting restorers, and in New York, some of the leading framers also offer museum-quality conservation. The close connection stems from the fact that both tasks, conservation and framing, are often done at the same time, usually at the point of a new acquisition. In many cases, the conservation may be a simple cleaning and re-varnishing, which is not considered an intervention, but rather an exercise in good long-term care. Frames, themselves, are very much art objects, and old ones can be extremely valuable and often in need of fixing, especially gilded ones, where the gilding has flaked off. Higher-end framers are dealers themselves, always looking to buy up inventory of interesting antique frames which they can resell at a significant mark-up. They furthermore develop clever strategies (resizing, matting, and floating canvas) to make an old frame work with a painting even if they do not initially size up.

PROCEDURES OF CONSERVATION

In the past, conservation and restoration were tasks picked up by painters looking for extra work, and they had the habit of often doing a good deal of inpainting and overpainting. Nowadays in the United States, and most Western countries, there exist established schools of higher education that train professional conservators in nearly all of the media in which artists work. Three universities in the United States, University of Delaware, New York University, and Buffalo State University, offer graduate programs in conservation. In Europe, the programs are more often based at national academies of fine art and begin at the undergraduate level, that is, accepting students straight out of high school. The training usually involves a strong immersion in art history and also the chemistry of art objects and their component parts before being allowed to begin work on any actual pieces. The intended employment for graduates will be at elite museums with budgets adequate to maintain a full-time conservation department. The sad reality, though, is that these jobs are scarce, and most conservators make do with part-time, poorly paid employment at a museum and use the prestige from such a position on their business card to secure better paying private-sector work on the side. Many museum directors of small institutions may find themselves and their curators playing the role of jack-of-all-trades, including sometimes having to play the role of conservator. The International Preservation Studies Center in Illinois had offered a range of short courses designed to train these people in professional conservation skills appropriate to their institution's profile and mission.[3]

A well-trained conservator, before beginning any cleaning, treatment, or intervention, will thoroughly document the work in its current state. They will use a high-quality digital camera to take images of all sides of the work and close-ups of significant areas where damage has occurred. They should also examine the work under ultraviolet light in order to determine where earlier interventions had been made. This will allow them to understand where the original portions of the work are, and where are latter-day insertions. If the restorer has access to a multi-spectral imaging camera, then they will be able to photograph in the ultraviolet and infrared spectrums (which can reveal underdrawing). If the conservator has access to a proper conservation science laboratory, then they can also request an X-ray of the piece, which might reveal an earlier underlying painting, referred to as a *pentimento*. They might also request materials analysis of the piece. For a painting, this would involve examining the pigments, which in the past would have been done by examining a (destructive) sample under a microscope, but now much data can be gathered on the pigments through X-ray fluorescence, which is non-destructive. Knowing the original pigments of the work can be enormously helpful in selecting the correct ones for the inpainting.

With a thorough documentation completed, a paintings conservator would next begin testing different solvents to remove dirt and old varnish. A careful conservator will proceed in small sections, and often relatively less important sections, giving time to see the effects of the chemicals being employed. Many painting dealers can tell nightmare stories of having sent out a painting for cleaning, only to find that the work had been carelessly over-cleaned, and crucial layers of original paint were removed. With the work cleaned, the conservator can proceed to any treatments that may have been requested, and someone experienced in the conservation business would know to have gotten clear written authorization to undertake these steps. Typical treatments for paintings might involve re-stretching (reattaching the canvas to the wooden stretcher or attaching it to an altogether new stretcher), inpainting, or fixing holes in the canvas. More invasive steps could include relining (applying a second canvas behind a weakened original canvas), vacuuming down craquelure, and even transferring to an altogether new support, such as from wooden panel to canvas. When the treatment is completed, the painting may be varnished again, if the original had been (many postwar paintings were not varnished). It will be replaced in its original frame (which might have also been conserved) or into a new one. Professional services such as these will easily cost over $1,000 and many thousands for significant treatments.

ETHICS OF CONSERVATION

The shift from the term "restoration" to the term "conservation" already says significant things about the evolving ethics of the field. If the old principle had been to "make it whole," then the new principle was "conserve but add nothing." Conservators entering the field are inculcated with a respect for the artist's original intent and their own humble desire for their hand to remain invisible in the conserved work. They are also shown how the work of earlier restorers' treatments caused much more damage to the work than had already been present. Therefore, everything an ethical conservator undertakes should ideally be reversible. These ideas emerged out of significant debates in the twentieth century about what were seen as destructive restorations. Joseph Duveen, the dominant secondary market dealer of the early twentieth century was notorious for commissioning over-restoration on Italian old master paintings, for example, having an older woman's portrait changed to appear that of a younger woman.[4] At this point, such restorations merge on the act of enhancement, which is essentially a form of forgery. When the frescos of Michelangelo's

Last Judgement were cleaned, many people were disappointed with the newly vibrant colors because they had been accustomed to its former smoky, opaque appearance.[5] It is worth remembering that the art of the past often gets remembered quite differently than it may have been to its contemporaries. We know now that true Hellenic Greek sculpture was painted, but by time it had been excavated in the fifteenth–eighteenth centuries, it had lost that paint. The Neo-Classical style it then inspired featured bare marble sculptures, similar to the way they looked when taken out of the ground.

Many extreme interventions that were standard in the past have become a step of last resort and to be avoided, if at all possible. Oil on canvas paintings usually had a second canvas glued to their backs after about 70–100 years because the original canvas would often stretch and weaken. This treatment was seen as ensuring the longevity of the piece, and the process often involved a vacuum table that pulled down paint that was developing concave craquelure in order to prevent it from flaking off completely. What current day curators have noticed, however, is how much this treatment can degrade the artwork, no more so than with canonical Impressionist paintings. The vast majority of important Impressionist works have already been relined, and we can now tell, when compared with the few that have not, that the relined ones have lost a certain luminosity. This is because, although we do not normally think of light passing through a painting, in fact, that is exactly what happened with Impressionist works. Adding a second layer of canvas, however, destroys that effect, and, furthermore, the glues used very often caused a darkening of the grounding, darkening the whole picture. If vacuuming was employed, it usually flattened out what had been an impasto with a great deal of plasticity. An important influence in the new ethics in conservation arrived from the archaeological field, where the early twentieth-century reconstructions of important sites had produced highly speculative interpretations and significant destruction to the actual material in the field. Adhering to the principle that treatments should be, as much as possible, non-invasive and reversible, conservators and curators are exploring the use of digital technology to allow visitors to appreciate how the intact work may have looked, without actually altering the work in its current state. At the Acquincum site in Budapest, a small late Roman (c.100–350 CE) town and fortress along the Danube, an imaging tool allows visitors to scan the site with a viewfinder that merges the existing ruins with a digital reconstruction of how the building would have looked intact.[6] At Harvard University, famous murals by Mark Rothko had faded significantly, and so colored lighting is shined on the works so that viewers can appreciate the colors as they originally looked.[7] Increasingly, artists are demanding a role in the conservation of their artworks during their own lifetimes, and if treatment is not something they have authorized, some have been known to try to legally disown the work, as Cady Noland has repeatedly try to do with her *Log Cabin*.[8]

CASE STUDY: THE RESTORATIONS OF LOTHAR MALSKAT

Conservations often go badly, and one, the story Cecilia Giménez's 2012 botched attempt at restoring a fresco, *Ecce Homo* by Elías García Martínez in the Sanctuary of Mercy church of Borja, Zaragoza, in Spain counts as a rare example of a conservation "gone bad" that has a happy ending. Giménez's restoration, which, to be fair, looks nothing like Martínez's original, was immediately mocked around the world with the monikers *Monkey Christ* or *Ecce Mono*. Then, precisely because of this notoriety, Borja became a pilgrimage site for tourists seeking something utterly ironic, and the sleepy town has suddenly acquired a tourism industry.[9] An opera has even been written about the story.

Restorations that profoundly corrupted knowledge, however, are more rare. In the middle of the Second World War, the bizarre story of Lothar Malskat and his restorations of the frescoes of the Marienkirche in the city of Lübeck serves as such an example. As a result of Allied bombing in 1942, the church was heavily damaged, but the heat of the explosion also removed plaster covering the remnants of the church's Gothic-era frescoes. It was regarded as a miracle that the bombs had revealed these lost treasures. A Professor Ernst Fey, an expert on German medieval churches, and his son Dietrich were hired to conduct the restoration, and the Feys had previously worked with a young painter, Lothar Malskat, as an assistant. On an earlier job, in the town of Schleswig, they had had to redo the Romanesque frescoes in city's cathedral, St. Petri-Dom, after an earlier disastrous restoration. In this case, Malskat ended up repainting himself what were mostly fragments of images. For the image of the Madonna, he used the face of Greta Garbo.[10] The apostles looked like Vikings, which appealed to the Nazi authorities. Furthermore, Malskat inserted a turkey, which should be a New World species, and so Third Reich historians took it as proof that Germanic Vikings had indeed made it to the New World and brought the bird back with them.

On the strength of their St. Petri-Dom restoration, the Feys won the contract to restore the frescoes of the Marienkirche of Lübeck. This time Malskat painted nearly the entire thing himself, essentially erasing the remnants of the recovered original Gothic images. However, when the restored church was unveiled in 1948, Malskat was not happy. He'd been paid only a small amount of the large fee the Feys had been paid for the project, and for which the Feys took all the credit. When Malskat tried to explain that he had created the frescoes, no one at first believed him. He tried confessing his earlier forgeries at Schleswig. Only when police found fake paintings ostensibly by Matisse, Degas, Chagall, and Beckmann (but by Malskat) in the Fey's home did the authorities began to take the whole restoration/forgery conspiracy seriously and realize that the frescoes in both churches were now entirely modern creations.[11]

CONSERVATION—TERMS

Restoration—the act of making a damaged art object whole and intact again. In the West, the term and its practice have fallen out of favor, and the term "conservation" is preferred, with emphasis being on not adding un-original material.

Inpainting—the practice of a conservator painting in areas that have lost their original paint. It can be a controversial practice if the inpainting amounts to a significant addition where the artist's original intentions are unclear.

Enhancement—an unethical practice where a restorer adds un-original elements to an artwork in order to increase its sale value.

Over-restoration—when a restorer removes original material or adds un-original elements in the attempt to make an intact artwork but ultimately ends up degrading the artwork.

Relining—a standard practice in the past involving adding another layer of canvas to an older painting in the interest of stabilizing it. Now realized to diminish the vibrancy of a painting, current-day conservators avoid the process if at all possible.

Craquelure—the phenomenon of a cracking pattern that forms on oil paint as it dries. It generally takes many decades for an oil painting to develop craquelure and is taken as a sign of age.

Cleaning—a basic conservation process that involves removing dirt, dust, and degraded varnish but must be done carefully with correctly chosen solvents so that none of the original paint is removed.

Matting—the placing of a work on paper within a cardboard frame, which is then set inside a wooden frame and usually covered with glass.

Stretcher—the wooden rectangle to which a canvas is attached in a way that makes the canvas taut.

Foxing—are small dots of oxidation and discoloration that appear on older paper.

Notes

1 *Apotropaion*, Hippopotamus tusk. c. 1773–1650 BCE. Collection of the Fine Arts Museum of Budapest. https://www.mfab.hu/artworks/apotropaion/.

2 Howard, S. "On the Reconstruction of the Vatican Laocoon Group." *American Journal of Archaeology*, vol. 63, no. 4, 1959, pp. 365–369.

3 Formerly called the Campbell Center, it has recently been absorbed by the Highland Community College.

4 Simpson, C. *Artful Partners: Bernard Berenson and Joseph Duveen*. New York: Macmillan, 1986, pp. 150–151.

5 Tagliabue, J. "Cleaned 'Last Judgment' Unveiled." *The New York Times*, Apr. 9, 1994.

6 Zsidi, P. "From the Plan Sheet to the Screen—Reconstructions in Aquincum." *Budapest Régiségei*, vol. XL, 2006, p. 328.

7 Sheets H. M. "A Return for Rothko's Harvard Murals." *The New York Times*, Oct. 23, 2014.

8 Kinsella, E. "Cady Noland Said a Collector Restored Her Log Cabin Sculpture Beyond Recognition. A Judge Has Thrown Out Her Lawsuit—for the Third Time." *Artnet*, June 3, 2020.

9 Jones, S. "How 'Monkey Christ' Brought New Life to a Quiet Spanish Town." *The Guardian*, Dec. 28, 2018.

10 Keats, J. "Pious Fraud: Art Forgery: Lothar Malskat Was a Master at Forging Restorations, Old-Master and Modern Paintings." *Art and Antiques Magazine*, Feb. 2, 2012.

11 Ibid.

Connoisseurship

Chapter 19

KNOWLEDGE IN ART

One of the greatest mysteries to those new to the art business is quite simply: how does the business agree to know what it knows? Especially in the most contentious sector of determining whether artworks are authentic or fake, the lack of any structure or standardized process for settling these disputes can seem perplexing to the outsider. In fact, the current system of establishing knowledge in art remains a hodgepodge of improvised arrangements for specific artists, but nothing exists in the form of an overarching authority. Although Interpol, the international police organization, did hold a landmark conference on art forgery in 2012, their role is limited to an advisory one, and domestic law enforcement must prosecute cases of fraud involving art. At the very heart of the problem lies the intersection of an academic discipline: art history with what are sometimes very, very large amounts of money. For this reason alone, the most contentious attribution disputes often end up being decided in court, often either a U.S. federal or a New York state court.

Almost as soon as art emerges as a phenomenon in the ancient world, it is followed closely by the phenomenon of art forgery. The Apollo of Piombino, for example, is a bronze sculpture cast in the style of a fifth century BCE kouros, but by two first century BCE sculptors who acknowledged as

DOI: 10.4324/9781003431756-20

much on a now-lost lead plate inside the bronze.[1] Pausanias, in his *Description of Greece*, provides an example of early connoisseurship when he describes the star artifact of Chaeronea, purporting to be the scepter of Agamemnon made by Hephaestus and referenced in Homer, and he deems it authentic, but he dismisses other works purporting to have belonged to Agamemnon because they are bronze, noting that the process of casting bronze was only invented by the Samians Theodorus and Rhoecus, which was after the age of Agamemnon. It may be our first reference of inauthenticity being determined through the presence of anachronistic materials.[2] The art forger's work often represents a resentment by latter-day contemporary artists who often believe that their work deserves equal praise and equal valuation to that of earlier masters, and their forgeries directly undermine that valuation hierarchy. For example, when Michelangelo created his *Sleeping Cupid*, he may have done so to prove he was as worthy as a classical sculptor, though it may have been Baldassare del Milanese, the dealer, who tried to pass it off as a classical piece.[3] Ultimately, the forger represents a rearguard, underdog counter-attack by the masses of underappreciated contemporary artists upon a market that pays super-prices for works by the canonical few. Time and time again, that resentment drives frustrated artists to become forgers.

The weakness that forgers exploit is the prevailing methods by which the art business decides how to determine the attribution of a given artwork. The seventeenth century painter and etcher Claude Lorrain recognized the threat of forgeries of his work even in his own lifetime, leading him to produce his own *Liber Veritatis*, which might represent a sort of first attempt at a *catalogue raisonné* (a complete compendium of an artist's work).[4] Most artists, however, have not had the prescience of Claude, and soon as they die, an immediate problem ensues as to how to determine if they executed an artwork or not. The French have a system of *droit moral* (Moral Rights), which derives from the 1928 Bern Convention on copyright and provides for the heirs of an artist to control the rights to that artist's works, thereby granting them control of the oeuvre and especially attributions. That said, only a tiny fraction of artists who have ever worked have families who have ever exercised that right and established authentication boards or *catalogue raisonné* committees. No clear method exists for how to determine the relevant authority for artists where there is no one to exercise *droit moral*, such as with long-dead old master artists. In some ways, the clearest indicator of widespread confidence that a piece is what it purports to be had been the de facto solution of whether Christie's or Sotheby's would sell it as such. That confidence, however, has been undermined by the on-going saga of the *Salvator Mundi* painting, which both auction houses sold as being by Leonardo da Vinci, but now both the Louvre and the Prado have essentially dismissed that attribution.[5]

To understand how fraught the current system of knowledge is, consider this one example. One day in 1985, the insured retail replacement value of a painting hanging in a West Berlin museum dropped from $8 million to approximately one twentieth of the value overnight. *Man with a Golden Helmet* had long been regarded as one of the finest works by Rembrandt van Rijn but was de-attributed (determined now not to be by Rembrandt) by the Rembrandt Research Project (RRP) in the first of a series of volumes that came out that year.[6] This project represented the single most expensive and exhaustive attempt to create accurate knowledge in the œuvre of a single artist. Begun in 1969, the RRP aimed to take full advantage of cutting-edge scientific techniques, using dendrochronology on the wood panels, X-rays of paint layers, and weave counts on the canvasses. However, in 1993, most members of the project's committee quit over disputes about its basic methodology, which had been to evaluate each potential Rembrandt (works that had been authenticated by earlier *catalogue raisonnés*) and assign a grade: A, by Rembrandt; B, doubtful; or C, not by Rembrandt. This trinary system essentially functioned as a binary one because the only result that actually mattered was whether it was A or not-A. Use of science did not, in the end, provide the certainty of conclusions that the committee had originally been expecting. Instead of weaning out the fakes, examinations more often showed that materials were entirely consistent with the work having been done in the seventeenth century. Shameless forgeries were not the problem, but rather co-productions of Rembrandt and his associates. Paintings were not so much A, B, or C, but rather some percent master and some percent assistant. Ernst van de Wetering, who remained in charge of the RRP, emphasized the group's new ethos which validated the importance of doubts and their honest expression:

> Most people want an authority who says, this is a Rembrandt and this is not a Rembrandt. But our work has little to do with money and with writing museum labels. It's doing the best we can to reconstruct a segment of art history.[7]

The example of the RRP remains so instructive because it clearly exposes the challenges of establishing how we know what we know in the art world. The market, especially auction houses, needs clear, unambiguous attributions, but the art historians, conservators, and connoisseurs studying these works may not honestly have developed a simple yes/no conclusion. What they may have is a series of observations that might not add up to a conclusive determination of authorship. This can especially be the case with seventeenth-century painters such as Rembrandt or Rubens, where separating the hand of the master from that of the assistant can be nearly impossible. And furthermore, the market is set up to sell works done solely by one artist. It does not know how to price a piece that is some percent master and some percent "workshop of the master." Museums, even if they are not selling ownership of the collection, are still selling it on an experiential level, and many of them felt they were suffering significant losses due to the RRP's de-attribution of their star Rembrandts.

The best way to understand how attributions are created across the art world is to turn to Karl Mannheim's concept of a sociology of knowledge, which describes how socially accepted knowledge is constructed in different formats:

1. On the basis of a consensus of opinion, called "consensus position;"
2. On the basis of the monopoly position of one particular group, called "monopoly position;"
3. On the basis of competition between many groups, called "atomistic competition;"
4. On the basis of a competition between a few groups, called "polar competition."[8]

We can find each of these examples present in the art world. Consensus position would represent any artwork for which, even though there may not exist a single monopoly expert, still no one seriously doubts the attribution, such as that Michelangelo painted the frescoes on the ceiling of the Sistine Chapel or that Raphael painted the altarpiece known as the *Sistine Madonna*. Monopoly position is that which is occupied by authentication boards and *catalogue raisonné* committees, which the market considers to be the only legitimate authority to give an attribution for that artist. Such is the case with the oeuvres of Pablo Picasso, Giorgio de Chirico, and Robert Motherwell, and generally is the case where an artist died within the last hundred years, and was famous enough, and the artist's works were worth enough, that their heirs exercised their *droit moral*. There are relatively few of these cases, however, which is surprising given that monopoly position is clearly what the market prefers. Leading auction houses prefer to hear from a single authority as to whether this is or is not by the artist, and then they can sell it as such with certainty. Atomistic competition would describe the situation with the vast, vast majority of all artists who have ever worked: that is, there is no authority. Generally, this would be the case for the simple reason that the artist's œuvre is simply not worth enough money for anyone to bother to be an expert on this artist. The last variant, polar competition, would describe many situations where there are experts, but no clear dominant one. Such would be the case with many of the canonical Old Masters: Leonardo, Caravaggio, and even some modernists such as Amedeo Modigliani.[9] This scenario can be the most bewildering to the market because it can result in competing authorities giving contradictory conclusions.

Establishing who has authority to make attributions regarding a certain artist represents one challenge, but an even more contentious challenge lies in determining the correct methodology for making an attribution. In the nineteenth century, alongside the emerging discipline of art history, arrived a parallel field called connoisseurship. It is inescapably associated with name of Giovanni Morelli, an Italian doctor who published *Die Werke italienischer Meister in den Galerien von*

München, Dresden und Berlin [the Work of the Italian Masters in the Galleries of Munich, Dresden and Berlin] in 1880 under a Russian penname Ivan Lermolieff, where he re-attributed Renaissance masterpieces in leading German museums to different authors.[10] In order to determine who was the actual true author of a piece, Morelli used his medical training to observe unnoticed details which would indicate who was the actual painter. The details he focused on were the particularly difficult features of the human anatomy for artists to render: the shape of the ears and the hands. He believed that in these peripheral details, the artist would reveal their personal solutions to these painterly problems. Morelli's method of connoisseurship would be adopted by his disciple Bernard Berenson, who would remain the authoritative figure on virtually all of painters of the Italian Renaissance for much of the first half of the twentieth century.[11] This vast expanse of authority over such an important period would be unthinkable in our current day, when an expert is generally an expert on, at most, one artist.

Berenson's prestige, however, diminished dramatically as a result of the most spectacular art trial in history, often referred to as the case of the American Leonardo. In many ways, this was the first public event to literally place the reigning connoisseurship system on trial. The lawsuit of Hahn v. Duveen centered on two versions of the purported Leonardo da Vinci *La Belle Ferronnière*, the one in the Louvre and the one that appeared in Kansas in 1920.[12] Joseph Duveen denounced the Kansas version, and its owner Harry Hahn had sued the dominant old master dealer for $500,000 USD for slander of title.[13] The trial would signal the formation of a dichotomy between Morellian connoisseurship, represented by the experts Duveen brought forward, especially Bernard Berenson, and new art forensics techniques such as microscopic study of pigment samples and x-rays.[14] Although Hahn's painting would never be accepted as a Leonardo nor ever able to be sold as one, Duveen lost the lawsuit and had to settle, and Berenson's reputation came out even worse. He admitted in court to being on Duveen's payroll, and while being questioned about a supposed Leonardo in the Prado, Berenson admitted that he did not know if the work was on panel or canvas, and believed the fact was no more important than the paper a Shakespeare play was written on. The lesson from the Hahn trial was that connoisseurship might work fine for the art market, but it did not hold up well in a court of law.

THE CRISIS OF FORGERY

Forgery has been a recurring problem since art's origins, but in the last twenty years the New York art world seems to have been shaken by one forgery scandal after another. Many of them have centered around the Abstract-Expressionist artists of the so-called New York School: Robert Motherwell, Mark Rothko, and especially Jackson Pollock. The fact that the œuvre of Pollock's should be the subject of so many disputes should come as no surprise. An artist who poured paint onto a canvas does not have a brushstroke and, furthermore, his abstract works did not represent figures with hands or ears. In other words, Morellian connoisseurship would be useless in authenticating a Pollock. The most spectacular of all forgery scandals exploded in 2011 with the abrupt closure of Knoedler, New York's oldest gallery (in operation for 168 years). They had been selling works by the Abstract-Expressionist masters for almost 20 years, with all of them coming through a little-known Long Island dealer who claimed to have connections to a mysterious collector who wished to remain anonymous. All of the works turned out to have been painted by one Chinese immigrant who promptly fled back to China when the scandal erupted [See Case Study: Knoedler].[15]

These and other forgery cases have caused the market to become skeptical of experts who vouch for an artwork simply by relying on their ability to visually recognize the hand of the artist based on their connoisseurship skills alone. The crisis, however, is not simply reserved to paintings. The serial print market faces its own threats, though different ones. Many people may have seen art galleries in resorts or casinos or cruise ships that seem to be selling prints by very canonical masters like Dalí, Miró, or Chagall. Somehow these works that in theory are over 50 years old and hand-signed by the artist are in fact in pristine condition. The suspect print market appears to run through the online marketplace first, where these galleries acquire their inventory, and thereby give themselves a fence (a plausible legitimate source for illicit goods) to explain how they acquired these pieces.[16]

Sometimes the artist's own worst enemy is themself, as would be the case with Andy Warhol. As an artist, Warhol set out to systematically destroy the modernist art market. One way he devised to achieve this was by reviving a seventeenth-century workshop technique at his studio, The Factory. He loved the idea that he often had little physical role in the production of his paintings (usually silkscreens with some paint applied to them). One problem was that Warhol gave scant supervision to his production systems, and especially his printers who were notorious for producing additional works beyond the official print-run. The Andy Warhol Art Authentication Board was the subject of two major lawsuits, which ultimately resulted in its dissolution. The working methodology that the board used to authenticate a work was essentially that it was a Warhol if Warhol had been aware of it.[17] But that dictum itself became impossible to enforce judiciously, and finally the costs of fighting lawsuits forced the board to end its operation. They are only one of many that have ceased giving authentications, along with the Keith Haring Foundation[18] and the Jean-Michel Basquiat authentication committee.[19]

TECHNIQUES OF THE MOST SUCCESSFUL FORGERS

At the center of every major forgery scandal of the last century stands a forger who not only could produce a very convincing fake, but who also understood how to corrupt the very systems of knowledge by which the art world agrees to know what it knows. The first great forger of the twentieth century, Han van Meegeren, had repeatedly failed to secure attribution for his fake Vermeers, but in 1937 succeeded spectacularly when the reigning old master expert, Abraham Bredius, authenticated the *Christ and the Disciples at Emmaus*.[20] This work, which looks absolutely nothing like a Vermeer, managed to convince Bredius because it manipulated his own constructed knowledge, which held out the possibility of a Vermeer "religious period."[21] Now approved by the expert, the painting became a sort of type specimen to the oeuvre, allowing it to then validate van Meegeren's subsequent attempts in the same implausible *Neue Sachlichkeit* style.[22] Forgers become good at foiling yesterday's forensic methods but fail to anticipate new ones. Van Meegeren mixed in Bakelite into his works to defeat the primary test of the first half of the twentieth century, which was simply rubbing alcohol on a painting and piercing it with a hot needle, to which new paint will yield but old will not. Current methods of testing, however, can quickly identify the presence of phenol formaldehyde, the main component of Bakelite, a material only van Meegeren was known to use.

When Elmyr de Hory confessed his crimes in a tell-all biography by Clifford Irving in 1969, he was referred to as "the greatest forger of our time." His example can serve as a template of the art forger in many ways. He was frustrated by his lack of success as a painter in his own right. His one exhibition in New York in 1948 generated little interest and only a faint praise review.[23] Elmyr had developed a familiarity for the *École de Paris* avant-garde and could effortlessly mimic the drawings of Picasso, Matisse, and Modigliani. He also painted convincing oil versions of the Fauves: Dufy, van Dongen. Producing fake artworks, however, remained only a portion of a life devoted to maintaining illusions. Even in the first two pages of Irving's book describing Elmyr's origins in Budapest, nine false claims have been discovered by subsequent research.[24] Elmyr's name was not Elmyr de Hory, but rather Elemér Hoffmann.[25] His family had no aristocratic title· nor a villa in the Buda hills.[26] To validate that lineage, though, he forged what he claimed was a double portrait of himself and his brother painted by the world famous Hungarian portraitist Philip de László.[27] The fact that Elmyr would forge a painting of himself by the painter of European plutocracy should give some indication of the importance he placed on his claim of aristocratic heritage. Elmyr even kept up illusions in death: his tombstone in Ibiza contains two falsehoods: his made-up name, Elmyr, and a year of birth that made him five years younger.[28]

His dealers further contributed to the corruption of knowledge that allowed his forgeries to be sold. They co-opted experts who could guarantee a work's authenticity, knowing who they could bribe, and who they could fool. They then made copies of the stamps used by these experts, allowing them to produce their own documents, doing the same with customs stamps, which both ensured ease of transport, and also provided an artificial provenance. Perhaps their nefarious genius is best shown by their technique of acquiring a pre-war monograph on Matisse which used "tipped-in" color plates (these were only attached with a small amount of glue). They removed the plate and replaced it with a photographic copy of an Elmyr forgery.[29]

All forgers learn from earlier ones, and Wolfgang Beltracchi represents the culmination of all these nefarious techniques. In French and German gallery exhibition catalogues dating from the 1910s to 1920s he searched for paintings considered lost and published without an image, producing counterfeits according to the title. Like the other forgers before him, as an artist he saw himself belonging to another era, and he considered himself a kindred soul to the early twentieth-century Expressionist painters to whose œuvre he made additions and did so very convincingly. But he also understood that artworks were judged on their provenance, and so he invented the art collection of the Cologne factory owner Werner Jaeger his wife's grandfather, and placed stamps "Sammlung Werner Jaeger Koeln" on the backs of his paintings. He also affixed forged collection stamps from *Sammlung Flechtheim*, the collection of Alfred Flechtheim, one of the most important modernist dealers during the Weimar period, as well as *Der Sturm*, Herwarth Walden's seminal gallery in Berlin. He even photographed his wife with a pre-war camera, posing as her grandmother, with period furniture and his forgeries hanging on the wall, since an archival photograph is the holy grail of provenance documentation. Increasingly, the Werner Jaeger collection designation served as its own validation.[30] His fakes would be exhibited at the Metropolitan Museum of Art[31] and sold at Christie's,[32] and elite collectors happily enjoyed them as if they were authentic. Beltracchi also knew exactly which paints to avoid and worked with only period pigments. He did not however realize that his tube of zinc white (a nineteenth-century pigment) might be mixed with titanium dioxide (a paint only available post-1920), and this was how he was caught. At the time of his arrest, he claims he had been sending his works out to labs to see if they were "science-proof." Beltracchi's attempts to manipulate both provenance and science illuminates the future of art forgery in the twenty-first century: the really dangerous forgers are going to be those who can corrupt knowledge itself.

STRATEGIES FOR FIGHTING FORGERIES

For much of the broader art world, little monopoly authority exists. This would be the case with nearly all sectors of antiques, as well as most of the area of fine arts. Monopoly authority largely only exists in the sector of paintings, and only for those artists whose market value merits the creation of a *catalogue raisonné* or to maintain an authentication committee. For everything else, in the absence of clear authority to determine what is authentic, it becomes almost impossible to eradicate fakes and forgeries. Furthermore, there exists a vast taxonomy of ways that an object can be in some way inauthentic. It can be a copy done in the manner of the master. The piece can be in the style of an earlier era, but done in a later period, which is often the case with furniture. For many of the applied arts that are collected, there can be a much sought-after firm's products, and then many copy-cat firms that produced similar, but not nearly so valuable versions. For prints, photographs, bronze castings, and other serially produced media, all can be easily copied and reproduced, resulting in unauthorized editions. Non-Fungible Tokens (NFTs) have only compounded the possibilities for appropriation and unauthorized usage of artworks.[33]

In the most contentious and high-value sector of paintings by canonical masters, we can observe that since the Hahn v. Duveen trial, the viability of Morellian connoisseurship has been repeatedly tested and shown to fail. The most recent forgery scandals occurring on the New York market have only confirmed that a more robust method to attribution is needed. Increasingly, the upper levels of the art world are embracing a model of a three-legged stool based on connoisseurship, provenance documentation, and scientific analysis, as the best practice for determining attribution.

With provenance itself becoming a target of forgeries (consider Beltracchi), more institutions are investing in professionals whose sole activity is to study and validate documents and sources related to the provenance of their collection. The Boston Museum of Fine Arts now has a full-time curator for provenance. Scientific analysis has increasingly become the means by which attribution disputes are being settled. The example of the conservator and fingerprint "expert" Peter Paul Biro, however, should serve to caution against working with "experts" who take a financial interest in the works they have studied.[34] Above all, art forensics laboratories should be operated by the principles of scientific method. Their results should be reproducible and based on pre-existing peer-reviewed knowledge.

With museum's holding a sort of canonizing power, especially through their possession of the crucial type specimens for a limited œuvre, inclusion and exhibition of newly discovered works can be regarded as de-facto authentication. This process remains at the heart of the *Salvator Mundi* narrative, both its initial inclusion in a show at the London National Gallery in 2011 which projected an imprimatur of autograph attribution, followed by the subsequent non-inclusion at the Louvre in 2019 and dismissal in the Prado's 2021 catalogue with a much downgraded designation in their list of "attributed works, workshop of authorized and supervised by Leonardo."[35] Collectors and dealers have sometimes managed to persuade museum directors to exhibit works that have not previously been fully authenticated. They can be attempting to exploit the lack of clear consensual monopoly authority in an œuvre and hope to use the museum setting and their labels to confirm the attribution. In 2017, the Museum of Fine Arts in Ghent showed the collection of Belgium-based Russians Igor and Olga Toporovsky featuring never-before seen works by Kazimir Malevich, Natalia Goncharova, and Wassily Kandinsky.[36] Outrage from a diverse group of experts and the art press, however, led to closure of the exhibit, the suspension of the museum director, and ultimately the arrest of the Toporovskys.[37] In 2022, the Orlando Museum of Art showed works by Jean-Michel Basquiat that were claimed to have been discovered in the storage locker of Thaddeus Mumford, a Hollywood screenwriter, who had supposedly bought them from the artist back in 1982, when he was living in Larry Gagosian's house.[38] The technique of placing the provenance running through an early or perhaps chaotic moment in the artist's career forms the basis of many significant forgery conspiracies. The exhibition was raided by the FBI shortly after opening, resulting in the ousting of the director, the resignation of the board chair, and the institution being placed on probation by the American Alliance of Museums.[39] Basquiat's two surviving sisters have now begun to reassert their *droit moral* over the estate both on questions of authenticity as well as licensing and rights of usage, for example, to prevent the auction of an unauthorized NFT.[40]

CASE STUDY: KNOEDLER

After suddenly closing in 2011 in the wake of massive lawsuits, Knoedler Gallery and its former director, Ann Freedman, were finally having their day in court in 2016: they were faced with a civil lawsuit levelled by collector (and Sotheby's chairman) Domenico De Sole, who thought he had bought an $8.3 million Mark Rothko from the gallery. It was actually painted by Pei-Shen Qian, a Chinese immigrant living in Queens. But the collapse of Knoedler, New York's oldest art gallery, was much more protracted and complex than the forgery trial taking place. The gallery's fall has much to do with profound changes in the gallery business over the last century and the increasing scarcity of profitable secondary market material.

When Michael Knoedler arrived in New York in 1852 to take over the representative outlet of the French lithographer Goupil & Cie, the city had virtually no art dealers to speak of. At that time, few Americans could afford to purchase one-of-a-kind oil paintings, and Knoedler's gallery would instead market inexpensive lithographs from Paris. Toward the end of the nineteenth century, the gallery began expanding, opening branches in Paris and London,[41] and they began working with the London gallery Colnaghi in the field of original Old Masters. Their clients included many of the robber barons of the era, including J.P. Morgan and Henry Clay Frick, allowing them to become a serious rival to the dominant dealer of the era, Joseph Duveen.[42] The 2011 lawsuits were not, however, the gallery's first brush with nefarious dealings.

In 1931, representatives of Knoedler purchased 21 masterpieces from Russia's Hermitage Museum for Andrew Mellon in a set of secret sales sanctioned by Joseph Stalin. The works included Jan van Eyck's *Annunciation* and an *Adoration of the Magi* by Sandro Botticelli, the latter

---

which was sold for over $800,000. The deal, brokered by Armand Hammer, an American with close business ties to Stalin, began the gallery's long, tragic involvement with the Hammer family.[43]

After the Second World War, they proved quite willing to deal in looted art, as the recent restitution of an El Greco has illuminated.[44] The recent case isn't their first brush with forgery either. In the 1958 edition of *Art News Annual*, the gallery took out a full-page ad with a 1948 Matisse that turned out to be a fake by the notorious forger Elmyr de Hory. After Elmyr's forgeries were exposed in 1969, Knoedler's top dealer, E. Coe Kerr, conceded: "It was a great painting....You would never dream it was a fake."[45]

Following the embarrassment of Elmy's forgery, Knoedler found itself close to bankruptcy. In 1971, the gallery was sold for $2.5 million—to their old partner in the Hermitage deals, Armand Hammer. Hammer made the excellent choice of appointing his business partner Maury Leibovitz to run the operation. Leibovitz, in turn, hired a well-connected art world figure, Lawrence Rubin, as gallery director.

Leibovitz and Rubin reversed flagging revenues by switching up the business model. They reoriented their focus, switching to mid-century and contemporary art and representing artists like Frank Stella, Richard Diebenkorn, and Robert Rauschenberg. Leibovitz also understood that galleries required multiple revenue streams to survive. He revived Knoedler's original business model—printing and selling serial artworks—and featured the prints of the immensely popular expressionist painter LeRoy Neiman. As one former employee of Leibovitz's explained:

> The main reason the Knoedler Gallery stayed afloat before 1993 was because of the genius of the president, Maury Leibovitz, and his strong relationship with LeRoy Neiman. The revenues from the lucrative publishing and printing deal between Neiman and Knoedler allowed the gallery to stay in business.[46]

When Armand Hammer died in 1990, his grandson, Michael A. Hammer, would assume control of the gallery. The full drama of the Hammer family has now entered the wider public's consciousness through that scandals of Michael's son Armie[47] and the Discovery+ documentary series House of Hammer.[48] Following Leibovitz's death in 1992, the gallery's profitable relationship with Neiman began to deteriorate. In a dramatic change in management, in 1994 Michael Hammer dismissed Rubin and turned over total control of the operation to his protégé Ann Freedman, which resulted in an exodus of artists led by Rauschenberg.[49] With the loss of their cash cow Neiman as well as their other late-career stars, the gallery needed to find new revenue streams, and for that they returned to their old profile in secondary market sales. They did so, however, right when a profound internet-driven paradigm shift was upsetting the balance between secondary market dealers and auction houses. Too much information and access to auctions were cannibalizing the dealers' opportunities for acquiring artworks that could be profitably resold. At this crucial moment, Knoedler initiated a business relationship with an obscure Long Island gallerist named Glafira Rosales, who represented a collection of previously unknown abstract-expressionist works belonging to an anonymous "Mr. X Jr." who had inherited them from a "Mr. X Sr." Rosales was willing to sell the pieces to Knoedler at dramatically below-market prices.[50]

Issues regarding the gallery's connoisseurship were already emerging by the early nineties when the estate of Richard Diebenkorn claimed two drawings from his Ocean Park series were fakes.[51] It seems, however, that the profits that Knoedler was earning from these secondary market sales were essential to their financial survival. One of the core questions that occurs when considering whether Ann Freedman knew the paintings were fake derives from the extraordinary profitability of these transactions. Many of their sales would achieve retail mark-ups of five to eight times their purchase price from Rosales. A gallerist would be thrilled to make that kind of opportunistic deal; but it becomes suspicious if it presents itself too often. Knoedler continued to receive indications that should have caused them to doubt the authenticity of the works, including the fact that a Pollock sold in 2002 was dismissed by the International Foundation for Art Research.[52] The provenance that had been given, that it had been acquired through a studio sale by a Filipino-American artist who had contemporaneously poured paint with Pollock, Alfonso Ossorio (who had also collected his works) was categorically dismissed by Ossorio's still living partner. Rosales and her co-conspirator José Carlos Bergantiños Diaz then concocted a provenance that originated through sales facilitated by a gallery assistant named David Herbert, and although he was indeed a fixture of the 57th Street art market at that time, no records of any sales to him could be located.[53] Knoedler nonetheless continued to sell works coming from the collection of Rosales' mysterious Mr. X Jr.

The full scale of the conspiracy only became apparent with two other works that could also not be authoritatively attributed. One was a purported Robert Motherwell painting from the artist's *Elegy to the Spanish Republic* series sold by Julian Weissman, a former Knoedler employee who knew of Rosales as a source. The Dedalus Foundation (which was at that time compiling the artist's *catalogue raisonné*) first wrote in 2007 that the work would be included in the upcoming edition. However, it wrote back two years later to say it would not; in the intervening years, the piece had been tested and found to contain anachronistic materials.[54] The other case involved another Pollock that Knoedler sold to hedge fund manager Pierre Lagrange with an assurance, apparently, that it would be included in the updated edition of Pollock's *catalogue raisonné*. In fact, the artist's authentication board had been disbanded since 1995. When Lagrange found that neither major auction house would accept the painting for sale, he filed suit in 2011, and the gallery promptly closed.[55]

CONNOISSEURSHIP—TERMS

Fake—an artwork which is not what it purports to be.

Forgery—an artwork which is not what it purports to be and is intentionally fraudulent with an intention to deceive, for example, having a forged signature.

Pastiche—a fake artwork composed of copied elements from the target artist's style.

Type specimen—a biology term for a specimen of an organism which represents a certain species. In the art world, these are artworks of uncontested authority (usually in public collections) that serve as representative examples of an artist's work and to which candidates for attribution will be compared.

Anachronistic material—material, such as a pigment, that was not in use at the time of an artwork's purported creation and therefore would indicate the object is probably a fake.

Connoisseur—is an expert in a certain artist, having studied a great amount of their work and has the ability to recognize authentic works through visual observation.

Provenance—is the history of ownership, commercial transactions, location, handling, usage, and exhibition of an artwork.

Art forensics—is the examination of artworks with scientific techniques with the purpose of determining a work's attribution, often with an identified master in question. The scientific examination can indicate the presence of anachronistic material which would determine the work to be fake.

Technical art history—is the examination of artworks with scientific techniques with the purpose of knowing more about the material components and production methods of a given artist.

Donor artwork—is a crude term used by art forgers to refer to the artworks that are used as the base materials in the making of a high-value forgery.

Notes

1 Ridgway, B. S. "The Bronze Apollo from Piombino in the Louvre." *Antike Plastik*, vol. 7, 1967, 43–75. Also see: https://www.louvre.fr/en/oeuvre-notices/apollo-piombino.

2 Pausanias. *Pausanias Description of Greece with an English Translation*. Trans. W. H. S. Jones, et al. Harvard University Press, 1918. 9.40.11- 9.41.1, 10.38.6. Pausanias is, however, not accurate in attributing the invention of the lost wax casting technique to these Sixth Century BCE sculptors. Examples of the technique pre-date them by millennia.

3 For a full narrative of the Sleeping Cupid and its source material, see: Norton, P. F. "The Lost Sleeping Cupid of Michelangelo." *The Art Bulletin*, vol. 39, no. 4, Dec. 1957, pp. 251–257.

4 Howard, D. "Review of Claude Lorrain: Liber Veritatis, by M. Kitson." *The Burlington Magazine*, vol. 121, no. 910, 1979, pp. 42–44.

5 Bailey, M. "Prado Museum Downgrades Leonardo's $450M Salvator Mundi in Exhibition Catalogue: Publication for Mona Lisa Show Puts the Painting in Category of Works That Are Attributed To, or Authorised or Supervised by the Renaissance Master." *The Art Newspaper*, Nov. 11, 2021.

6 Russel, J. "In search of the Real Thing." *The New York Times*, Dec. 1, 1985.

7 Hochfield, S. "What is a Real Rembrandt." *Art News*, Feb. 2004.

8 Mannheim, K. *Competition as Cultural Phenomenon, Essays Sociology Knowledge*, Volume 5, Routledge, (1929) 2013, p. 198.

9 Esterow, M. "The Art Market's Modigliani Forgery Epidemic." *Vanity Fair*, May 3, 2017.

10 Lermolieff, I. *Die Werke italienischer Meister in den Galerien von München, Dresden und Berlin*. Trans. J. Schwarze. Seemann, 1880.

11 See: Berenson, B. *The Venetian Painters of the Renaissance with an Index to their Works*. G. P. Putnam's sons, 1894. Berenson, B. *The Florentine Painters of the Renaissance with an Index to their Works*. G. P. Putnam's sons, 1896. Berenson, B. *The Central Italian Painters of the Renaissance*. G. P. Putnam's sons, 1897.

12 Brewer, J. *The American Leonardo: A Tale of Obsession, Art and Money*. New York: Oxford UP, 2009, provides the full narrative up until its recent sale.

13 "$500,000 Suit Hangs on da Vinci Fingers: Impressions on Canvas Said to Prove Master Painted Picture Denounced by Duveen." *The New York Times*, Nov. 5, 1921.

14 Brewer, J. "Art and Science: A Da Vinci Detective Story." *Engineering & Science*, vol. 68, no. 1/2, 2005, 37–40.

15 Miller, M. H. "The Big Fake: Behind the Scenes of Knoedler Gallery's Downfall." *ARTnews*, Apr. 25, 2016.

16 Levin, H. "Confessions of Art Fraud King Michael Zabrin." *Chicago Magazine*, Oct. 25, 2011.

17 Dorment, R. "What is a Warhol? The Buried Evidence." *The New York Review of Books*, June 20, 2013.

18 Burns, C. "Haring Market in Turmoil – Prolific Artist's Foundation Is Latest to Close Its Authentication Board." *The Art Newspaper*, Oct. 12, 2012.

19 Kinsella, E. "Basquiat Committee to Cease Authenticating Works." *ARTnews*, Jan. 24, 2012.

20 Bredius, A. "A New Vermeer." *Burlington Magazine*, vol. 71, 1937, p. 211.

21 Blankert, A. "The Case of Han van Meegeren's Fake Vermeer Supper at Emmaus Reconsidered." In Golahny, A., Mochizuki, M.M., Vergara, L. eds. *In His Milieu: Essays on Netherlandish Art in Memory of John Michael Montias,* Amsterdam University Press, 2006. pp. 47-58.

22 Morris, E. "Bamboozling Ourselves (Part 2)." *The New York Times*, May 28, 2009.

23 Keats, J. *Forged: Why Fakes are the Great Art of Our Age*. Oxford University Press, 2013, p. 114.

24 Irving, C. *Fake! The Story of Elmyr De Hory, the Greatest Art Forger of Our Time*. McGraw-Hill, 1969, pp. 15–16.

25 Birth Record for Hoffmann Elemér, Folyó-szám [Registration Number]: 1034. "Kivonat: A Budapest Zsidó Hitközseg Születési Anyakönyvéböl." It reports April 14, 1906 as his date of birth.

26 Birth Certificate. The address was Sétatér 2 in District V. This would have been on the edge of a massive building project going on around today's Szabadsag tér, and so the address was probably constantly cacophonous and dusty.

27 Forgy, M. *The Forger's Apprentice: Life with the World's Most Notorious Artist* CreateSpace Independent Publishing Platform, 2012.

28 His gravestone on the Spanish island of Ibiza is engraved: "14 de Abril 1911-11 de Diciembre de 1976 ELMYR."

29 Taylor, J. "The Artifice of Elmyr de Hory." *Intent to deceive exhibition catalogue.* 2012 http://www.intenttodeceive.org/forger-profiles/elmyr-de-hory/the-artifice-of-elmyr-de-hory/.

30 Hammer, J. "The Greatest Fake-Art Scam in History?" *Vanity Fair*, Oct. 10, 2012.

31 The work was a fake Max Ernst that was shown at *Max Ernst: A Retrospective.* Exhibition dates: Apr. 7–July 10, 2005.

32 Ernst, M. *La Horde* (1927). Christie's London: Tuesday, June 20, 2006 [Lot 00158] Impressionist and Modern Art (Evening Sale).

33 Batycka, D. "Counterfeit NFTs Are Creating Major Problems for Digital Platforms— but New Tools to Spot Fakes Are on the Rise: Image Recognition and Data Scraping Technology Are Increasingly Being Used by the NFT Community to Protect Intellectual Property Online." *The Art Newspaper*, Apr. 1, 2022.

34 Grann, D. "The Mark of a Masterpiece: The Man Who Keeps Finding Famous Fingerprints on Uncelebrated Works of Art." *The New Yorker*, July 12, 2010.

35 Bailey, M. "Prado museum downgrades Leonardo's $450m Salvator Mundi in exhibition catalogue: Publication for Mona Lisa show puts the painting in category of works that are attributed to, or authorised or supervised by the Renaissance master." *The Art Newspaper*, Nov. 11, 2021.

36 Hewitt, S. "Russian Art Critics Challenge Director of Ghent Museum over Show of Dubious Russian Avant-Garde Works. De Standaard Newspaper Reports That the Contract Allowed Any Piece in the Display To Be Sold." *The Art Newspaper*, Feb. 28, 2018.

37 Pes, J. "The Collectors Who Lent Two Dozen Allegedly Fake Artworks to a Major Belgian Museum Have Been Arrested: Igor and Olga Toporovsky Were Taken into Custody Late Last Month." *Artnet*, Jan. 3, 2020.

38 Velie, E. "Is the Orlando Museum of Art Displaying Fake Basquiats? The FBI is Investigating the Authenticity of Works That Are Said to Have Been Found in the Storage Unit of a Hollywood Screenwriter." *Hyperallergic*, June 1, 2022.

39 Velie, E. "Orlando Museum of Art on Probation after Disputed Basquiat Show. The American Alliance of Museums's Sanction Comes after the FBI Raided the Museum and Seized 25 Disputed Paintings." *Hyperallergic*, Jan. 23, 2023.

40 Crow, K. "The Basquiat Sisters on Managing One of Art's Hottest Brands." *The Wall Street Journal.* [Interview]. Apr. 8, 2022.

41 Goldstein, M. *Landscape with Figures: A History of Art Dealing in the United States.* Oxford University Press, 2003, p. 167.

42 Ripps, M. J. "Chapter 11: The London Picture Trade and Knoedler & Co.: Supplying Dutch Old Masters 1900–1914." In I. Reist, ed., *British Models of Art Collecting and the American Response: Reflections Across the Pond.* Henry Ling Ltd, Dorset Press. pp. 163–180.

43 Williams, R. C. "Dumping Oils: Soviet Art Sales and Soviet-American Relations, 1928–1933." Washington, DC: Kennan Institute for Advanced Russian Studies, Woodrow Wilson International Center for Scholars, May 25, 1977.

44 Boucher, B. "El Greco Stolen by Nazis and Sold by Knoedler Returns to Rightful Owners." *Artnet*, Mar. 24, 2015.

45 Keats, p. 120.

46 Taylor, J. "The Rise and Fall of the Knoedler, New York's Most Notorious Art Gallery." *The Conversation*, Feb. 5, 2016.

47 Miller, J. "The Fall of Armie Hammer: A Family Saga of Sex, Money, Drugs, and Betrayal." *Vanity Fair*, Mar. 11, 2021.

48 Hakami, E. and Hobbs, J. P. *House of Hammer*. Three-part documentary series. Discovery+, 2022.

49 Shnayerson, M. "A Question of Provenance." *Vanity Fair*, Apr. 23, 2012.

50 Avrich, B. *Made You Look: A True Story About Fake Art*. Documentary Film. *Netflix*, 2020.

51 Cohen, P. "Artist's Family Says Gallery Ignored Warning of Fakes." *The New York Times*, May 6, 2012.

52 Warnica, R. "How Did David Mirvish End up in the Decade's Most Shocking Art Forgery Scandal? *Canadian Business*, Dec. 17, 2013.

53 Shnayerson, 2012.

54 Cohen, P. "Possible Forging of Modern Art Is Investigated." *The New York Times*, Dec. 2, 2011.

55 Warnica, 2013.

Art Advising, Art Finance, NFTs

Chapter 20

ART ADVISING

An art advisor can describe a professional who provides a broad range of services within the art business. The term can frequently be used interchangeably with art consultant and art agent, though, in fact, the terms all reflect somewhat different roles and relationships with regards to their clients. In all cases, however, their primary function will always be to serve as intermediary party for art market transactions. Art advisors are usually engaged by collectors to help them assemble their collection. In that role they may accompany their clients to galleries, artists' studios, and especially art fairs. They also are expected to follow the auction market and know when desired works might be coming up for sale, alert the client, preview the work, and possibly bid on it. In the case of secondary market purchases, they should provide some degree of connoisseurship and be sure that the work is authentic. During the acquisition process, their primary value-added comes through guiding the client toward the artworks that best suit their collecting strategy. They then handle purchasing negotiations and arrange for payment, shipping, and installation of the acquisitions.[1] They can also make arrangements for pieces to be cleaned, conserved, or re-framed. Their input on framing and placement decisions represents an area where they apply their expertise, acting as a sort of curator for the collector. Since an art advisor is engaged

DOI: 10.4324/9781003431756-21

to enhance the prestige of the collection, they will work to try to get works loaned to prestigious temporary museum exhibitions, and these activities might find them filling a role similar to a museum registrar. With larger collections, numbering hundreds and even thousands of objects, this registrar role, knowing the status and location of everything: whether on loan, in transit, under consideration, in placement, or in storage, can easily be someone's full-time job.

Art advisors can be self-standing firms. Gallerists, however, will also often take of this role for clients who trust their advice and judgment. Because art advisors are frequently giving advice on market valuations and also arranging for works to be insured or donated, they frequently will also be qualified appraisers. Serving as an art advisor and as an appraiser, however, are distinctly different roles, and they should always be clear at any given moment which role they are currently playing. There is a membership organization for art advisors, the Association of Professional Art Advisors, and they maintain a code of ethics that include a number of important provisions, including not maintaining one's own inventory for sale and not accepting compensation from service providers or vendors.[2] This solicitation of "kickbacks" nonetheless remains a widespread phenomenon in the art and antiques business. Art advisors may work under a number of compensation structures, either a percentage-based commission, possibly somewhere between 5 and 10 percent of purchase prices, or they might instead bill on an hourly or monthly retainer fee, but they should be ethical in only being paid by their client and not by those who do business with their client. Their ability to guide the purchasing of high-net-worth individuals led to Sotheby's acquisition of the art advisory firm Art Agency, Partners for $85 million in 2016.[3] The relative low overhead required to enter the field means that numerous former gallery workers become art advisors with the hope of exploiting their access to the market's most precious asset: collectors with the capacity and inclination to buy. The over-abundance of art advisors has led to the derisive term "Gmail art advisors," who seek to make easy commissions from escorting clients through art fairs but provide little in the way of long-term guidance and management of their collection.[4]

A similar but slightly different profession would be that of art consultant. Though no firm distinction exists, the term has come to apply to those specialists who deal primarily in contemporary art and in commissioning artists to produce work for the private or public sector. They often guide the acquisition of a corporate art collection. An example would be the firm NINE dot ARTS based in Denver, Colorado, who provide an entire curatorial scheme that allows, for example, a hotel to brand itself as an art destination.[5] Given an art consultant's authority to purchase significant amounts of art on a company's budget, the profession is even more so expected to operate strictly on a retainer from their client, and not be influenced or paid by the suppliers of the market.

An art agent could describe a variety of roles. There are agents for artists who represent them the way other cultural industries, for example, film and literature, have agents who represent the talent and secure them profitable contracts. They will frequently represent in-demand illustrators and those working in more commercial industries. Some dealers will leave the field of operating a retail gallery but will still continue to represent artists through some sort of representational space.[6] They differ from art advisors and consultants who serve the demand side of the market (collectors), though, because their primary relationship is with the market's supply side (artists they represent).

The trans-Atlantic antiques trade would frequently be facilitated by agents who could serve as guides through the flea markets, fairs, and wholesalers of England, France, Belgium, and Central Europe. Their clients would be larger antiques dealers in the United States, and they would be expected to know the sources where large quantities of inventory could be quickly located, and once prices negotiated, could be tagged, photographed, and a purchase order written up with a promise to wire the money in a week. They work closely with the fine art transport industries (packing, trucking, crating, warehousing, customs, cultural heritage permits, air cargo, container brokers) required to ship the merchandise back to the buyer's retail location. These agents may also bid for their clients at auction as well as supervise conservation and framing work prior to shipping. They also play a role that is often called a "picker," who is someone who spots objects for sale that might interest a buyer, either a collector or a dealer, and now they might send them a picture from their phone. In the past, the process would have been transacted with polaroids.

ART FINANCE

The phenomenon that art can accrue value over time forms one of the foundational premises of an art market. The key point to remember is that this occurs sometimes, and in other situations, art does not become more valuable. In fact, very often it loses value relative to its initial purchase price. The market's intersection with art history and its capacity for canonizing a select group of artists and their works remains the essential, and largely uncontrollable, element necessary for dramatic rises in value. Nonetheless, the market has become increasingly sophisticated in measuring the means by which canonization occurs so that speculators can read an artist's potential trajectory. *Kunstkompass* has been ranking the world's contemporary artists since 1970 based on a highly objective methodology including museum exhibitions, reviews in specialist magazines, acquisitions by leading museums, and awards.[7]

A foundational narrative that often appears in the marketing materials for investments in contemporary art would be what could be the considered the first art investment fund, *La Peau de L'Ours*, led by collector and critic André Level. Over the period of 1904–1914, the fund acquired early works by modernists Picasso and Matisse, as well some by now deceased post-impressionists van Gogh and Gauguin. Using a subscription fee from 12 members, he had 2,750 Francs to purchase artworks each year, ultimately acquiring 232 pieces. After ten years of collecting, *La Peau de L'Ours* auctioned off 145 works at Hôtel Drouot in March of 1914.[8] They presciently did so right at the peak of the pre-WWI Paris art market, which would subsequently crash with onset of the war a few months later. They earned over 100,000 Francs at the auction achieving returns of approximately 400 percent over a period ten years with only selling part of the collection.[9] A contrary narrative, however, that of the two large-scale works, *Christ before Pilate* and *Golgotha* by the Hungarian painter

Mihály Munkácsy, might serve as a cautious counterpoint. Although readers might not know Munkácsy, during the 1880s he was nearly the most famous artist in the world, and these two paintings would be two of the best-known artworks of the era, having earned millions of Francs in entrance fees from exhibitions across Europe and the United States. Eventually, they were sold to the American retail magnate John Wanamaker for reputedly 160,000 and 175,000 US Dollars[10] and were possibly the two most expensive contemporary artworks sold in the nineteenth century. The new owner, however, displayed them in his luxurious Philadelphia department store, and they never entered the collection of a major museum.[11] When Wanamaker's department store came under new ownership the paintings were auctioned in 1988 for what was approximately 2 percent of their original purchase price in real dollar terms. They represent two of the greatest examples of price collapse in the history of the art market, and it was not the result of de-attribution (the usual cause for loss of value), but simply that the market had forgotten who Munkácsy was and demand for his œuvre had evaporated.

From the time, Sheridan Ford published his survey of the late nineteenth century American art market under the title *Art: A Commodity*,[12] the phrase has been widely used to express the fact that artworks have come to be regarded as a luxury asset class that retains and even accrues value. In key ways, however, art remains something that does not fit the definition of a commodity, at least in the more precise usage of the term in economics. Typical commodities derive from agricultural and extraction industries and are considered fungible, meaning that they are essentially interchangeable. In the case of art, though, quite the opposite is true: artworks are unique.[13] Paintings and hand-carved sculpture are produced in a one-off method, and even serial artworks like prints and castings bear numberings that make them distinct from the other pieces from the series. Headline-grabbing news of record-setting prices may give the impression that art should be a profitable investment, but the relative opacity of data on the market and the infrequency of trades relative to financial markets means that it is nearly impossible to say whether it actually is. William Baumol, however, argued at the peak of the 1980s art boom that it categorically was not, at least relative to traditional securities.[14]

Nonetheless, numerous indices will chart the valuations of artists in a way similar to how the securities industry follows stocks, commodities, and currencies. The problem with indices will be that they cannot reliably capture the full scope of the market, since much of it occurs out of view through private sales and in galleries, and only the public auctions can be reliably tracked,[15] and sometimes even their data can be unreliable if the hammer prices do not represent completed transactions.[16] Furthermore, much of the very functioning of the art market relies of "informational asymmetry" which by its very essence produces highly imperfect data, at best.[17] For overall market trends, however, *The Art Basel and UBS Global Art Market Report* report by Clare McAndrew and Art Economics, uses a methodology of surveying dealers to compensate for the general inscrutability of the gallery sector.[18]

Despite these deficiencies a robust sector of art finance has grown up in recent years, which has only done more to highlight the way the art market does not conform to the standards of highly regulated financial industries. Among these problems are whether art investing should be treated as, and marketed as, a security, which would place it under the regulation of the Securities and Exchange Commission (SEC).[19] Following the trend of making financial services more accessible to younger, new investors, firms are offering fractional ownership in artworks.[20] Some funds try to concentrate on under-valued areas of the market, such as focusing on women and minority artists.[21] With the recent emergence of secondary market contemporary art auctions, art investors have become notorious for "flipping" recent Chelsea gallery purchases, which can pose serious peril to artists' careers. If an auction sale hammers at something significantly below what their gallerist is currently retailing their work for (or even worse, it is "bought in"), that can send their prices into a death spiral.[22] As with financial industries, the art market is likely to follow wider macroeconomic trends, which means that art funds might outperform in good times. But in bad times, the asset can seem almost illiquid, and institutional investors have been recently leaving the sector.[23]

In addition to art being used as an investment vehicle, it is also increasingly employed as collateral for loans, and now even that type of finance is being securitized so that many investors can pool their lending.[24] The weakness in the sector lies in the problem of title (ownership) of art, and its lack of a central registry comparable to what exists for real estate. In fact, the market does not even have any sort of standardized document, as for example with automobiles, that proves title to an artwork. Bills of sale, invoices, estate filings, appraisals, and contracts all might be used to designate who has the right to dispose of the property. This lack of a reliable system to verify title and its possible claimants lies at the heart of the fraudulent schemes employed by Inigo Philbrick.[25] [See: Case Study: Inigo Philbrick]

NON-FUNGIBLE TOKENS (NFTs)

Very much simultaneous with the art world's pivot from the physical to the virtual during the COVID pandemic, the disruptive technology of NFTs emerged quite suddenly in early 2021. Although digital art had existed for decades, almost since the onset of the computer age, the collecting of it remained essentially impossible in the sense of one collector claiming ownership over something infinitely reproducible. With the development of blockchain technology spurred by the crypto currency industry, digital artworks now could be "minted" and sold and their ownership and provenance tracked on a visible ledger. NFTs seemed to capture a moment during the pandemic which appeared to signal a transformation from the art market's obsession with the ownership consumption of physical unique objects to non-material forms of "liquid consumption."[26]

When Christie's sold in March 2021 what it billed as the first ever "purely digital NFT-based work of art offered by a major auction house," with Beeple's *Everydays: The First 5,000 Days*, the sale price of $69 million attracted the art world's full attention.[27] A month later Yuga Labs launched what would become the most widely known crypto art project The Bored Ape Yacht Club. The series of 10,000 computer-generated apes featured accessories, such as gold fur, a sailor hat, laser eyes, 3D glasses, a cigarette, a prison jumpsuit, and a pith helmet, that served to differentiate one from the other 9,999. Numerous celebrities touted their acquisition of editions, in theory for prices of hundreds of thousands of dollars. A recent lawsuit, however, alleges that those celebrities may have been acting as promoters for Yuga Labs, as well as the crypto payment service MoonPay, and also possibly did not really pay for their Bored Apes.[28]

The wider fallout from the Crypto Winter, which began with the collapse of Terra Luna in May 2022 and set in motion the eventual bankruptcy of FTX, has also exposed NFTs' many inherent flaws. Being that rarity forms the basis of art market valuations, the medium has been trumpeted in terms of its ability to provide verified rarity, and to pay artists resale royalties, though now several marketplaces have stopped honoring that promise.[29] Still, the largest cause for their popularity lies in their perceived speculative investment value. The medium, in many ways, represented the convergence of art finance with crypto currencies. Real-time market data can be followed on artists, projects, and the valuations of their NFTs. Like art finance for paintings, NFTs can be leveraged as collateral for loans of crypto currency.[30] Fractional ownership has also arrived in the form of Decentralized Autonomous Organizations which allow members to vote on acquisitions of NFTs. Nadya Tolokonnikova, a member of the Russian protest and performance art group Pussy Riot, co-founded UnicornDAO to redistribute "wealth and visibility in order to create equality for women-identified and lgbtq+ people."[31]

When the buyer of *Everydays: The First 5,000 Days* was revealed, the new owner turned out to be Metakovan, a Singapore-based crypto trader (who battled another crypto trader to the $69 million price) and was himself launching a new crypto art fund.[32] In other words, this record price for an NFT was achieved through the bidding by two parties who each had a vested interest in portraying effervescent valuations. In fact, wash trading, a fraudulent technique of linked parties systematically bidding up assets, is a practice banned in most mature securities markets, but from its onset the NFT platforms have been rife with the practice.[33] Manipulation in traditional art auctions have long been known, such as chandelier bidding, hidden reserve, or other forms of giving the false appearance of completed sales transactions, and wash trading appears to be the NFT market's variant of those abuses.

Furthermore, what must be most clearly emphasized: the NFT is unique, not the artwork. Unless the artist has agreed to limit their edition, then they have not. In other words, the Token is Non-Fungible. The artwork remains very much Fungible. More troubling and perplexing would be concepts of copyright and title, especially in the case of digital artwork created years ago on work for hire contracts, which might be minted by the artist or the rights holder with no clear concept of how such disputes over title should be resolved. Even if the NFT guarantees good title once it has been minted, there is no guarantee that the minter had good title to the artwork in the first place.[34] Numerous cases have already emerged of artists having their artwork inappropriately lifted and sold as an NFT by another party.[35] Despite the claims that blockchain would prevent theft, in fact, hackers have already made off with over $100 million in stolen NFTs.[36]

Those who continue to be bullish on the medium also fully understand that long-term values can only be achieved by canonization, which occurs through inclusion in museum collections. The Centre Pompidou recently announced the acquisition of 18 works,[37] and the Los Angeles County Museum of Art (LACMA) received the gift 22 works, which might be the donation of the rapper Snoop Dogg, a crypto evangelist.[38] NFTs are often referred to as collectables since, like coins, stamps, and baseball cards, other than being essentially another jpeg on a digital screen, they have little display value as compared to, for example, oil on canvas paintings. Without a means to enjoy the artwork that is attached to an NFT, it takes on a secondary role relative to the NFT's exchange potential. In this way the NFT sector resembles an art market without much consideration for the art itself. Or more simply: an art market without art.

CASE STUDY: INIGO PHILBRICK

Successful art forgers understand the importance of the corruption of knowledge. Although Inigo Philbrick dealt in authentic artworks, his fraud schemes clearly demonstrated his ability to exploit the market's weak points for knowing and establishing title. Philbrick employed all of the latest trends, including, flipping, fractional ownership, and art financing, and he serves as a cautionary tale to the perils of all of them. In particular, he showed how easily the documentation of title can be forged to allow for the reselling of the same work multiple times.[39]

Until his sudden disappearance in 2019, he had been something of a wunderkind in the business, having a stellar pedigree of a museum director father, an education at Goldsmiths in London, and protégé to alpha dealer Jay Jopling of the White Cube, moving quickly from interning to managing their secondary market sales.[40] By 2013, he had opened his own contemporary art gallery in Mayfair and, after generating earnings of supposedly $130 million in 2017, he opened another gallery in Miami. Like other notable art fraudsters and forgers, however, his opulent lifestyle and penchant for substance abuse necessitated an income stream that honest business could not provide. He formed a close friendship with critic and dealer Kenny Schachter, who he also scammed, but also continued to message with even while hiding out on the South Pacific island of Vanuatu.[41]

One of his schemes involved a 1982 painting by the artist Jean-Michel Basquiat *Humidity* he purchased for $18.4 million, to which he sold fractional interests over 100 percent and then also borrowed against it. German firm Fine Art Partners filed suit in October 2019 over an untitled 2012 painting by Rudolf Stingel of Pablo Picasso, which Philbrick sold multiple times while at the same time telling others that he still owned it. He had the audacity to peddle a Yayoi Kusama installation that was then on show at the Institute of Contemporary Art in Miami to Mohammed bin Salman (aka MBS) the Crown Prince of Saudi Arabia (and owner of the *Salvator Mundi*). According to the prosecutors in New York, he had built his business by collateralizing and reselling fractional shares artworks in a way that the concealed the true ownership interests, as well as employing fake documents, including a Christie's consignment agreement, a purchase and sale agreement, and a Christie's invoice.

In June of 2020, U.S. law enforcement arrested Philbrick in Vanuatu, and in May of 2022, he was sentenced to seven years in prison.[42] A co-conspirator, British Dealer Robert Newland, was also extradited from the U.K. and pled guilty to conspire to commit wire fraud.[43] The total scale of his Philbrick's scam is estimated at $86 million, and numerous lawsuits continue to try to sort out a tangle of competing claims over the subject artworks. Described as an art world "mini-Madoff," he serves as another reminder that the future art fraud, much like forgery, lies in the fabrication and manipulation of the supporting documents and processes that determine ownership. To emphasize the point, high-end art advisor, Lisa Schiff, recently just declared bankruptcy in what has been described as a "ponzi scheme."[44] As the art world becomes more liquid both through art finance and through the consumption of NFTs, these perils will only become more pronounced.

ART ADVISING, ART FINANCE, NFTS—TERMS

Kickback—a payment received by the agent of a commercial transaction from a supplier, usually in compensation for the agent having facilitated their client's business with the supplier.

Title—a term for ownership. In the art world, title has no centralized registry as with real estate and no official documents designating ownership, as with automobiles.

Commodity—commercial good that is fungible, or interchangeable, with other goods of the same type. Commodities often derive from agriculture and extraction industries and serve as the raw materials for manufactured goods.

Security—tradable financial assets that present themselves as investments that will accrue value or generate income. Common securities can be equities like shares of companies or debt securities that function like complex loans. Securities are regulated by the SEC, and both art finance instruments and NFTs are being scrutinized as to whether they also may be regarded as and regulated as securities.

Collateral—an asset provided to a lender as a guarantee of repayment, and which can be seized in the event of default. A sector of art finance has now emerged that uses artworks as collateral to secure loans.

Blue-Chip—a term derived from the equities market referring to a well-established publicly traded company with a long-term record of profitability and stable growth. Blue-chip art refers to a select group of artists who have canonical status and proven sales histories at the leading auction houses.

Gas Fee—payments from NFT creators to those who have staked crypto currency to the blockchain in order for it to remain secure. All blockchain transactions incur a gas fee including minting of NFTs.

Crypto—a shortening of crypto currency, which is digital currency that serves as alternative means of exchange created using encryption algorithms, referred to as blockchain.

Blockchain—a ledger of transactions, developed particularly for crypto currency, that is maintained across computers linked in a peer-to-peer network.

Ponzi Scheme—an investment fraud that uses funds from new investors to pay existing investors and would therefore be an ultimately unsustainable business model.

Notes

1 Neuendorf, H. "Art Demystified: What Is the Role of Art Advisors?" *Artnet*, Aug. 11, 2016.
2 Association of Professional Art Advisors (APAA) website. https://www.artadvisors. org/association-of-professional-art-advisors-mission.
3 Forbes, A. "Why Sotheby's Just Bought an Art Advisory for $85 Million." *Artsy*, Jan. 12, 2016.
4 Kazakina, K. "'Gmail Art Advisors' Are a Pestilence on the Market. Luckily, They Are Starting to Melt Away, One by One." *Artnet*, Feb. 3, 2023.
5 Navarro, C. "Now Is the Best Time for Stylish Travelers to Visit Denver: Colorado's Mile High City is in the Midst of an Unexpected Art and Design Boom." *Architectural Digest*, Nov. 1, 2021.

6 Trezzi, N. "The Art Dealers Finding Alternatives to the Gallery Model." *Artnet*, Sep. 14, 2016.

7 "Art Compass: Gerhard Richter Remains the Most Important Artist." *Zeit Online*, Oct. 20, 2022.

8 *Collection de la Peau de L'Ours Tableaux Modernes.* Exhibition Catalogue Hôtel Drouot for auction, Mar. 2, 1914.

9 Richetti, A. "La Peau de L'Ours: Avant-Garde Art as an Investment." *Daily Art Magazine*, Jan. 17, 2022.

10 Huemer, C. "Charles Sedelmeyer's Theatricality: Art and Speculation in Late 19th-Century Paris." In J. Bakoš, ed., *Artwork through the Market: The Past and the Present.* Slovak Academy of Sciences, 2004, pp. 109–124.

11 Morowitz, L. "A Passion for Business: Wanamaker's, Munkácsy, and the Depiction of Christ." *The Art Bulletin*, vol. 91, no. 2, June 2009, pp. 184–206.

12 Ford, S. *Art: A Commodity.* Rogers & Sherwood, 1888.

13 McAndrew, C. "An Introduction to Art and Finance." In C. McAndrew, ed., *Fine Art and High Finance: Expert Advice on the Economics of Ownership.* Bloomberg Press, 2010, p. 18.

14 Baumol, W. "Unnatural Value: Or Art Investment as a Floating Crap Game." *American Economic Review*, vol. 78, no. 2, 1986, pp. 10–14.

15 Kräussl, R. "Art Price Indices." In C. McAndrew, ed., *Fine Art and High Finance: Expert Advice on the Economics of Ownership.* Bloomberg Press, 2010, p. 68.

16 Barboza, D., Bowley, G., and Cox, A. "A Culture of Bidding: Forging an Art Market in China." *The New York Times*, Oct. 28, 2013.

17 van Miegroet, H. "Imperfect Data, Art Markets and Internet Research. *Art Markets and Digital Histories*, MDPI (Multidisciplinary Digital Publishing Institute), 2020.

18 McAndrew, C. *The Art Market 2022.* Art Basel / Union Bank of Switzerland, 2022, pp. 271–272.

19 Villa, A. "Rising Startup Masterworks Beset by Internal Rifts, Alleged Recklessness, and Staff Cuts." *ARTnews*, Dec. 27, 2022.

20 Anapur, E. "Fractional Ownership - A New Model of Art Collecting." *Widewalls*, Sep. 7, 2022.

21 Lindeberg, R. "Ex-Tate Modern Boss Builds New Fund Targeting Minority Artists." *Bloomberg*, Sep. 22, 2022.

22 Cohen, A. "Why 'Flipping' Art Is so Controversial." *Artsy*, Feb. 10, 2020.

23 Bainbridge, A. "Art Investing Loses Its Appeal for a $44 Billion Pension Fund." *Bloomberg*, Oct. 17, 2022.

24 Grant, D. "Would You Invest in Art without Seeing It? New Scheme Invites Users to Buy Into Securitised—but Unnamed—Art Loans." *The Art Newspaper*, Nov. 25, 2022.

25 Kinsella, E. "What Did Inigo Philbrick Do? How One Precocious Dealer Allegedly Swindled the Art Market's Savviest Players Out of Millions." *Artnet*, Mar. 12, 2020.

26 Bardhi, F. and Eckhard, G. "Liquid Consumption." *Journal of Consumer Research*, vol. 44, no. 3, Oct. 2017, pp. 582–597.

27 Kastrenakes, J. "Beeple Sold an NFT for $69 Million. Through a First-Of-Its-Kind Auction at Christie's." *The Verge*, Mar. 11, 2021.

28 Reeve, E. and Guff, S. "A Twisted Tale of Celebrity Promotion, Opaque Transactions and Allegations of Racist Tropes." *CNN*, Feb. 11, 2023.

29 Akers, T. "Crypto Winter Is Here—and NFT Artist Royalties Are under Threat." *The Art Newspaper*, Dec. 3, 2022.

30 Kelly, L. J. "Borrowing Against a Bored Ape NFT—What Could Go Wrong? *Decypt*, Feb. 25, 2023.

31 Andrew, G. "What Are DAOs? How Blockchain-Governed Collectives Might Revolutionise the Art World." *The Art Newspaper*, Feb. 23, 2023.

32 Gottsegen, W. "$69 Million Beeple Art Buyer Revealed as NFT Whale Metakovan." *Decrypt*, Mar. 12, 2021.

33 Kochkodin, B. "Market Manipulation Chatter Rises as Digital Art Scene Explodes." *Bloomberg*, Mar. 13, 2021.

34 Sloane, K. and Taylor, J. "Art Markets without Art, Art without Objects." *The Garage Journal: Studies in Art, Museums & Culture*, vol. 2, 2021, pp. 152–175.

35 Kwan, J. "An Artist Died. Then Thieves Made NFTs of Her Work." *Wired*, July 28, 2021.

36 Solomon, T. "More Than $100 M. Worth of NFTs Have Been Stolen This Year, a New Report Finds." *ARTnews*, Aug. 25, 2022.

37 Batycka, D. "Paris's Centre Pompidou Breaks New Ground by Acquiring 18 NFTs." *The Art Newspaper*, Feb. 14, 2023.

38 Voon, C. "Mysterious NFT Collector—Who May Actually Be the Rapper Snoop Dogg—Gifts 22 Blockchain Works to Lacma." *The Art Newspaper*, Feb. 13, 2023.

39 Kinsella, E. Mar 12, 2020.

40 Douglas, S. and Tully, J. "Who Is Inigo Philbrick? Meet the Man Behind One of the Biggest Potential Modern Art Scandals." *ARTnews*, Dec. 3, 2019.

41 Schachter, K. "Where's Inigo? As a Furious Art World Searches for the Disappeared Dealer, Kenny Schachter Finds Him… on Instagram." *Artnet*. Dec. 10, 2019.

42 Alberge, D. "'He's Sabotaged His Entire Life for Greed': The $86M Rise and Fall of Inigo Philbrick." *The Guardian*, May 25, 2022.

43 Cassady, D. "British Art Dealer Robert Newland Pleads Guilty to Conspiring with Inigo Philbrick to Defraud Collectors and Financiers." *The Art Newspaper*, Sep. 26, 2022.

44 Nayyar, R. "New York Art Advisor Lisa Schiff Files for Bankruptcy: Schiff was hit with two lawsuits in the span of a week accusing her of embezzling funds and running a 'Ponzi scheme.'" *Hyperallergic*. May 18, 2023

Works Cited

Abrams, A.-R. 'Why Are Antiques Fairs Showcasing Contemporary Art?" *Artnet*, Aug. 3, 2016.

Actman, J. "U.S. Adopts Near-Total Ivory Ban." *National Geographic*, June 3, 2016.

Adam, G. "Show and Sell: The Added Value of a Museum Exhibition." *The Art Newspaper*, June 12, 2018.

Addley, E. and Smith, H. "British Museum in Talks with Greece over Return of Parthenon Marbles." *The Guardian*, Jan, 4, 2023.

Ahlstrom Christy, C. "Art Market Transformed by Shifting Boundaries." *Property Journal*, July 15, 2022.

Akers, T. "Crypto Winter Is Here—and NFT Artist Royalties Are under Threat." *The Art Newspaper*, Dec. 3, 2022.

Alberge, D. "Antiquities for Auction Could Be Illicitly Sourced, Archaeologist Claims." *The Guardian*, Dec. 7, 2021.

————. 'He's Sabotaged His Entire Life for Greed': The $86M Rise and Fall of Inigo Philbrick." *The Guardian*, May 25, 2022.

Alsop, J. *The Rare Art Traditions: The History of Art Collecting and Its Linked Phenomena Wherever These Have Appeared*. New York: Harper & Row, 1987, pp. 28–29.

Alvarez, A. "Santa Fe Arts District Faces an Uncertain Future." *Axios Denver*, Oct 11, 2021.

Anapur, E. "Fractional Ownership - A New Model of Art Collecting." *Widewalls*, Sep. 7, 2022.

Andrew, G. "What Are DAOs? How Blockchain-Governed Collectives Might Revolutionise the Art World." *The Art Newspaper*, Feb. 23, 2023.

Apollinaire, G. *Les peintres cubistes, méditations esthétiques*. Paris: Eugène Figuière Éditeurs, 1913.

Apotropaion, Hippopotamus tusk. c. 1773–1650 BCE. Collection of the Fine Arts Museum of Budapest. https://www.mfab.hu/artworks/apotropaion/

Arkell, R. "Furniture Index Falls Another 7%: Hopes of a Recovery in the Value of Antique Furniture Have Been Dealt a Blow after the Antiques Collectors' Club's Annual Furniture Index (AFI) Saw Prices Fall by Seven per Cent during 2009." *Antiques Trade Gazette*, Jan. 25, 2010. https://www.art-appraisals.net/value-definitions

Arp, J., Mondrian, P., Guggenheim, P., and Andrea, B. *Art of This Century*. Art of This Century & Art Aid Corporation, 1942.

Art of the Steal. Documentary film. Maj Productions, 9.14 Pictures, Sep. 12, 2009.

Art Research Staff. "The Mystery of the Hungarian 'Gold Train'", Presidential Advisory Commission on Holocaust Assets in the United States, Oct. 14, 1999.

Art Review Power 100: The Annual Ranking of the Most Influential People in Art, 2022, Dec. 5, 2022.

Artnet News and Morgan Stanley. "From the Studio to the Auction Block: How the Path Between These Two Poles Shrank in the 21st Century—and What It Means for the Art Market." Nov. 3, 2022.

Ashenfelter, O. and Graddy, K. "The Rise and Fall of a Price-Fixing Conspiracy: Auction at Sotheby's and Christie's." *Journal of Competition Law and Economics*, vol. 1, 2005, pp. 3–20.

The Associated Press. "Federal Court Approves Deal with U.S. in Nazi 'Gold Train' Case: A Federal Judge Approved a $25.5 Million Settlement between the U.S. And Hungarian Jews Dispossessed during WWII." *Haaretz*, Sep. 27, 2005.

Association of Professional Art Advisors (APAA) website. https://www.artadvisors. org/association-of-professional-art-advisors-mission

Auction catalogue for sale of Leonardo da Vinci. Salvator Mundi. Christie's, Nov. 15, 2017.

Avrich, B. *Made You Look: A True Story About Fake Art*. Documentary Film. Netflix, 2020.

Bailey, M. "Prado Museum Downgrades Leonardo's $450M Salvator Mundi in Exhibition Catalogue: Publication for Mona Lisa Show Puts the Painting in Category of Works That Are Attributed To, or Authorised or Supervised by the Renaissance Master." *The Art Newspaper*, Nov. 11, 2021.

Bainbridge, A. "Art Investing Loses Its Appeal for a $44 Billion Pension Fund." *Bloomberg*, Oct. 17, 2022.

Barboza, D., Bowley, G., and Cox, A. "A Culture of Bidding: Forging an Art Market in China." *The New York Times*, Oct. 28, 2013.

Bardhi, F. and Eckhard, G. "Liquid Consumption." *Journal of Consumer Research*, vol. 44, no. 3, Oct. 2017, pp. 582–597.

Barnett, V., Rosenblum, R., and Salmen, B. *Art of Tomorrow: Hilla Rebay and Solomon R. Guggenheim*. Guggenheim Museum, 2005.

Bar-Yosef, O. "The Known and the Unknown about the Acheulean." In: N. Goren-bar, G. Sharon, eds, *Axe Age: Acheulian Tool-Making from Quarry to Discard*. Equinox, pp. 479–494.

Barr, A. *Cubism and Abstract Art*. Modern Museum of Art, 1936, back cover.

Bashkoff, T. R., Hanhardt, J., and Quaintance, D. *The Museum of Non-Objective Painting: Hilla Rebay and the Origins of the Solomon R. Guggenheim Museum*. Guggenheim Museum, 2009.

Batycka, D.—. "Counterfeit NFTs Are Creating Major Problems for Digital Platforms—But New Tools to Spot Fakes Are on the Rise: Image Recognition and Data Scraping Technology Are Increasingly Being Used by the NFT Community to Protect Intellectual Property Online." *The Art Newspaper*, Apr. 1, 2022.

———. "Paris's Centre Pompidou Breaks New Ground by Acquiring 18 NFTs." *The Art Newspaper*, Feb. 14, 2023.

———. "Volta Finds Its Niche in Basel, Offering Exciting New Work by Emerging Artists at Affordable Price Points." *Artnet News*, June 16, 2022.

Baumgardner, J. "At the Venice Biennale, Simone Leigh Embraces Sovereignty." *Hyperallergic*, May 1, 2022.

Baumol, W. "Unnatural Value: Or Art Investment as a Floating Crap Game." *American Economic Review,* vol. 78, no. 2, 1986, pp. 10–14.

Bayer, T. M. and Page, J. R. "The Formation of a Nexus: A Story of Christie's." In: *The Development of the Art Market in England: Money as Muse, 1730–1900*. London: Pickering and Chatto, 2011, pp. 143–151.

Bell, A. R. and Dale, R. S. "The Medieval Pilgrimage Business." *Enterprise & Society*, vol. 12, no. 3, 2011, pp. 601–627.

Behrman, S. N. "The Days of Duveen: A Legendary Art Dealer and his Clients." *The New Yorker*, Sep. 22, 1951.

Benjamin, W. "The Work of Art in the Age of Mechanical Reproduction." In: H. Arendt, ed., H. Zohn, trans., *Illuminations: Essays and Reflections*. Schocken, 1969, pp. 218–242.

Bennet, C. and Gus, C. "Croatia to Join Schengen Free-Travel Zone In 2023; But Romania and Bulgaria Were Left Out as Austria Objects to Their Inclusion." *Politico*, Dec. 8, 2022.

Benzine, V. "Highlights from the Other Art Fair: The Bright and Boozy Arts Bonanza Returned to Brooklyn This Weekend, Allowing Artists and Their (Potential) Customers to Rub Elbows." *Brooklyn Magazine*, Nov 7, 2022.

Berenson, A. and Vogel, C. "Ex-Tyco Chief Is Indicted in Tax Case." *The New York Times*, June 5, 2002.

Berenson, B. *The Central Italian Painters of the Renaissance*. G. P. Putnam's sons, 1897.

———. *The Florentine Painters of the Renaissance*. Putnam & Sons, 1896.

———. *The Venetian Painters of the Renaissance with an Index to Their Works*. Putnam & Sons, 1894.

Berning Sawa, D. "Bourse de Commerce: Opening of Pinault's Long-Awaited Paris Museum Is — Pandemic Permitting — Finally around the Corner." *The Art Newspaper*, Jan. 5, 2021.

Billcliffe, R. and Vergo, P. "Charles Rennie Mackintosh and the Austrian Art Revival." *The Burlington Magazine*, vol. 119, no. 896, Special Issue Devoted to European Art Since 1890, Nov. 1977, pp. 739–746.

Birnie Danzker, J.-A., Salmen, B., and Vail, K. *Art of Tomorrow: Hilla Rebay and Solomon R. Guggenheim*. Guggenheim Museum, 2005.

Birth Record for Elemér Hoffmann, Folyó-szám [Registration Number]: 1034. "Kivonat: A Budapest Zsidó Hitközseg Születési Anyakönyvéből."

Blankert, A. "The Case of Han van Meegeren's Fake Vermeer Supper at Emmaus Reconsidered." In: *His Milieu: Essays on Netherlandish Art in Memory of John Michael Montias*. Amsterdam University Press, 2006, pp. 47–58.

Blondin, J. E. "Power Made Visible: Pope Sixtus IV as 'Urbis Restaurator' in Quattrocento Rome." *The Catholic Historical Review*, vol. 91, no. 1, 2005, pp. 1–25.

Blumenthal, R. and Vogel, C. "Auction Case Takes Turn to Documents." *The New York Times*, July 11, 2001.

Bode, W. V. and de Groot, C. H. *The Complete Work of Rembrandt, History, Description and Heliographic Reproduction of all the Master's Pictures, with a Study of His Life and Work*. C. Sedelmeyer, 1897–1906.

Boerner, L., van Bochove, C., and Quint, D. "Anglo-Dutch Premium Auctions in Eighteenth-Century Amsterdam." *Modern and Comparative Seminar*, Nov. 22, 2012, London, UK.

Bogner, D. *Peggy Guggenheim & Frederick Kiesler: The Story of Art of This Century*. Guggenheim Museum Publications, 2004.

Boime, A. "Entrepreneurial Patronage in Nineteenth-Century France." In: E. C. Carter II, R. Forster and J. N. Moody, eds., *Enterprise and Entrepreneurs in Nineteenth- and Twentieth-Century France*. Johns Hopkins University Press, 1976, pp. 137–207.

————. "The Salon des Refusés and the Evolution of Modern Art." *Art Quarterly*, vol. 32, Winter, 1969, pp. 411–426.

Boman, D. and Fusselman, A. "On Writing and Criticism: An Interview with Jerry Saltz." *Ohio Edit*, Sep. 8, 2016.

Boucher, B. "El Greco Stolen by Nazis and Sold by Knoedler Returns to Rightful Owners." *Artnet*, Mar. 24, 2015.

Bourdieu, P. *Distinction: A Social Critique of the Judgment of Taste* (Nice, R. trans.). Harvard University Press, 1984.

Bowley, G. "Art Collectors Find Safe Harbor in Delaware's Tax Laws." *The New York Times*, Oct. 25, 2015.

Bowley, G. and Rashbaum, W. "Sotheby's Tries to Block Suit over a Leonardo Sold and Resold at a Big Markup." *The New York Times*, Nov. 28, 2016.

Bowlt, J. E. "Stage Design and the Ballets Russes." *The Journal of Decorative and Propaganda Arts*, Vol. 5, Russian/Soviet Theme Issue (Summer, 1987), pp. 28-45.

Bowron, E. P. and Rishel, J. J. *Art in Rome in the Eighteenth Century* [Exhibition Catalogue]. Philadelphia Museum of Art (Rizzoli), 2000.

Brady, A. "What Does a $450m Leonardo Mean for the Old Master Market?" *The Art Newspaper*, Dec. 1, 2017.

Brauer, F. *Rivals and Conspirators: The Paris Salons and the Modern Art Centre*. Newcastle upon Tyne: Cambridge Scholars Publishing, 2013, pp. 138–157, 347–348.

Bredius, A. "A New Vermeer." *Burlington Magazine*, vol. 71, 1937, p. 211.

Brettell, R. R. "Monet's Haystacks Reconsidered." *Art Institute of Chicago Museum Studies*, vol. 11, no. 1, Autumn, 1984, pp. 4–21.

Brewer, J. *The American Leonardo: A Tale of Obsession, Art and Money*. New York: Oxford UP, 2009.

————. "Art and Science: A Da Vinci Detective Story." *Engineering & Science*, vol. 1/2, 2005, pp. 37–40.

Brodie, S. "The Case for Title Insurance." *Art and Advocacy*, vol. 15, Spring/Summer 2013, pp. 1–11..

Brown, K. "A Startling Exhibition on the History of Documenta Reveals the Political Moves—and Nazi Ties—of Its First Curators." *Artnet News*, June 25, 2021.

————. "The Organizers of Berlin's Most Important Art Fair Have Canceled All Future Editions Due to Financial Shortfalls." *Artnet News*, Dec. 11, 2019.

Brown, M. W. *The Story of the Armory Show*. Abbeville Press, 1988, pp. 45–62, 244–327.

Burckhardt, J. *The Civilisation of the Period of the Renaissance in Italy* [Die Kultur der Renaissance in Italien]. Trans. S. G. C. Middlemore. C. K. Paul & Co., 1878 (1860).

Burns, C. "Haring Market in Turmoil – Prolific Artist's Foundation Is Latest to Close Its Authentication Board." *The Art Newspaper*, Oct. 12, 2012.

Calvera, A. "The Influence of English Design Reform in Catalonia: An Attempt at Comparative History." *Journal of Design History*, vol. 15, no. 2, 2002, pp. 83–100.

Campbell, L. "The Art Market in the Southern Netherlands in the Fifteenth Century." *The Burlington Magazine*, vol. 118, no. 877, 1976, pp. 188–198.

Carrigan, M. "Dealer Mary Boone Pleads Guilty to $1.6m in Tax Fraud." *The Art Newspaper*, Sep. 5, 2018.

Cascone, S. "Art Basel Completes Hong Kong Art Fair Buy-Out." *Artnet News*, Oct. 28, 2014.

Cassady, D. "The Armory Show, 'New York's Art Fair', Is an Increasingly Global Juggernaut." *The Art Newspaper*, Sep. 9, 2022.

———. "British Art Dealer Robert Newland Pleads Guilty to Conspiring with Inigo Philbrick to Defraud Collectors and Financiers." *The Art Newspaper*, Sep. 26, 2022.

———. "Tefaf, Back in New York after Years of Cancellations, Takes Visitors outside of Time." *The Art Newspaper*, May 7, 2022.

Casson, M. and Lee, J. S. "The Origin and Development of Markets: A Business History Perspective." *Business History Review*, vol. 85, no. 1, 2011, pp. 9–37.

Charbonneau, L. "UNESCO Sounds Alarm about Illicit Syria Archeology Digs." *Reuters*, Dec. 14, 2013.

Chen, X. "Can Tribeca Avoid Repeating the Boom-And-Bust Cycle of Previous New York City Gallery Districts?" *The Art Newspaper*, Sep. 23, 2022.

Chow, J. "UBS Secures Global Art Basel Sponsorship." *The Wall Street Journal*, May 26, 2013.

Chrisafis, A. "Attack on 'Blasphemous' Art Work Fires Debate on Role of Religion in France." *The Guradian*, Apr 18, 2011.

Cohen, A. "Why 'Flipping' Art Is so Controversial." *Artsy*, Feb. 10, 2020.

Cohen, P. "Art's Sale Value? Zero. The Tax Bill? $29 Million." *The New York Times*, July 22, 2012.

———. "Artist's Family Says Gallery Ignored Warning of Fakes." *The New York Times*, May 6, 2012.

———. "Possible Forging of Modern Art Is Investigated." *The New York Times*, Dec. 2, 2011.

Cole, D. B. "Artists and Urban Redevelopment." *Geographical Review*, vol. 77, no. 4, Oct. 1987, pp. 391–407.

Collection de la Peau de L'Ours Tableaux Modernes. Exhibition Catalogue Hôtel Drouot for auction, Mar. 2, 1914.

Coqueugniot, G. "Where Was the Royal Library of Pergamum?: An Institution Found and Lost Again." In: Jason König et al., eds., *Ancient Libraries*. Cambridge: Cambridge University Press, 2013, pp. 109–123.

Coulson, W. D. E. "The Reliability of Pliny's Chapters on Greek and Roman Sculpture." *The Classical World*, vol. 69, no. 6, 1976, pp. 361–372.

Crenshaw, P. *Rembrandt's Bankruptcy: The Artist, His Patrons, and the Art Market in Seventeenth-Century Netherlands*. Cambridge University Press, 2006.

Crow, T. *Painters and Public Life in 18th Century Paris*. New Haven, CT: Yale University Press, 1987.

Dafoe, T. "Christie's Pulled a $25 Million T-Rex Skeleton from Auction After Experts Pointed Out That Most of Its Bones Are Replicas." *Artnet*, Nov. 21, 2022.

———. "New York City Has Returned $14 Million in Stolen Antiquities to Italy, Including Dozens Recovered from a Hedge-Fund Billionaire." *Artnet*, July 21, 2022.

Davidson, S. and Rylands, P., eds. *Peggy Guggenheim & Fredrick Kiesler: The Story of Art of This Century*. Peggy Guggenheim Collection, 2005.

Davies, C. and Addley, E. "Art Dealers Claim Droit de Suite Levy Threatens London's Art Trade." *The Guardian*, Dec. 22, 2011.

Davis, J. H. *The Guggenheims: An American Epic*. William Morrow, 1978, pp. 238–239.

Dawkins, R. M. "Ancient Statues in Mediaeval Constantinople." *Folklore*, vol. 35, no. 3, Sep. 30, 1924, pp. 209–248.

De Beer, G. *Sir Hans Sloane and the British Museum*. Oxford University Press, 1953.

De Roover, R. "The Three Golden Balls of the Pawnbrokers." *Bulletin of the Business Historical Society*, vol. 20, no. 4, Oct. 1946, pp. 117–124.

De Smet, C. "Marketing the French Revolution? Revolutionary Auction Advertisements in Comparative Perspective (Paris, 1778–1793)." *French History*, vol. 36, no. 1, Mar. 2022, pp. 68–99.

Deutsche, R. and Cara Gendel, R. "The Fine Art of Gentrification." *October*, vol. 31, 1984, pp. 91–111.

DeVerteuil, G. "Evidence of Gentrification-Induced Displacement among Social Services in London and Los Angeles." *Urban Studies*, vol. 48, no. 8, June 2011, pp. 1,563–1,580.

Dillon, A. "Collecting as Routine Human Behavior: Motivations for Identity and Control in the Material and Digital World." *Information & Culture*, vol. 54, pp. 255–280.

Dorment, R. "What Is a Warhol? The Buried Evidence." *The New York Review of Books*, June 20, 2013.

Dortch, V., ed. *Peggy Guggenheim and Her Friends*. Berenice Art Books, 1994, p.11.

Douglas, S. and Tully, J. "Who Is Inigo Philbrick? Meet the Man Behind One of the Biggest Potential Modern Art Scandals." *ARTnews*, Dec. 3, 2019.

Dumas, A. "Ambroise Vollard Patron of the Avant-Garde." In: R. Rabinow, ed., *Cézanne to Picasso: Ambroise Vollard, Patron of the Avant-Garde*. New York: Metropolitan Museum of Art, 2006, pp. 3–27.

Durand-Ruel, P. "Catalogue de la vente qui aura lieu par suite du décès de Jean-François Millet." *Hôtel Drouot*, May 10–11, 1875.

Duray, D "Christie's Nets $705.8 M. at 'Looking Forward' Sale, Led by Picasso and Giacometti Record Setters." *ARTnews*, May 12, 2015.

Duron, M. "Mana Contemporary Launches 'Decentralized' Platform for Artists to Sell Work Directly to Collectors." *ARTnews*, Apr. 26, 2019.

Earlom, R. *The Exhibition at the Royal Academy in Pall Mall in 1771*, May 20, 1772. Mezzotint. Collection of the Royal Academy.

Eckardt, S. "Hilde Lynn Helphenstein Wants to Be the Art World's Anthony Bourdain: The Brains Behind @jerrygogosian is Building a New Kind of Creative Career." *W Magazine*, Sep. 20, 2022.

Egan, M. "The Art World Has a Money Laundering Problem." *CNN*, July 29, 2020.

Eidelberg, M. and Henrion-Giele, S. "Horta and Bing: An Unwritten Episode of L'Art Nouveau." *The Burlington Magazine*, vol. 119, no. 896, Special Issue Devoted to European Art Since 1890, Nov. 1977, pp. 747–752.

Elliott, J. E. "The Cost of Reading in Eighteenth Century England: Auction Sale Catalogues and the Cheap Literature Hypothesis." *ELH*, vol. 77, no. 2, 2010, pp. 353–384.

Esterow, M. "The Art Market's Modigliani Forgery Epidemic." *Vanity Fair*, May 3, 2017.

European Commission. *Communication from the Commission to the European Parliament, the Council, the European Economic and Social Committee and the Committee of the Regions on the EU Action Plan against Trafficking in Cultural Goods*, Dec. 13, 2022.

————. "Directive 2001/84/EC of the European Parliament and of the Council of 27 September 2001 on the Resale Right for the Benefit of the Author of an Original Work of Art." *Official Journal L*, vol. 272, Oct. 13, 2001, pp. 0032–0036.

Explication des Ouvrages de Peintre, Sculpture, Gravure, Lithographie, et Architecture des Artistes Vivants Exposés au Palais des Champs-Élysées -1861. Charles de Mourges Freres, 1861.

Ewing, D. "Marketing Art in Antwerp, 1460–1560: Our Lady's Pand." *Art Bulletin*, vol. 72, no. 4, 1990, pp. 558–584.

Fabrikant, G. "The Good Stuff in the Back Room." *The New York Times*, Mar. 12, 2009.

Fahrner, R. and Kleb, W. "The Theatrical Activity of Gianlorenzo Bernini." *Educational Theatre Journal*, vol. 25, no. 1, Mar. 1973, pp. 5–14.

Feinstein, L. "'Beginning of a New Era': How Culture Went Virtual in the Face of Crisis." *The Guardian*, Apr. 8, 2020.

Felch, J. and Frammolino, R. *Chasing Aphrodite: The Hunt for Looted Antiquities at the World's Richest Museum.* Boston and New York: Houghton Mifflin Harcourt, 2011, pp. 265–66,

Fensterstock, A. *Art on the Block: Tracking the New York Art World from SoHo to the Bowery, Bushwick and Beyond.* St. Martin's Press, 2013.

Fenton, L. "Why the World Is Obsessed with Midcentury Modern Design: The Story behind the Ubiquity." *Curbed*, Apr 8, 2015.

Fisman, R. and Wei, S-J. "The Smuggling of Art, and the Art of Smuggling: Uncovering the Illicit Trade in Cultural Property and Antiques." *American Economic Journal: Applied Economics*, American Economic Association, vol. 1, no. 3, 2009, pp. 82–96.

Fleming, O. "Why the World's Most Talked-About New Art Dealer Is Instagram." *Vogue*, May 13, 2014.

Forbes. "Bonhams Buys Butterfields." Aug. 6, 2002.

Forbes, A. "German Dealers Forced to Make Up Tax Law." *Artnet*, July 21, 2014.

———"Why Sotheby's Just Bought an Art Advisory for $85 Million." *Artsy*, Jan. 12, 2016.

Ford, S. *Art: A Commodity.* Rogers & Sherwood, 1888.

Forgy, M. *The Forger's Apprentice: Life with the World's Most Notorious Artist,* CreateSpace Independent Publishing Platform, 2012.

Fratello, B. "France Embraces Millet: The Intertwined Fates of 'The Gleaners' and 'The Angelus.'" *The Art Bulletin*, vol. 85, no. 4, Dec. 2003, pp. 685–701.

Freifeld, K. "Ex-Tyco CEO Kozlowski Says He Stole Out of Pure Greed." *Reuters*, Dec. 5, 2013.

Fuchsgruber, L. "The Hôtel Drouot as the Stock Exchange for Art. Financialization of Art Auctions in the Nineteenth Century." *Journal for Art Market Studies*, vol. 1, no. 1, 2017, pp. 34–46.

Gaie, S. Dilemmas of Public Art: (Strolling Around Richard Serra's Tilted Arc). *Cultura. International Journal of Philosophy of Culture and Axiology*, vol. VII, no. 2, 2010, pp. 21–37.

Galenson, D. and Jensen, R. "Careers and Canvases: The Rise of the Market for Modern Art in the Nineteenth Century." In: Stolwijk, C., ed., *Van Gogh Studies: Current Issues in 19th-Century Art.* Van Gogh Museum, Waanders Publishers, 2007, pp. 146–147.

Geary, P. J. "10. Sacred Commodities: The Circulation of Medieval Relics." *Sacred Commodities: The Circulation of Medieval Relics*, Cornell University Press, 2018, pp. 194–218.

Geraldine, D., Huemer, C., and Oosterlinck, K. "Art Dealers' Inventory Strategy: The Case of Goupil, Boussod & Valadon from 1860 to 1914." *Business History*, Nov. 2020, pp. 1–32.

Gerard, J. "New York Times & Wall Street Journal Prepare to Slash Entertainment Coverage and Staff as Print Ads Vanish." *Deadline Hollywood*, Nov. 9, 2016.

Ghassemitari, S. "The 2022 ADAA Art Show Is Back at New York's Park Avenue Armory." *Hypebeast*, Nov. 4, 2022.

Gilbert, L. "Legal Battle over Modigliani Painting Rumbles On." *The Art Newspaper*, Apr. 20, 2018.

Gilmore Holt, E. *The Expanding World of Art, 1874–1902*. Yale University Press, 1988.

Goldstein, C. "In a Major Shift, Museums Can Now Use the Proceeds from Deaccessioning for More Than Just Buying Art." *Artnet*, Oct. 3, 2022.

———. "The Museum of the Bible Must Once Again Return Artifacts, This Time an Entire Warehouse of 5,000 Egyptian Objects." *Artnet*, Jan. 29, 2021.

Goldstein, M. *Landscape with Figures: A History of Art Dealing in the United States.* Oxford University Press, 2003.

Gottsegen, W. "$69 Million Beeple Art Buyer Revealed as NFT Whale Metakovan." *Decrypt*, Mar. 12, 2021.

Grann, D. "The Mark of a Masterpiece: The Man Who Keeps Finding Famous Fingerprints on Uncelebrated Works of Art." *The New Yorker*, July 12, 2010.

Grant, D. "Would You Invest in Art without Seeing It? New Scheme Invites Users to Buy Into Securitised—but Unnamed—Art Loans." *The Art Newspaper*, Nov. 25, 2022.

Gray, C. "When Elegance Sold Art." *The New York Times*, Mar 8, 2012.

Greenberger, A. "Black Women Reign Victorious at Venice Biennale as Simone Leigh, Sonia Boyce Win Top Awards." *ARTnews*, April 23, 2022.

———. "Documenta's Anti-Semitism Controversy, Explained: How a German Art Show Became the Year's Most Contentious Exhibition." *ARTnews*, July 22, 2022.

———. "Paris+, Explained: Why Art Basel Arrived in Paris, and What's Happening to FIAC." *ARTnews*, Oct. 16, 2022.

Greenberg, C. "Avant-Garde and Kitsch." *Partisan Review*, vol. 6, no. 5, 1939, pp. 34–49.

Grimes, W. "Ernst Beyeler, Top Dealer of Modern Art, Dies at 88." *The New York Times*, Feb. 26, 2010.

Hakami, E. and Hobbs, J. P. *House of Hammer.* Three-part documentary series. Discovery+, 2022.

Hamilton, A. "Christie's Is Bought out by the French." June 1, 1998.

Hammer, J. "The Greatest Fake-Art Scam in History?" *Vanity Fair*, Oct. 10, 2012.

Hanson, S. "The Great Artists' Estates Race." *The Art Newspaper*, May 17, 2017.

Harrison C. White and Cynthia A. White, *Canvases and Careers: Institutional Change in the French Painting World*, rev. ed., University of Chicago Press, (1965) 1993.

Harwell Celenza, A. "Music and the Vienna Secession: 1897–1902." *Music in Art*, vol. 29, no. 1/2, Music in Art: Iconography as a Source for Music History Volume I, Spring–Fall 2004, pp. 203–212.

Hemmings, F. W. J. "Zola, Manet, and the Impressionists (1875–80)." *PMLA*, vol. 73, no. 4, 1958, pp. 407–417.

Hern, A. "More than $100M Worth of NFTs Stolen since July 2021, Data Shows." *The Guardian*, Aug. 24, 2022.

Heslin, P. *The Museum of Augustus: The Temple of Apollo in Pompeii, the Portico of Philippus in Rome, and Latin Poetry*, J. Paul Getty Museum, 2015.

Hevesi, L. *Acht Jahre Secession*. Vienna: Carl Koregen, 1906, pp. 120–121.

Hewett, I. "Did the Rite of Spring Really Spark a Riot?" *BBC*, May 29, 2013.

Hewitt, S. "Russian Art Critics Challenge Director of Ghent Museum Over Show of Dubious Russian Avant-Garde Works. De Standaard Newspaper Reports That the Contract Allowed Any Piece in the Display To Be Sold." *The Art Newspaper*, Feb. 28, 2018.

Hickley, C. "New Evidence Cited in Restitution Claim for Panama Papers Modigliani." *The Art Newspaper*, Jan. 9, 2020.

Hill, D. K. "A Copy of the Athena Parthenos." *The Art Bulletin*, vol. 18, no. 2, June 1936, pp. 150–167.

Hochfield, S. "What is a Real Rembrandt." *Art News*, Feb. 2004.

Howard, D. "Review of Claude Lorrain: Liber Veritatis, by M. Kitson." *The Burlington Magazine*, vol. 121, no. 910, 1979, pp. 42–44.

Howard, C. *The Jean Freeman Gallery Does Not Exist*. MIT Press, 2018.

Howard, S. "On the Reconstruction of the Vatican Laocoön Group." *American Journal of Archaeology*, vol. 63, no. 4, 1959, pp. 365–369.

Huemer, C. "Charles Sedelmeyer's Theatricality: Art Speculation in Late Nineteenth Century Paris." In: Bakoš, J. ed., *Artwork through the Market: The Past and the Present*. Bratislava: VEDA, 2004.

———. "Historicizing the Avant-Garde: The 1903 Impressionist Exhibition at the Vienna Secession." Database of Modern Exhibitions (DoME), European Paintings and Drawings 1905–1915, July 9, 2018.

Husslein-Arco, A. and Weidinger, A. *Gustav Klimt und die Kunstschau 1908*. Vienna: Prestel, 2008.

Impey, O. R. and MacGregor, A. *The Origins of Museums: The Cabinet of Curiosities in Sixteenth- and Seventeenth-Century Europe*. House of Stratus, 2001.

irs.gov *Sole Proprietorships*. 2018, www.irs.gov/businesses/ small-businesses-self-employed/sole-proprietorships.

Internal Revenue Service (IRS). Treasury Regulation. §20.2031 (b).

Irving, C. *Fake! The Story of Elmyr De Hory, the Greatest Art Forger of Our Time*. McGraw-Hill, 1969, pp. 15–16.

Jacobs, H. and Villa, A. "U.K.'s National Portrait Gallery Is Raising Funds to Purchase $58 M. Joshua Reynolds Portrait." *Artnews*, Aug. 31, 2022.

Jaspers, K. *Vom Ursprung und Ziel der Geschichte*. München: Piper, 1949. p. 2.

Jhala, K. "Bonhams owner floats sale of auction house at $1bn." *The Art Newspaper*, Feb. 7, 2023.

———. "'Fatal for the French art market': Dealers Decry New EU Sales Tax That Could Wipe Out Paris's Booming Commercial Scene." *The Art Newspaper*, Feb. 24, 2023.

———. "WTAF? Beeple NFT Work Sells for Astonishing $69.3M at Christie's after Flurry of Last-Minute Bids Nearly Crashes Website." *The Art Newspaper*, Mar. 11, 2021.

Jenson, R. *Marketing Modernism in Fin-de-Siècle Europe*. Princeton University Press, 1996, pp. 22–46.

———"Vollard and Cezanne: Anatomy of a Relationship." In: R. Rabinow, ed., *Cézanne to Picasso: Ambroise Vollard, Patron of the Avant-Garde*. New York: Metropolitan Museum of Art, 2006, pp. 29–47.

Jochum, U. "The Alexandrian Library and its Aftermath." *Library History*, vol. 15, no. 1, 1999, pp. 5–12.

Jones, J. "Artists v Critics, Round One." *The Guardian*, June 26, 2003.

Jones, S. "How 'Monkey Christ' Brought New Life to a Quiet Spanish Town." *The Guardian*, Dec. 28, 2018.

Kachur, L. *Displaying the Marvelous.* MIT Press, 2001, pp. 195–197.

Kaplan, I. "Why Impressionist and Modern works Are Losing Ground at the Top End of the Auction Market." *Artsy*, Aug. 8, 2016.

Karakatsanis, C. G. "G. David Thompson: A Pittsburgh Art Patron and His Collection." *Storyboard. Carnegie Museum of Art*, Apr. 7, 2015.

Karmon, D. *The Ruin of the Eternal City: Antiquity and Preservation in Renaissance Rome.* Oxford University Press, 2011, p. 69.

Karnes, K. C. "'All of Vienna Has Become Secessionistic:' Longings of an Organization." *A Kingdom Not of This World: Wagner, the Arts, and Utopian Visions in Fin-de-Siecle Vienna.* Oxford Academic, 2013, pp. 66–92.

Kastrenakes, J. "Beeple Sold an NFT for $69 Million. Through a First-Of-Its-Kind Auction at Christie's." *The Verge*, Mar. 11, 2021.

Kaye, N. "The Dedicatory Inscription of the Stoa of Attalos in the Athenian Agora: Public Property, Commercial Space, and Hellenistic Kings." *The Journal of the American School of Classical Studies at Athens*, vol. 85, no. 3, July September 2016, pp. 537–558.

Kazakina, K. "'Gmail Art Advisors' Are a Pestilence on the Market. Luckily, They Are Starting to Melt Away, One by One." *Artnet*, Feb. 3, 2023.

Keats, J. *Forged: Why Fakes are the Great Art of Our Age.* Oxford University Press, 2013, p. 114.

——. "Pious Fraud: Art Forgery: Lothar Malskat Was a Master at Forging Restorations, Old-Master and Modern Paintings." *Art and Antiques Magazine*, Feb. 2, 2012.

Kelly, L. J. "Borrowing Against a Bored Ape NFT—What Could Go Wrong? *Decypt*, Feb. 25, 2023.

Kenney, N. "Philanthropist Marie-Josée Kravis Will Replace the Embattled Leon Black as MoMA's Board Chairman." *The Art Newspaper*, Apr. 28, 2021.

Kerr, D. "How to Get Your Gallery into Art Basel in 5 Not-So-Easy Steps." *Artspace*, June 16, 2015.

Kettles, N. "Mistakes That Will Earn You a Small Fortune: Look out for Stamps with Errors in Them If You Want to Make a Really Lucrative Investment in Philately." *The Guardian*, Nov. 30, 2003.

Kim, H. "Diving into Rauschenberg's Canyon." *Inside/Out: A MoMA/MoMA PS1 Blog*, Jan. 24, 2014.

Kinsella, E. "Basquiat Committee to Cease Authenticating Works." *ARTnews*, Jan. 24, 2012.

——. "Cady Noland Said a Collector Restored Her Log Cabin Sculpture Beyond Recognition. A Judge Has Thrown Out Her Lawsuit—for the Third Time." *Artnet*, June 3, 2020.

——. "Ending a Seven-Year Dispute, a US Court Rules That Artists Aren't Entitled to Royalties for Artworks Resold at Auction." *ARTnews*, July 9, 2018.

——. "French Media Tycoon Patrick Drahi Has Acquired Sotheby's for $3.7 Billion, Taking the Publicly Traded Auction House Private." *ARTnet*, June 17, 2019.

_____. "It's a 'Leaser's Market' With 'Unheard-Of' Rents: Why Blue-Chip Galleries Are Doubling Down in New York's Chelsea." *Artnet*, Sep. 6, 2018.

_____. "What Did Inigo Philbrick Do? How One Precocious Dealer Allegedly Swindled the Art Market's Savviest Players Out of Millions." *Artnet*, Mar 12, 2020.

Kishkovsky, S. "First Cosmoscow Fair since Russian Invasion of Ukraine to Open with No Foreign Galleries and Internal Complaints of Censorship." *The Art Newspaper*, Sep. 13, 2022.

Knöfel, U. "The German Artist Who Inspired the Museum Gets Her Due in New Show." *Spiegel*, Mar. 21, 2005.

Kochkodin, B. "Market Manipulation Chatter Rises as Digital Art Scene Explodes." *Bloomberg*, Mar. 13, 2021.

Koerner von Gustorf, O. "Theaster Gates: Inner city blues." *ArtMag*, vol. 76, June 14, 2013.

Koncius, J. "Antique and Vintage Sales Have Soared, Thanks to Supply Chain Issues: Consumers Are Finding That Secondhand Furniture Is Both Sustainable and Available." *The Washington Post*, Jan. 26, 2022.

Koss, J. *Modernism after Wagner*. University of Minnesota Press, 2009.

Kozinn, A. "From a Moving Van to an Arts Complex." *The New York Times*, May 16, 2013.

Kramer, H. "3-year-old Basel Art Fair Lures Some Top Dealers." *The New York Times*, June 27, 1972.

Kräussl, R. "Art Price Indices." In: C. McAndrew, ed., *Fine Art and High Finance: Expert Advice on the Economics of Ownership*. Bloomberg Press, 2010, p. 68.

Kwan, J. "An Artist Died. Then Thieves Made NFTs of Her Work." *Wired*, July 28, 2021.

labiennale.org *Biennale Arte history*. The Beginning of the 20th Century. www.labiennale.org/en/history-biennale-arte

Laird, M. "No Easy Solutions for Swiss Museums." *Swissinfo.ch.*, Nov. 7, 2013.

Landois, P. "*Academy of Painting*. 1751." In: R. Benhamou and A. Arbor, trans., *The Encyclopedia of Diderot & d'Alembert Collaborative Translation Project*. Michigan Publishing, 2003.

Lee, R. L. "Cochineal Production and Trade in New Spain to 1600." *The Americas*, vol. 4, no. 4, Apr. 1948, pp. 449–473.

Lermolieff, I. *Die Werke italienischer Meister in den Galerien von München, Dresden und Berlin*, trans. Johannes Schwarze. Seemann, 1880.

Leroy, L. "L'Exposition des Impressionnistes." *Le Charivari*, Apr. 25, 1874.

Levin, H. "Confessions of Art Fraud King Michael Zabrin." *Chicago Magazine*, Oct. 25, 2011.

Levinson, M. *The Box: How the Shipping Container Made the World Smaller and the World Economy Bigger*. Princeton University Press, 2006.

Ley, D. "Artists, Aestheticisation and the Field of Gentrification." *Urban Studies*, vol. 40, no. 12, special issue: The Gentry in the City: Upward Neighbourhood Trajectories and Gentrification, Nov. 2003, pp. 2527–2544.

Lindeberg, R. "Ex-Tate Modern Boss Builds New Fund Targeting Minority Artists." *Bloomberg*, Sep. 22, 2022.

Loos, T. "Frieze New York Sticks with a Winning Formula: The Art Fair, to Be Held Again at the Shed, Will Have 'More of an International Feel' This Year — And at Least One Surprise." *The New York Times*, May 17, 2022.

Los Angeles Times. "Sotheby's to Pay $148.8 Million for N.Y. Gallery." Apr. 26, 1990.

Louie Sussman, A. "The Strategies Art Dealers Use to Discount Artists' Work." *Artsy*, Aug. 21, 2018.

Lu, J. "How a Parasitic Fungus Turns Ants into 'Zombies.'" *National Geographic*, Apr. 18, 2019.

Luhn, A. "Billionaire Us Art Dealer Hillel "Helly" Nahmad Admits to Running $100M Global Gambling Ring." *The Independent*, Nov. 14, 2013.

Lycett, S. J. "Acheulean Variation and Selection: Does Handaxe Symmetry Fit Neutral Expectations?" *Journal of Archaeological Science*, vol. 35, 2008, pp. 2640–2648.

Maakela, M. *The Munich Secession: Art and Artists in Turn-of-the-Century Munich.* Princeton University Press, 1990, pp. 58–60.

Mackrell, J. "Sex and Art by the Grand Canal: How Peggy Guggenheim Took Venice." *The Guardian*, May 10, 2017.

Mann, J. "How Duchamp's Urinal Changed Art Forever." *Artsy*, May 9, 2017.

Mannheim, K. *Competition as Cultural Phenomenon, Essays Sociology Knowledge*, Volume 5, Routledge, (1929) 2013, p. 198.

Markowitz, D. "Is Nothing Sacred? Andres Serrano's Piss Christ Becomes NFT." *Miami New Times.* December 2, 2022.

Martin-Gropius-Bau "Frederick Kiesler: Architect, Artist, Visionary at Martin-Gropius-Bau Berlin." *Bigmat International Architecture Agenda*, Mar. 22, 2017.

Martini, V. and Collicelli Cagol, S. "The Venice Biennale at Its Turning Points: 1948 and the Aftermath of 1968." In: de Haro García, Noemi, et al., eds., *Making Art History in Europe After 1945.* Routledge, 2020, pp. 90–97.

McAndrew, C. "An Introduction to Art and Finance." In: C. McAndrew, ed., *Fine Art and High Finance: Expert Advice on the Economics of Ownership.* Bloomberg Press, 2010, p. 18.

————. *The Art Market 2022.* Art Basel / Union Bank of Switzerland, 2022, pp. 271–272.

McCarthy, D. and Wallace, A. "Open Access to Collections Is a No-Brainer – It's a Clear-Cut Extension of any Museum's Mission." *Apollo*, June 1, 2020.

McClellan, A. "Edme Gersaint and the Marketing of Art in Eighteenth-Century Paris." *Eighteenth-Century Studies*, vol. 29, no. 2, Winter 1995/1996, pp. 218–222.

————. *Inventing the Louvre: Art, Politics, and the Origins of the Modern Museum.* University of California Press, 1999.

Melion, W. S. *Shaping the Netherlandish Canon: Karel Van Mander's Schilder-Boeck.* University of Chicago Press, 1991.

Merian, W. "Bonifacius Amerbach." *Basler Zeitschrift für Geschichte und Altertumskunde*, vol. 16, 1917, pp. 144–162.

Middleton, W. "Is Brexit Going to Cause a Crisis in the London Art Scene?" *Town and Country*, Nov. 5, 2019.

van Miegroet, H. "Imperfect Data, Art Markets and Internet Research." *Art Markets and Digital Histories*, MDPI (Multidisciplinary Digital Publishing Institute), 2020.

Miller, J. "The Fall of Armie Hammer: A Family Saga of Sex, Money, Drugs, and Betrayal." *Vanity Fair*, Mar. 11, 2021.

Miller, M. H. "The Big Fake: Behind the Scenes of Knoedler Gallery's Downfall." *ARTnews*, Apr. 25, 2016.

Mintz Messinger, L. ed., *Stieglitz and His Artists: Matisse to O'Keefe.* New York: The Metropolitan Museum of Art, 2011.

Mitter, S. "Art Biennials Were Testing Grounds. Now They Are Being Tested." *The New York Times*, May 1, 2020.

Molotch, H. and Treskon, M. "Changing Art: SoHo, Chelsea and the Dynamic Geography of Galleries in New York City." *International Journal of Urban and Regional Research*, vol. 33, no. 2, June, pp. 517–541.

Moncrieff, E. "Christie's Close Down Spink and Take over the Building for Corporate Headquarters." *The Art Newspaper*, Mar. 1, 2000.

Monroe, R. "Can an Art Collective Become the Disney of the Experience Economy?" *New York Times*, May 1, 2019.

Montais, J. M. "Art dealers in the Seventeenth-Century Netherlands." *Simiolus: Netherlands Quarterly for the History of Art*, vol. 18, no. 4, 1998.

Montias, J. "The Guild of St. Luke in 17th-Century Delft and the Economic Status of Artists and Artisans." *Simiolus: Netherlands Quarterly for the History of Art*, vol. 9, no. 2, 1977, pp. 93–105.

Montias, J. M. *Art at Auction in 17th Century Amsterdam*. Amsterdam University Press, 2002.

Moore, R. "The Bilbao Effect: How Frank Gehry's Guggenheim Started a Global Craze." *The Guardian*, Oct. 1, 2017.

Morcillo, M. G. "Staging Power and Authority at Roman Auctions." *Ancient Society*, vol. 38, 2008, pp. 153–181.

Morgenthau, R. *Supreme Court of the State of New York—Grand Jury Indictment for Dennis Kozlowski*. ind. no. 3418/02.

Morowitz, L. "A Passion for Business: Wanamaker's, Munkácsy, and the Depiction of Christ." *The Art Bulletin*, vol. 91, no. 2, June 2009, pp. 184–206.

Morris, E. "Bamboozling Ourselves (Part 2)." *The New York Times*, May 28, 2009.

Morton, E. "An Art Biennial in a Pandemic? How Latvia's RIBOCA2 Embraced COVID-19 as Its Co-curator." *The Calvert Journal*, Sep. 3, 2020.

Moss, C. and Baden, J. "Feds Investigate Hobby Lobby Boss for Illicit Artifacts." *The Daily Beast*, July 12, 2017.

Movius, L. "Seoul's Art Market Ascent Reaches New High with First Frieze Fair." *The Art Newspaper*, Aug. 29, 2022.

Moxey, K. "Panofsky's Concept of "Iconology" and the Problem of Interpretation in the History of Art." *New Literary History*, vol. 17, no. 2, Interpretation and Culture, Winter 1986, pp. 265–274.

Mravik, L. *The "Sacco Di Budapest" and Depredation of Hungary, 1938–1949: Works of Art Missing from Hungary as a Result of the Second World War*. Hungarian National Gallery, 1998.

Mravik, L. and Bereczky, L. *The "Sacco Di Budapest" and Depredation of Hungary, 1938–1949: Works of Art Missing from Hungary as a Result of the Second World War: Looted, Smuggled, Captured, Lost and Destroyed Art Works, Books and Archival Documents: Preliminary and Provisional Catalogue*. Hungarian National Gallery for the Joint Restitution Committee at the Hungarian Ministry of Culture and Education, 1998.

Nagin, C. "First the 'Hotpot'- Now, the Uncup." *New York Magazine*, Dec. 7, 1981, pp. 61–74.

Navarro, C. "Now Is the Best Time for Stylish Travelers to Visit Denver: Colorado's Mile High City Is in the Midst of an Unexpected Art and Design Boom." *Architectural Digest*, Nov. 1, 2021.

Nayyar, R. "New York Art Advisor Lisa Schiff Files for Bankruptcy: Schiff was hit with two lawsuits in the span of a week accusing her of embezzling funds and running a 'Ponzi scheme.'" *Hyperallergic.* May 18, 2023.

Neuendorf, H. "The Armory Show Lures Gagosian Back to the Piers for a Slimmed-Down 2018 Edition." *Artnet News*, Nov. 6, 2017.

———. "Art Demystified: What Is the Role of Art Advisors?" *Artnet*, Aug. 11, 2016.

———. "May Oppose Building on Site of Arsenal; Secretary Watrous of Academy of Design Says No Offer Has Been Made and No Vote Taken. Some of the Members Might Object -- Bill in Legislature Permits the Arrangement." Feb. 17, 1909.

———. "Sotheby's Acquires 75% of Parke-Bernet." July 15, 1964.

———. "$500,000 Suit Hangs on da Vinci Fingers: Impressions on Canvas Said to Prove Master Painted Picture Denounced by Duveen." Nov. 5, 1921.

Newell-Hanson, A. "Why New York's Young Artists Are Leaving the City and Moving Upstate." i-D [Vice], June 12, 2016.

Ng, B. "Why Everything at Major Art Fairs Seems to Be Pre-Sold." *Artsy*, Nov. 18.

Noce, V. "Leading Parisian Antiques Dealers Arrested for Forgery: Ministry of Culture Is Investigating Authenticity of Furniture Bought by Versailles since 2008." *The Art Newspaper,* July 1, 2016.

———. "Wanted in the US, Lebanese Antiquities Collector Maintains His Innocence, Says His 'Big Mistake' Was Trusting New York Art Crime Official." *The Art Newspaper*, Sep. 9, 2022.

Norton, P. F. "The Lost Sleeping Cupid of Michelangelo." *The Art Bulletin*, vol. 39, no. 4, Dec. 1957, pp. 251–257.

O'Connor, F., Quaintance, D., and Sharp, J. *Peggy Guggenheim & Frederick Kiesler: The Story of Art of this Century.* Guggenheim Museum, 2005.

Olson, D. "Dating Impression, Sunrise." *Monet's Impression, Sunrise: A Biography of a Painting.* Paris: Musée Marmottan Monet, 2014, pp. 11–15.

Osborn, A. and Kennedy, M. "Sotheby's Fined £13m for Price-Fixing Scandal with Christie's." *The Guardian*, Oct. 31, 2002.

Ovenell, R. F. *The Ashmolean Museum, 1683–1894.* Clarendon Press, 1986.

Pakiam, R., Chanjaroen, C., and Huang, Z. "Chinese Crypto Tycoon-Backed Bitdeer Buys Asia's 'Fort Knox:' Le Freeport Sold to Jihan Wu's Company for S$40 Million. Wu Is One of the Most Influential People in Crypto Market." *Bloomberg*, Sep. 19, 2022.

Parker, K. "An Introduction to the Künstlersozialkasse (KSK)." *Redtape Translation*, Aug. 2, 2017.

Pausanias. *Pausanias Description of Greece with an English Translation.* Trans. W.H.S. Jones, et al. Harvard University Press, 1918. 9.40.11–9.41.1, 10.38.6.

Patry, S., ed., *Inventing Impressionism: Paul Durand-Ruel and the Modern Art Market.* London: National Gallery Company, 2015.

Perlson, H. "Hildebrand Gurlitt Built a Brilliant Trove of Art Under the Nazis. Two New Exhibitions Show His Taste, and His Duplicity." *ARTnews*, Nov. 3, 2017.

Pes, J. "The Collectors Who Lent Two Dozen Allegedly Fake Artworks to a Major Belgian Museum Have Been Arrested: Igor and Olga Toporovsky Were Taken into Custody Late Last Month." *Artnet*, Jan. 3, 2020.

Pliny the Elder. Ed. John Bostock, M. D., F.R.S. H. T. Riley, Esq., B.A. "Book XXXV: An Account of Paintings and Colours, Chapter 8 — At What Period Foreign Paintings Were First Introduced at Rome." *The Natural History.* Taylor and Francis, 1855.

Povoledo, E. "Ancient Vase Comes Home to a Hero's Welcome." *The New York Times*, Jan. 19, 2008.

———. "Photographs of Getty Griffins Shown at Antiquities Trial in Rome." *The New York Times*, June 1, 2006.

Prak, M. "Guilds and the Development of the Art Market during the Dutch Golden Age." *Simiolus: Netherlands Quarterly for the History of Art*, vol. 30, no. ¾, 2003, pp. 236–251.

Premiere Exposition 1874, Catalogue. Société Antonyms des Artistes, Peintres, Sculpteurs, Graveurs, etc., 1874.

Quarmby, K. "Meet the Gypsy Entrepreneurs: Travelling People Are Putting Their Business Skills to Increasingly Impressive Use." *The Spectator*, Aug. 24, 2013.

Rębała, M. and Miller Llana, S. "Legend Realized? Discovery of Lost Nazi 'Gold Train' Invigorates Polish Town." *The Christian Science Monitor*, Sep. 4, 2015.

Reeve, E. and Guff, S. "A Twisted Tale of Celebrity Promotion, Opaque Transactions and Allegations of Racist Tropes." *CNN*, Feb. 11, 2023.

Rehn Wolfman, U. "Richard Wagner's Concept of the 'Gesamtkunstwerk.'" *Interlude*, Mar. 12, 2013.

Rewald, J. *The History of Impressionism*. New York: Metropolitan Museum of Art, 1961, p. 314.

Reyburn, S. "Five Years Since the $450m Salvator Mundi Sale: A First-Hand Account of the Nonsensical Auction." *The Art Newspaper*, Nov. 15, 2022.

———. "How Online Buyers of Luxury Collectibles Reshaped Auctions in an Economic Slump." *The Art Newspaper*, Feb. 23, 2023.

———. "Is the Old Masters Market in Terminal Decline?" *The Art Newspaper*, Dec. 7, 2022.

———. "Market for Chinese Art Is Increasingly in China." *The New York Times*, Mar. 25, 2016.

———. "Why Sotheby's Agreed to Be Bought by a Telecom Executive for $3.7 Billion." *The New York Times*, June 17, 2019.

Ricci, B. "The Shows That Made Contemporary Art History: The International Surrealist Exhibition of 1938." *Artland Magazine*.

Richard, P. "Bernard Berenson — Portrait of a Connoisseur: The Life of a Renaissance Man, the Rewarding Life of a Self-Made Aristocrat." *The Washington Post*, Jan. 21, 1979.

Richardson, J. *Two Discourses: I. an Essay on the Whole Art of Criticism, as It Relates to Painting. Ii. an Argument in Behalf of the Science of a Connoisseur: Certainty, Pleasure, and Advantage of It*. HardPress Publishing, 2020.

Richetti, A. "La Peau de L'Ours: Avant-Garde Art as an Investment." *Daily Art Magazine*, Jan. 17, 2022.

Ridgewell, R. "Music Printing in Mozart's Vienna: The Artaria Press." *Fontes Artis Musicae*, vol. 48, no. 3, 2001, pp. 217–236.

Ridgway, B. S. "The Bronze Apollo from Piombino in the Louvre." *Antike Plastik*, vol. 7, 1967, pp. 43–75.

Riding, A. "Dutch to Return Art Seized by Nazis." *The New York Times*, Feb. 7, 2006.

Ripps, M. J. "Chapter 11: The London Picture Trade and Knoedler & Co.: Supplying Dutch Old Masters 1900–1914." In: I. Reist, ed., *British Models of Art Collecting and the American Response: Reflections Across the Pond*. Henry Ling Ltd, Dorset Press, pp. 163–180.

Robertson, I. "The International Art Market." In: I. Robertson, ed., *Understanding International Art Markets and Management.* Routledge, pp. 13–60.

Roche, J. F. "Louis Sullivan's Architectural Principles and the Organicist Aesthetic of Friedrich Schelling and S. T. Coleridge." *Nineteenth Century Studies*, vol. 7, 1993, pp. 29–55.

Romain, L. "Zur Geschichte des deutschen Kunstvereins. In: Arbeitsgemeinschaft deutscher Kunstvereine." In: *Kunstlandschaft Bundesrepublik.* Stuttgart: Klett-Cotta, 1984, pp. 11–37.

Roodt, C. "Private International Law, Art and Cultural Heritage." Cheltenham: Edward Elgar Publishing, 2015, pp. 293–297.

Rubinstein, R. "Pius II and Roman Ruins." *Renaissance Studies*, vol. 2, no. 2, 1988, pp. 197–203.

Russel, J. "In Search of the Real Thing." *The New York Times*, Dec. 1, 1985.

Russeth, A. "The Venice Biennale: Everything You Could Ever Want to Know." *ARTnews.* April 17, 2019.

Saltzman, C. *Old Masters New World: America's Raid on Europe's Great Pictures, 1880-World War I.* Viking. 2008, p. 77.

Salz, J. "A Modest Proposal: Break the Art Fair." *New York Magazine*, May 1, 2018.

———. "2 Big Things Wrong with the Art World as Demonstrated by the September Issue of Artforum." *New York Magazine*, Sep. 2, 2014.

Samuels, E. and Samuels, J. N. *Bernard Berenson, the Making of a Legend.* Belknap Press, 1987, p. 216.

Schellenberg, R. "Museums and Museality." *Journal of Austrian Studies*, vol. 51, no. 2, Summer 2018, pp. 31–50.

Sansom, A. "After the Arrival of Paris+, Is There a Future for FIAC? Its New Director Is Plotting a Return." *Artnet News*, Nov. 21, 2022.

Sawbridge, P. *A Little History of the Royal Academy.* London: Royal Academy of Arts, 2019 (2022).

Sayej, N. "The Guerrilla Girls: 'We Upend the Art World's Notion of What's Good and What's Right.'" *The Guardian*, Oct. 19, 2020.

Schachter, K. "Where's Inigo? As a Furious Art World Searches for the Disappeared Dealer, Kenny Schachter Finds Him... on Instagram." *Artnet*, Dec. 10, 2019.

Schaefer, B. "1912 – Mission Moderne." In: B. Schaefer, ed., *1912 – Mission Moderne. Die Jahrhundertschau des Sonderbunds.* Wienand, 2012, p. 21.

Scher, R. "'Round 57th Street: New York's First Gallery District Continues (for Now) to Weather Endless Changes in the Art World." *ARTnews*, July. 19, 2016.

Schneider, T. "Virtual Art Fairs Were Seen as a Lifeline in the Lockdown Era. A New Study Shows They Are Failing New York's Art Market." *Artnet*, Nov. 18, 2020.

Schorske, C. E. *Fin-de-siècle Vienna: Politics and Culture.* New York: Vintage Books, 1981, pp. 208–278.

Schultheis, F. "The Art, the Market, and Sociology: Concluding Remarks." In: A. Glauser, P. Holder, T. Mazzurana, O. Moeschler, V. Rolle and F. Schultheis, eds., *The Sociology of Arts and Markets: New Developments and Persistent Patterns.* Palgrave Macmillan, 2020. pp. 411–419.

———. *Talking Prices: Symbolic Meanings of Prices on the Market for Contemporary Art.* Princeton University Press, 2005.

Scott, D. and Kliff, S. "Republicans Have Finally Repealed a Crucial Piece of Obamacare." *Vox*, Dec. 20, 2017.

Seal, T. "The Recline and Fall of Antique Furniture." *Financial Times*, Mar. 10, 2016.

Secrest, M. *Duveen: A Life in Art*. New York: Alfred A. Knopf, 2004.

Segal, D. "Pulling Art Sales out of Thinning Air." *The New York Times*, Mar. 7, 2009.

Sennewald, J. E. and Timm, T. "Im Bunker der Schönheit." *Zeit Online*, Apr. 25, 2013.

Seymour, T. "Tainted Gifts: As British Museum and the Met Disavow the Sackler Name, Museums Rethink Donation Deals." *The Art Newspaper*, Mar. 28, 2022.

Shaw, A. "Art Basel Introduces New Booth Pricing Structure to Subsidise Younger Galleries." *The Art Newspaper*, Sep. 3, 2018.

Sheets H. M. "A Return for Rothko's Harvard Murals." *The New York Times*, Oct. 23, 2014.

Shelley, M. *The Care and Handling of Art Objects: Practices in the Metropolitan Museum of Art*. New York: The Metropolitan Museum of Art, 1987, pp. 68–69.

Shephard, T., Lea, S., and Hempel de Ibarra, N. "The Thieving Magpie'? No Evidence for Attraction to Shiny Objects." *Animal Cognition*, vol. 18, no. 1, Aug. 2014.

Shnayerson, M. "A Question of Provenance." *Vanity Fair*, Apr. 23, 2012.

si.edu [Smithsonian website]. "Smithsonian Fiscal Year 2022 Federal Budget Tops $1 Billion." Mar. 29, 2022.

Simpson, C. *Artful Partners: Bernard Berenson and Joseph Duveen*. New York: Macmillan, 1986, pp. 150–151.

Singer, L. and Lynch, G. "Public Choice in the Tertiary Art Market." *Journal of Cultural Economics*, vol. 18, no. 3, 1994, pp. 199–216.

Sisa, J. *Motherland and Progress: Hungarian Architecture and Design 1800–1900*. Birkhäuser, 2016.

Sloane, K. and Taylor, J. "Art Markets without Art, Art without Objects." *The Garage Journal: Studies in Art, Museums & Culture*, vol. 2, 2021.

Small, Z. "Push to Return 116,000 Native American Remains Is Long-Awaited." *The New York Times*, Aug. 6, 2021.

Smith, A. *An Enquiry into the Nature and Causes of the Wealth of Nations*. Random House, 1947, pp. 3–5.

Smith, R. "Art Review: Combining People and Machines in Venice." *The New York Times*, July 8, 2011.

Solomon, T. "More Than $100 M. Worth of NFTs Have Been Stolen This Year, a New Report Finds." *ARTnews*, Aug. 25, 2022.

Stapley-Brown, V. and Kenney, N. "Met Hands over an Egyptian Coffin That It Says Was Looted." *The Art Newspaper*, Feb. 15, 2019.

Stowe, S. "Storm Leaves Residue of Questions." *The New York Times*, May 9, 2013.

Stromberg, M. "Are Art Fairs Necessary?" *KCET*, Feb. 4, 2016.

Sussman, A. L. "How the Scull Sale Changed the Art Market." *Artsy*, Apr. 26, 2017.

Sutton, B. "Pensioners Revolt: Patrick Drahi Winds up Sotheby's 'Defined Benefit' Pension Plan, and Former Employees Are Not Happy." *The Art Newspaper*, Feb. 9, 2021.

———. "Sotheby's Owner Patrick Drahi Reportedly Considering Taking Auction House Public." *The Art Newspaper*, Dec. 15, 2021.

Suykerbuyk, R. "Chapter 2 The Image of Piety at the Dawn of Iconoclasm." *The Matter of Piety*. Series: Studies in Netherlandish Art and Cultural History, vol. 16. Brill. July 17, 2020, pp. 74–107.

Szabolcsi, H. "A Bécsi Artaria Magyar Kapcsolatairól." In: E. András, ed., *Angyalokra Szükség Van. Tanulmányok Bernáth Mária Tiszteletére*. Budapest: MTA Műv. Tört. Kutatóintézet, 2005, pp. 15–19.

Tagliabue, J. "Cleaned 'Last Judgment' Unveiled." *The New York Times*, Apr. 9, 1994.

Takac, B. "The Controversy Behind Edouard Manet's Olympia Masterpiece." *Wide Walls*, Oct. 28, 2018.

Tarmy, J. "Your Unloved Heirlooms Might Mean Serious Money: The Market for Fine Antiques and Decorative Arts Is Still Well Below Former Highs, Which—for Some—Is a $100 Million Opportunity." *Bloomberg*, July 1, 2021.

Taylor, J. "Art Forgers and the Deconstruction of Genius." *Journal for Art Market Studies*, vol. 1, 2021, pp. 2–3.

———. *In Search of the Budapest Secession: The Artist Proletariat and the Modernism's rise in the Hungarian Art Market, 1800–1914*. Helena History Press, 2014, pp. 185–192.

———. "The Artifice of Elmyr de Hory." *Intent to Deceive Exhibition Catalogue*, 2012. http://www.intenttodeceive.org/forger-profiles/elmyr-de-hory/the-artifice-of-elmyr-de-hory/.

———. "The Rise and Fall of the Knoedler, New York's Most Notorious Art Gallery." *The Conversation*, Feb. 5, 2016.

Thaddeus-Johns, J. "Can New York Have Too Many Art Fairs?" *Artsy*, May 11, 2022.

Tharp, Paul. "Auction House Bombshell; Exec's Affair with Socialite Led Scandal to Surface." *New York Post*, Oct. 1, 2000.

Thompson, D. *The $12 Million Stuffed Shark: The Curious Economics of Contemporary Art*. Macmillan, 2010, pp. 1–3.

Thompson, J. A. "Durand-Ruel and America." In: S. Patry, ed., *Inventing Impressionism: Paul Durand-Ruel and the Modern Art Market*. London: National Gallery Company, 2015, pp. 136–151.

Thucydides. *History of the Peloponnesian War*, Eds. M. I. Finley, Trans. R. Warner. New York: Penguin, 1972.

Tollebeek, J. "'Renaissance' and 'fossilization': Michelet, Burckhardt, and Huizinga." *Renaissance Studies*, vol. 15 no. 3, 2001, pp. 354–366.

Tompkins, C. *Merchants & Masterpieces: The Story of the Metropolitan Museum of Art*. E. P. Dutton & Co., 1970, pp. 15–94.

Topazio, V. W, and May, G. Diderot's Art Criticism: A Controversy. *The French Review*, vol. 37, no. 1, part 1, Oct., 1963, pp. 3–21.

Tremlett, G. "Anarchists and the Fine Art of Torture." *The Guardian*, Jan. 27, 2003.

Trezzi, N. "The Art Dealers Finding Alternatives to the Gallery Model." *Artnet*, Sep. 14, 2016.

Troncoso, V. A. "The Hellenistic Gymnasium and the Pleasures of Paideia." *Symbolae Hilologorum Posnaniensium Graecae et Latinae*. Adam Mickiewicz University Press, Poznan, XIX, 2009, pp. 71–84.

Tucker, P. "The First Impressionist Exhibition in Context." In: C. Moffett, ed., *The New Painting: Impressionism*. San Francisco: The Fine Arts Museum of San Francisco, 1986.

Twitchett, D. and Loewe, M., eds., *The Cambridge History of China: Volume I: The Ch'in and Han Empires, 221 B.C. – A.D. 220*, Cambridge: Cambridge University Press, pp. 223–290.

UNESCO *Convention on the Means of Prohibiting and Preventing the Illicit Import, Export and Transfer of Ownership of Cultural Property*. Paris: UNESCO, 1970.

United Nations. *Customs Convention on the International Transport of Goods under Cover of Tir Carnets (TIR CONVENTION, 1975)*. Tenth Revised Edition, 2013.

van Mander, K. *The Lives of the Illustrious Netherlandish and German Painters, from the First Edition of the Schilder-boeck (1603–1604)*. Davaco, 1994.

Vasan, K., Janosov, M., and Barabási, A.L. "Quantifying NFT-Driven Networks in Crypto Art." *Sci Rep*, vol. 12, no. 2769, 2022.

Vasari, G. *Lives of the Most Eminent Painters Sculptors & Architects*. Trans, Du C. De Vere, G. Macmillan and Co. & the Medici Society, 1912–1914.

Veblen, T. *The Theory of the Leisure Class: An Economic Study of Institutions*. MacMillan, 1899, p. 59.

Velie, E. "Is the Orlando Museum of Art Displaying Fake Basquiats? The FBI Is Investigating the Authenticity of Works That Are Said to Have Been Found in the Storage Unit of a Hollywood Screenwriter." *Hyperallergic*, June 1, 2022.

———. "Orlando Museum of Art on Probation After Disputed Basquiat Show. The American Alliance of Museums's Sanction Comes After the FBI Raided the Museum and Seized 25 Disputed Paintings." *Hyperallergic*, Jan. 23, 2023.

Vergo, P. *Art in Vienna, 1898–1918*. Ithaca, NY: Cornell University Press, 1975, p. 23.

Vottero, M. "To Collect and Conquer: American Collections in the Gilded Age." *Transatlantica*, vol. 1, 2013.

Villa, A. "Rising Startup Masterworks Beset by Internal Rifts, Alleged Recklessness, and Staff Cuts." *ARTnews*, Dec. 27, 2022.

Vogel, C. "Lauder Pays $135 Million, a Record, for a Klimt Portrait." *The New York Times*, June 19, 2006.

Vogel, C. and Eaton, L. "Sotheby's and Christie's Face Lawsuits from Angry Customers in Antitrust Case." *New York Times*, Feb. 21, 2000.

von Vegesack, A., ed. *Czech Cubism: Architecture, Furniture, and Decorative Arts, 1910–1925*. Princeton Architectural Press, 1992.

Voon, C. "Mysterious NFT Collector—Who May Actually Be the Rapper Snoop Dogg—Gifts 22 Blockchain Works to Lacma." *The Art Newspaper*, Feb. 13, 2023.

Warburg, A. *Bilderatlas Mnemosyne – The Original*. Ed. der Welt, H. D. K., The Warburg Institute, Ohrt, R. and Heil, A. Hatje Cantz, 2020.

Warnica, R. "How Did David Mirvish End up in the Decade's Most Shocking Art Forgery Scandal?" *Canadian Business*, Dec. 17, 2013.

Watson, P. and Todeschini, C. *The Medici Conspiracy: The Illicit Journey of Looted Antiquities: From Italy's Tomb Raiders to the World's Greatest Museums*. New York: Public Affairs, 2006.

Weber, B. "Robert Hecht, Antiquities Dealer, Dies at 92." *The New York Times*, Feb. 9, 2012.

Weschler, L. *Mr. Wilson's Cabinet of Wonder*. New York: Vintage Books, 1995.

Whitaker, L. and Clayton, M. "'Art Becomes a Piece of State': Italian Paintings and Drawings and the Royal Collection." The Art of Italy in the Royal Collection: Renaissance & Baroque. Royal Collection Publications, 2007, pp. 11–41.

Williams, R. C. "Dumping Oils: Soviet Art Sales and Soviet-American Relations, 1928–1933." Washington, D.C.: Kennan Institute for Advanced Russian Studies, Woodrow Wilson International Center for Scholars. May 25, 1977.

Wölfflin, H. *Renaissance und Barock: eine Untersuchung über Wesen und Entstehung des Barockstils in Italien*. Theodor Ackermann, 1888.

Woodham, D. "Common Mistakes of Rookie Auction Guarantors." *The Art Newspaper*, Nov. 12, 2018.

Xenophon. *Memorabilia*. Ithaca, NY: Cornell University Press, 2001, Book 3, Chapter 10.

Young, L. "The Fierce, Forgotten Library Wars of the Ancient World: The Dark Trade of Collecting Books Used to Get Really Messy." *Atlas Obscura*, Aug. 26, 2016.

Zarobell, J. *Art and the Global Economy*. Oakland: University of California Press, 2013, p. 143.

Zeit Online. "Art Compass: Gerhard Richter Remains the Most Important Artist." Oct. 20, 2022.

Zsidi, P. "From the Plan Sheet to the Screen—Reconstructions in Aquincum." *Budapest Régiségei*, vol. XL, 2006, p. 328.

Zweig, R. W. *The Gold Train: The Destruction of the Jews and the Looting of Hungary*. William Morrow & Co., 2002, pp. 99–118.

Index

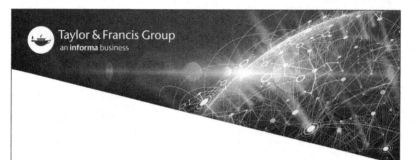

Printed in the United States
by Baker & Taylor Publisher Services